1st edition

Getting Paid

How to Collect from Bankrupt Debtors

by Attorney Stephen R. Elias

NOLO

First Edition	NOVEMBER 2003
Editor	ILONA BRAY
Book Design	SUSAN PUTNEY
Cover Design	TONI IHARA
Index	ELLEN DAVENPORT
Proofreading	SUSAN CARLSON GREENE
Printing	ARVATO SERVICES, INC.

Elias, Stephen.

    Getting paid : how to collect from bankrupt debtors / by Stephen Elias.-- 1st ed.

        p.   cm.

    Includes index.

    ISBN 0-87337-978-0

      1. Collecting of accounts--United States 2. Bankruptcy--United States.   I. Title.

HG3752.7.U6E45 2003

346.73'07'8--dc21   2003052495

For information on bulk purchases or corporate premium sales, please contact the Special Sales Department. For academic sales or textbook adoptions, ask for Academic Sales. Call 800-955-4775 or write to Nolo at 950 Parker Street, Berkeley, CA 94710.

Acknowledgments

Thank you Ilona for your scrupulous editing, Albin for your always helpful contributions and wisdom about bankruptcy, Jaleh and Susan for getting the book into physical form, and Jake, Linda, Toni, Mary, David, Janet, John, Jack, Lulu, Barbara, and my other friends at Nolo for keeping the ship afloat and on course so that this book could be published and distributed to the many folks who can really use it.

Table of Contents

10 Filing Motions and Complaints in Bankruptcy Court

11 Responding to Motions and Complaints

12 How To Torpedo an Undeserving Bankruptcy

13 The Creditor's Role in a Reorganization Case

14 Conversions Between Bankruptcy Chapters

15 Prepetition Transfers: How to Keep Payments You've Already Received

How to Use This Book

People who go bankrupt and can't pay their bills are a fact of life for business owners and others. This is true in good times and in bad—though the numbers definitely rise during bad times. In the early 2000s, for example, with rising unemployment and stock market nosedives, record numbers of people filed for bankruptcy—more than 1.5 million a year. The number of large companies seeking bankruptcy protection also reached record highs. In fact, seven of the largest companies ever to file for bankruptcy filed their petitions in 2002, and 2003 brought more major filings. Every person or company that goes bankrupt results in an even larger number of people who don't get paid what they're owed.

A. Who Should Use This Book

If you're among the ones left holding the bag after someone who owes you goes bankrupt, this book's for you.

- It's for the owner of a small business whose customer has filed for bankruptcy.
- It's for the spouse going through a divorce from a partner who is threatening to file for bankruptcy.
- It's for the employee or retiree from a company that has gone belly up.
- It's for the victim of negligence or wrongdoing who isn't getting compensated because the perpetrator has gone bankrupt.

In short, it's for everybody who is owed money by a person or business that has turned to bankruptcy as a solution to his, her, or its economic difficulties.

What this book doesn't do is show you how to file for bankruptcy. There are plenty of other books on the market for that. We'll be looking through the other side of the bankruptcy lens, so that instead of explaining how to fill out a bankruptcy petition, we'll explain what the petition and other papers filed by the debtor mean. Instead of telling debtors how to protect property by claiming it as exempt, we'll show you how to check the legitimacy of the exemptions claimed by the debtor. And, instead of describing how to create a reorganization plan, we'll tell you how to make sure you get the most out of the reorganization plan proposed by the debtor.

If you're looking for a guide to filing for bankruptcy, see, for example:

- *How to File for Chapter 7 Bankruptcy*, by Stephen R. Elias, Albin Renauer, Robin Leonard and Kathleen Michon (Nolo), or

- *Chapter 13 Bankruptcy: Repay Your Debts*, by Robin Leonard (Nolo).

Is there anyone who shouldn't rely on this book alone, but should also consult an attorney? Yes. While many of the procedures for protecting your right to be paid—like filing a proof of claim or attending a creditors' meeting—can be done without an attorney's help, others aren't so straightforward. For example, asking the court to refuse to allow a debtor to wipe out his debt to you, or to force a debtor into involuntary bankruptcy are best done with an attorney's help. Throughout this book, we've done our best to point out the situations in which you'd benefit from hiring an attorney. How to find a good one is discussed in Chapter 19.

B. Choosing Which Chapters to Read

You may not have to read this entire book. For example, we've written some material covering situations in which the debtor is still merely threatening bankruptcy—material that you can skip if your debtor is already deep in bankruptcy court proceedings.

You can also narrow down your reading based on the type of claim you hold. If your claim is secured—that is, the law or the debtor has given you the ability to take the debtor's property if he doesn't pay the bill—you'll be interested in Chapter 8, which explains how to get the debtor to pay secured claims. If your claim is not secured, then you'll want to focus on the chapters dealing with the rights of unsecured creditors (Chapters 7 and 9).

The following chapter summary will help you decide what to read and when to read it.

Chapter 2: How Bankruptcy Works. If this is the first time you've been involved with a bankruptcy, start here. This chapter reviews the different types of bankruptcy relief available, including Chapters 7, 11, 12, and 13 bankruptcy. You'll also find this chapter useful if you've dealt with bankruptcy before but want to review the differences between these types of relief.

Chapter 3: Finding Out the Debtor Has Gone Bankrupt. Everyone should read this chapter, though not necessarily the whole chapter. If you're concerned that someone who owes you money might file for bankruptcy, then read the sections covering what kind of notification to expect and how to respond once you receive it. This chapter also explains what happens if the debtor fails to notify you. If you've already received the notice of bankruptcy, read the sections clarifying your current rights and responsibilities and how to train your staff to respond to future bankruptcy notices.

Chapter 4: The Automatic Stay. This chapter is a must-read for everyone. The very moment a debtor files for bankruptcy, something called the automatic stay goes into effect. Anything you do to collect your claim after that violates federal law. Read this chapter so you don't waste time and money by improperly pursuing the debtor.

Chapter 5: Examining the Bankruptcy Papers. After filing for bankruptcy, debtors must make lengthy and detailed disclosures to the bankruptcy court. This chapter takes you through all the forms and schedules, explains what's supposed to be revealed on them and helps you understand the significance of each disclosure. You'll definitely want to read this chapter if this is the first time you've been involved in a bankruptcy. And even if you're an experienced creditor, you may benefit from the checklists and other analytical advice provided.

Chapter 6: The Meeting of Creditors and Other Communications With the Debtor. The automatic stay creates real dangers for creditors who need to talk with debtors. This chapter lays out what you can and cannot do—what you can say, when you can say it, and when you're better off talking to the debtor's lawyer. It's important information for everyone.

Chapter 7: Filing and Defending Your Proof of Claim. This chapter addresses the crucial question of how to bring the court's attention to the amount that the debtor owes you. In fact, the entire book was written around answering this question and it's companion question, "How can I collect on my claim without ending up losing money in attorneys, fees or paying court penalties because I did something incorrectly?"

Chapter 8: Getting Payment for Secured Claims. You can skip this chapter if you don't hold a lien against (or security interest in) the debtor's property. If you do have a lien, this chapter will explain whether and how you can preserve or enforce it during the bankruptcy.

Chapter 9: Claims That Can't Be Wiped Out Through Bankruptcy. This chapter applies to both secured and unsecured creditors. However, it is particularly important if you're an unsecured creditor, because your claim represents your sole right to payment. (Secured creditors can pursue their liens in addition to their claims, provided that their liens survive the bankruptcy.) The debtor's goal in filing for bankruptcy is to "discharge," that is, wipe out your claim against him. Your goal is to see that this doesn't happen. Your best way of attaining this goal is to point to portions of the bankruptcy law that list types of obligations that individual debtors can't walk away from. In this chapter you'll learn what those obligations are, and what you'll need to show the bankruptcy court in order for your claim to be excepted from discharge.

Chapter 10: Filing Motions and Complaints in Bankruptcy Court. At some point in the bankruptcy case, you may need to ask the bankruptcy judge for a ruling in order to protect your rights as a creditor. You might, for example, ask the court to lift the automatic stay so you can foreclose on your collateral, to limit the debtor's ability to protect property, to deny the debtor's discharge, or any one of a number of other actions. Read this chapter before you ask the court for help or hire an attorney to do this work for you.

Chapter 11: Responding to Motions and Complaints. Over the course of the bankruptcy proceedings, the debtor or the trustee may ask the court to make rulings that affect you or your claim. Read this chapter if the court notifies you that a motion or complaint has been filed against you, to learn how to respond.

Chapter 12: How to Torpedo an Undeserving Bankruptcy. Read this chapter if you think the debtor doesn't deserve a bankruptcy discharge. It will explain when and how the debtor's bankruptcy can be terminated and the debtor held to his obligations.

Chapter 13: The Creditor's Role in a Reorganization Case. Read this chapter if the debtor filed under bankruptcy Chapter 11, 12, or 13. You'll learn what goes into the creation of a reorganization plan and what you should expect to receive from it.

This book doesn't have a separate chapter covering the creditor's role in a Chapter 7 case. That's because Chapter 7 is generic bankruptcy. All the general rules and concepts described in other chapters apply to Chap-

ter 7 cases. However, reorganization bankruptcies present exceptions that require a separate discussion.

Chapter 14: Conversions Between Bankruptcy Chapters. Debtors are not locked into the type of bankruptcy they initially filed under. Read this chapter if your debtor is planning to change chapters—or if you believe the debtor should be in a different chapter and you would like to force the issue.

Chapter 15: Prepetition Transfers: How to Keep Payments You've Already Received. Read this chapter if the trustee or the debtor has asked you to give back money or property you received prior to the bankruptcy filing. You'll learn the circumstances under which these requests are proper and your possible defenses.

Chapter 16: Creditors' Rights After the Bankruptcy Ends. Read this chapter if the debtor's case was dismissed or the debtor was unable to discharge your claim. You should also read this chapter if you hold a security interest that the court didn't void. You may be able to resume efforts to collect what's owed you.

Chapter 17: Minimizing Future Bankruptcy Losses. This chapter is primarily for business owners. It contains suggested practices for getting customers to pay up well before they go bankrupt.

Chapter 18: Forcing Debtors Into Bankruptcy. Would you have a greater chance of getting paid if the person who owes you money just went ahead and filed for bankruptcy? There are rare situations in which this is true. This chapter explains when you might want to file an involuntary bankruptcy on the debtor's behalf.

Chapter 19: Legal Help Beyond This Book. Read this chapter for information on doing your own legal research or finding a good attorney to assist you with issues too complex to be covered in this book.

Icons Used in This Book

To aid you in using this book, we use the following icons:

 The caution icon warns you of potential problems.

 This icon indicates that the information is a useful tip.

 This icon refers you to helpful books or other resources.

This icon indicates when you should consider consulting an attorney or other expert.

This icon refers you to a further discussion of the topic somewhere else in this book.

Minding our "he's" and "she's." It's almost impossible to write a book of this nature without using personal pronouns. In an effort to reach some measure of gender neutrality, we have alternated the use of "he" and "she." This wasn't done mathematically, however, so we apologize in advance for any imbalances.

Legal Citations Used in This Book

At times, we include references to the law or case on which we're basing a particular discussion point. However, we use a standard legal shorthand for these. For example, a reference to a statute (law) will look something like this: "11 U.S.C. § 362." That means volume 11 of the U.S. Code (federal law), Section 362. Or, a reference to a case that a court has decided may look something like this: *In Re Jamo*, 283 F.3d 392 (1st Cir. 2002). You can ignore these references if you wish—but if you want to use them to check the original source, just ask any legal librarian for help. Also see Chapter 19 for more on do-it-yourself legal research. ■

CHAPTER

2

How Bankruptcy Works

Before we explain what you can and can't do to collect your money, you should know something about what bankruptcy is and how it works. This chapter will stick to the basics—the need-to-know stuff—so that you can get on with the task at hand. We'll cover:

- the basic procedures and players in a bankruptcy (Section A)
- some key features common to all bankruptcies (Section B), and
- the particular features of each type of bankruptcy (Section C).

A. Introduction to Bankruptcy Procedures and Players

Bankruptcy exists to help debtors (the people who owe money) while simultaneously protecting their creditors (the people to whom the money is owed). Bankruptcy helps debtors by allowing them to avoid paying some or all of their bills or debts. In technical terms, the law allows them to "discharge" their legal obligation to pay. Bankruptcy protects creditors by setting limits on the types of debts that can be discharged and by making sure all creditors are treated fairly.

As a creditor, you'll refer to the money that the debtor owes you as your "claim." Much of this book is dedicated to showing you how to protect that claim. The best type of claim to have is a "secured"

one. A claim is secured when you hold a "lien" against the debtor's property for the amount of the claim. A lien enables you to take and sell the debtor's property ("collateral") if the debtor doesn't pay the debt. Liens may be created by contract (for example, a home mortgage or a car loan), by law (for example, a mechanic's lien for work done to improve real estate) or by court order (for example, a judgment lien created to secure the payment of a property distribution in a divorce). If you are owed more than the debtor's collateral is worth, then you have a secured claim to the extent of the collateral's value and an unsecured claim for the balance.

If none of the possibilities just described gives you the right to collect from the debtor's property, then your claim is unsecured. Cash loans and unpaid bills for services are usually unsecured claims. They can still be collected on in a bankruptcy, but unsecured claims are usually the last to get paid.

The bankruptcy laws try to balance the debtor's need for an economic fresh start against the creditor's contractual right to be paid. Whether the law achieves this balance depends on your perspective. Debtors tend to see the law as favoring creditors, while creditors usually see the law as favoring debtors. Over the years, the law has been changed several times to make it more favorable to creditors, so perhaps it truly did start out tilted in the debtor's favor.

No matter who ultimately gets the fairest treatment, however, you'll notice that all bankruptcy cases revolve around the debtor. That's not too surprising, since it's usually the debtor who starts the case, and it's the debtor's financial condition that is the focus of the legal proceedings. In consumer cases where the debtor is not represented by an attorney, the judge may have to spend a significant amount of extra time with the debtor. Try to realize that this attention to the debtor does not necessarily represent a bias against your interests

1. How Federal Law Governs Bankruptcies

Bankruptcies are governed by federal law, namely the U.S. Bankruptcy Code. If you want to look up the law, go to Title 11 of the U.S. Code. (See Chapter 19 of this book for more on doing your own legal research.) Title 11 is divided into chapters, some of whose numbers you may recognize, because they correspond to different types of bankruptcy: Chapter 7, Chapter 11, Chapter 12, and Chapter 13.

If you end up going to court over a bankruptcy case, it won't be in the usual state or federal court system. Bankruptcy cases are filed in special bankruptcy courts that don't hear any other kind of case. Their rulings govern all actions filed against the debtor in other courts any-

where in the country. So, if you have a claim against the debtor, you must present it in the bankruptcy court or risk losing it. In fact, the mere filing of a bankruptcy petition is enough to bring all litigation against the debtor (the person who filed the bankruptcy petition) to a halt. This is true no matter what part of the United States the other litigation is filed in, or in what type of court. This is known as the "automatic stay." It's so important we've devoted all of Chapter 4 to it.

2. Who's Who in a Bankruptcy Case?

Let's look at who the major players are in a bankruptcy proceeding, including the debtor, creditor, trustee, and bankruptcy court judge.

a. Debtor

The person or company who files for bankruptcy is called the "debtor."

b. Creditor

You—a person or business owner owed money by the debtor—are referred to as a "creditor." Creditors are separated into two categories, those holding secured claims and those holding unsecured claims.

c. Trustee

After someone files for bankruptcy, the federal bankruptcy court will appoint a "trustee" to directly oversee the handling of the bankruptcy case. In Chapter 7 cases, the trustee for a particular case is selected from a panel of trustees. In Chapters 12 and 13 cases, one trustee handles all cases filed in that trustee's jurisdiction. (A jurisdiction is all or a portion of a federal court district.) In Chapter 11 cases, the court doesn't appoint a trustee at all, unless it finds that special circumstances warrant it.

You may also hear the term "U.S. trustee." This is a federal agent who keeps tabs on all bankruptcies. The Executive Office for U.S. Trustees is a division of the U.S. Attorney's office, which is part of the Department of Justice. One U.S. trustee oversees several bankruptcy courts. Individual cases within those courts are assigned to assistant U.S. trustees, who also employ attorneys, auditors and investigators. U.S. trustees work closely with their Department of Justice colleagues from the FBI and other federal agencies to ferret out fraud and abuse in the bankruptcy system.

The most likely setting in which you, as a creditor, might encounter a U.S. trustee is in a Chapter 11 case, where they take center stage because they oversee the administration of these cases (unless a separate trustee is appointed). U.S. trustees are also visible in cases that involve allegations of bad faith or fraud. U.S. trustees work behind the scenes in consumer cases, where their primary role is as the supervisor of the panel and the standing trustees who administer the cases.

d. Bankruptcy Court Judge

The bankruptcy judge has ultimate control over the debtor's case. In routine cases, the judge's role can be almost clerical, simply signing standard orders after little or no review. But don't let this lack of involvement fool you. The bankruptcy judge is in every way a federal judge. He or she knows the subject matter inside and out, has the power to punish abusive behavior, and can take action that permanently affects your ability to collect on your claim or to sell the collateral.

3. The Different Bankruptcy Chapters

Not all bankruptcies are the same. In fact, debtors may choose from four different types of bankruptcy protection. Each one is named for the chapter of the Bankruptcy Code where it is found. These include Chapter 7, Chapter 9, Chapter 11, Chapter 12, and Chapter 13. The numbering scheme may strike you as odd—Congress skipped chapters so that there would be room to add more of them later.

Chapter 9 Bankruptcy for Cities

Chapter 9 of the Bankruptcy Code allows municipalities to file for bankruptcy. However, we won't discuss Chapter 9 in this book because it probably won't be useful to our readers. Should a city or town that owes you money file for bankruptcy, however—as happened to many creditors in 1994 when Orange County, California, filed for bankruptcy—the basic rules we discuss elsewhere in this book will apply.

From your perspective, one of the major features distinguishing the different types of bankruptcy is whether the debtor's property can be sold so that creditors can collect on the proceeds, or whether creditors must instead rely primarily on the debtor's future income.

Chapter 7 is the only chapter that allows the debtor's property to be sold in order to pay off creditors' claims. However, don't count on selling the property of an individual—as opposed to a business—Chapter 7 debtor. The Bankruptcy Code allows individual debtors to exempt certain property, such as a home or car, from sale. Furthermore, the trustee won't sell loan collateral property unless it's worth more than is owed on the debt. So, the only property the trustee can realistically sell is stuff the debtor can't claim as exempt and that isn't pledged against a loan. The typical debtor doesn't have much property that fits into this category, and what they do have is seldom worth selling.

The other three chapters (11, 12, and 13) allow debtors to hang onto their property while reorganizing their debts. The focus of the case is the debtor's available income, which the debtor must use to fund a repayment plan. The debtor drafts the plan and submits it to the court for approval. Creditors and the trustee have a chance to object to the plan's provisions. Once the court finds the debtor's plan to be acceptable, it confirms the plan and the creditors should begin receiving payments from the debtor consistent with the plan's terms.

B. What All Bankruptcies Have in Common

Before detailing the differences between the four main chapters of bankruptcy, let's look at what features they have in common. This section will cover:

- the petition that starts off the case (Section 1)
- the automatic stay (Section 2)
- how creditors normally learn about the bankruptcy (Section 3)
- what property will be subject to the bankruptcy (Section 4)

- what property the debtor can keep (Section 5)
- how the property will be distributed to creditors (Section 6), and
- how the case will probably end (Section 7).

1. How a Bankruptcy Case Begins—the Petition

Regardless of which bankruptcy chapter the debtor will use, every voluntary bankruptcy case begins the same way, with the debtor filing a bankruptcy petition. The petition gives basic information about the debtor and the type of bankruptcy relief the debtor hopes to obtain. Along with the petition, the debtor must give the court a list of creditors, a schedule of assets and liabilities, and a summary of financial affairs (the debtor's economic transactions for the last several years before the filing). (See Chapter 5 for more information on the bankruptcy petition and related documents.)

2. The Automatic Stay—Bringing Creditors to a Halt

Debtors receive protection from their creditors as soon as they file for bankruptcy. This protection is known as the "automatic stay." It mandates that all creditors immediately stop all their collection efforts against the debtor. The automatic stay goes into effect upon the filing of the bankruptcy petition (regardless of whether all the accompanying paperwork is complete). The stay remains in effect until the case is closed, the bankruptcy is dismissed or the debtor receives or is denied a discharge. (See Chapter 4 for a full discussion of the automatic stay.)

3. How You'll Learn About the Bankruptcy

As a creditor, you are most likely to learn of the debtor's bankruptcy filing from a notice sent to you by the bankruptcy court. The notice will tell you the debtor's name, address, and the last four digits of his Social Security number. It will also give you the names of the debtor's attorney (if any) and the trustee—the person responsible for gathering the debtor's assets. You will be given a date and place when the debtor will be available for questioning by creditors and the trustee. The notice will also state a deadline by which you must take any action to preserve your claim or challenge the debtor's discharge. (See Chapter 3 for details on the bankruptcy notice.)

The notice isn't, however, the only way you might hear about the bankruptcy filing. If you have been actively trying to collect on your claim, you may be told about the bankruptcy even before you receive the official notice. If this happens, you must stop what you are doing and make a reasonable attempt to confirm what you've heard. That means contacting the debtor's attorney or the bankruptcy court to learn the status of the case. Sometimes debtors will say they filed when all they did was hire an attorney to prepare the bankruptcy petition. On the other hand, any action you take to collect your claim after the case has been filed is a violation of the automatic stay. Actions taken with knowledge of the filing are willful violations that could get you into very hot water.

4. What Property Goes Into the Bankruptcy Estate

The imposition of the automatic stay isn't the only thing that happens as soon as the debtor files for bankruptcy. The filing also triggers the creation of the bankruptcy "estate," a legal concept defining what property will be at issue—that is, fought over by creditors during the proceedings. The estate includes all the debtor's legal and equitable interests in any property. That's everything the debtor owns or has a right to own as of when the petition is filed. The estate also includes property the debtor acquires after filing for bankruptcy if the debtor had an interest in that property when the petition was filed. For example, in a Chapter 7 case, any wages that the debtor had worked to earn before filing but had not

yet received are added to the estate. However, wages the debtor earns after the filing date would not become part of the estate.

The bankruptcy estate does not include property that was unavailable to pay a creditor's claim when the debtor filed for bankruptcy. That property might have been unavailable because the debtor didn't yet own it, as would be the situation with income that had yet to be earned. Or, it might have been unavailable because state or federal law shields such property from creditors' claims. For example, money held in a retirement account such as an IRA, Keogh, or 401(k) plan is typically beyond the reach of creditors and, therefore, doesn't become a part of the debtor's bankruptcy estate. Whether property is or is not part of the bankruptcy estate is determined as of the time when the bankruptcy petition was filed. So, too, are creditors' rights to the debtor's property. It's as if that moment in time is frozen for purposes of determining who gets what in the bankruptcy.

5. What Property the Debtor Can Keep

While, in concept, most of what the debtor owns gets heaped into the bankruptcy estate, the law actually allows debtors to keep some of their possessions. To hang onto any particular item of property, the debtor must show that it falls into one of the various exemption categories. Of course, the debtor can only claim an exemption in as much of the property as she owns free and clear of debt—that is, her equity in the property.

> **EXAMPLE:** Davina owns a house worth $100,000 with a $75,000 mortgage. That means she has $25,000 of equity in the house. If she files under Chapter 7, she will be allowed to keep her house only if she is current on her mortgage payments and has filed in a state that has a homestead exemption of at least $25,000. (Homestead exemptions differ from state to state.)

In a Chapter 11, 12, or 13 reorganization case, the law similarly allows the debtor to keep any property that qualifies as exempt. In fact, she can keep property that doesn't qualify as exempt by paying more money into her reorganization plan. The amount of extra money must be at least as much as the value of the equity minus available exemptions.

> **EXAMPLE:** Delilah has a house worth $100,000 with a $75,000 mortgage, and therefore $25,000 in equity. She files for Chapter 13 bankruptcy. In the state where she lives, there is no homestead exemption. However, she is able to keep her house by paying at least $25,000 to her unsecured creditors through her plan.

Although the Bankruptcy Code is part of the federal law, it defers to the law of the debtor's home state when it comes time to determine the type and amount of property that the debtor may claim as exempt. (Some states, however, turn around and allow debtors to choose the federal exemption scheme.) Most states, as well as the federal law, allow debtors to exempt a specified amount of equity in their home, car, and common household possessions.

6. How Property in the Estate Gets Distributed

Property that the debtor can't keep may be used to pay creditors' claims. How this process works depends on the type of bankruptcy and the nature of the property. In a Chapter 7 case, once the exempt property has been removed from the bankruptcy estate, the trustee looks at what's left and determines whether there is anything of value. If there is, the trustee collects and sells it. If there isn't, the trustee abandons it and closes the estate.

In a reorganization case (Chapter 11, 12, or 13), the value of the debtor's non-exempt property is one of the criteria the bankruptcy judge considers when determining whether to approve the debtor's plan. The judge's object is to ensure that unsecured creditors will receive the value of the nonexempt property through the plan.

In cases where the debtor owns property that can be distributed to unsecured creditors, you may have to take action in order to claim your share. In either a Chapter 7 case where property will be sold and the proceeds distributed, or a Chapter 12 or 13 where unsecured creditors will be paid through the execution of the debtor's reorganization plan, only creditors who file proofs of claim will be paid. (See Chapter 7 of this book regarding how to file a proof of claim.) You need not file a proof of claim in a Chapter 11 case if your claim is listed in the debtor's bankruptcy schedules and there is no dispute as to the amount of your claim and the debtor's liability for its payment. The notice of the bankruptcy filing you receive from the court will tell you whether you need to file a proof of claim, and if so, by when.

7. How the Case May End

Once a case has successfully gotten underway, its three most likely ending scenarios include:
- discharge (Subsection a)
- conversion (Subsection b), and
- dismissal (Subsection c).

a. The Debtor Receives a Discharge

If all goes as it should, every bankruptcy case, regardless of chapter, will end the same way. Once the trustee has finished administering the estate, he will recommend to the bankruptcy judge that the case be closed and the debtor be discharged of—that is, forever freed from the legal obligation to pay—his debts. As a creditor, you may never again go after the debtor to collect any claims that were discharged in the course of this bankruptcy. Nor may you collect your claim from the debtor's property, unless you have a lien against that property that survived the bankruptcy.

On the other hand, if your claim is of the type that cannot be discharged in bankruptcy (detailed in Chapter 9), or you have obtained an order from the bankruptcy court determining that your claim should survive the bankruptcy, you will be able to try to collect on the debt as soon as the discharge is granted or the case is closed, whichever happens first.

b. Converting Between Bankruptcy Chapters

Debtors are normally allowed one free chance to voluntarily convert their cases to a different chapter of the Bankruptcy Code. Debtors might choose to do this because of a change in their financial circumstances. Conversion doesn't go so far as to end the case, but it does set it back near square one, under a mostly different set of rules. The main restriction on conversion is that the newly chosen chapter must be one under which the debtor could have filed originally. After the debtors use up their one free pass, they are not allowed to convert again without court approval.

Conversion isn't always voluntary. Creditors and trustees may ask the bankruptcy court to convert a reorganization case to a Chapter 7, though they can't ask to convert a Chapter 7 case to a Chapter 12 or 13. The court can also force a debtor to convert from Chapter 7 to Chapter 11 if appropriate. (See Chapter 14 for details on how conversion works, how it affects your claim, and when you should seek it or oppose it.)

c. Dismissal

The bankruptcy court may "dismiss" a case, which means that all previous court orders are vacated (canceled) and the parties are returned to whatever position they held on the date the case was first filed.

Dismissal at the debtor's request is widely available in Chapter 13 cases and only sometimes available in Chapter 7 cases. If a case is dismissed after one of the creditors has requested relief from the automatic stay, the debtor may not file another bankruptcy petition for 180 days. This prohibition gives the creditor a chance to foreclose on the debtor's property without the debtor being able to stop the foreclosure by refiling for bankruptcy protection.

Chapter 13 debtors may have their cases dismissed at any time, so long as their case has not previously been converted from another chapter. Although the Bankruptcy Code seems to require the courts to dismiss a Chapter 13 case any time the debtor asks for it, some courts impose additional requirements on the debtor nonetheless. Courts like to consider the circumstances motivating the debtor's dismissal request. If the motivation was improper, then the court may deny the request or order the case converted to a Chapter 7. A court's decision to keep the debtor in bankruptcy is usually motivated by a desire to protect the interests of unsecured creditors. The court deems it better to have a single trustee liquidate the debtor's assets than to leave all the creditors to haphazardly pursue those assets in state court.

Chapter 13 cases that have been converted from other chapters and bankruptcy cases filed under Chapter 7 may be dismissed only if the court believes it would be in the creditors' best interests to allow dismissal. It comes as a surprise to many debtors to learn that, having voluntarily filed for Chapter 7 relief, they can't also voluntarily "un-file." However, bankruptcy courts will usually deny debtors' request for dismissal if unsecured creditors stand to receive something on their claims if the case is kept open.

Trustees and creditors may also ask the bankruptcy court to dismiss debtors' cases. Usually, a motion to dismiss is filed by the trustee, based on the debtor's failure to obey the rules of the bankruptcy court. For example, Chapter 7 trustees ask the court to dismiss cases when debtors do not show up for their meetings with creditors.

C. What Distinguishes Each Type of Bankruptcy

Now that we've considered how all bankruptcies are similar, let's look at what makes them different. We'll look at the different chapters in the order you're most likely to encounter them, including:

- Chapter 7 (Subsection 1)
- Chapter 13 (Subsection 2)
- Chapter 11 (Subsection 3), and
- Chapter 12 (Subsection 4).

1. Chapter 7 Bankruptcy

Chapter 7 is by far the most frequent type of bankruptcy relief chosen by debtors. More than two out of every three debtors file under Chapter 7. You may hear Chapter 7 referred to as "straight bankruptcy" because it is what most people think of when they hear the word "bankruptcy." Chapter 7 is simply a process for gathering up everything the debtor owns, allowing him to keep what is exempt, enabling

secured creditors to recover property that was pledged as collateral and selling the rest to pay the claims of unsecured creditors.

In the typical Chapter 7 case, the debtor has no assets of any value, so the trustee has nothing to sell. These bankruptcies are referred to as "no-asset" cases. The notice you receive from the bankruptcy court will identify the case as either a "no-asset" or an "asset" case. The court will make this determination based on the information the debtor provided. The notice will also advise you whether you should file a proof of claim.

a. The Role of the Chapter 7 Trustee

The Chapter 7 trustee controls the flow of the case. This person is appointed from a panel of trustees maintained by the U.S. Trustee. It's the trustee's job to look out for the best interests of creditors, particularly unsecured creditors. The trustee is paid a commission, based on how much money he distributes to the creditors. This money comes from assets he collects from the debtor and sells. If the creditors end up with nothing, the trustee receives a flat fee of $60. As you can see, this system creates an incentive for trustees to collect whatever property is available and sell it for as much as possible. A maximum return to you means a maximum fee to the trustee.

A few weeks after the debtor files for bankruptcy, the trustee will hold a "meeting of creditors." The purpose is to examine the debtor and review the bankruptcy schedules and statements. Any creditor may appear (with or without an attorney) and question the debtor at this meeting. (See Chapter 6 for more on preparing for the creditors' meeting.)

Most trustees handle a number of cases at the same time. They may not have time to review the debtor's paperwork in as much detail as you would like. They also don't know the debtor as well as you might. So, if you find something suspicious—we'll talk about what should raise your suspicions in Chapter 5—you should bring it to the trustee's attention. If the area of suspicion is only relevant to your claim, you may have to file your own challenge to the debtor's ability to discharge your claim. But if dealing with it would benefit all creditors, then the trustee should be willing to handle it.

Trustees are going to be especially interested in property that the debtor owns or owned but didn't reveal on the bankruptcy schedules. Even if the debtor doesn't have the property any more, the trustee may be able to get it back from the person who does. (Even an unwitting buyer will need to prove that he didn't know about the bankruptcy, had no reason to suspect there was a bankruptcy, and paid fair value for the property—otherwise, the trustee may retrieve it.) A debtor who fails to disclose property on the bankruptcy schedules can also be barred from receiving a bankruptcy discharge.

Trustees are also going to be very interested in whether the debtor correctly stated her income and expenses. You may be able to help out in this investigation. Give the trustee any financial information you got from the debtor when the debt was incurred. Debtors whose income is more than enough to live on may be forced to choose between withdrawing their bankruptcy and converting their case to a reorganization (under Chapter 11, 12, or 13).

Once the trustee is satisfied that he has collected all the property he can, and that the debtor is qualified to receive a discharge, he submits a final report to the court. The court then issues the bankruptcy discharge. If the trustee instead believes that the debtor should not receive a discharge, he files a complaint to that effect and the court decides whether to grant the discharge or dismiss the case.

b. Your Role as a Chapter 7 Creditor

Most creditors, upon hearing that their claims have been listed in a Chapter 7 bankruptcy case, simply write them off as a lost cause. They seldom even bother to file a proof of claim. You'll have to use your own business judgment—but before jumping to conclusions, look at some of the ways that an alert creditor can turn the outcome of a Chapter 7 case to her advantage:

- **Identifying missing assets.** Do you know whether the debtor owned anything of value that wasn't mentioned in the bankruptcy schedule? Perhaps you sold it to the debtor. Perhaps it was listed on the debtor's loan application.
- **Identifying extra income.** Does the debtor make more money than is listed in the schedules? Does the debtor get paid in cash? Does the debtor work a second job?
- **Pointing out errors in the schedules and statements.** Does everything the debtor told the bankruptcy court jibe with what you know about the debtor?
- **Raising discharge exceptions.** The debtor may not have the right to discharge every debt. For example, debts that the judge determines were incurred by fraud cannot be discharged—the debtor remains on the hook for these.

Of course, you may not have any of this valuable information, and the case may end with your claim being discharged. If, however, you hold a secured claim and the debtor hasn't avoided your lien (see Chapter 8), you will be able to foreclose on the collateral after bankruptcy. Still, you won't be able to collect the balance from the debtor if you sell the property for less than what the debtor owes you.

2. Chapter 13 Bankruptcy

Chapter 13 bankruptcy is available to any consumer debtor with regular income who owes less than $290,525 in unsecured debts and less than $871,550 in secured debts.

⚠ The debt ceilings for Chapter 13 eligibility are adjusted every three years. The amounts just quoted are as of April 1, 2001. The next adjustment will occur on April 1, 2004.

Chapter 13 allows debtors to keep all their property if they pay their creditors' claims pursuant to a court-approved plan. This plan must:

- **Include all of the debtor's "projected disposable income."** Disposable income is what the debtor has left over every month after paying all necessary expenses. If you take this amount and extend it over the life of the plan, you arrive at projected disposable income. (See Chapter 13 of this book for more information.)
- **Pay unsecured creditors at least as much as they would have gotten if the debtor had filed under Chapter 7.** As we've seen, unsecured creditors would ordinarily end up with nothing under Chapter 7, so this requirement is either easily met or completely irrelevant. However, if the debtor's motive for choosing Chapter 13 was to protect the property that he

owned—which the trustee would have sold in a Chapter 7—then this requirement might help you, by guaranteeing that you will receive no less than you would have if the debtor's property had been sold. In legal terms, you will receive the "present value" of your claim. "Present value" is the amount you would have received today if the property were sold, plus interest to compensate you for your inevitable wait for payment.

Only debtors may propose Chapter 13 plans. However, the trustee and creditors are free to object to what the debtor proposes. The plan goes into effect when the bankruptcy judge confirms that it satisfies the Bankruptcy Code's requirements. To find out when the judge will consider confirming the plan, check the bankruptcy notice.

Regardless of when the judge actually confirms the debtor's plan, the debtor must begin making payments to the Chapter 13 trustee shortly after the petition is filed. The trustee will hold this money until the plan is confirmed, at which time the trustee will begin disbursing it to creditors according to the plan's terms.

Chapter 13 debtors, trustees and unsecured creditors may, under certain circumstances, ask the court to modify the terms of a confirmed plan. For example, they can ask the court to shorten or lengthen the plan, or to decrease or increase the amount of payments. Bank-

ruptcy judges disagree on what circumstances warrant modification of a confirmed plan. Usually, however, they require that the person seeking modification show a change in the debtor's circumstances that wasn't anticipated when the plan was being confirmed. Winning the lottery, changing jobs, or receiving an inheritance are examples of unexpected income increases that could warrant modifying the plan.

After a Chapter 13 debtor has made all the payments called for in the confirmed plan, the debtor can ask the court for a discharge. This discharge is broader than what the debtor would receive under a Chapter 7 bankruptcy. For example, debts incurred by fraud are discharged under Chapter 13 but not under Chapter 7.

It is possible for Chapter 13 debtors to ask the bankruptcy judge to grant them a discharge before they complete their payments. The condition is that completing the plan would impose a hardship on the debtor. A hardship discharge carries the same benefits as a Chapter 7 discharge.

a. The Role of the Chapter 13 Trustee

Chapter 13 trustees are known as "standing" trustees because they oversee all the Chapter 13 cases filed in their jurisdictions. Some bankruptcy courts have three or four bankruptcy judges but only one Chapter 13 trustee. Other courts have multiple trustees who are responsible for all the Chapter 13 cases filed within the same geographic area.

Chances are, of all the people you encounter in the bankruptcy process, the Chapter 13 trustee will be your most kindred spirit. That's because Chapter 13 trustees run their offices like private shops doing contract work for the bankruptcy court. Yes, the trustee is appointed by the U.S. Trustee, who oversees the trustee's operation. But trustees have a fair degree of autonomy when it comes to the daily operation of their offices.

For starters, Chapter 13 trustees do all the things Chapter 7 trustees do—review the debtor's petition, schedules, and statement for accuracy, conduct the creditors' meeting, and bring actions against the debtor and others when necessary to maximize the money available to repay creditors' claims.

However, the Chapter 13 trustee's primary activity is serving as a conduit for plan payments, collecting them from debtors and disbursing them to creditors. Many trustees handle more than $1 million every month. Last year, Chapter 13 trustees distributed about $4 billion to creditors.

In order to fulfill all these roles, Chapter 13 trustees normally hire full-time staffs, including data entry personnel, accountants, lawyers, and managers. Like Chapter 7 trustees, Chapter 13 trustees are paid by commission, that is, a percentage of the money paid to them by debtors.

Chapter 13 trustees tend to operate very cost-effective operations—their average commission is a reasonable 6%-plus. The maximum commission allowed by law is 10%. The rest of the money paid to Chapter 13 trustees goes to pay the claims filed against the estate.

b. Your Role as a Chapter 13 Creditor

When you receive the court's notice that your debtor has filed for Chapter 13, you are presented with a choice: file a proof of claim by the stated deadline, or ignore it as a lost cause. You'd be surprised how many creditors do the latter. The secured creditors have some justification for their decision, since they may still be able to proceed against the collateral. (However, some secured creditors get pulled into the proceedings anyway, when the debtor files a proof of claim on a secured creditor's behalf so as to avoid having the collateral exposed to foreclosure.)

Unsecured creditors who don't file a proof of claim may save a few minutes of their time, but could lose big later on. The debtor may have more money available to pay claims than was originally expected—but you'll share in it only if you filed a claim. Or, the debtor's financial situation might undergo a dramatic improvement after confirmation of the plan, as occurred in the following cases:

- A couple in Tennessee filed for bankruptcy after the husband lost his job. Under their Chapter 13 plan, unsecured creditors were to receive a mere 1% of their claims. But while their bankruptcy was proceeding, the husband settled a wrongful termination action—providing enough money to pay all their creditors in full.
- A Missouri man died after filing for Chapter 13 bankruptcy with his wife. The wife was the primary beneficiary of his life insurance policy. The court ordered the wife to modify her plan to include the proceeds from that policy.
- A Nevada couple sold their home after filing for Chapter 13 protection. The sale was made possible because the creditor holding the mortgage on the property agreed to be paid less than it was owed. The bankruptcy court ruled that the loan forgiveness was a property interest that should be used to pay the claims of unsecured creditors.

As mentioned above, secured creditors have two ways of getting paid—at least, in theory. Just like an unsecured creditor, you can look to the debtor for payment of your claim. If that's what you want to do, you must file a proof of claim. You can also look to the collateral for payment, which would mean getting possession of the property, selling it, and using the proceeds to pay your claim. If that's what you want to do, you don't need to file a proof of claim. Instead, you foreclose on the collateral once it is no longer protected by the automatic stay. If the debtor wants to avoid this result, however, he will file a claim for you in order to force you to get paid on your claim.

If your claim is to be paid through the debtor's reorganization plan, either because you filed a claim or because the debtor filed one for you, the bankruptcy rules require that you receive at least as much through the plan as you could have received if you had foreclosed. For example, if you could have sold the collateral for $10,000 and your claim is worth $10,000 or more, then the plan must pay you at least $10,000 plus interest. The rules also require that you keep your lien at least until your secured claim is fully paid.

If you believe the proposed reorganization plan doesn't pay the present value of your claim, then you should object to confirmation. (See Chapter 13 of this book.)

If you don't receive the payments to which you are entitled, or if the debtor does not meet the terms of your agreement—such as maintaining insurance on your property—you have the right to ask the bankruptcy court for permission to go after the collateral. (See Chapter 4 regarding repossessions or foreclosures.)

A Chapter 13 case usually ends in one of two ways: The debtor either completes the plan and receives a discharge, or doesn't complete the plan (and receives either a hardship discharge, which gives the same benefits as a Chapter 7 discharge, or no discharge at all). We'll cover how you would be affected by each of these two possible outcomes in Subsections i and ii, below.

i. If the Debtor Completes the Plan

If the debtor receives a Chapter 13 discharge after making all the planned-for payments, that's the end of the story for creditors whose claims were provided for in the plan. These creditors may not collect any unpaid balance due on their claims. Their unpaid balances are precisely what were discharged in the Chapter 13 proceeding.

How do you tell for sure whether your claim was provided for in the debtor's plan? If you are mentioned by name in the plan or if your claim is part of a group of claims identified by the plan—that is, if you can tell by reading the plan how your claim is going to be paid—you were provided for. Here are two common ways that claims are identified within a plan:

- **By name:** Each creditor is individually identified.
- **By class:** Creditors are not named, but the plan says that all holders of unsecured claims will receive a certain percentage of their claims or will share in a certain amount of money.

If the plan did, in fact, provide for the payment of your claim, then your claim was discharged even if you didn't file a proof of claim.

EXAMPLE: Dempsey's attorney agreed to represent him in his divorce even though Dempsey was broke. Dempsey did, however, own a hunting cabin that the attorney agreed to accept as collateral for his fees. Things went from bad to worse for Dempsey, and he ended up filing for bankruptcy. He chose Chapter 13, because it allowed him to pay his support arrearages over time. Dempsey listed his divorce attorney as an unsecured creditor, which was incorrect because the attorney held a lien against the hunting cabin. Dempsey's plan provided for the payment of his support obligation to his ex-wife and 10% of the claims of unsecured creditors who filed claims. The divorce attorney didn't file a claim and Dempsey didn't file one for him. After Dempsey finished making his plan payments, he received a discharge, but his debt to his attorney survived because Dempsey's plan didn't provide for the payment of any secured claims.

ii. If the Debtor Doesn't Complete the Plan

If the debtor fails to complete the plan, then your luck depends on whether the debtor seeks a discharge (either a hardship discharge under Chapter 13 or a discharge under another chapter that the debtor converts to) or has the case dismissed. If the case is dismissed, then you and the debtor return to your prebankruptcy positions. However, if the debtor receives a discharge, then what happens depends on whether your claim was secured and whether you filed a proof of claim. If your claim is secured by the debtor's property, your lien will survive the bankruptcy unless the court rules otherwise. It's often said that secured creditors can ignore bankruptcy and look to their lien for payment. While this statement is partially true, many secured creditors discover that their decision to ignore the bankruptcy costs them both their right to seek payment from the debtor and their ability to foreclose on the debtor's property.

How does this happen? As you'll see in Chapter 15, there are a number of ways that debtors can avoid liens. And Chapter 13 debtors have a bonus method at their disposal—they can pay secured claims in full through their plans, and have the court void the lien as soon as the secured claim is paid. If you didn't file a proof of claim, and if the debtor's plan called for your secured claim to be paid in full through the plan, the debtor may file a proof of claim *on your behalf*. This makes sure that your claim is paid and that your lien is no longer good.

3. Chapter 11 Bankruptcy

Chapter 11 is the common choice for corporations in need of bankruptcy relief. This explains why it's the chapter you'll most often hear about in the national media. Despite its visibility, however, Chapter 11 is not used as commonly as you might think. For every Chapter 11 case filed, other debtors file a whopping 39 cases under Chapter 13 and 96 cases under Chapter 7.

Another misconception is that Chapter 11 can be used only for the restructuring of major corporations. Technically, anyone can file under Chapter 11. However, Chapter 11 is very complicated and expensive for the debtor, and tends not to be as beneficial as Chapter 13. Consequently, Chapter 11 is used by individuals only when they don't qualify for Chapter 13 because of the size of their debts.

Corporations and partnerships, on the other hand, cannot file for Chapter 13 relief. Chapter 11 provides them their only opportunity to reorganize.

a. Who Fulfills the Trustee Role in a Chapter 11?

From your standpoint, one of the most important features of a Chapter 11 bankruptcy is that, unlike bankruptcies under Chapters 7 and 13, no trustee is normally appointed. Instead, the debtor retains possession and control of all his property. However, the debtor now owns this property in a different capacity—as a so-called "debtor in possession" (DIP). The DIP title lets anyone who deals with the debtor know that, although the person or corporation exercising control over the property is the same as before the bankruptcy, that person's or corporation's legal capacity has changed.

A DIP has all the powers and duties of a trustee. There are, however, a few times when the debtor can't successfully wear the dual hats of DIP and trustee. One is at the creditors' meeting, where the DIP obviously can't interrogate itself. The creditors' meeting will be conducted by the U.S. Trustee. In addition, however, the U.S. Trustee may find that it's not appropriate for the debtor to wear two hats in a particular case, and ask the court to assign a regular trustee—for example, if there are indications that the DIP has not disclosed all his or her assets.

If you know of any such tomfoolery by the DIP, bring this to the U.S. Trustee's attention immediately. It may lead to the appointment of a trustee to run the case or an examiner to audit the DIP's financial dealings.

Despite the relative low frequency of Chapter 11 filings, they can affect a large number of people. Employees owed wages, former employees paid from a company-run pension fund, professionals who provided services, vendors who provided goods, holders of stock in the bankrupt company and others will all become creditors in a Chapter 11.

In order to keep this large number of people organized, the creditors' interests in a Chapter 11 filing are represented by committees formed according to the type of claim. The U.S. Trustee must organize a committee representing unsecured creditors as soon as possible after the bankruptcy filing. The U.S. Trustee may also organize other committees to represent other creditor constituencies as needed. For example, the U.S. Trustee may create a committee to represent stockholders when a publicly traded company files for bankruptcy.

The U.S. Trustee normally asks the holders of the seven largest claims of each type to serve on the relevant committee. These committees may hire attorneys, accountants, appraisers or whatever professional counsel they need to represent the committees' interests in the bankruptcy. The DIP is responsible for paying the fees and costs charged by these professionals.

The committees are charged with looking out for the common good of all their members. If the members of a committee have too many competing interests to achieve this goal, the group can be further subdivided. Any creditor or the DIP may ask the U.S. Trustee to create smaller committees.

The Enron bankruptcy of 2002 provides a good example of how committees may be carved out of the larger group. Here, the U.S. Trustee determined that a special committee was needed to represent the interests of Enron's current and former employees. The employees had concerns such as the continuation of their health care benefits, the payment of termination bonuses, and the prosecution of various legal actions against the company. Concerns of this nature could not have been properly considered by a committee representing the claims of all unsecured creditors.

Lawyers Benefit Most From a Chapter 11

Back in 1989, publisher Sol Stein described his experience as the owner of a company that went into Chapter 11 bankruptcy, in a book called *A Feast for Lawyers*. The title accurately described his impression of Chapter 11 then—and pretty much accurately describes what happens today. The Chapter 11 process is so expensive and time consuming that the lawyers walk away with most of the spoils—and few businesses successfully reorganize.

For example, six months into the Enron bankruptcy, the *Houston Chronicle* reported that Enron was spending $22 million per month in attorneys' fees. The law firm representing Enron had assigned 120 attorneys to the case and was billing more than $6 million per month. On top of this, Enron was responsible for paying the attorneys and accountants representing the creditors' committee and the two examiners who were investigating the company's finances.

Concerned about escalating fees, the judge appointed a committee to review the professional expenses. Guess what—after a mere month on the job, the chairman of that committee billed Enron $20,500 for the work he'd done so far.

Not every bankruptcy is on the scale of Enron—but every dollar that goes to pay an attorney is one dollar that doesn't go to pay creditors. The result is that most Chapter 11 bankruptcies—about 70% of them—end in dismissal or conversion. While these cases may have looked viable at the beginning, the debtors' obligations to pay attorneys' fees wipe out their few remaining financial resources, so that a reorganization plan cannot be confirmed. Dismissal or conversion to another bankruptcy chapter then becomes the debtors' only option.

b. Your Role as a Chapter 11 Creditor

As a creditor in a Chapter 11 case, your main concerns include seeing that your claim is correctly listed and scheduled, deciding how to vote on the debtor's plan for making payments on your claim, and tracking the debtor's payments until the case is finished.

i. Establishing Your Claim

When you get a copy of the debtor's schedules, you'll need to check to see that your claim is listed in the correct amount and that the debtor admits liability on the claim. If both these things are true, you do not need to file a proof of claim. If the case is large, the court may appoint an independent claims processing agent to handle the mailing of notices and the collection of proofs of claims. Such an agent will also be able to tell you how your claim is scheduled.

There is an advantage to having a relatively small claim against the debtor. The debtor may well concede liability in the correct amount and/or offer to pay the claim in full, as a way of getting your vote of acceptance for the plan. Also, paying small claims in full is usually more convenient and economical for the debtor than haggling with creditors over pennies. Check the paperwork carefully nonetheless—you're the one most interested in seeing that your claim is correctly set forth.

If your claim is on the larger end of the scale, or if the debtor seems to have empty pockets, you'll likely need outside assistance. An experienced bankruptcy attorney can help you decide whether to accept the debtor's proposal, back a competing plan or propose a plan of your own. You may also be able to sell your claim, either to an enterprise that speculates in bankruptcy claims or to another creditor who is looking to acquire a stronger bargaining position.

ii. Your Input Into the Reorganization Plan

Creditors in Chapter 11 cases are paid on the basis of the debtor's reorganization plan (similar to Chapter 13 cases). Unlike in Chapter 13 cases, however, creditors have the opportunity to propose their own plan if the debtor doesn't propose a confirmable plan within 120 days after filing. Also unlike a Chapter 13, creditors can cast their vote for or against the confirmation of a proposed plan.

When you receive a copy of a Chapter 11 plan, it will be accompanied by a disclosure statement. This is intended to convey enough information for you to decide whether to accept or reject the proposed plan. The bankruptcy court approves the contents of these disclosure statements before soliciting your vote. For more on deciding how to cast your vote, see Chapter 13 of this book.

In a fair number of cases, the debtor is ultimately unable to confirm a plan. The fate of your claim then depends on the outcome of the debtor's bankruptcy. If the case is converted to another type of bankruptcy (for example, from Chapter 11 to Chapter 7), then you'll start over under the rules of whichever new chapter the debtor chooses. That may mean you have to file a proof of claim for the first time, assuming that the debtor believes there will be money available to pay unsecured claims. (The court will tell you how to proceed.) If the case is simply dismissed, then you can act as though it was never filed—and once again go after the debtor for payment.

iii. Proceeding Under the Plan

Once confirmed, the Chapter 11 plan becomes a contract between the debtor and the creditors. As a creditor, you're supposed to get paid according to the plan's terms and you won't be allowed to sue the debtor for payment of the prior debt.

Chapter 11 debtors don't receive a discharge at the end of the case like Chapter 7 and Chapter 13 debtors do. The plan survives the bankruptcy, and the debtor's relief from indebtedness depends on the terms and arrangements made in those plans—with one exception. If the plan calls for a debtor corporation or partnership's assets to be liquidated, the case is treated like a Chapter 7. This clears the way for the enterprise to be dissolved under state law. Under these circumstances, the debtor's assets would be sold through the bankruptcy with the proceeds applied to pay creditors' claims. Creditors whose claims are secured by property would get paid first. The remaining creditors would be paid in accordance with the Bankruptcy Code's priority scheme. (See Chapter 5 for a list of priority claims.)

4. Chapter 12 Bankruptcy

A brief word on Chapter 12 bankruptcy: Unless you do business in an agricultural area, your debtors are unlikely to file for Chapter 12. It provides relief for "family farmers"—people who earn more than 80% of their income from farming. To make use of Chapter 12, they must not owe more than $1.5 million, and at least 80% of their debt must be attributable to their farming operation.

Another factor reducing your chances of encountering Chapter 12 is that it's a temporary provision in the law. Over the years, it has repeatedly expired and then been revived by Congress. At some point, however, Congress may get tired of bringing it back to life. The chapter's expiration does not affect cases that were properly filed while the relief was available, but it prevents new cases from being filed under it.

The Chapter 12 bankruptcy law is modeled on that of Chapter 13. Therefore, everything discussed in Subsection 2, above, regarding Chapter 13 also applies to Chapter 12.

Bankruptcy by the Numbers		
The chart below reviews the main Bankruptcy Code chapters under which a debtor can seek relief and how a debtor's choice will affect her and you.		
Code Chapter	**Effect on Debtor**	**Effect on Creditors**
Chapter 7	The debtor is protected from creditors, while the debtor's nonexempt, unencumbered assets are liquidated.	Secured creditors get paid the value of their liens (assuming the debtor has sufficient assets), while unsecured creditors get whatever is left over.
Chapter 11	The debtor, which is usually a corporation or partnership, is protected from creditors while the debtor is reorganized.	Secured creditors get paid the value of their liens, while unsecured creditors get whatever is needed to gain their acceptance of the reorganization plan.
Chapter 13	The debtor, an individual, will be reorganized.	Secured creditors get paid the present value of their secured claims, while unsecured creditors get whatever the debtor can afford to pay, provided it's at least as much as the creditors would get under a Chapter 7 bankruptcy. ■

Finding Out the Debtor Has Gone Bankrupt

The entire debtor-creditor relationship changes when the debtor files for bankruptcy. One second before the filing, you may do whatever you please (so long as it's legal) to get paid. One second afterward, you can't do anything—and something as innocent as sending a collection letter to the debtor may expose you to court-imposed penalties for violating the automatic stay (discussed in Chapter 4). Why such a dramatic shift?

The bankruptcy law assumes that the debtor is entitled to bankruptcy protection. There's no need for the debtor to prove insolvency at the filing stage. The debtor doesn't even need to prove an inability to pay her bills, although Congress has discussed creating such a requirement. All that's necessary to start the bankruptcy ball rolling is that the debtor file a few sheets of paper asking the court for bankruptcy protection.

Under these circumstances, you can see why it's important that you know exactly when a debtor files for bankruptcy. Since you can be penalized for violating the automatic stay even if you don't know about it, you might as well take steps to ensure that you will know about it. You also have a positive incentive for learning about the bankruptcy. Once you know, you can start working to protect your claim from discharge and preserve your liens from elimination by the bankruptcy court. If you ignore the bankruptcy and your claim is discharged, you'll never be able to collect your claim from the debtor and you may lose your ability to foreclose on your liens against the debtor's property.

This chapter focuses on the formal and informal ways you may learn of a debtor's bankruptcy filing. You're probably going to learn about the bankruptcy filing in one of two ways:

- the court will notify you (Section A), or
- you'll find out about it by chance, most likely from the debtor (Section B).

A. Notice from the Bankruptcy Court

The usual way to learn about a bankruptcy filing is by getting an official notice from the court. The clerk of the court will send the official notice a few days after the debtor's bankruptcy filing. (Or, in some very large cases, the court may appoint an independent claims processing agent to handle the mailing of notices.) The recipients will include all creditors listed in a mailing matrix provided by the debtor.

The primary notice form will look like the sample shown below, titled "Notice of Chapter 7 Bankruptcy Case, Meeting of Creditors, & Deadlines." (The notices for the other bankruptcy chapters look quite similar—you can view or download them online, from the U.S. Courts website at www.uscourts.gov/bankform/index.html.) However, the notice will be just the first thing you see in a packet of forms.

⚠️ **Here come the forms.** Bankruptcy is a form-oriented practice, so we'll be introducing you to an alphabet soup of form names and titles. Using standardized forms whenever possible provides consistency and predictability from one court to another across the country.

In this section, we'll explain:

- what information you'll find in the court notice (Subsection 1)
- why some court notices never reach you (Subsection 2), and
- how to ensure that future bankruptcy court notices reach you (Subsection 3).

1. What You'll Learn from the Court Notice

The first thing you'll see when you open the packet from the bankruptcy court is the official notice of the bankruptcy filing on Form B9. This form has several variations, to cover filings under each chapter of the Bankruptcy Code as well as filings by individuals, partnerships and corporations.

Don't expect the notice to contain much information that's specific to you and your claim. However, it will give you and all other creditors important information about the bankruptcy case itself. It

will tell you, for example, when the meeting of creditors will be held, the deadlines for filing certain actions, and whether creditors should file a proof of claim. From the front of the notice alone, you'll learn:

- **Which chapter of the Bankruptcy Code the petition was filed under.**
  If it was filed under Chapter 7, the notice will also say whether the debtor claims or admits to having assets that can be sold to pay the claims of unsecured creditors. Most Chapter 7 debtors have no assets, so you're most likely to see notice of a "no-asset" Chapter 7. In a no-asset case, you'll be instructed not to file a proof of claim. You'll also be advised that if assets turn up that might result in some type of payment to you, you'll be notified and invited to file a proof of claim.

- **The date when the case was filed—and therefore when the automatic stay went into effect.**
  Check to see whether you or anyone working for you carried on with any collection activity on the debtor's account after the petition date. If you received a payment, recorded a lien, or repossessed any collateral after the filing date, you may have violated the stay. To avoid being penalized, you'll probably need to undo whatever you did. (See Chapter 4.)

Notice of Chapter 7 Bankruptcy Case, Meeting of Creditors, & Deadlines

FORM B9A (Chapter 7 Individual or Joint Debtor No Asset Case (9/97))

UNITED STATES BANKRUPTCY COURT	_____ District of _____

Notice of
Chapter 7 Bankruptcy Case, Meeting of Creditors, & Deadlines

[A chapter 7 bankruptcy case concerning the debtor(s) listed below was filed on _____ (date).]

or [A bankruptcy case concerning the debtor(s) listed below was originally filed under chapter _____ on _____ (date) and was converted to a case under chapter 7 on_____.]

You may be a creditor of the debtor. **This notice lists important deadlines.** You may want to consult an attorney to protect your rights. All documents filed in the case may be inspected at the bankruptcy clerk's office at the address listed below. NOTE: The staff of the bankruptcy clerk's office cannot give legal advice.

See Reverse Side For Important Explanations.

Debtor(s) (name(s) and address):	Case Number:
	Social Security/Taxpayer ID Nos.:
Attorney for Debtor(s) (name and address):	Bankruptcy Trustee (name and address):
Telephone number:	Telephone number:

Meeting of Creditors:

Date: /   /   Time: (   ) A.M.   Location:
                              (   ) P.M.

Deadlines:

Papers must be *received* by the bankruptcy clerk's office by the following deadlines:

Deadline to File a Complaint Objecting to Discharge of the Debtor *or* to Determine Dischargeability of Certain Debts:

Deadline to Object to Exemptions:

Thirty (30) days after the *conclusion* of the meeting of creditors.

Creditors May Not Take Certain Actions

The filing of the bankruptcy case automatically stays certain collection and other actions against the debtor and the debtor's property. If you attempt to collect a debt or take other action in violation of the Bankruptcy Code, you may be penalized.

Please Do Not File A Proof of Claim Unless You Receive a Notice To Do So.

Address of the Bankruptcy Clerk's Office:	For the Court:
	Clerk of the Bankruptcy Court:
Telephone number:	
Hours Open:	Date:

Notice of Chapter 7 Bankruptcy Case, Meeting of Creditors, & Deadlines, page 2

EXPLANATIONS

FORM B9A (9/97)

Filing of Chapter 7 Bankruptcy Case	A bankruptcy case under chapter 7 of the Bankruptcy Code (title 11, United States Code) has been filed in this court by or against the debtor(s) listed on the front side, and an order for relief has been entered.
Creditors May Not Take Certain Actions	Prohibited collection actions are listed in Bankruptcy Code § 362. Common examples of prohibited actions include contacting the debtor by telephone, mail or otherwise to demand repayment; taking actions to collect money or obtain property from the debtor; repossessing the debtor's property; starting or continuing lawsuits or foreclosures; and garnishing or deducting from the debtor's wages.
Meeting of Creditors	A meeting of creditors is scheduled for the date, time and location listed on the front side. *The debtor (both spouses in a joint case) must be present at the meeting to be questioned under oath by the trustee and by creditors.* Creditors are welcome to attend, but are not required to do so. The meeting may be continued and concluded at a later date without further notice.
Do Not File a Proof of Claim at This Time	There does not appear to be any property available to the trustee to pay creditors. *You therefore should not file a proof of claim at this time.* If it later appears that assets are available to pay creditors, you will be sent another notice telling you that you may file a proof of claim, and telling you the deadline for filing your proof of claim.
Discharge of Debts	The debtor is seeking a discharge of most debts, which may include your debt. A discharge means that you may never try to collect the debt from the debtor. If you believe that the debtor is not entitled to receive a discharge under Bankruptcy Code § 727(a) *or* that a debt owed to you is not dischargeable under Bankruptcy Code § 523(a)(2), (4), (6), or (15), you must start a lawsuit by filing a complaint in the bankruptcy clerk's office by the "Deadline to File a Complaint Objecting to Discharge of the Debtor or to Determine Dischargeability of Certain Debts" listed on the front side. The bankruptcy clerk's office must receive the complaint and the required filing fee by that Deadline.
Exempt Property	The debtor is permitted by law to keep certain property as exempt. Exempt property will not be sold and distributed to creditors. The debtor must file a list of all property claimed as exempt. You may inspect that list at the bankruptcy clerk's office. If you believe that an exemption claimed by the debtor is not authorized by law, you may file an objection to that exemption. The bankruptcy clerk's office must receive the objection by the "Deadline to Object to Exemptions" listed on the front side.
Bankruptcy Clerk's Office	Any paper that you file in this bankruptcy case should be filed at the bankruptcy clerk's office at the address listed on the front side. You may inspect all papers filed, including the list of the debtor's property and debts and the list of the property claimed as exempt, at the bankruptcy clerk's office.
Legal Advice	The staff of the bankruptcy clerk's office cannot give legal advice. You may want to consult an attorney to protect your rights.

—Refer To Other Side For Important Deadlines and Notices—

- **The case's docket number.** This is the number the bankruptcy court assigns to the debtor's case. Any document filed in the case, including your proof of claim, must include this identifying number.

- **Whether the case was originally filed under another chapter of the Bankruptcy Code, but has since been converted.** When a debtor converts from Chapter 7 to one of the reorganization chapters (11, 12, or 13), it's a good sign for creditors—it usually means they will receive something on their claims. While you might have been instructed not to file a proof of claim back when the original Chapter 7 was a no-asset case, you'll need to file a proof of claim if the case has been converted to Chapter 12 or 13. You may or may not need to file a proof of claim if the case was converted to Chapter 11, depending on whether your claim was accurately listed in the debtor's schedules.

- **The deadline for filing a proof of claim.** Courts operate on strict deadlines, so make a note of this date. Filing a proof of claim before the deadline is one of the simplest things you can do to protect your claim. But you'll recall that if the case is a no-asset Chapter 7 case, the notice will tell you not to file a proof of claim unless you later receive a notice to do so.

- **If the debtor filed under Chapter 12 or 13, the date and time of the plan confirmation hearing.** While creditors can't propose Chapter 12 or 13 reorganization plans and don't get to vote on them, they can object to them. The confirmation hearing is the event at which the court considers the debtor's plan and the creditors' objections.

- **The debtor's name, address, and Social Security number (last four digits only).** If the listed name doesn't ring a bell and doesn't match with anything you have on file, call the debtor's attorney to find out why you were listed as a creditor. Maybe the debtor was a cosigner on a loan or changed her name. There are many reasons why you may not recognize the name of a person who owes you money, so don't ignore the notice.

- **The name, address, and telephone number of the debtor's lawyer.** Your relationship with the debtor may be adversarial, but that doesn't mean your relationship with the debtor's counsel should be. If you've got a question about the case, the lawyer listed here—or a member of the lawyer's office staff—may be the best person to ask. Most debtors' attorneys have a paralegal or another staff person dedicated to answering questions from creditors. Lawyers who make their living representing debtors know that the best way to maximize their earnings is to avoid trouble with creditors. (See Chapter 6 for communication do's and don'ts.)

- **The name, address, and telephone number of the trustee.** Like the debtor's attorney, the trustee assigned to the case will have a staff member available to assist you. The trustee represents all creditors and is very interested in any information you can provide that will benefit all creditors.

- **The address, telephone number, and office hours of the bankruptcy clerk's office.** All documents in the bankruptcy case are filed at the clerk's office. (Don't make the mistake of sending court pleadings such as your proof of claim or objection to discharge to the trustee for filing. That's not the trustee's job.) Clerks can usually help you with procedural matters or basic information, but they can't provide legal advice. For example, they can tell you when the deadline is to file your proof of claim, but they can't tell you how to file the proof of claim. Also, the clerk's office is where the case files are kept, so it's where you'd go to examine the debtor's filing.

- **The time and place of the creditors' meeting.** The Bankruptcy Code requires debtors to submit to an examination by their creditors, moder-

ated by the trustee. If you have any reason to be suspicious about any aspect of the bankruptcy, you won't want to miss the chance to attend the meeting and ask the debtor your questions. (See Chapter 6 for more about the creditors meeting; and Chapter 5 to find out the types of information [or lack thereof] that should raise your suspicions.)

- **The deadline for filing complaints challenging the debtor's ability to discharge your claim through bankruptcy.** Certain types of bills can't be wriggled out of using bankruptcy. (See Chapter 9 for details.) In some cases, these debts survive the bankruptcy automatically—you wouldn't have to take any action. In other cases, however, you will need to challenge the debtor's ability to discharge the debt by filing a dischargeability complaint in the bankruptcy court.

- **The deadline for filing complaints challenging the debtor's very eligibility to receive a discharge.** Some debtors are not entitled to discharge any of their debts, period. (See Chapter 12.)

- **The deadline for filing objections to the property exemptions being claimed by the debtor.** Debtors sometimes attempt to protect and keep more property than the law allows. These unfounded exemptions become valid if no one objects. (See Chapter 5 for more on spotting unfounded exemptions.)

EXAMPLE: On debtor David's bankruptcy paperwork, he lists his occupation as construction worker, and claims his pickup truck as an exempt tool of his trade. This all looks logical to the trustee, who is ready to accept David's statement that he uses the truck in his work. But a creditor who lives near David has watched David's wife drive the truck to her teaching job for the last few years. The creditor successfully objects to the exemption.

That's it for the front of the notice. On the back of the notice, you'll find a brief explanation of bankruptcy.

➡️ **Many of you reading this book are doing so because you've received notice of the filing.** You may skip ahead to the next chapter, unless you are curious about what would have happened had you not received the notice.

2. When Bankruptcy Notices Go Astray

Court notices that never reach the creditor are more common than you might think—leading to unwitting violations of the automatic stay. One reason is that most debtors, when creating the mailing matrix

they'll give to the court, use either the return address from the last letter they received from their creditors or the address where they were sending their payments. Because anyone working for you is considered your "agent," and therefore a legitimate person to receive your mail, this causes scenarios such as the following:

EXAMPLE: Catherine the creditor hands debtor Devon's claim over to her attorney for collection. The attorney sends Devon a demand letter. After Devon files for bankruptcy, he gives the court the attorney's address. Meanwhile, the attorney has taken off on a month-long vacation and his secretary has quit, so the notice languishes in the attorney's Inbox. The creditors' meeting comes and goes without Catherine. She, meanwhile, gets frustrated and leaves a message on Devon's voice mail saying that she'll accept partial payment if he'll come up with a check by the end of the month. Catherine is now in violation of the automatic stay.

A similar result could have occurred if Catherine, in the example above, had turned her claim over to a collection agency. An attorney or a collection agency counts as your "agent," so the court won't look with any sympathy if your agent received the notice instead of you. It's as if the notice had come to you directly.

EXAMPLE: Carl the creditor manages a large office supplies company with a separate billing department. Dina the debtor orders a leather chair and some fancy pens. Carl has met Dina a few times in person, and always figured she was wealthy, since she dripped with sparkling—and obviously real—diamonds. The trouble is, Dina doesn't pay her bills. Carl's billing department sends her two notices, with no reply. Dina then files for bankruptcy. The notice is sent to Carl's billing department. Unfortunately, the person who opens the mail has never seen one of these notices before, and puts it in Dina's file for normal collection activities.

By the time the error is discovered, Carl has missed the creditors' meeting—at which Dina showed up wearing no jewelry at all. What's more, the statements she filed with the court claimed she owned only a wedding ring and some inconsequential costume pieces. Had Carl known of the creditors' meeting, he could have asked her what happened to all those diamonds.

Carl's situation isn't the worst that could happen to a creditor—but it's one that's worth avoiding, by training your staff and developing a system for handling incoming bankruptcy notices (see Subsection 3, below).

To make sure you get prompt notice of any bankruptcy filings, give specific instructions to anyone collecting debts for you. Tell the person to call you or fax you the bankruptcy notice immediately upon receiving it. If your office has multiple locations, make sure someone in each location knows what to do with the notice. The first meeting of creditors may be held just a few days after the notice finally gets to you, and you'll want to prepare for it if you're going to attend.

If, however, the court notice was sent someplace completely inappropriate, you will not be held responsible for knowing of the bankruptcy. If, for example, the debtor typed your address wrong, and it ended up where neither you, your business, nor anyone acting as your agent is located, this doesn't count as your having received notice. Such an errant delivery will not mean that the automatic stay doesn't apply to you—it does. However, anything you do that violates the stay will be an innocent violation. As long as you undo your action without delay, you won't be penalized for your violation. The one caveat is that if you learned of the bankruptcy by other means, or should have learned of it through your own investigation, you will still be held responsible.

3. Developing Office Procedures for Handling Bankruptcy Notices

By setting up a system within your office for responding to bankruptcy notices, you'll reduce the chances of missing important steps in the bankruptcy case or violating the automatic stay. We suggest designating one person or a team of people to be in charge of all your bankrupt accounts. An advantage to this centralized control is that it may prevent an over-enthusiastic manager from taking actions that violate other areas of the Bankruptcy Code.

Even if you and your entire operating staff are at close quarters, you should take the following steps as soon as a bankruptcy notice comes in the door:

- **Flag the account.** Mark the debtor's account in a clear and conspicuous manner to show that a bankruptcy has been filed.
- **Remove the account from regular collections.** Don't take the chance that a bill or collection letter could be automatically sent to the debtor. Accidents happen, but failing to guard against them is not an accident in the eyes of the bankruptcy court.
- **Review the file for outside collection activity.** Make sure everyone doing debt collection for you is aware of the bankruptcy. Remind them to cease all collection activity until you tell them it's okay to start up again. You may need to contact collection agents, repo professionals, court officials, and attorneys.
- **Turn the debtor's file and the bankruptcy notice over to the person responsible for bankruptcy filings.** That person can then monitor and participate in the bankruptcy proceedings.
- **Deal with any address problems.** If the bankruptcy notice was sent to the wrong address or the wrong person, correct this error as soon as you learn of it. Do so by either filing a proof of claim with the correct address or asking the clerk of the court to change your address, depending on the type of bankruptcy proceedings. If you will be filing a proof of claim, this is your method of first choice—and once you've filed it, all notices must be sent to the address you've listed. If you received a notice of a no-asset Chapter 7, which instructs you not to file a proof of claim, you'll have to ask the clerk, in writing, to change your address in the court's records. Also send a copy of your request to the debtor's attorney, so the attorney's records may also be corrected.

What If You Can't Identify the Customer Account?

Everything we've discussed doing regarding the bankruptcy notice assumes you can figure out which of your customers the notice is referring to. The notice gives a lot of information, but it may not tally with your internal records. For example, if you keep track of customers using account numbers, don't expect to see that number on the bankruptcy notice. Such information might be found in the schedules and statements filed with the court (assuming your customer knows his account number), but you don't get a copy of the schedules and statements along with the notice. If you can't figure out why you received the notice, call the debtor's attorney (who is listed on the notice), ask why your claim was included in the bankruptcy and get the account number. Or, you could go to the courthouse and look at the filing for yourself.

Whatever you do, don't assume the notice was sent to you by mistake. You could expose yourself to liability for violating the automatic stay, and possibly throw away your only chance to collect on your claim.

B. Informal Notice

All the information that's in the official court notice won't do you any good if you don't receive it. But you'll only get the notice if the debtor gave your address to the court correctly—and how much do you trust the debtor at this point? There's also a chance that someone connected to you did receive the notice, but didn't pass it along to you. This section will discuss what to do as soon as you find out that:

- the case has recently been filed (Subsection 1)
- the case has been filed and is well underway (Subsection 2), or
- the case is over and done with (Subsection 3).

1. You Happen to Hear About a Recent Bankruptcy Filing

If you are actively seeking collection of your claim, you're likely to hear about the debtor's bankruptcy filing even before you receive the official court notice. You'll most likely hear about it from the debtor, in response to your telephone call, repossession effort, or attempted foreclosure sale. The debtor may say, "Stop! I filed for bankruptcy and my lawyer says you can't call me any more/take my car/sell my house!" Until you can confirm whether the debtor is telling the truth, you'll have to take his words at face value and stop trying to collect, as detailed below.

Even if you hear that the debtor has filed for bankruptcy from someone other than the debtor—perhaps a relative, a neighbor, or another creditor—you should accept it as true. The law doesn't care how you learned about the bankruptcy. It only asks whether you actually knew about the bankruptcy. If you choose to ignore the information, you do so at your own risk.

a. Stop Collection Activities

By now, you know that the filing of a bankruptcy petition requires you to stop all attempts to collect your claim. This is true even if you find out about the filing informally. Though it may turn out the debtor was lying, if he turns out to have been telling the truth, you're on the hook for violating the automatic stay.

b. Attempt to Confirm the Filing

Your next step is to find out, as quickly as possible, whether the debtor is selling you a line or not. If you can find out the court docket number, it should be a simple matter to check out the situation with the court.

If you learn of the bankruptcy filing in a face-to-face encounter with the debtor, ask to see a time-stamped copy of the

bankruptcy petition. If the petition was filed with the bankruptcy court it will have a docket number stamped on it along with the date and time the clerk of the bankruptcy court received it. A copy of the petition without these markings doesn't tell you anything, but suggests that the petition wasn't filed. However, it may just be that the debtor's attorney gave the debtor an unfiled copy of the petition.

If the debtor can't produce a time-stamped copy of the petition, or you're told of the filing over the telephone, ask for the docket number or the name of the debtor's attorney. If you get the docket number, call the bankruptcy court to confirm the filing. If you get the attorney's name, call the attorney's office, get the docket number, and then call the bankruptcy court.

⚠ Don't take anyone's word except the court's. Debtors will lie to you to save their property. Attorneys will lie to you to cover the fact that they didn't do what they should have, namely filed the bankruptcy petition when they said they would. The only place to find out whether a bankruptcy petition was truly filed, and when, is the bankruptcy court.

If you are unable to confirm the bankruptcy filing after making a reasonable attempt to do so, you may resume your collection attempts. However, what's considered "reasonable" depends on the circumstances. For example, trying to call the court at 8 p.m., when it's closed, and then giving up, is not at all reasonable.

But what if you learn about the bankruptcy late one evening, and the debtor's home is scheduled to be sold by the county sheriff the very next day? You should still try to reach the bankruptcy court in the morning, before the sale occurs. If you confirm there is a filing, you can postpone the sale without violating the automatic stay. If you can't confirm the filing, despite your best efforts to do so, you should let the sale proceed.

2. You Hear About a Bankruptcy That's Well Underway

If the court notice went astray and you haven't happened to talk to the debtor recently, it could be weeks or even months before you find out about the debtor's bankruptcy. However, regardless of how much time has gone by, you are not excused from taking prompt, appropriate action. That includes contacting the court to confirm that a bankruptcy petition was filed and how far along the case has gotten.

If you're lucky, you may learn of the bankruptcy before the deadline for filing objections to the debtor's discharge or the dischargeability of your claim. If that deadline is coming up fast, you can ask the court to extend it. However, if the deadline passes and you knew about it but didn't ask for an extension, you'll

probably lose your ability to file these objections. It doesn't matter that you didn't have sufficient time to review the debtor's paperwork, you missed the chance to question the debtor at the creditors' meeting and you don't have enough time to negotiate a settlement of your claim. If you had enough time to ask the court for an extension, the deadline will apply to you. (See Chapter 10 for procedures on requesting an extension.)

3. You Hear About a Completed Bankruptcy Case

It may happen that you remained completely in the dark throughout the whole bankruptcy. Creditors who were not listed on the bankruptcy schedules typically find out about the filing when they try to get a judgment against the debtor in state court long after the bankruptcy case has been put to rest.

The good news is that as long as you truly knew nothing, the fact that you may have proceeded with your normal collection activity means you won't be subject to punishment for violating the automatic stay. The bad news is that your lack of knowledge about the bankruptcy doesn't necessarily mean that your claim survived. In fact, many courts have found that when a debtor with no assets receives a discharge under Chapter 7, the fact that an unsecured claim wasn't scheduled doesn't mean it survives the bankruptcy.

If you do fall into the classic situation of a creditor who finds out about the filing when trying to get a judgment in state court, here's what to expect next: The debtor may respond that your claim was discharged in bankruptcy, and ask the state court to dismiss your complaint. Or, the debtor may ask the bankruptcy court to reopen the case to hold you in contempt of the discharge order (if the debtor says you knew about the bankruptcy) or to determine whether your claim was discharged (if the debtor acknowledges that you didn't know about the bankruptcy).

The bankruptcy court will be faced with two issues. First, the court will need to determine whether you knew or should have known about the bankruptcy. This will include consideration of whether your claim was scheduled, whether the notice was sent to the correct location, and whether you should have known about the bankruptcy without receiving official notice. Second, if the court finds that you were wholly unaware of the bankruptcy, the court will consider whether your claim is excepted from discharge. We'll talk about what goes into that determination in Chapter 9.

Summary of Your First Steps After Receiving Notice of Bankruptcy

1. You find out the debtor has filed for bankruptcy.
2. Mark account as being in bankruptcy.
3. Stop all collection efforts against the debtor (see Chapter 4).
4. Note important dates:
   - deadline for filing proof of claim (if any)
   - deadline for filing complaint challenging debtor's discharge or the discharge of your claim, and
   - time and place of creditors' (Section 341) meeting.
5. Prepare proof of claim (if needed).
6. Review bankruptcy schedules and your internal files, looking for irregularities (as discussed in Chapter 5). ■

CHAPTER

4

The Automatic Stay

The instant a debtor files a bankruptcy petition, it triggers a standing court order. (See 11 U.S.C. § 362.) This order is popularly known as the automatic stay. The stay forces you and other creditors to lay off your collection efforts until further order of the bankruptcy court. This order isn't something you'll see on paper, but it exists nonetheless, and you violate it at your peril.

Though you may bridle at this restriction on your ability to collect on your debts, it has certain advantages. With the stay holding back all creditors equally, you are freed from worrying about whether a competing creditor will get paid ahead of you. The stay ultimately fosters the orderly treatment of all creditors' claims. And, looking at the even-bigger picture, bankruptcy without the automatic stay would offer little relief to the harried debtor pursued by vigilant creditors. With it, debtors have a chance to stop suits against them, quiet the telephone, and get a rest from bill collectors. That allows debtors a chance to decide the best way to deal with their unpaid bills, while assuring creditors that they will not be prejudiced by the delay.

Because the automatic stay goes into effect immediately upon the debtor's filing, there's basically no time for anyone to consider whether the debtor is actually eligible for bankruptcy protection. Hence, it is truly automatic. It doesn't matter whether the debtor filed for bankruptcy in good faith or in bad. Nor does it matter whether the debtor timed the bankruptcy filing deliberately, to stop your or another creditor's collection efforts. All of these issues will be hashed out in court later. But, in the meantime, the stay will remain in effect until the debtor receives a discharge, the bankruptcy case is closed, or the court orders the stay to be lifted.

The discussion in this chapter will cover:

- what the automatic stay stops you from doing (Section A)
- exceptions to the automatic stay (Section B)
- what happens if you violate the automatic stay (Section C)
- how to ask the court to lift the stay and allow you to take action against the debtor (Section D), and
- when the automatic stay will come to an end (Section E).

A. What the Automatic Stay Stops You From Doing

The automatic stay is quite comprehensive in its protection of the debtor and the debtor's property. Under Section 362(a) of the Code, as soon as the debtor files for bankruptcy you must abide by all of the following:

- **You can't sue the debtor regarding any matter that you could have sued over before the bankruptcy was filed.** Even if you could have sued the debtor over an unpaid bill one minute before he filed for bankruptcy, a minute later, when the automatic stay has kicked in, you can no longer sue him for the same bill. This rule applies to almost any type of lawsuit you'd want to file against a debtor. (See Section B, below for exceptions.) If your claim against the debtor survives the bankruptcy, you'll be allowed to sue the debtor after the conclusion of the proceedings. In fact, even if the time period for suing the debtor (the "statute of limitations") expired while the automatic stay was in force, the Bankruptcy Code keeps your right to sue alive—briefly. You'll have 30 days after the stay is lifted to file your suit in these circumstances. (See 11 U.S.C. § 108(c).)

- **You can't pursue a lawsuit that you filed against the debtor prior to the bankruptcy filing.** However, your suit will remain open, although inactive, pending the outcome of the bankruptcy. Any time limits based on that lawsuit will be put on hold for as long as the automatic stay remains in effect. If your claim against the debtor survives the bankruptcy, you may then continue the lawsuit where you left off.

- **If you obtained a court judgment against the debtor before the bankruptcy was filed, you can't enforce it against the debtor or the debtor's property during the bankruptcy.** That means you can't garnish the debtor's wages or ask the local sheriff to seize the debtor's property. If the debtor receives a discharge, you'll never be able to enforce the judgment against the debtor unless the judgment is excepted from discharge (see Chapter 9). However, any lien against the debtor's property that is created by the judgment will survive the bankruptcy unless it is voided by the bankruptcy court (see Chapter 8).

- **You can't repossess your collateral or exercise control over the debtor's property.** And there's more: If you repossessed the collateral before the bankruptcy was filed, you may need to return it to the debtor. State laws differ on this matter, but some states actually say that the collateral continues to be the debtor's property even after it has been repossessed. (See Section D3, below, for details.)

- **You can't acquire a lien against property that the debtor owned at the time of filing for bankruptcy.** By way of reminder, liens can normally be created by entry or enforcement of a court judgment (judicial liens), by action of law (statutory liens such as a mechanic's lien), or by agreement of the parties (consensual liens, as in a mortgage or second deed of trust). Since the automatic stay stops any pending judicial actions, it already prevented the creation of a judicial lien, but the law adds other type of liens to the list. The purpose is to ensure that property that entered bankruptcy unencumbered by liens remains that way during the bankruptcy.

- **You can't record ("perfect") a lien against property that the debtor owned when the bankruptcy was filed.** This means that you can't ordinarily take action to make your lien enforceable against other persons who might claim an interest in the debtor's property. There are exceptions to this rule, however, in cases where the Bankruptcy Code or state law treats your action as having taken place prior to the bankruptcy filing. (See the sidebar, below "How Consensual Liens Are Perfected," for a complete explanation of these exceptions.)

- **You can't foreclose or enforce any lien that was created prior to the bankruptcy filing.** This means you can't exercise the rights you had to seize or repossess the collateral. Nor can you enforce any other rights you have against the debtor's property.

For example, if the debtor owns an apartment building and you have a lien against the rent paid by the tenants, you can't demand that the tenants pay the rent to you instead of to the debtor.

- **If your claim against the debtor arose prior to the bankruptcy filing, you can't assert a lien against any property that the debtor obtained after the filing.** If, prior to filing for bankruptcy, the debtor gave you permission to take a lien against property that she was to acquire after the bankruptcy was filed, you can't perfect your lien or enforce it.

- **You can't do anything outside of the legal process to collect your claim from the debtor.** No calling the debtor up, no letters, no casual requests as you pass each other on the street. The automatic stay forbids any—and that means any—action to collect, assess, or recover a claim against the debtor that came into existence before the debtor filed for bankruptcy.

- **You can't reduce a debt you owe to the debtor by an amount that the debtor owes you.** When you owe money to the debtor and the debtor owes money to you, everyday non-bankruptcy law provides two ways for these mutual obligations to be reconciled. Setoff involves mutual obligations that arose out of separate transactions. Recoupment involves mutual obligations that arose out of the same transaction. Within a bankruptcy, you may reduce your obligation to a debtor by way of recoupment without violating the automatic stay, but you can't do so by way of setoff. For a more detailed discussion, see the sidebar, below, "Recoupment vs. Setoff."

How Consensual Liens Are Perfected

When a debtor gives you an interest in his property as security for a loan, that interest is a consensual lien. State law may require you to record your lien in a public place so that, for example, someone interested in buying the collateral from the debtor will know that the debtor doesn't own it free and clear. A typical situation is where your loan to the debtor is secured by the debtor's car. If you don't get the lien noted on the car's certificate of title, someone could come along and buy the car from the debtor without first paying off your claim. Or, the debtor might pledge the car as collateral for another loan—and the new lender might record the lien on the car's title, making the new lender's claim against the car superior to yours. With an inferior claim, if the car ends up being sold for less than enough to pay off the two claims against it you'll get what's left over after the new claim is paid. The same analysis works for the recording of liens against real property.

It's not uncommon for real property to serve as collateral for multiple loans.

The process by which you make a public record of your lien against the debtor's property is known as "perfection." Perfection procedures are determined by state law. In most states, you perfect your lien against a car by having the lien noted on the car's title. You usually perfect a lien against a home by having the lien recorded at the county courthouse.

There are situations in which your state's laws may not require you to do anything to protect your lien. For example, if you loan someone money for the purpose of purchasing an item of personal property, it automatically creates a lien in that property. This lien is known as a "purchase-money security interest." Most states do not require these liens to be recorded in a public place in order to be effective. However, you must be able to clearly identify the purchased property in order to prove that it is collateral for your loan.

Recoupment vs. Setoff

Outside of bankruptcy, no one worries much about the difference between recoupment and setoff. If I owe you $10 and you owe me $5, and then I pay you $5, we're square, end of story. But once matters enter the bankruptcy realm, transactions like ours will be examined to see whether the mutual debts were part of the same or different transactions—that is, whether my payment to you was a recoupment or a setoff. Only a recoupment would pass legal muster once the automatic stay was in effect.

Creditors may exercise their recoupment rights at any time without violating the automatic stay. They must, however, get the stay lifted before exercising their right to take a setoff. Hence, it's imperative that creditors who want to reduce what they owe to a debtor by what the debtor owes them know the difference between recoupment and setoff—or seek the advice of someone who does.

EXAMPLE: Monty owns a motel, and hires Grasslands landscaping company to maintain the grounds. One day, the landscaper's mower runs out of gas while working on the lawn around the motel's kiddie pool. Monty happens to have five gallons of gas handy, which he offers Grasslands for refilling the mower. When it's time for Monty to pay Grasslands for its services, Monty deducts the value of the gas from the bill. This is an example of recoupment. Monty's obligation to pay the landscaper arose from the same transaction—the mowing job—that created Grasslands' gas debt to Monty.

Now assume that Monty is out running errands and sees Grasslands' truck pulled off to the side of the road, out of gas. Monty again gives them five gallons of gas. The next time Grasslands sends Monty a bill, Monty deducts the cost of the gas before he pays it. This is a setoff. Monty owed money to Grasslands for its services. Grasslands owed Monty money for the gas. Although the two obligations are mutual, they didn't arise out of a single transaction.

Special Rules Protecting Codebtors in Chapters 12 and 13 Cases

Generally, the automatic stay applies to the debtor and to the debtor's property. However, when the debtor files under Chapter 12 or Chapter 13, the automatic stay also protects anyone who cosigned with the debtor on a loan, provided that the debtor was the one who incurred the liability.

You can get relief from the automatic stay in order to proceed against a codebtor, by showing the following:

- The person you want to sue is the one who received the benefit of the loan. In this situation, the debtor is the person commonly viewed as the "cosigner."
- The plan will not fully repay your claim.
- Your claim will be irreparably harmed if you are prevented from going after the cosigner for payment. This can be shown where there is no security for the loan or the cosigner is also in financial trouble.

B. Exceptions to the Automatic Stay

There are a few exceptional situations in which you can sue or take other action against a debtor even though the automatic stay is already in effect.

⚠ These exceptions are tricky.
Unless your planned action against the debtor clearly and squarely fits within an exception, you should not sue the debtor without getting the bankruptcy court's permission first, as discussed in Section D, below.

The actions you can take against a debtor at any time include:

- **Suing to establish paternity.** If you think the debtor is the father of your child, you may sue him for the purpose of establishing this, without regard for whether he's in bankruptcy.
- **Suing to establish or modify an order of alimony, maintenance, or support.** However, collecting on this order may be another matter. You can't sue the debtor to collect on an order of alimony, maintenance, or support if the money is supposed to come from property that is being administered in the bankruptcy case. This means you can sue the debtor to establish the fact that you, your children, or both are entitled to receive support, and you can get a state court to order the debtor to pay that support. But you can't force the debtor to pay with money that's under the bankruptcy court's control. Wages earned after the debtor filed for bankruptcy are not subject to the bank-

ruptcy court's control if the debtor filed under Chapter 7. Wages are, however, subject to the court's control if the debtor filed under Chapter 13.

- **Suing to evict the debtor from commercial property.** Such evictions are allowed only in cases where the lease expired prior to the bankruptcy filing. Also, the tenant must be a commercial one—residential tenants receive full protection from eviction under the automatic stay.

- **Perfecting certain liens.** A bankruptcy filing cannot be used to interrupt the process of perfecting a lien (see the sidebar, above, "How Consensual Liens Are Perfected") if the law says perfection was achieved prior to the bankruptcy filing. The following examples show the most common situations in which the law would make this allowance:

  ✓ Consensual liens that secure repayment of a purchase-money loan. If you loaned the debtor money with which to buy something, that's a purchase-money loan. Purchase-money loans are secured by the property purchased. In most situations, you don't need to take any action to perfect a purchase-money loan. However, if state law requires some act of perfection, and you successfully perfected your purchase-money security interest within 20 days of the debtor taking

possession of the property, the law says your lien was "perfected" on that possession date. For example, if the debtor buys a car today using a bank loan, drives it home, and files for bankruptcy tomorrow, the bank may file the necessary papers to complete the perfection process without violating the stay, so long as it does so within 20 days of the purchase. The bank's act of perfection will relate back to the day before the bankruptcy filing. (Note: Although the general UCC rule is that you don't need to take any action in order to perfect a purchase-money security interest, most states require that liens against vehicles be recorded on the title.)

  ✓ **Other consensual liens.** When a debtor voluntarily gives a creditor a security interest in an item of property she already owns, the law says the lien is perfected on that same day, so long as the creditor perfects the lien within ten days. For example, let's say an unsecured creditor is pressing a debtor for payment. The debtor, who has no cash on hand, gives the creditor a lien against her home. If the creditor perfects the lien within ten days, it is treated as if it was perfected when the debtor granted the security interest—even if the debtor files for bankruptcy between when the lien was received and when it was perfected.

✓ **Nonconsensual liens.** State and federal law allow creditors to acquire an interest in property without the debtor's permission. These interests can take the form of statutory liens such as mechanic's liens, or they can be transfers of ownership rights, as in foreclosure sales. In either event, if the law treats a postpetition action that perfects the creditor's interest as relating back to a prepetition event, then the action doesn't violate the stay. For example, if state law requires the provider of a service to sue the debtor in order to perfect a mechanic's lien, the provider won't be violating the stay by filing such a lawsuit.

- **Maintaining the perfection of a lien that was perfected when the debtor filed for bankruptcy.** You may do whatever is necessary to comply with renewal requirements to preserve your perfected lien.

- **Cashing a check from a debtor who later filed for bankruptcy.** You may, however, find that the bank doesn't honor the check, because it has placed an administrative freeze on the debtor's account in order to preserve the debtor's assets. Nevertheless, you may demand payment without violating the stay.

Any action included on this list may be started or continued without first seeking permission from the bankruptcy court. If, however, there is any doubt as to whether your action qualifies under one of these exceptions, ask the court to lift the automatic stay. This is one of those situations where it's much better to ask permission now than to say "I'm sorry" later.

If the debtor protests that your action violates the automatic stay, either the bankruptcy court or the state court may rule on whether it does.

C. Results of Violating the Automatic Stay

If you take any action in violation of the stay, you face a number of possible consequences. First, your action will be void, which means it will be treated as if it didn't happen (see Subsection 1, below). Second, you may face criminal or other penalties (see Subsection 2, below).

1. Your Actions Become Void

If you attempt to collect from the debtor after the automatic stay is in effect, your actions will be rendered utterly useless. It won't matter whether you acted in good faith or bad, or whether you knew of the bankruptcy or not. All that matters is whether you acted after the bankruptcy had been filed. If you did, your action is invalid and has no legal significance (except to expose you to penalties, which we'll discuss in Subsection 2).

The examples below illustrate how actions are rendered void.

EXAMPLE 1: Daphne the debtor is sued in state court, for nonpayment of bills she ran run up on an Internet site. She files for bankruptcy eight days later, and proceeds to ignore the state court lawsuit. The state court, seeing that Daphne wasn't in court (but having no knowledge of the bankruptcy), rules against her (a "default judgment"). However, when the creditor tries to collect on the judgment, he discovers that the state court's judgment is void, since it violated the automatic stay.

EXAMPLE 2: Darth the debtor files for bankruptcy in order to stop a foreclosure sale of his home. The court finds that Darth isn't eligible for bankruptcy protection, however, and dismisses his case. The lender goes ahead and reschedules the foreclosure sale. Darth then refiles for bankruptcy without bothering to tell the lender. The lender proceeds with the foreclosure sale. Even though the lender didn't know about the second filing, the rescheduled foreclosure sale is void. (The lender would prob-

ably discover what happened when the buyer tried to evict Darth, and Darth headed into court to deal with this.)

EXAMPLE 3: Devorah the debtor fails to pay her property taxes, and the tax authorities sell her home as a result. Under the law, Devorah has a certain amount of time during which she can pay up and redeem her home from the buyer. Devorah fails to redeem on time—but she does file for bankruptcy. The buyer, seeing that Devorah has missed the redemption deadline, records title to the property. However, this act of recording the title is void because it violates the automatic stay.

By now, we hope you're convinced that all manner of actions can become void when done in violation of the automatic stay. But you should also know that bankruptcy courts have the power to retroactively lift the automatic stay. If the circumstances at the time your action was taken were such that the court would have lifted the stay to allow the action to take place, then the court may—and we emphasize may—okay your action after the fact. For this reason, you may hear some bankruptcy attorneys or judges say that actions taken in violation of the automatic stay are "voidable" rather than "void."

Consider our earlier example of the lender who foreclosed on Darth's home after his first bankruptcy case was dismissed. We said that the lender's action violated the automatic stay in the debtor's second case, even though the lender didn't know there was a second case. However, if the bankruptcy court found that Darth filed the second case for no purpose other than to stop the foreclosure sale and that he intentionally didn't tell the lender about it, then the court could have validated the sale by retroactively granting stay relief to the lender.

⚠ **Don't count on the court making it okay.** You don't want to take a chance on doing something that violates the automatic stay, and we don't want to leave you with the impression that you can wiggle around it. In fact, if you're looking for a way around the automatic stay, you've already demonstrated enough bad faith that the bankruptcy court will rule against you. To win the court's favor, you generally need to show an innocent stay violation coupled with bad faith by the debtor. If you want to push the boundary between acceptable actions and stay violations, hire a lawyer.

2. You Face Penalties

There's only one thing worse than not getting paid—and that's not getting paid and being ordered by the court to hand money over to the person who stiffed you. But you could easily find yourself in this position by violating the automatic stay. In the previous sections, we outlined what the stay prevents you from doing, and explained that those prohibitions kick in the very second the debtor files for bankruptcy. In the next section, we're going to talk about the nasty things that happen to creditors who ignore the automatic stay. We'll discuss innocent violations in Subsection a. But take heart, the truly nasty stuff is saved for those who intentionally violate the stay (see Subsection b).

a. Penalties for Innocent Violations of the Automatic Stay

The automatic stay has teeth. Even innocent stay violations are not immune from its bite.

EXAMPLE: CalBeach Bank schedules a foreclosure sale of Derwin's house for Tuesday at 2:00 p.m. Derwin files for bankruptcy on Tuesday at 1:59 pm. CalBeach doesn't hear about the bankruptcy, but its sale is nonetheless invalidated by the automatic stay. It doesn't matter that the sale was conducted properly and legally. It doesn't matter that the buyer paid fair value for the property. The sale is nullified by the bankruptcy.

In a Chapter 13 bankruptcy, debtors can pay mortgage arrearages through their reorganization plan while resuming their regular mortgage payments. This means that in the example above, Derwin's Chapter 13 filing returned his relationship with CalBeach to exactly where it was in the minutes before the foreclosure sale. If Derwin fails to resume making payments after filing for bankruptcy, the bank can ask the court to lift the stay to allow it to reschedule the foreclosure sale (see Section D, below).

CalBeach's penalty for its innocent violation of the automatic stay was the loss of the sale. If CalBeach believes this penalty is unjust, perhaps because Derwin has repeatedly filed for bankruptcy just before foreclosure sales, then the bank may ask the bankruptcy court to retroactively lift the stay and allow the sale to stand.

b. Penalties for Willful Violations of the Automatic Stay

While innocent violations of the automatic stay merely result in the invalidation of the offending act, willful violations of the automatic stay expose the violator to punishment. The court may require the violator to pay the debtor actual damages (reflecting monetary loss as a direct result of the violation), punitive damages (a sum set by the court to separately punish the violator), as well as attorneys fees.

With the stakes this high, you're probably wondering what sorts of violations the court will consider willful. In this context, willful means you knew that the debtor had filed for bankruptcy. Having known that, you are also presumed to have known that the automatic stay was in effect—and that you'd be violating it by trying to collect from the debtor.

From the creditor's point of view, what is willful and what isn't may not look completely clearcut. Below are some actual cases demonstrating where courts have drawn these lines.

- A husband and wife were indebted to a credit union in Maine on two separate loans. Both loans had been made prior to the bankruptcy filing, and were of types that can be discharged in bankruptcy. One loan was secured by the debtors' home and the other was not secured. The debtors wanted to keep ("reaffirm") their secured loan to the credit union so they could keep their home. However, they hoped to discharge the unsecured loan in the bankruptcy. The credit union refused to allow the debtors to do this, demanding that they reaffirm both loans. The bankruptcy judge found that the credit union's bargaining position violated the automatic stay because it coerced the debtors into paying a debt they wanted to discharge. A review panel made up of three bankruptcy judges agreed. However, a subsequent review panel composed of three federal circuit judges said what the credit union did was okay. The credit union's use of its superior bargaining position was an acceptable negotiating tactic, the federal judges said. (See *In re Jamo*, 283 F.3d 392 (1st Cir. 2002).)

- A creditor began garnishment proceedings before the debtor filed for bankruptcy. After the bankruptcy was filed, the creditor failed to tell the county sheriff to stop enforcing the garnishment order. The creditor also took its time in giving the debtor back the money that was garnished after the bankruptcy filing. The court held that both acts were violations of the stay. Creditors are expected to move quickly to restore debtors to the position they were in prior to filing for bankruptcy. (See *Sucre v. MIC Leasing Corp. (In re Sucre)*, 226 B.R. 340 (Bankr. S.D.N.Y. 1998).)

- In a variety of cases, creditors have repossessed property the debtors used in their businesses prior to the bankruptcy—and then kept the property after the bankruptcy, while waiting for the debtors to provide assurance that the creditor's interest in the property would be protected. Courts have found that keeping property in these circumstances willfully violates the automatic stay. While creditors may ordinarily condition the return of repossessed collateral on such assurance—such as proof of insurance—the courts found that the collateral involved in these cases was so central to the debtor's business that its continued deprivation unjustly diminished the debtor's opportunity for a fresh start. (See Section D3 for a discussion of adequate protection.) In one case, the creditor had seized a jeep used in the debtor's part-time snow removal business—at the beginning of the winter season. The court required the creditor to reimburse the debtor for lost business, to the tune of $4,270. (See *In re Jackson*, 251 B.R. 597 (Bankr. D. Utah 2000).) In another case, the creditor had seized perishable food from the debtor's small market. The creditor allowed the food to spoil rather than return it to the debtor. That was a pricey mistake—the court awarded the debtor damages of $244,473. (See *Foust v. Seal (In re Foust)*, No. 98-50774 SEG, Adv. No. 98-5032 SEG. This is an unreported decision out of the Southern District of Mississippi.)

3. How Damages Are Computed

Creditors who willfully violate the stay can be ordered to pay damages to the debtor. These damages reimburse the debtor for any out-of-pocket losses (actual damages), any costs related to enforcing the stay (attorneys fees and court costs) and any additional amount the court feels is necessary to dissuade the creditor from violating the stay again (punitive damages). The bigger the creditor and the more egregious the violation, the higher these punitive damages can go. For example, a Texas bankruptcy judge in 2003 ordered First USA Bank to pay $100,000 for violating the stay, because, he said, the creditor had exhibited "an irresponsible and cavalier attitude." Here are some more real-life examples of damage awards:

- A creditor who repossessed the debtor's car in violation of the automatic stay was ordered to pay $500 for the debtor's emotional distress, $642 in actual damages and $2,340 in attorney's fees. The actual damages were the difference between the higher finance charges on the loan the debtor had to take out to buy a replacement car versus the lower finance charges that the debtor was paying on the loan for the repossessed car. The emotional distress award was somewhat unusual—many courts won't award damages for emotional distress, especially when the debtor can't prove any actual dam-

ages. (See *Manufacturers & Traders Trust Co. v. Alberto (In re Alberto)*, 271 B.R. 223 (N.D.N.Y. 2001). This case was reversed on appeal, but on unrelated grounds.)

- In the case mentioned earlier, concerning the creditor who didn't return perishable collateral to the debtors who operated a small grocery store, the creditor was ordered to pay $144,473 in actual damages plus $100,000 in punitive damages. The court said the creditor shouldn't have ignored the perishable nature of the inventory items it seized and the importance of these items to the operation of the debtor's business—the loss had forced the debtors to close down shop. The damage award represented the value of the business as an ongoing enterprise. (See *Foust v. Seal (In re Foust)*, No. 98-50774 SEG, Adv. No. 98-5032 SEG.)

- A creditor who didn't take the steps necessary to end the garnishment of the debtor's wages was ordered to pay $6,669 in actual damages and $1,000 in punitive damages, plus another $1,000 to compensate the debtors for their emotional distress. Although the creditor claimed that his attorney was at fault, this simply resulted in the court holding the creditor and his attorney equally liable for payment of the award. (See *In re Johnson*, 253 B.R. 857 (Bankr. S.D. Ohio 2000).)

D. Asking the Court to Lift the Automatic Stay

If you, as a creditor, believe that the automatic stay is not appropriate in a particular context, you can ask the bankruptcy court to "lift the stay." You're most likely to succeed at this if you're a secured creditor who wants to foreclose on your collateral. Unsecured creditors rarely have anything to gain by seeking stay relief, with the common exception of residential landlords who want to evict debtor-tenants. The Bankruptcy Code says that relief from the automatic stay shall be granted "for cause" or when the debtor has no equity in property that is not necessary to the debtor's reorganization. (11 U.S.C. § 362(d).)

Procedurally speaking, you would make your request by filing what's called a motion for relief from the automatic stay. It's also known as a motion to lift the automatic stay. Procedures for filing motions are discussed in Chapter 10. This section will augment that chapter, however, by discussing:

- what you can ask for (Subsection 1)
- specific situations in which you might seek stay relief (Subsection 2), and
- procedures for seeking stay relief (Subsection 4).

1. What You Can Ask For

Relief from the stay can take a number of forms, and can be initiated by a single creditor or a group of creditors, depending on the facts of the case:

- **Termination as to one creditor.** The stay may be terminated so that it no longer protects the debtor from actions by the particular creditor seeking relief. This would be a solo effort by one creditor, seeking the court's permission to do something that would otherwise violate the stay. The most common example is a bank asking the court's permission to foreclose on its collateral.

- **Termination as to all creditors.** The stay may be terminated as to all creditors. Blanket stay relief requires either a cooperative effort of creditors or an action by the trustee that benefits all creditors. For example, multiple creditors whose claims are all secured by the same collateral might seek broad stay relief.

- **Annulment.** The stay may be annulled so that it is treated as if it never came into effect. Annulling the stay is the retroactive relief we referred to previously that validates actions already taken in violation of the stay. In effect, a single creditor who violated the stay goes to the court and argues that the action should be allowed to stand despite the stay violation.

- **Modification.** The stay may be modified in a way that provides relief to the creditor while preserving some aspects of the stay for the debtor's protection. For example, a creditor may need to prove the debtor's liability in order to present a claim to a third party for payment. Because suing to establish the debtor's liability would violate the stay, the creditor needs to ask for stay relief. The bankruptcy court would grant the relief with the proviso that the creditor only look to the third party for payment of the judgment—any attempts to enforce the judgment against the debtor would still be forbidden.
- **Conditional grant.** The stay may be granted conditionally, so that its continued vitality will depend on future events. This usually arises as a compromise, in a situation where the creditor initially requested full stay relief, perhaps because the debtor is in violation of the terms of a loan agreement. The debtor may concede the breach but promise to correct it. The parties can agree that the debtor will correct the problem by a certain date—and that if the debtor fails, the creditor will be entitled to immediate stay relief. Thus, stay relief is triggered by a future event—the debtor's failure to cure the breach.

2. Specific Scenarios in Which You Might Seek Stay Relief

Creditors might seek relief from the automatic stay in a wide range of situations—sufficiently wide that we've decided to cover the most common ones in depth, rather than attempting broad generalizations. The subsections below describe the most common scenarios in which creditors seek stay relief.

a. Landlords Wishing to Evict Residential Tenants With Expired or Unwritten Leases

If your debtor is a residential tenant whose lease expired before the bankruptcy was filed, you can ask for stay relief in order to regain possession of the property. As long as your sole intended action is to evict the debtor, the court will likely lift the stay. However, if you make any attempt to go beyond the eviction—for example, to establish the debtor's personal liability for breaching the lease agreement—you will be violating the automatic stay.

If your lease agreement is merely oral, and was never committed to paper, you'll need to show that eviction is proper under your state's law in order for the bankruptcy court to lift the stay and allow you to evict the debtor.

b. Landlords Wishing to Evict Residential Tenants with Valid Leases

If you wish to evict a residential tenant with a lease that hasn't yet expired, your rights depend on what chapter the bankruptcy was filed under and what the trustee decides to do with your lease.

If the tenant-debtor filed for Chapter 7 bankruptcy, then the trustee has 60 days after the filing within which to decide what the estate's going to do with the lease. The trustee may decide to honor ("assume") it, because that's what the debtor wants or the lease itself adds value to the estate. If the trustee does nothing, then the lease is canceled ("rejected"). Most trustees try to follow the debtor's wishes. If the trustee chooses to assume the lease, then the debtor must bring the lease payments current. If the trustee chooses to reject the lease, or doesn't state any intention within 60 days, then the landlord may obtain stay relief to recover the leased property.

If the tenant-debtor filed for Chapter 11, 12, or 13 bankruptcy, then the debtor must assume or reject the lease prior to the confirmation of the reorganization plan. Although the law says this decision is to be made by the trustee in a Chapter 11 case, recall that Chapter 11 debtors usually carry all the rights and powers of a trustee. In Chapter 12 and 13 cases, the law specifically allows debtors to provide for the assumption or rejection of a lease that the trustee hasn't already rejected. So, if the trustee doesn't reject the lease (and it's unlikely the trustee would if the debtor wants to keep the apartment) then the debtor can assume the lease and make up missed payments through the plan.

Ask the court to set a deadline for the trustee to assume or reject the lease. This is especially important in Chapters 11 and 12 cases, where confirmation of the debtor's plan may not happen for months after the bankruptcy filing. You can avoid being stuck in limbo waiting and wondering what the debtor is going to do about the lease by filing a motion asking the court to direct the trustee to make a decision.

c. Landlords Wishing to Evict Commercial Tenants With Expired Leases

If your tenant is a commercial one, and the lease term expired before the bankruptcy was filed, you're in good shape. Landlords may evict nonresidential tenants with expired leases without seeking stay relief. It won't matter whether or not you started the eviction process prior to the bankruptcy filing. But this exception works only in cases where the lease term expired on its own, as opposed to having been triggered into termination because of some action by the tenant. For example, the debtor's payment default, bankruptcy filing, or violation of another lease term may have triggered an early end to the lease. In the latter types of case, the landlord must ask the court for stay relief before evicting the tenant.

d. Landlords Wishing to Evict Commercial Tenants With Valid Leases

If your commercial tenant's lease did not expire prior to the bankruptcy filing, your rights depend on what chapter the bankruptcy was filed under and what the trustee decides to do with your lease. The rules are the same as those that apply to residential tenants; see Subsection b, above.

Bankruptcy Cannot Be Called a Breach of Contract

Does your lease or other agreement with the debtor treat the debtor's financial condition, insolvency, or bankruptcy filing as a default? If it does, don't count on using this clause. According to Section 363(l) of the Bankruptcy Code, such provisions (referred to as *ipso facto* clauses) are unenforceable in bankruptcy—in other words, if you were to sue the debtor for breach of contract, the court would refuse to honor the *ipso facto* clause. These *ipso facto* provisions are still found in many contracts, for obvious reasons—creditors want to be able to get out of an agreement if the debtor gets into financial trouble. However, if the debtor's financial trouble leads to bankruptcy, a creditor's attempt to void the contract based on the *ipso facto* clause will violate the automatic stay.

e. Creditors Who Hold Security Interests in Depreciating Assets

If you're watching the value of your loan collateral depreciate as the bankruptcy proceedings drag on, you're probably concerned—especially if the collateral's value is declining faster than the loan is being repaid. In such situations, you may be able to obtain stay relief "for cause," based on a lack of adequate protection for the collateral. Typically this occurs with car loans, since cars are famous for rapid declines in value.

Ideally, you'd like the court to lift the stay and allow you to foreclose on your collateral before it loses any more value. The court, however, may respond by allowing the stay to remain in effect so long as the debtor provides you with adequate protection for your secured claim. This adequate protection can take one of three forms.

One possibility is for the debtor to make adequate protection payments to you. In other words, the debtor would retain the stay's protection by compensating you for the deterioration in the collateral's value. If the debtor fails to make these payments, then the stay will be terminated. This is an example of what's called conditional stay relief.

Another option is for the court to order the debtor to provide substitute or additional collateral. Allowing you to take a new lien is a form of adequate protec-tion usually associated with business bankruptcies. Perhaps a lender whose loan was secured by machinery in the debtor's business can be granted an additional lien in the debtor's accounts receivable.

A third alternative is for the court to order the debtor to provide something to you that is the "indubitable equivalent" of your interest in the collateral. The Bankruptcy Code doesn't tell us what constitutes indubitable equivalency. At the very least, it means insuring the property against loss. What else it can mean is debated each time that it's used.

You can ask for any of these remedies by filing a motion with the court. If it later turns out that the adequate protection awarded by the court is inadequate—that is, you recover less than the value of your secured claim—the Bankruptcy Code will protect your claim as an administrative priority. That means if there's any money to pay claims, your claim will be paid along with the claims of professionals working for the bankruptcy estate.

f. Creditors Who Hold Security Interests That Exceed the Collateral's Value

In some situations, the debtor has borrowed 100% of the property's purchase price—but as soon as the debtor got the property, it was no longer worth what was paid for it. This is commonly the case with cars and household property such as televisions, computers, and other electronic equipment. From day one, you are owed more than the collateral is worth. (However, unlike the situation described in Subsection e, above, these items don't necessarily depreciate rapidly after the day you buy them—they may drop in value initially, then hold firm for awhile.) Also, from day one the debtor has no equity in the property, since its decline in value probably more than offset any of the debtor's loan payments. Luckily for you as a creditor, the law requires the bankruptcy courts to grant stay relief if the debtor has no equity in the collateral and the collateral is not necessary for the debtor's reorganization. (11 U.S.C. § 362(d)(2).)

Figuring out whether the debtor has equity in the property is a simple matter of arithmetic. Figuring out whether the property is necessary for the debtor's reorganization can be a thornier matter. If the debtor filed for Chapter 7 relief, it's easy—the debtor is not attempting to reorganize, so the question doesn't come into play. However, if the debtor filed under Chapter 11, 12, or 13, you must prove that the success of the debtor's reorganization plan is not conditioned on his retention of your collateral. If the item in question is the debtor's home, then your success is going to turn on how this particular dwelling fits into the debtor's reorganization scheme. If the item is a car, then your success will turn on whether this particular car is needed for the debtor to complete his plan payments. Expect the debtor to argue that he can't make any progress without a home or a car!

g. Creditors Who Are in Possession of the Collateral

Perhaps you repossessed items of collateral before the debtor filed for bankruptcy. Unfortunately, that doesn't mean that the property is yours to do with as you wish. Repossessed collateral comes under the protection of the automatic stay. Before you sell the collateral, you must ask the court's permission. Meanwhile, the debtor can file a motion seeking to have you return the property as part of the bankruptcy estate.

Who will win depends on how your state's law treats a debtor's interest in repossessed collateral. If the law says that a debtor completely loses her ownership of the collateral when you repossess it, then you should win. The exception would be if the debtor can show that she has the ability to redeem the property by paying you its fair market value (and the proceedings are taking place in a state whose law allows for redemption). If, however, your state's law says that a debtor still owns collateral subject to the creditor's right to repossess it, then whether you will be allowed to sell it will depend on how much the debtor needs the property in order to reorganize and whether the debtor can adequately protect your interest in the property—either by making protection payments or by providing additional collateral. If the court finds in favor of the debtor, you'll have to return the property.

h. Creditors Whose Loans Are Secured by Cash Collateral

Many business lenders ask debtors to put up not only their property, but also their accounts receivable and inventory as security for a loan. Then, when the debtor receives payments in the course of his or her business operations, this money belongs to the creditor. In an ongoing business relationship, the debtor is allowed to use the cash collateral so long as the business is current on its loan payments. Still, the creditor has a continuing lien against new accounts receivable and inventory.

Of course, when the debtor files bankruptcy, this ongoing business relationship is interrupted. As a creditor, you would now look to accounts receivable and inventory as your only possibility for getting paid—and would therefore want to file for stay relief to collect your cash collateral. The business, meanwhile, will be eager to return to business as usual, especially if it has filed under one of the reorganization chapters. The debtor business will likely ask the court's permission to use the cash collateral to fund its business operations. The court is more likely to rule in favor of the debtor if:

- the bankruptcy was filed under Chapter 11, 12, or 13 rather than Chapter 7
- the chances of a successful reorganization are good, and
- you, the creditor, have a security interest in assets other than the cash collateral.

i. Creditors Wishing to Act Upon a Debtor's Intent to Surrender the Collateral

A consumer debtor's bankruptcy papers will tell you exactly what the debtor plans to do with property that was pledged as collateral for a secured debt. Is the debtor going to keep the property and reaffirm the debt (meaning the debt will be unaffected by the bankruptcy)? Or will the debtor claim the collateral as exempt and attempt to avoid the lien (discussed in Chapter 8)? Or is the debtor planning to surrender the collateral or redeem it with a lump sum payment equal to its fair market value? If the debtor's stated intention is to surrender or abandon his interest in the property, it is imperative that you, the creditor, act quickly. You'll need to recover the property before it is damaged or lost through the debtor's neglect. You can accomplish this by seeking stay relief to recover the collateral.

j. Creditors Wishing to Pursue Nonestate Property

If the debtor won't be able to discharge your claim because it fits within one of the exceptions to discharge (listed in Chapter 9), that means you'll be entitled to collect your claim after the bankruptcy is over. If you can't or don't want to wait that long, you'll need to seek stay relief in order to sue the debtor to collect your claim early. You'll probably be anxious to get paid sooner rather than later. Remember, the automatic stay applies to all creditors, not just to those holding claims that can be discharged. You can't sue the debtor unless the bankruptcy court lifts the automatic stay.

In a Chapter 7 case, you can ask the court to lift the stay in order to sue the debtor or collect your claim from property not being administered in the bankruptcy estate. For example, if your claim is excepted from discharge because it is for alimony, maintenance, or support, you can collect your claim from exempt property. Creditors holding other types of claims that are excepted from discharge

can't collect their claims from exempt property, but they can go after property the debtor acquired after filing for bankruptcy. They will, however, need stay relief in order to do so. In Chapter 7 cases, you can also go after money the debtor has earned subsequent to filing for bankruptcy. (See Chapter 2 for an explanation of what property is and is not included in the bankruptcy estate.)

If the debtor filed under a reorganization chapter, you may wish to sue the debtor if your claim is not being fully paid through the plan or if the debtor has property that you can reach outside of bankruptcy. Since the debtor's property will not be sold to fund the plan, you may be able to seize it to satisfy your claim. Whether you can do this depends on whether the property remains protected by the bankruptcy even though it's not being used to fund the debtor's plan. Generally speaking, once the debtor's plan is confirmed, the only property that remains in the bankruptcy estate is whatever property is needed to fund the plan. Most often, this is the debtor's postpetition income. Everything else is fair game. That's not saying it's a slam dunk that the court will grant stay relief. The court may find that fairness requires preserving the stay in order to protect the debtor's reorganization.

k. Creditors Trying to Collect From the Debtor's Insurance Company or Cosigner

Your claim against the debtor may be one that another entity should ultimately pay—but will pay only after you've proven the debtor's liability, usually through a lawsuit. The most common example is where your claim is for damages caused by the debtor's negligent operation of an automobile. In order to collect from the debtor's insurance carrier, you'll have to prove that the debtor was at fault. In such cases, the bankruptcy court is likely to lift the stay for the sole purpose of allowing you to prove the debtor's liability.

A similar situation arises when you have sued multiple people, one of whom files for bankruptcy. While the bankruptcy stays the action against the debtor, it has no effect on the debtor's codefendants. You may resolve this dilemma in one of two ways: either by asking the bankruptcy court to lift the stay to allow the litigation to proceed, or by asking the judge hearing the litigation to stay that action as to all defendants until the debtor's bankruptcy is resolved.

And then there's the situation where the creditor's right go against a third party is based on a cosigned loan. For example, a debt might be owed by both spouses, but only one spouse filed for bankruptcy. In most bankruptcies, other than in Chapter 13, you can get stay relief to proceed against the codebtor. However, if the debtor filed for Chapter 13 bankruptcy and the debtor, not the cosigner, was the one who borrowed the money, then the automatic stay prevents the creditor from collecting the debt from the cosigner. This rule applies only in Chapter 13 cases, and only when the loan was made to the debtor. The impact of the codebtor stay will be discussed in Chapter 13 of this book.

l. Creditors Who Are Victims of Serial Bankruptcy Filers

Some debtors make a game of filing for bankruptcy relief just before the creditor forecloses on the collateral. These frequent filers have no more hope of reorganizing than they have any intention of repaying their debts. They've basically found a way to stay in their homes without paying rent. But you're not without recourse: If you can show that the debtor's bankruptcy filing was an abuse of the system, you can obtain stay relief for cause. In fact, a growing number of bankruptcy courts are ruling that the property of debtors who have abused the system in this way (or that portion of their property which is subject to a creditor's lien) can never again be protected by the automatic stay, for as long as it is owned by the debtors. This is called *in rem* relief, meaning that the order stays with the property and applies to all creditors who have liens secured by that property.

EXAMPLE: A Pennsylvania couple stopped two foreclosure actions in a row by filing for bankruptcy. The wife's filing stopped the first foreclosure—which was rescheduled after her case was dismissed. The husband then filed, which stopped the second foreclosure. The frustrated lender asked the court to bar both the husband and the wife from filing another bankruptcy for 180 days. The court became suspicious that the couple was planning another bankruptcy when the husband agreed not to file for 180 days but argued that this injunction should not apply to his wife. In order to prevent the couple from abusing the Bankruptcy Code by filing under Chapter 13 without intending to reorganize, the court said the automatic stay would not apply to the debtor's home in any bankruptcy filed by the debtor or his wife within 180 days of the court's order. That gave the lender 180 days in which to complete the foreclosure process, free of interruption by the automatic stay.

The Bankruptcy Code attempts to discourage serial filings by making debtors ineligible for bankruptcy within 180 days after they've had a case dismissed for cause or had one of their creditors file a stay relief motion. Remember, however, that the automatic stay always goes into effect without regard to the debtor's eligibility for bankruptcy relief. Furthermore, a debtor who files before his 180 days are up wouldn't be blocked at the courthouse door. That means that a debtor could file before his 180-day limit, and you, as a creditor, would have to abide by the automatic stay until the court got around to invalidating the bankruptcy. Still, creditors who violate the stay in these circumstances might not be penalized, since most courts will sympathize enough to retroactively lift the stay. In fact, the bankruptcy court in the District of Columbia went so far as to say in one case that no stay was triggered because no legitimate bankruptcy filing had occurred.

Don't take the action of one bankruptcy judge in one particular different case as permission to violate the stay in your case, however. If you know that your debtor has filed for bankruptcy, no matter how inappropriately, get relief from the stay before acting. The fact that the debtor's filing was out of line should allow you to get expedited relief from the court.

3. Procedures For Seeking Stay Relief

Before making any attempt to obtain stay relief, contact the debtor's attorney. Both of you have an interest in avoiding the time and paperwork involved in having the court decide who's right. You and the debtor's attorney may be able to simply settle whatever problem gave rise to your need for stay relief. The only times when this initial step should be skipped are when the debtor's filing is abusive, as in the case of a serial filing, or when speed is important, as in the case of rapidly depreciating collateral.

Once you have decided you have no choice but to seek stay relief, your first step is to file the appropriate motion with the clerk of the bankruptcy court. (See Chapter 10 for more on filing motions.) Motions for stay relief may be filed at any time. Some situations demand immediate attention, such as when the collateral is rapidly losing its value. This would be the case with a car or with perishable goods. Or, if you lawfully repossessed collateral prior to the bankruptcy filing, you face a choice of either giving it back or quickly asking that the stay be lifted. In these types of situations, you should seek stay relief as soon as you learn of the bankruptcy.

A motion for stay relief should:
- identify the parties involved, typically you (the movant) and the debtor (the respondent)
- tell the court what you, the creditor, want to do, and
- explain why you should be allowed to do it.

Since everyone's motion for stay relief will involve slightly different facts and needs, we've chosen to illustrate how the procedure would play out with an extended example.

EXAMPLE: When Daphne the debtor files for Chapter 7 bankruptcy, she is behind on her mortgage payments. The lawyer for the mortgage company sends a letter demanding that she immediately bring her account current or surrender the property. Daphne's lawyer doesn't respond, so the mortgage company files a motion for stay relief that states the following:

a) The debtor filed for Chapter 7 protection.

b) The mortgage company is a secured creditor holding a mortgage against the property.

c) The total amount owed on the mortgage is $100,000.

d) At the time the debtor filed for bankruptcy, she was two months behind on her mortgage payments, owing $1,500 in prepetition arrearages.

e) The property is worth $80,000.

f) Cause exists under Section 362(d)(1) of the Bankruptcy Code to terminate the stay to allow the mortgage company to proceed with foreclosure, given that the debtor has breached the mortgage contract by failing to maintain monthly payments.

g) Cause exists under Section 362(d)(2) of the Bankruptcy Code to terminate the stay to allow the mortgage company to proceed with foreclosure, in that the debtor has no equity in the property and the property is not necessary to the debtor's reorganization.

h) Based on the facts above, the mortgage company asks the court to terminate the automatic stay as to the property so that the mortgage company can proceed with foreclosure pursuant to state law. The motion includes a proposed order granting the relief requested.

Now the ball is in Daphne's court. If she ignores the creditor's motion, the court will grant it and the mortgage company will be able to proceed with foreclosure as if Daphne weren't in bankruptcy. If Daphne responds to the creditor's motion, that response will take one of five forms, as detailed below. Note that in some courts, a debtor does not need to file a written response in order to preserve her ability to appear in court to defend against the requested relief. The clerk of the bankruptcy court can tell you whether the court will hear the debtor's opposition to your motion without filing a written response. Also, even if the debtor doesn't file a written response or appear in court, the court will review your motion for stay relief to make sure there is a legal basis for granting the motion.

Here is what might happen next:

• Daphne can file an answer refuting some or all of the facts laid out by the mortgage company in its motion. Chances are, however, that the factual basis for the creditor's motion is fairly black and white. If Daphne was behind on her mortgage payments, she will have trouble denying this fact, although the amount of the arrearage may be disputed. Similarly, there's usually little room for argument about the balance owed on the debt. The only allegation subject to legitimate debate may be the property's value, but if the debtor concedes the other issues, then it doesn't matter how much the property is worth, because the debtor has admitted that there is cause to lift the automatic stay.

- Daphne may know full well that she is in default or that the creditor's claim is not adequately protected, in which case the creditor truly would be entitled to stay relief under Section 362(d)(1). Faced with this reality, Daphne may attempt to negotiate a settlement with the creditor. For example, Daphne may promise to cure the prepetition arrearage within 30 days and ask the creditor to agree to a 30-day postponement of the hearing to allow her this opportunity. Other promises may be exchanged that would allow the debtor to keep the property subject to making some concessions to the mortgage company.

- If negotiations prove unsuccessful, Daphne can file an answer to preserve her right to a hearing, where she will attempt to achieve by court order what the mortgage company wouldn't give her. She may ask for a 30-day continuance (time extension of the court proceedings), with the idea that by then she will be able to cure the arrearage and eliminate that

prepetition delinquency as a cause for stay relief. Failing that, she may ask the court to condition stay relief on her failure to pay the arrearage within 30 days. Unless there is a reason to give the mortgage company immediate relief or reason to deny the debtor's request, courts will usually give the debtor a chance—so long as the negative impact on the creditor is minimized. Conditional orders for relief serve this purpose.

- Daphne can file an answer and convert her case to one of the reorganization chapters (so long as she could have originally filed under that chapter). Assuming the conversion attempt is successful, Daphne tells the court that the prepetition arrearage will be resolved through the plan. Here again, the court will usually enter a conditional order giving the debtor a chance to confirm a plan and save her home. But the order will also allow the mortgage company to receive stay relief without returning to court if the debtor fails to do so.

- Daphne's last option, which is a highly questionable one, is to ask the court to dismiss the entire bankruptcy case. Because the stay terminates when the case is dismissed, this action expedites the relief sought by the creditor. And the debtor would be unable to file another bankruptcy petition for 180 days, because she asked the court for the dismissal after a motion for stay relief was filed (11 U.S.C. § 109). Although the dismissal option would seem to be a questionable strategy, debtors employ it with surprising frequency—especially when they are unaware that they can't refile for 180 days.

If no settlement is reached and the debtor has filed an answer, the court will hold a hearing to determine whether and what form of relief to grant. This is a full evidentiary hearing in which the creditor must prove that it is entitled to the relief sought. At the end of the hearing, the court usually announces its decision from the bench.

E. When the Automatic Stay Will End

If the bankruptcy court doesn't lift the stay in response to a creditor's motion, the stay lasts until the earliest of the following events:

- **The court orders that the debtor's obligations be discharged.** This means that the debtor has successfully completed the bankruptcy.
- **The court closes the case.** This is an administrative procedure that literally closes the bankruptcy file in the bankruptcy clerk's office. When debtors succeed in receiving a discharge, the discharge is entered while the case is open, and the case is closed later, after all the loose ends have been tied up.
- **The court dismisses the case.** This means that the court ends the case without ruling on the debtor's discharge. Even when the debtor voluntarily submits to a dismissal, the case isn't technically dismissed until the court says so. ■

Examining the Bankruptcy Papers

When debtors file for bankruptcy, they are required to file not only a basic petition, but also a comprehensive set of schedules and statements (either along with the petition or soon after). You can learn a lot from these documents, including:

- what property the debtor claims to own
- which items of property the debtor believes are exempt
- which items of property are collateral for secured debts
- how the debtor plans to deal with any secured debt, and
- the name of every creditor to whom the debtor owes money.

The documents also provide a detailed (if not always reliable) picture of the debtor's current financial situation. From the information you receive, you should be able to see what the debtor has been doing with his money over the months and years leading up to the bankruptcy. This treasure trove of information can help you do such things as get your claim paid during the bankruptcy, have your claim excepted from discharge, or convince the court to deny the debtor a bankruptcy discharge.

No matter what, a careful review of the debtor's schedules and statements should provide a solid foundation for protecting your claim. In this chapter, we'll explain:

- how to obtain a copy of all the paperwork (it's not automatic) (Section A)
- what's in the petition, schedules, and statements (Section B)
- how to glean the information you need from these papers (Section C), and
- what to do with the information you find (Section D).

A. Obtaining the Bankruptcy Schedules and Statements

You're allowed to see all the papers that the bankrupt debtor has filed—but you won't be sent them automatically. Most creditors are surprised that bankruptcy courts don't send the debtor's bankruptcy petition, schedules, and statements to them. Instead, there are three possible ways to get them:

(1) Go to the courthouse. Every document in the debtor's bankruptcy case will be kept in a case file in the bankruptcy clerk's office. The clerk will help you access it. You'll not only find the schedules and statements, you'll also find the fee disclosure filed by the debtor's attorney, the proofs of claim filed by other creditors, the case assignment to a trustee, and any documents filed in relation to the litigation in the bankruptcy court. Most bankruptcy clerks' offices do a good job at making recent filings easily accessible to all interested parties, including creditors.

(2) Hire someone to go to the courthouse for you. This person could be your attorney or other agent such as a collection agency or claims representative, sent to review the documents and report back to you. Or you could hire a document collection service to simply copy the schedules and statements.

(3) Mail a request that the bankruptcy clerk copy the file and send it to you. Plan on spending $25 to $75 for this service, depending on whether the bankruptcy clerk does the work or uses an outside service.

Electronic Filing Is on the Horizon

The bankruptcy courts are in the process of creating an electronic filing system. As more filings are made electronically, you, too, will be able to access them online, via the Internet. You'll need to register for this service, but it promises to be the least expensive way to see the debtor's paperwork. Most courts in the initial phases of rolling out electronic case filings are charging seven cents per page view.

B. What the Debtor's Paperwork Should Include

Assuming you've now gotten a copy of the debtor's petition, schedules, and statements, let's go through them, item by item, to see what you're looking at.

⚠️ **Sometimes debtors fail to include all the schedules and statements with their initial filings.** Under the court rules, any missing information must be filed with the court within 15 days after the initial filing or the case may be dismissed.

1. The Bankruptcy Petition

You may surprised to see that the bankruptcy petition itself is only two pages long. It's filed on a government form called "Official Form 1." See, for example, the petition filed by WorldCom, Inc., included below (without the various attachment pages). The petition length doesn't vary, no matter which chapter the bankruptcy was filed under, who the debtor is, or how many creditors are listed. The Chapter 11 bankruptcy petition of a huge conglomerate is of the same length as a Chapter 7 petition filed by a lone person with only a rusty car to his name.

Voluntary Petition of WorldCom, Inc.

(Official Form 1) (9/01)

FORM B1	United States Bankruptcy Court Southern District of New York	Voluntary Petition

Name of Debtor (if individual, enter Last, First, Middle): **WorldCom, Inc.**	Name of Joint Debtor (Spouse) (Last, First, Middle):
All Other Names used by the Debtor in the last 6 years (include married, maiden, and trade names): **MCI WORLDCOM, Inc., LDDS WorldCom**	All Other Names used by the Joint Debtor in the last 6 years (include married, maiden, and trade names):
Soc. Sec./Tax I.D. No. (if more than one, state all): **58-1521612**	Soc. Sec./Tax I.D. No. (if more than one, state all):
Street Address of Debtor (No. & Street, City, State & Zip Code): **500 Clinton Center Drive** **Clinton, Mississippi 39056**	Street Address of Joint Debtor (No. & Street, City, State & Zip Code):
County of Residence or of the Principal Place of Business: **Hinds County, Clinton, Mississippi**	County of Residence or of the Principal Place of Business:
Mailing Address of Debtor (if different from street address):	Mailing Address of Joint Debtor (if different from street address):

Location of Principal Assets of Business Debtor
(if different from street address above):

The Debtor and its affiliates own and operate a global telecommunications network with substantial assets throughout North America, Europe, the Middle East, Africa, Latin America, Australia, and Asia.

Information Regarding the Debtor (Check the Applicable Boxes)

Venue (Check any applicable box)
☐ Debtor has been domiciled or has had a residence, principal place of business, or principal assets in this District for 180 days immediately preceding the date of this petition or for a longer part of such 180 days than in any other District.
☒ There is a bankruptcy case concerning debtor's affiliate, general partner, or partnership pending in this District.

Type of Debtor (Check all boxes that apply)		**Chapter or Section of Bankruptcy Code Under Which the Petition is Filed** (Check one box)
☐ Individual(s) ☐ Railroad ☒ Corporation ☐ Stockbroker ☐ Partnership ☐ Commodity Broker ☐ Other_____		☐ Chapter 7 ☒ Chapter 11 ☐ Chapter 13 ☐ Chapter 9 ☐ Chapter 12 ☐ Sec. 304 - Case ancillary to foreign proceeding

Nature of Debts (Check one box)	**Filing Fee** (Check one box)
☐ Consumer/Non-Business ☒ Business	☒ Full Filing Fee attached
Chapter 11 Small Business (Check all boxes that apply) ☐ Debtor is a small business as defined in 11 U.S.C. § 101 ☐ Debtor is and elects to be considered a small business under 11 U.S.C. § 1121(e) (Optional)	☐ Filing Fee to be paid in installments (Applicable to individuals only) Must attach signed application for the court's consideration certifying that the debtor is unable to pay fee except in installments. Rule 1006(b). See Official Form No. 3.

Statistical/Administrative Information (Estimates only)	THIS SPACE IS FOR COURT USE ONLY
☒ Debtor estimates that funds will be available for distribution to unsecured creditors. ☐ Debtor estimates that, after any exempt property is excluded and administrative expenses paid, there will be no funds available for distribution to unsecured creditors.	

Estimated Number of Creditors	1-15	16-49	50-99	100-199	200-999	1000-over
(consolidated basis)	☐	☐	☐	☐	☐	☒

Estimated Assets (consolidated basis)							
$0 to $50,000	$50,001 to $100,000	$100,001 to $500,000	$500,001 to $1 million	$1,000,001 to $10 million	$10,000,001 to $50 million	$50,000,001 to $100 million	More than $100 million
☐	☐	☐	☐	☐	☐	☐	☒

Estimated Debts (consolidated basis)							
$0 to $50,000	$50,001 to $100,000	$100,001 to $500,000	$500,001 to $1 million	$1,000,001 to $10 million	$10,000,001 to $50 million	$50,000,001 to $100 million	More than $100 million
☐	☐	☐	☐	☐	☐	☐	☒

Voluntary Petition of WorldCom, Inc., Page 2

(Official Form 1) (9/01)		FORM B1, Page 2
Voluntary Petition *(This page must be completed and filed in every case)*	Name of Debtor(s): WorldCom, Inc.	

Prior Bankruptcy Case Filed Within Last 6 Years (If more than one, attach additional sheet)		
Location Where Filed: N/A	Case Number:	Date Filed:

Pending Bankruptcy Case Filed by any Spouse, Partner or Affiliate of this Debtor (If more than one, attach additional sheet)		
Name of Debtor: See attached list of Affiliated Chapter 11 Debtors	Case Number:	Date Filed: 7/21/02
District: S.D.N.Y.	Relationship:	Judge:

Signatures

Signature(s) of Debtor(s) (Individual/Joint)	**Exhibit A**

Signature(s) of Debtor(s) (Individual/Joint)

I declare under penalty of perjury that the information provided in this petition is true and correct.

[If petitioner is an individual whose debts are primarily consumer debts and has chosen to file under chapter 7] I am aware that I may proceed under chapter 7, 11, 12 or 13 of title 11, United States Code, understand the relief available under each such chapter, and choose to proceed under chapter 7.

I request relief in accordance with the chapter of title 11, United States Code, specified in this petition.

_____
Signature of Debtor

_____
Signature of Joint Debtor

_____
Telephone Number (If not represented by attorney)

_____
Date

Exhibit A
(To be completed if debtor is required to file periodic reports (e.g., forms 10K and 10Q) with the Securities and Exchange Commission pursuant to Section 13 or 15(d) of the Securities Exchange Act of 1934 and is requesting relief under chapter 11)

☒ Exhibit A is attached and made a part of this petition.

Exhibit B
(To be completed if debtor is an individual whose debts are primarily consumer debts)

I, the attorney for the petitioner named in the foregoing petition, declare that I have informed the petitioner that [he or she] may proceed under chapter 7, 11, 12, or 13 of title 11, United States Code, and have explained the relief available under each such chapter.

_____
Signature of Attorney for Debtor(s)   Date

Exhibit C

Does the debtor own or have possession of any property that poses or is alleged to pose a threat of imminent and identifiable harm to public health or safety?

☐ Yes, and Exhibit C is attached and made a part of this petition.

☒ No

Signature of Attorney

X /s/ Marcia L. Goldstein
_____
Signature of Attorney for Debtor(s)

Marcia L. Goldstein
_____
Printed Name of Attorney for Debtor(s)

Weil, Gotshal & Manges LLP
_____
Firm Name

767 Fifth Avenue
_____
Address

New York, New York 10153

(212) 310-8000
_____
Telephone Number

7/21/02
_____
Date

Signature of Non-Attorney Petition Preparer

I certify that I am a bankruptcy petition preparer as defined in 11 U.S.C. § 110, that I prepared this document for compensation, and that I have provided the debtor with a copy of this document.

_____
Printed Name of Bankruptcy Petition Preparer

_____
Social Security Number

_____
Address

_____
Names and Social Security numbers of all other individuals who prepared or assisted in preparing this document:

Signature of Debtor (Corporation/Partnership)

I declare under penalty of perjury that the information provided in this petition is true and correct, and that I have been authorized to file this petition on behalf of the debtor.

The debtor requests relief in accordance with the chapter of title 11, United States Code, specified in this petition.

X /s/ Susan Mayer
_____
Signature of Authorized Individual

Susan Mayer
_____
Printed Name of Authorized Individual

Senior Vice President
_____
Title of Authorized Individual

7/21/02
_____
Date

If more than one person prepared this document, attach additional sheets conforming to the appropriate official form for each person.

_____
Signature of Bankruptcy Petition Preparer

_____
Date

A bankruptcy petition preparer's failure to comply with the provisions of title 11 and the Federal Rules of Bankruptcy Procedure may result in fines or imprisonment or both 11 U.S.C. §110; 18 U.S.C. §156.

Below, we describe what you'll see on the bankruptcy petition, section by section.

In the first seven rows, you'll find the debtor's name, address, and Social Security number as well as all other names used by the debtor during the previous six years. The **Name of Joint Debtor** box will tell you whether the debtor is filing jointly with a spouse. If the debtor has operated a business and used a fictitious name for that business, it will be listed here, preceded by a shorthand reference such as "d/b/a" for "doing business as" or "f/k/a" for "formerly known as." Similarly, if the debtor has recently changed legal names (for marriage or other reasons), or lived under an assumed identity, these aliases should be disclosed here. Even nicknames must be disclosed.

Under **Information Regarding the Debtor,** see the box titled **Venue.** This tells you why the debtor chose the city it did in which to file the bankruptcy case. The Bankruptcy Code allows individuals to file the bankruptcy petition in the city where they have lived for the previous 180 days or for the greater part of these 180 days. Usually people file for bankruptcy where they live. However, if the debtor is a corporation, partnership, or sole proprietorship, the bankruptcy may be filed where the principal business or principal assets have been located for the greater part of the last 180 days. A business may also file for bankruptcy in the

district where an affiliate, general partner, or partnership has a bankruptcy pending.

Businesses, especially big businesses, seem to file wherever they please. Enron, which most people associate with Texas, filed in New York City. Many other large corporations file in Wilmington, Delaware. The reasons for their choice and the merits of allowing them to make such choices are not our concern here. However, if one of these behemoths owes you money, don't be surprised to find that the bankruptcy case is pending far away from where you did business with it.

The box labeled **Type of Debtor** will tell you whether the debtor is filing as an individual or a business. If the debtor is a business, you'll learn whether it is filing as a partnership, corporation, railroad, stockbroker, commodity broker, or clearing bank.

In the box **Nature of Debts,** you'll see whether the debtors' obligations are primarily consumer- or business-related. Some issues—for instance, whether granting a Chapter 7 discharge to the debtor would be a substantial abuse of the Bankruptcy Code—depend on whether the debtor's obligations are primarily consumer or business debts. However, the debtor's declaration on the petition doesn't govern this determination—the court will ultimately make its own decision about this. So why is this information required here? It gives the courts a quick source from which to estimate the number of consumer bankruptcies versus business bankruptcies.

Next you'll see a box called **Chapter or Section of Bankruptcy Code Under Which the Petition is Filed.** That's pretty self-explanatory—the choices include Chapter 7, 9, 11, 12, or 13. If the debtor chooses Chapter 11, he or she may also choose to fill in the box called **Chapter 11 Small Business.** Small businesses are entitled to use a different and relatively simpler procedure in Chapter 11.

The box called **Filing Fee** tells you whether the fee was paid along with the petition. If the debtor is an individual, the filing fee may be paid in installments, provided the debtor hasn't already made payments to an attorney or bankruptcy petition preparer (BPP). Note that the automatic stay goes into effect immediately, regardless of whether the debtor has paid all of the filing fee.

The boxes under the heading **Statistical/Administrative Information** are more significant than they sound. The first one tells you whether the debtor thinks there will be any money available to pay unsecured creditors' claims. If the debtor has filed for Chapter 7 protection, then the answer on this line determines whether the bankruptcy clerk sends you a notice of a "no-asset" or "asset" case. No-asset doesn't mean the debtor has no assets at all. Rather, it usually means that the debtor believes all his or her assets are exempt and therefore not available

for distribution to creditors. Remember, in no-asset Chapter 7 cases there is no need for creditors to file a proof of claim. You will, however, be notified to file a proof of claim at a later time if it turns out that the debtor has assets available for distribution after all. (See Chapter 3 for a discussion of the notice process, and Chapter 7 for a discussion of how to file a proof of claim.)

⚠️ **This statement of whether there will be assets available is only the debtor's estimate.** The trustee hasn't even gotten involved in the case yet. Don't take what the debtor says on the petition as the final word. In fact, your review may uncover assets that will pay your claim and others.

The second box in this section lists the **Estimated Number of Creditors.** Below this, under **Estimated Assets,** the debtor must approximate the dollar value of the assets he owns. Under **Estimated Debts,** the debtor must approximate how much he owes.

On Page 2 of the form, under **Prior Bankruptcy Case Filed Within Last 6 Years,** the debtor must give a bit of his history, including the location where each petition was filed, the case number, and the filing date. In addition, under **Pending Bankruptcy Case Filed by any Spouse, Partner or Affiliate of this Debtor,** the debtor must disclose the name of the debtor in the related case, the nature of the relationship, the court where the case is pending, the date it was filed and the judge to whom it is assigned.

The various entries under the heading **Signatures** contain important information as well. If the debtor is an individual, that's the signature you'll see first. And, if the debtor is not represented by an attorney or law firm, you'll find the debtor's telephone number. Things can get dicey for you when the debtor files without the benefit of legal counsel. Since you are a creditor, some types of contacts with the debtor may be interpreted as violations of the automatic stay. However, there may be times when you'll need to contact the debtor in the course of your legitimate participation in the bankruptcy. (See Chapter 4 for a rundown on when you can and can't contact debtors directly.)

Next, you'll find the name, address and telephone number of any law firm or attorney representing the debtor. If the debtor is represented by a law firm rather than by an individual attorney, the firm must designate one attorney as the debtor's counsel. If you learned of the debtor's bankruptcy by receiving a notice from the bankruptcy court, then you already have the information regarding the debtor's attorney. If, however, you're reviewing the court records to confirm or deny a rumor that the debtor filed for bankruptcy, then you'll want to record this information in a prominent spot in your collection file. You'll need to access this information often.

Debtors that are corporations or partnerships sign in the next box.

If the debtor is not represented by counsel, but had help in preparing the bankruptcy petition, then the helper—termed bankruptcy petition preparer or BPP—must sign the petition in the lower right box, and disclose his address, telephone number, and Social Security number.

The signatures on this form carry some legal weight. The debtor signs under penalty of perjury. The attorney signs under penalty of professional sanctions (Bankruptcy Rule 9011). If the debtor is a consumer, she must also declare her understanding of the various forms of bankruptcy relief available to her; and her attorney must declare that the debtor was informed of these various forms of possible relief.

2. Bankruptcy Schedules and Statements

Supporting the debtor's bankruptcy petition are a number of schedules and statements. In this section, we'll describe what each one should contain. Also see the Appendix to this book, where we've reprinted all the schedule and statement forms. (These forms can also be found on the federal court website at www.uscourts.gov/bankform/index.html.)

a. Schedule A—Real Property

Schedule A should be included with every bankruptcy filing. (See the reprinted form in the appendix.) It gives the debtor a place to list and describe all the real estate that she owns or may someday own. For each property listed, the debtor should have stated:

- where the property is located
- whether the debtor owns the property outright, or shares ownership with others
- whether the debtor's ownership interest currently exists or will come into existence only after something else happens. For example, the property deed may say that ownership won't pass to the debtor until the property's current occupant dies.
- if the petition was filed by a husband and wife, whether the property is titled in the husband's name, the wife's name, both names or held as community property regardless of how it is titled
- how much the debtor thinks the property is worth, before considering any liens against the property. In other words, what is its market value or the most likely amount that someone would pay for it?
- who holds a lien against the property (if anyone) and how much the lienholders are owed. If the property's market value exceeds the amount of the liens, then the debtor has equity in the property. Unless this equity is protected by an exemption, the property is available for sale by a Chapter 7 trustee to pay unsecured claims. If the debtor files under one of the reorganization chapters, the debtor's plan must pay the creditor at least as much as would have been paid if the debtor had filed under Chapter 7. That means that the amount of the debtor's nonexempt equity plays an indirect role in determining whether the debtor's plan is approved.

b. Schedule B—Personal Property

Schedule B asks the debtor to list all the personal property (as opposed to real estate) that she owns. (See the reprinted form in the Appendix.) This schedule designates 32 types of personal property, and has a category for "other" types of property. Nothing is supposed to be left out. For each category of property listed on the schedule, the debtor must state:

- specifically what each item of property is. For example, under the "furs and jewelry" category, the debtor would have to state whether the property is mink or sheepskin, emeralds or tinted crystals. The debtor must provide enough detail for you to reasonably judge each item's value. "A ring" is not an adequate answer. If the debtor's information is incomplete or vague, you or the trustee should ask the debtor for details.

- where the property is located. This information is especially important for property that the debtor owns but doesn't have in his possession. For example, the debtor may own a car that is being driven by a daughter away at college. If the property is valuable, the trustee may wish to have that property returned to the debtor or to a safe location. Also, if the debtor is holding property that doesn't belong to him, this fact must be disclosed so that other person's property won't be mistakenly swept into the bankruptcy proceedings.

- if the petition was filed by a married person or couple, whether property is titled in the husband's name, the wife's name, both names, or held as community property regardless of how it is titled. Many debtors don't designate which spouse owns property. However, this question will need to be answered eventually, because when only one spouse files for bankruptcy, property belonging entirely to the nonfiling spouse won't usually be included in the bankruptcy estate.

- how much the debtor thinks the property is worth, without taking into consideration any liens against the property. This means how much the property would sell for. Unlike real estate, this can be a hard number to come up with. While there's a stable market for real estate, there's not much of a market for used silverware. Most debtors will list their used property at a minimal value. As we'll see in Section c, part of your detective work will be to sleuth out any gems hidden among the debtor's old trinkets.

c. Schedule C—Property Claimed as Exempt

On Schedule C, the debtor must list all the exemptions being claimed in an effort to protect property that's in the bankruptcy estate from being sold by the trustee. (See the reprinted form in the Appendix.) You'll only find a Schedule C if it's an individual bankruptcy—business entities can't claim exemptions.

An exemption won't always shield the entire piece of property. The various exemption laws allow the debtor to keep property only up to a certain value. So, for example, a debtor won't be able to shield his $2 million Picasso painting while creditors go away with nothing. And, of course, the debtor can't shield any more of the property than he actually owns, or his "equity." If the liens against the property are equal to or exceed the property's market value, the debtor doesn't need to claim the property as exempt, because there's no equity to protect. If the property's value exceeds the debtor's available exemption plus the amount of liens, then this excess equity is available to pay at least part of your claim—if your claim is unsecured.

Although the federal Bankruptcy Code provides an exemption scheme for debtors, states are allowed to opt out of the federal exemption scheme—and most have. Even in the few states that allow their citizens to claim the federal exemptions, debtors may select the state exemptions instead. (They can't claim exemptions piecemeal, but must choose to go with either the federal or their state's scheme.) So, in addition to telling you what property is being claimed as exempt, the debtor must tell you the statutory basis for that exemption.

The debtor must also tell you the value or amount of the exemption being claimed in the property and remind you of the property's market value.

d. Schedule D—Creditors Holding Secured Claims

On Schedule D, the debtor must list all the "secured" creditors—that is, those whose right to payment is secured by liens on the debtor's property. (See the reprinted form in the Appendix.) For each secured creditor, the debtor must state:

- the creditor's name and mailing address
- the debtor's account number with the creditor
- whether another person or business (besides the debtor and the debtor's spouse) is liable on this debt
- if the bankruptcy petition was filed jointly by a husband and wife, who is responsible for paying the debt—the husband, the wife or both
- when the debtor became indebted to the creditor—in other words, the date when the loan was made, the property was purchased or the debtor become legally obligated to repay the creditor
- what kind of lien the creditor has... was it created by an agreement, such as a mortgage? Was it created by statute, as with a mechanic's lien? Or, was it created following a judgment or court order, such as might be issued in a divorce proceeding?
- whether the claim is contingent on a future event. A contingent claim is one in which the debtor will owe the debt only if something else happens. For example, if the debtor pledged her home as security for a bail bond to get her brother out of jail, she will only be liable if her brother jumps bail. The claim, therefore, is a contingent one, based on the bond's forfeiture.

- whether the amount owed on the claim can be determined. If it's clear how much the debtor owes you or there's a formula by which you can make the calculation, then the claim is referred to as "liquidated." If, however, you claim that the debtor owes you money but you don't know how much, the claim is "unliquidated"— and the debtor must disclose this fact. For example, a claim that the debtor caused you personal injury is unliquidated until a court determines the amount of damages.
- whether the debtor contests the claim's legitimacy. The debtor must list all creditors' claims in this schedule, but gets an opportunity here to state that the claim is in dispute.
- the amount owed to the creditors (listed creditor by creditor, with a total figure at the end). The total figure should correspond to the amount of secured claims listed in Schedule A.
- how much of each creditor's claim exceeds the value of the collateral securing it. To the extent you're owed more than your collateral is worth, your claim is unsecured and will be treated the same as other unsecured claims.

e. Schedule E—Creditors Holding Unsecured Priority Claims

On Schedule E, the debtor must list all the creditors whose claims should receive payment priority under the Bankruptcy Code. (See the reprinted form in the Appendix.) Being on this list doesn't mean you're sure to get paid. Instead, in Chapter 7 cases, it means that if there is money available to pay claims, priority claims get paid first. In reorganization cases, it means that priority claims must be paid in full through the confirmed plan.

Priority claims include:

- money lent or credit given to a debtor after an involuntary petition was filed against him and before a trustee was appointed or the court declared the debtor to be bankrupt. (See Chapter 18.)
- in cases where the creditor was an employee of the debtor, up to $4,650 per employee for wages, salaries, and commissions earned within 90 days prior to the bankruptcy filing or the closing of the business, whichever occurred first
- also for employee creditors, employer contributions to employee benefit plans that went unpaid within the 180 days prior to the bankruptcy filing or the closing of the business, whichever occurred first

- in cases where the creditor is a farmer or fisherman, up to $4,650 per person for unpaid products provided to the debtor
- up to $2,100 per claim for deposits made by people who were buying or renting goods or services from the debtor for personal, family, or household use. This priority designation is meant to protect people from dress shop owners and travel agencies who close up shop while holding deposits for such things as wedding gowns and family vacations
- most taxes owed to any government, along with the penalties imposed for nonpayment

For each priority claim, the debtor must state:

- the creditor's name and mailing address
- the debtor's account number with the creditor
- whether another person or business is liable on this debt besides the debtor and the debtor's spouse
- if the bankruptcy petition was filed jointly by a husband and wife, which of them is responsible for paying the debt—the husband, the wife, or both—or whether the debt is a marital community obligation, regardless of which spouse incurred it
- when the debtor became indebted to the creditor

- why the debt is entitled to priority status
- whether the claim is contingent on a future event
- whether the claim is for an amount that cannot be calculated
- whether the debtor contests the claim's legitimacy
- the amount owed to the creditor, and
- how much of the creditor's claim is entitled to priority status.

f. Schedule F—Creditors Holding Unsecured Nonpriority Claims

On Schedule F, the debtor must list all the creditors who didn't appear on the previous schedules—that is, those who don't have liens on the debtor's property and who aren't otherwise entitled to priority payment. (See the reprinted form in the Appendix.) For each holder of a general unsecured claim, the debtor must state:

- the creditor's name and mailing address
- the debtor's account number with the creditor
- whether another person or business (besides the debtor and the debtor's spouse) is liable on this debt
- If the bankruptcy petition was filed jointly by a husband and wife, which of them is responsible for paying the debt—the husband, the wife, or

both—or whether the debt is a marital community obligation, regardless of which spouse incurred it

- when the debtor became indebted to the creditor
- what the debtor received from the creditor that created the repayment obligation
- whether the creditor owes any money to the debtor. If so, the creditor may be entitled to reduce the amount of money owed to the debtor by the amount of money that the debtor owes to the creditor. This is known as a setoff
- whether the claim is contingent on a future event
- whether the claim is for an amount that cannot be calculated
- whether the debtor contests the claim's legitimacy, and
- the amount owed to the creditor.

g. Schedule G—Executory Contracts and Unexpired Leases

On Schedule G, the debtor must list all the currently valid and unexpired agreements into which she has entered. (See the reprinted form in the Appendix.) For example, the debtor must disclose any timeshare interests here. Unexpired leases for cars, equipment, buildings, and the like must also be disclosed. With regard to each contract, the debtor must state:

- the name and address of the other party to the contract
- the contract and the nature of the debtor's involvement
- whether any lease is for nonresidential real estate, and
- the contract number of any government contract.

h. Schedule H—Codebtors

On Schedules D, E, and F, the debtor stated whether there are people who are obligated on debts along with her. Now, on Schedule H, the debtor must provide the names and addresses of those codebtors. (See the reprinted form in the Appendix.)

i. Schedule I—Current Income of Individual Debtor(s), and Schedule J – Current Expenditures of Individual Debtor(s)

Schedule I requires the debtor to provide a statement of income, while Schedule J requires a statement of the debtor's expenses. (See the reprinted forms in the Appendix.) Both statements need be filed only by individual, as opposed to business debtors. (Partnerships and corporations must also make income and expense disclosures, but they don't use Schedules I and J to do it.)

The debtors must disclose the amount of their monthly earnings, payroll deductions, and expenses. If the filing is a joint petition under Chapter 7, both spouses must provide the required information. In a Chapter 12 or 13 filing, both spouses must provide the information even if only one spouse filed for bankruptcy.

j.   Statement of Financial Affairs

All debtors must complete a Statement of Financial Affairs form. (See the reprinted form in the Appendix.) However, questions 19 through 25 of the form need to be answered only by debtors that are businesses or who were in business at some point in time during the previous six years. Below is what you should see on the Statement of Financial Affairs.

In **Questions 1 and 2,** the debtor must report all recent income. This includes income received from the beginning of the calendar year up to the bankruptcy filing, as well as income received during the previous two calendar years.

In **Question 3,** the debtor must reveal any payments in excess of $600 made to creditors within the 90 days leading up to the bankruptcy filing. The debtor must also reveal all payments to family members and close business associates made during the 12 months leading up to the bankruptcy filing. The trustee may be able to force those who received these pay-

ments to return them to the estate so they can be distributed to unsecured creditors.

In **Question 4,** the debtor must describe any litigation in which the debtor was involved during the 12 months leading up to the bankruptcy filing, such as a divorce or any other lawsuit in which the debtor was a plaintiff or defendant. Question 4 also asks the debtor to reveal any liens placed against the debtor's property within the 12 months leading up to the bankruptcy filing date.

In **Question 5,** the debtor must reveal whether any of the debtor's property has been repossessed, foreclosed upon or returned to creditors within the 12 months leading up to the bankruptcy.

In **Question 6,** the debtor must describe any assignments and receiverships created within the 120 days leading up to the bankruptcy filing. Assignments and receiverships are state equivalents to bankruptcy. An assignment is the transfer of some or all of a debtor's property to a creditor. An assignment for the benefit of creditors is the transfer of all a debtor's property to a neutral party who sells the property to pay creditors' claims. A receivership is a proceeding by which a debtor's property is placed under the control of a receiver for the benefit of creditors.

In **Question 7,** the debtor must list any gifts made within the 12 months leading up to the bankruptcy filing. Ordinary gifts to family members totaling less than

$200 do not need to be listed. Nor do charitable contributions totaling less than $100, so long as they're made to IRS-recognized tax-exempt religious organizations or charitable entities. While charitable contributions of more than $100 must be listed, the Bankruptcy Code prohibits trustees from recovering these contributions if they accounted for less than 15% of the debtor's gross annual income. A debtor can protect an even greater percentage if it is consistent with her previous level of giving. In other words, if the debtor gave 20% of her gross income to charity during the 12 months prior to the bankruptcy filing, the trustee cannot recover any of this money if debtor gave that amount in previous years.

In **Question 8,** the debtor must reveal any property lost within the 12 months leading up to the bankruptcy filing and explain the circumstances surrounding the loss. If the property was insured, the debtor must tell what company provided the insurance, whether a claim for loss was filed with the company and what happened to the claim.

In **Question 9,** the debtor must state when and how much was paid to bankruptcy attorneys and debt counseling services prior to filing for bankruptcy.

Question 10 is a catch-all question, asking the debtor to reveal any transfers made within the 12 months leading up to the bankruptcy filing. It's important to know about all these transfers for a

couple of reasons, the primary one being to discover any transfers that can be recovered by the bankruptcy trustee. As we'll discuss in Chapter 15, the trustee may be able to bring back into the bankruptcy estate certain payments and transfers the debtor made shortly before filing for bankruptcy. This information also gives the trustee and you an idea of how the debtor was handling her finances in the months leading up to the bankruptcy. This information could form a basis to challenge the debtor's eligibility for a discharge or lead to the discovery of undisclosed assets.

In **Question 11,** the debtor must reveal financial accounts and instruments (such as certificates of deposit) that were closed or sold within the 12 months leading up to the bankruptcy filing.

In **Question 12,** the debtor must reveal whether she has any safe deposit boxes or had any safe deposit boxes that were closed within the 12 months leading up to the bankruptcy filing. If she did, she must disclose the contents of the safe deposit box or boxes. While the debtor must reveal details regarding the box and who had access to it, this statement doesn't ask debtors to say what happened to the property disclosed as being kept in the box.

In **Question 13,** the debtor must reveal any debts that were reduced by the creditor in an amount of money equal to what the creditor owed to the debtor. For example, if Dan owes you $400 and you owe Dan $150, Dan may pay you $250 and called it even. This is a setoff of mutual debts and, for bankruptcy purposes, it is a transfer that may be pulled back into the estate (avoided). Review any setoffs disclosed by the debtor in the same manner you reviewed transfers disclosed in Questions 3 through 6 and 10.

In **Question 14,** the debtor must describe any property that she is holding for someone else.

In **Question 15,** the debtor must state where she has lived over the past two years.

Question 16 applies only to debtors who are living or who have lived with a spouse in a community property state within the six years leading up to the bankruptcy filing. If the question applies, the debtor must reveal the spouse or former spouse's name.

In **Question 17,** the debtor must reveal whether he owns property that is or may be in violation of environmental law.

In **Question 18,** the debtor must list the names and addresses of all business with which the debtor is involved. The debtor must also disclose the nature of those businesses.

Question 19 must be answered by debtors who are either engaged in business, or were engaged in business at any point during the past six years. It asks the debtor for the name and address of the debtor's bookkeeper and accountant. It

also asks for a list of everyone who received a copy of the debtor's financial statements within the two years leading up to the bankruptcy filing.

In **Question 20,** the business debtor must list the last two times that the company's property was inventoried and by whom. The debtor must also state the total value of the property turned up in that inventory.

If the debtor is a partnership, **Question 21** asks the debtor for the names, addresses, and percentage interest of each partner. If the debtor is a corporation, Question 21 asks for the names, addresses, title, and ownership interest of each stockholder who owns at least a 5% share of the corporation's voting stock.

Question 22 repeats the inquiry of Question 21, but for former partners, officers, directors, and shareholders whose relationship with the debtor ended within the 12 months leading up to the bankruptcy filing.

In **Question 23,** the debtor must describe any withdrawals from partnership accounts and distributions by a corporation.

In **Question 24,** debtors who joined with other businesses in order to make group purchases of supplies and services must disclose the name of the parent corporation for their buying group. It's not unusual for businesses to pool their resources to gain purchasing power, but look for unusual transfers between the participants.

In **Question 25,** debtors who are employers must disclose the name and taxpayer identification number of any pension fund to which the debtor has been contributing. The purpose of this disclosure is to verify the debtor's status with its pension contributions.

k. Statement of Intention

The Statement of Intention form need be completed only by individuals who owe money on secured consumer debts. (See the reprinted form in the Appendix.) The debtor must state:

- what the collateral is
- who the creditor is, and
- whether the debtor intends to surrender the collateral.

If the debtor plans to keep the collateral, she must state whether she plans to reaffirm her debt, pay the creditor the cash value of the collateral, or avoid the creditor's lien and claim the property as exempt. Whichever choice the debtor makes must be acted upon within 45 days of filing the statement with the court (unless the court grants an extension of time). (See Chapter 8 for more about Statements of Intention.)

l. The Debtor's Reorganization Plan

If the debtor filed under one of the reorganization chapters—9, 11, 12, or 13—you may find the debtor's plan for repaying debts along with the schedules and statements. If you don't find the plan, you might receive it within days—or months. If the debtor filed under Chapter 13, the debtor will have to file a plan within 15 days of the initial filing. Chapter 12 debtors have 90 days within which to file their plans. In Chapters 9 and 11, there is no set deadline for filing plans. The court will establish a deadline for the Chapter 9 debtors. Chapter 11 debtors file plans when they think they can get them confirmed, or when they think they're at risk of having their cases dismissed for not filing a plan.

3. Amendments to the Paperwork After Filing

Though extensive, the paperwork that the debtor initially files with the court may not be all that the court eventually receives from the debtor. If, within the 180 days following the bankruptcy filing, the debtor acquires property via inheritance, a marital property settlement, or as the beneficiary of a life insurance policy, the debtor must amend the schedules and statements to reflect this. Debtors may also amend their schedules and statements at any time while the case is open to correct mistakes made in the original filing. Don't worry, Rule 1009 requires the debtor to notify the trustee and creditors of any amendments to the schedules.

C. Playing Detective With the Debtor's Paperwork

Now we get to the meat of the matter—how you, as a creditor, can use the information in the debtor's paperwork to shake some money out of the bankruptcy tree. If you do nothing, you may get nothing, especially if your claim is unsecured (and not automatically excepted from discharge). Even if your claim is secured, in which case your lien may survive bankruptcy (see Chapter 8), you can't afford to ignore the debtor's documents.

To improve your chances of getting paid, we'll give you tips on how to:

- Find evidence of property that the debtor owns and can't exempt. If the debtor filed under Chapter 7, this property can be sold by the trustee, and the proceeds put towards paying your claim. If the debtor filed under one of the reorganization chapters, the court will consider the value of this property when determining whether to confirm the debtor's proposed plan.

- Uncover inaccuracies and omissions in the debtor's schedules. We're not talking mere typos here—if you know that the debtor owns property or assets that you don't see listed on the schedules, you may not only provide the trustee with something to sell, but also expose the debtor as an abuser of the bankruptcy system. Debtors who abuse the system are not eligible to receive a discharge.

- Discover that the debtor understated her income or overstated her living expenses. Either way, it means she has more money that can be used to pay unsecured creditors. If the debtor filed under Chapter 7, the trustee can ask the court to dismiss her case if she can repay a significant percentage of her unsecured claims. If she filed under one of the reorganization cases, the court will consider the amount of her disposable income when deciding whether to confirm her proposed plan.

- Uncover facts that show your claim can't be discharged (wiped out) through the bankruptcy. For example, if you loaned money to the debtor, you may learn that the debtor lied to you. This information can enable you to challenge the entire discharge. If you hold a claim against the debtor that was not created by your voluntary decision to loan him money—for example, you hold a state court judgment against the debtor—you may already know all you need to in order to reveal the debtor's true nature to the court.

Although some of the above-mentioned ways of derailing the debtor's plans involve using your outside knowledge, you'll want to start with a thorough review of the debtor's bankruptcy petition, schedules, and statements. You'll be looking for apparent errors and inconsistencies in the schedules—for example, claims of pension plan deductions without any listing of the pension plan as an asset. When you find anything that doesn't look right, note it so you will remember to ask the debtor about it at the creditors' meeting.

Hidden assets that won't pay you may still help you. Although many assets, such as pensions, are excluded from the bankruptcy estate, the debtor's failure to list an asset can be the basis for denying the discharge. The debtor must list all property, regardless of whether it will yield any payment to creditors.

Don't sit back and figure the trustee will do the work for you. If the debtor filed under Chapter 7 and stated that he had no assets, then the trustee will make a cursory examination of the debtor's paperwork, looking for obvious errors. But the trustee is going to depend on interested creditors to help find hidden treasures.

If the debtor filed under Chapter 11, there is no trustee—just the debtor, acting as a debtor-in-possession with the powers of a trustee. He's not exactly going to be bending over backwards to protect your interests. You'll get some oversight from the U.S. Trustee, who supervises the debtor's actions and conducts the creditor's meeting. And if evidence of fraud or mismanagement emerges, you or the U.S. Trustee can ask the court to appoint a trustee, but this rarely happens.

If the debtor filed under Chapter 12 or 13, the trustee is going to be more interested in the debtor's repayment plan than in what the debtor owns or what financial shenanigans he engaged in before filing for bankruptcy. If the debtor appears able to make the payments called for in his plan and the plan appears to meet the Bankruptcy Code's approval requirements, then the trustee will probably be satisfied. But you may still be able to create a better deal for you and other creditors through an aggressive investigation of the debtor.

There's Gold in Them Thar Documents

In 1999, Steven Rhodes, a bankruptcy judge in Michigan, performed an interesting investigative exercise. He took a close look at 200 consumer bankruptcy petitions that had been filed in his court, scrutinizing them in the same way we're talking about in this chapter. The result: Judge Rhodes found potential errors in a whopping 198 out of 200 cases. That's 99% of the cases. Within each case, the average number of apparent errors was nearly four. With statistics like that, you've got every incentive to get your hands on the debtor's paperwork and take your cat's flea comb to it.

But finding errors is a meaningless exercise unless it leads to cash for creditors. Recognizing this, Judge Rhodes conducted a second survey. This time he looked at 103 cases that were filed in his court under Chapter 7 over a six-month period, and that were closed with money paid to unsecured creditors. In 41% of those cases, the debtor had declared "no assets" upon filing—which would have meant zilch for the unsecured creditors. But lo and behold, fifty-one pieces of property worth nearly $1 million were uncovered in these supposed "no-asset" cases. In 14 of the 103 cases, sufficient assets were found that all creditors who had filed claims allowed by the court were paid in full. Undisclosed assets included boats, jewelry, and collectibles. In one case, a debtor left a Rolex watch behind at the creditors' meeting. Talk about finding an asset!

Does this mean that most debtors are liars? Not really—the number of errors and the manner in which the documents were prepared seemed to indicate that the debtor or the attorney simply didn't take the bankruptcy filing very seriously. In Judge Rhodes' study, 21% of the petitions were not dated and 19% were dated more than 15 days before they were filed. The debtor is required to sign and date the petition and schedules after reviewing them. If the petition was dated more than 15 days before it was filed, the information disclosed could be stale. If the petition is undated, you have no idea how old the information is. Such carelessness is a serious matter all its own—and one that the law attempts to deal with by giving the court the right to deny the debtor's discharge if the debtor has shown an indifferent attitude toward the bankruptcy. The court looks with particular disfavor on debtors who are slow to correct their mistakes.

1. Reviewing the Bankruptcy Petition

As you review the bankruptcy petition, see if you can find justification for asking the court to:

- dismiss the case, either because the debtor filed in the wrong court (Subsection a), or
- because the debtor isn't eligible for bankruptcy (Subsection b).

a. Spotting a Filing in the Wrong Court

Look at the top of the bankruptcy petition to see what court the debtor chose to file in. If that court is far away from where you did business with the debtor, consider that a red flag. Individuals may file for bankruptcy in the district where they reside or have been residing for most of the 180 days prior to the filing. Businesses may file where their principal location is, where their assets are, or where their affiliate has filed bankruptcy. When a conglomerate files bankruptcy, it can file just about wherever it wants to, by having a subsidiary file first, and then filing where the subsidiary did business, based on the fact that the subsidiary has a pending bankruptcy there.

Filing in the wrong court is primarily a concern in Chapter 11 cases. Debtors seem to find a way to file in Delaware or New York regardless of where their company is located. They're looking for advantages like a slow court docket, which gives debtors leverage against the creditors. However, individual debtors and companies filing under Chapter 7 have also been known to file in the wrong court.

If you determine that the case was filed in the wrong court, send a letter to the U.S. Trustee pointing out the problem. The trustee should take care of asking the court to dismiss the case.

Even if the debtor did file in the right court, it's possible for you to challenge the so-called venue—that is, the debtor's choice of a particular local court within the larger jurisdiction—as being inconvenient. However, your chances of success are slim if the debtor is eligible for bankruptcy in the court where the case was filed. Courts won't transfer a case to another court that's more convenient for creditors unless it's crystal clear that the case belongs somewhere else.

b. Spotting the Debtor's Ineligibility for Bankruptcy

It sometimes happens that the debtor isn't even eligible for relief under the chosen bankruptcy chapter. Eligibility is generally based on what type of entity the debtor is and whether the debt level is below a certain limit. The eligibility rules for each chapter can be summarized as follows:

- **Chapter 7:** Nearly anyone can be a debtor under Chapter 7. The most notable exceptions are railroads, banks, and insurance companies. However, holding companies for these types of enterprises may file under Chapter 7.
- **Chapter 9:** Only municipalities may reorganize under Chapter 9.
- **Chapter 11:** Any debtor who is eligible for Chapter 7 relief may file under Chapter 11. In addition, railroads may file under Chapter 11.
- **Chapter 12:** Only individual debtors who do not owe more than $1.5 million and who earn most of their income from farming may file under Chapter 12.
- **Chapter 13:** Only individuals with regular income who owe less than $290,525 in unsecured debt and $871,550 in secured debt may file under Chapter 13. (These dollar figures are adjusted for inflation every three years. The next scheduled adjustment will occur on April 4, 2004.)

If you believe the debtor is ineligible to receive a discharge under the chapter chosen, bring your doubts to the trustee's attention or file a motion asking the court to dismiss the case. The basis for your motion would be the debtor's ineligibility for relief. (See Chapter 10 for information on how to file a motion to dismiss. It can be done without an attorney.)

2. Reviewing Schedule A—Real Property

In reviewing the debtor's Schedule A, look for:

- real estate that you know the debtor owns, but that wasn't listed (Subsection a)
- equity in real estate that the debtor failed to list (Subsection b), and
- indications that the debtor believes your claim is higher than the collateral is worth (Subsection c).

a. Spotting Unscheduled Real Estate

Look over the real estate that the debtor mentions on Schedule A. Compare it to any loan applications the debtor filed with you previously, to make sure that nothing was left out. Also compare it to your own knowledge. If you have any personal contact with the debtor, recall whether you've heard of any summer homes or inheritances that should have been mentioned here.

If the Schedule A is blank, ask yourself where the debtor is living. If the debtor doesn't own a home, chances are he rents one. Turn to Schedule B and see if the debtor has listed a security deposit (number 3 on the property list). Most landlords demand security deposits. Also check Schedule G to see if an apartment lease is listed, and check Schedule J for a rent expense.

If nothing is listed on Schedule A and there's nothing listed that indicates the debtor is a renter, then make a note to ask the debtor about his living arrangement. The answer may be an innocent one—he may live rent-free with relatives or friends. On the other hand, you may learn about a home that the debtor improperly transferred to others and left off Schedule A for that reason.

If you turn up any unscheduled real estate, ask the debtor about it at the creditors' meeting or tell the trustee about it. In a Chapter 7 case, the trustee can add it to the bankruptcy estate, and sell it to pay claims. In a Chapter 11, the property must be sold to benefit creditors, unless the debtor has no equity in it or the debtor's plan calls for unsecured creditors to be paid in full. In a Chapter 12 or 13, the court will consider the amount of equity the debtor has in this property when deciding whether to approve the debtor's proposed plan. The failure to schedule a valuable asset is also a reason for the court to deny the debtor's discharge.

b. Spotting Unscheduled Equity in Real Estate

Even if the debtor has listed real estate on Schedule A, he may not have confessed its full value. See if it passes your own reasonableness test. If you know the property address, you can get a rough appraisal online. For example, at www.domania.com you can find out the prices of homes sold in the same neighborhood, within a time frame of your choosing (don't choose any more than one year). Or, you can look at the prices of homes currently for sale at http://houseandhome.msn.com. Be aware, however, that homes may sell for much more or less than the list price, depending on the market.

If you don't know the property's address, check the real estate records, usually kept at the county recorder's office, to see when the debtor acquired the property and how much was paid. If your initial inquiry makes you suspicious, call a friend in the real estate business or do a drive-by appraisal. Make a note to ask the debtor how he valued the property.

Now look at the total amount listed for all secured creditors' claims. Is it the same as the value of the property? If so, the debtor may be up to something. When the debtor shows no equity in the property, the debtor doesn't need to use an exemption to protect it. That's an advantage in states whose exemption system allows "wildcard exemptions." With a wildcard system, the debtor can take some of his unused homestead exemption and apply it to other types of property—including property that wouldn't have qualified for an exemption on its own. For example, in states that allow the use of the federal exemptions, debtors can use up to one-half of the unused portion of the homestead exemption to protect any other property. The federal wildcard exemption allows debtors to protect $9,650 in any asset. (This is the 2003 figure; it is modified every three years. See 11 U.S.C. § 522(d)(5).) This extra exemption could be used to protect a second car, stock or any property that otherwise would be available to pay unsecured creditors' claims. Now you can see why the debtor might have fudged the value of the property downward or the value of the liens upward in order to make them come out equal.

EXAMPLE: Daisy states on Schedule A that her house is worth $125,000 and that the liens against her house also equal $125,000. In the state where Daisy lives, she's allowed to use half of her unused homestead exemption to protect anything. The homestead exemption in her state is $15,000. Daisy has an antique doll collection, which she says is worth $5,000. She shields this collection with the unused homestead exemption. A savvy creditor would have reason to question the value of Daisy's home and the liens against it to see if she's hiding equity in order to create an exemption for the doll collection.

You should also be suspicious if the full amount of the homestead exemption plus the liens against the debtor's residence neatly equals the property's value. This would mean that the amount of the debtor's equity in the property is exactly the same as the amount of equity the debtor can protect. What a lucky coincidence! The debtor has no equity in his house that would tempt the trustee to sell it.

EXAMPLE: Dirk says his home is worth $300,000. He has $100,000 in equity in it, which is exactly the same amount as the state's homestead exemption. Not willing to accept these numbers at face value, Catya, a creditor, learned the following just from checking the title records in the county courthouse:

- Dirk bought his house four years ago, for $300,000. Since home prices in the area have increased by 20% during the past four years, that means that Dirk's home could easily be worth $360,000 by now.

- Dirk borrowed $200,000 to buy his home. While most of the payments at the beginning of a mortgage go to pay interest and not principal, Catya believes that the principal balance owed is less than $200,000. With potentially only about $100,000 in debt on a $360,000 home, it looks like Dirk may have plenty of equity.

Catya forwards this information to the trustee, who asks the court to deny Dirk's discharge based on Dirk's misrepresentations. Catya also objects to Dirk's homestead exemption by filing a motion with the court.

There is one similar situation that shouldn't excite your suspicion, however. If the debtor states an amount of liens against the property that exceeds the property's value, then the debtor is probably telling the truth. It is not unusual for a person in financial trouble to pledge her home as collateral in order to borrow more money (in a last ditch effort to avoid bankruptcy). In fact, payment of these loans, which often carry high rates of interest, may be one of the factors contributing to the debtor's need for bankruptcy protection.

If you uncover undisclosed equity in real estate, ask the debtor about it at the creditors' meeting or tell the trustee about it. In a Chapter 7 case, the trustee can sell the real estate to pay creditors' claims. In a Chapter 11 case, the property will be sold unless the debtor's plan fully pays unsecured creditors. In a Chapter 12 or 13, the court will consider the value of the property when ruling on confirmation of the debtor's plan. Also, the debtor's failure to correctly schedule the value of real estate can be a reason for the court to deny the debtor's discharge.

c. **Spotting Undersecured Claims**

If you hold a secured claim, look at Schedule A to make sure your claim is properly scheduled. Your only concern at this point is that the debtor hasn't said that the property is worth less than you're owed. That would mean that your claim is undersecured. The mere fact that Schedule A shows your claim as being undersecured doesn't mean you lose anything, but it does put you on guard for an attempt by the debtor to reduce the secured value of your claim.

In a Chapter 7 bankruptcy, if your collateral is worth less than what you are owed, and it is personal property that is primarily used for a personal, family or household purposes, the debtor is entitled to pay you the collateral's value and discharge the balance of your claim.

In a Chapter 11, 12, or 13 bankruptcy, the debtor is allowed to pay you the collateral's value through the plan and discharge the balance of your claim.

3. **Reviewing Schedule B—Personal Property**

Schedule B is supposed to contain a comprehensive list of the debtor's personal property. In reviewing the debtor's Schedule B, you'll want to look for:

- unscheduled assets (Subsection a)
- undervalued assets (Subsection c), and

- evidence that the debtor isn't really bankrupt (Subsection c).

a. Spotting Unscheduled Assets

Start by using your common sense to root out obvious omissions. If the debtor is an individual, make sure he has listed the type of stuff that a normal person keeps around, such as clothing and appliances. If the debtor is a business, make sure it has listed the types of materials you would expect such a business to have, such as computers or other equipment. If obvious items are missing, the debtor may be hiding less obvious ones.

Even if your imagination is running dry as to things an ordinary person or business would have, you may be the best person to know certain items the debtor must have—because you sold them to him. Check for those items. Then, go one step further and make sure that the debtor listed anything that he'd need along with the items you sold him. For example, if you sold the debtor tires, check the list for the car that should be sitting atop those tires. If you sold him a printing press, look for printing supplies. If you sold the debtor bed sheets, look for the bed!

Another way to play detective is to look for internal inconsistencies within the Schedule B or between the various schedules. For example, if the debtor's budget on Schedule J says he's paying money for car insurance, look for a car.

If the debtor is married but filing as an individual, look for inappropriate claims that the other spouse owns the property. It's not unusual for a great deal of personal property—the type of property for which there is no recorded title and it is difficult to prove ownership—to be omitted from the debtor's schedules because it is alleged to belong to the nonfiling spouse. For example, the debtor may say she listed no furnishings because they all belong to her husband, who didn't file for bankruptcy. To find out whether this is true, ask her when the furniture was purchased and who paid for it. If the property was purchased during the marriage, chances are that it belongs to both spouses jointly. Whether it does depends on how your state treats property acquired during marriage.

If you find unscheduled assets, ask the debtor about them at the creditor's meeting or bring them up with the trustee. In a Chapter 7 case, the trustee can sell these assets to pay creditors' claims. In a Chapter 11, the debtor cannot keep the assets unless his plan fully pays unsecured creditors (otherwise, the assets will have to be sold, and the proceeds used to pay unsecured creditors' claims.) In a Chapter 12 or 13, the value of the assets will be considered by the bankruptcy court when deciding whether to approve the debtor's proposed repayment plan. In addition, the court may use the debtor's failure to disclose all assets as grounds to deny the debtor's discharge.

b.   Spotting Undervalued Assets

Though it's hard to gauge the value of the debtor's property without seeing it, certain signs of trouble may stand out. Be skeptical of any property that the debtor has valued in the same amount as the available exemption. Just as with real property, the debtor may be hiding equity by undervaluing property so that it doesn't exceed the exemption amount.

Also look hard at any property that seems to be lumped together in a manner that hides the true nature and value of the individual items. While it's acceptable for a consumer debtor to list everyday clothing as a single asset, it's not acceptable to list all jewelry the same way. Similarly, furniture should not be lumped together under a description like "living room furniture," but should be described separately, piece by piece.

c.   Spotting Evidence that the Debtor Isn't Really Bankrupt

The nature of the assets that the debtor admits to owning can also yield interesting information. Question any asset that doesn't fit the profile of a bankrupt debtor. Boats and expensive cars are signs that the debtor isn't taking the bankruptcy seriously. In order to receive a discharge, debtors must approach bankruptcy in good faith. At the very least,

that means sacrificing a luxurious lifestyle in an attempt to pay one's creditors. Bankruptcy judges, who have an annual salary of about $150,000, joke that they won't grant a discharge to any debtor driving a nicer car than they do. All kidding aside, many of them won't.

If the debtor filed under one of the reorganization chapters, any money the debtor is spending on a luxury item should be going to pay creditors' claims. Make a note to question the debtor's need for the item at the Section 341 creditors' meeting. Remember, any reduction in the debtor's expenses means more money the debtor can use to fund the reorganization plan.

⚠️ **Use your judgment when deciding whether to challenge how a debtor scheduled his assets.** If you think he's hiding something, go after it with bulldog determination. If the trustee doesn't like you using time at the creditor's meeting for your interrogation, then schedule a Rule 2004 examination to do it (see Chapter 6, Section C). But do this only if you have a sincere belief that the debtor isn't being honest.

4.   Reviewing Schedule C

In looking at the debtor's Schedule C, you'll want to verify that the exemptions being claimed are available to the debtor and are of the proper amount. First, you'll need to figure out which system of exemptions the debtor is using—either the federal exemptions or, if your state has adopted an alternate system, possibly your state's exemptions. In a few states, however, debtors may choose either the federal bankruptcy or state exemptions (but not both—they can't mix and match exemptions). These states are listed in the sidebar below, "States Allowing Debtors to Choose Federal Exemptions." Debtors in states offering a choice must declare on Schedule C which system of exemptions they are using to protect their property.

States Allowing Debtors to Choose Federal Exemptions

In addition to the exemptions provided under state law, the following states allow their citizens to use the exemptions provided in Section 522 of the Bankruptcy Code.

Arkansas	New Mexico
Connecticut	Pennsylvania
District of Columbia	Rhode Island
Hawaii	South Carolina
Massachusetts	Texas
Michigan	Vermont
Minnesota	Washington
New Jersey	Wisconsin

In every state not listed above, debtors cannot use the federal exemptions.

Next, you'll need to compare the debtor's exemptions against what the appropriate law says. For the federal exemptions, see 11 U.S.C. 522(d). For charts summarizing the federal and state exemptions, see *How to File for Chapter 7 Bankruptcy*, by Stephen Elias, Albin Renauer, Robin Leonard and Kathleen Michon (Nolo). For an explanation of exemptions being claimed under a "wildcard" rather than under a particular category, see the sidebar below, "Understanding the Wildcard Exemption."

If you believe the debtor has claimed an exemption to which he is not entitled, you may file a motion with the court objecting to that exemption. (See Chapter 10 for information on filing motions.)

If the debtor claims that the value of the exemption is "unknown," or claims that an asset of unknown value is totally exempt, you'll need to file an objection. Ask the court to value the asset and to determine whether the debtor can exempt its entire value. This issue arises most frequently where the asset is a pending lawsuit. Most applicable exemption statutes allow debtors to protect some, but not all, of the proceeds from a lawsuit. So, an attempt to exempt the entire, unknown value of the lawsuit would be invalid. A copy of such an objection is shown at the end of this chapter.

In a Chapter 7 bankruptcy, any property that a debtor claims as exempt will be considered exempt if no one challenges it. A successful challenge will make the exemption unavailable, so that the trustee can sell the property to pay creditors' claims. In a Chapter 11, note that only individual debtors can claim property as exempt. That means that you won't have to worry about exemptions in cases where the debtor is a corporation or partnership. But in cases involving a person, you should challenge any improperly claimed exemption, since the debtor can't keep nonexempt property without fully paying creditors' claims.

In a Chapter 12 or 13, any property that the debtor claims as exempt will remain exempt if no one raises a challenge—though exemption challenges are rare in reorganization cases, because property is generally not sold to pay creditors' claims. However, improper exemptions should be challenged for two reasons:

- The court will consider the nonexempt value of the debtor's property when deciding whether to confirm the plan. The more nonexempt property the debtor has, the more money the debtor will need to pay into the plan in order to receive the court's approval.
- If the debtor subsequently converts the case to a Chapter 7, you may not be able to challenge the exemption, because you had a chance to do so while the debtor was in Chapter 12 or 13.

Understanding the Wildcard Exemption

No one wants to lose a home—and for a bankrupt debtor, the home is usually the biggest asset and the one that seems most crucial for getting a fresh start. That's why the homestead exemption is, dollar-wise, the largest exemption available under the Bankruptcy Code and in most states' exemption schemes.

But not everyone owns a home—and the homestead exemption creates some potential inequity between debtors who own homes and those who don't. In an effort to address this, the federal exemption scheme and some states' schemes provide what's called a wildcard exemption. Debtors can use the wildcard to protect any asset. Under the federal Bankruptcy Code, the wildcard exemption equals one half the unused homestead exemption. In addition, a husband and wife can both claim it if they file jointly. Some states' schemes use the homestead exemption to fund the wildcard exemption, while other states create a separate wildcard exemption that's available to all debtors.

5. Reviewing Schedules D, E, and F

In Schedules D, E, and F, you have an opportunity to discover whether the debtor acted fraudulently when running up credit, perhaps not revealing to new creditors how deeply into debt he already was. If you manage to collect any evidence of fraud, you may use it to challenge the debtor's ability to discharge your claim. However, you can do this only if your claim was voluntarily incurred.

To ferret out fraud, look for claims as old as yours. Did you know that the debtor was borrowing money from these sources or incurring these debts? If you asked, the debtor should have disclosed this information to you.

Fraud also can be deduced by looking for a trend in the debtor's obligations. For example, debtors who have a number of credit card accounts that were opened in succession may have been shuffling their debts around, basically using the creditors' money to pay their bills. The schedules will tell you when accounts were first opened and what they were used for. If they don't—and many debtors conveniently forget to include this information even though it's required—you can ask about it at the creditors' meeting.

6. Reviewing Schedules G and H

Schedules G and H—which list pending contracts and codebtors—give you another opportunity to uncover assets that the debtor is hiding. Look for consistency between the information on these and the various other schedules. If the debtor says she is renting property, see if she schedules a rental agreement and a security deposit. (In Judge Rhodes' study, discussed in the sidebar, above, "There's Gold In Them Thar Documents," he found that nine out of ten debtors who were renters didn't list one or the other.)

If you discover any unscheduled assets, ask the debtor about them at the creditors' meeting or bring it up with the trustee. In a Chapter 7, the trustee can sell unscheduled assets to pay creditors' claims. In a Chapter 11, the debtor can only protect these assets from sale if the debtor's plan fully pays unsecured creditors. In a Chapter 12 or 13, the bankruptcy court will consider the value of the total assets in deciding whether to approve the debtor's proposed repayment plan. In addition, remember that debtors who fail to disclose all their assets may not be entitled to receive a bankruptcy discharge.

7. Reviewing Schedules I and J

Schedules I and J, which contain the debtor's income and expense statements, offer you a chance to discover instances of unreported income and unnecessary expenses.

Start by checking to see what deductions are being taken out of the debtor's paycheck. Question any deduction that's not for taxes or the debtor's own medical insurance. In fact, you can even challenge the tax deductions, if the debtor is claiming fewer exemptions than allowed so that he can get a larger refund. More particularly, make sure the debtor isn't contributing to his retirement fund when he can't afford to pay his debts.

Also make sure that the debtor's listed expenses are consistent with the other information provided in the schedules. For example, if the debtor claims an expense for property insurance, make sure the insurance can be matched to a piece of property on one of the other schedules.

Be on your guard for redundant expenses. For example, a debtor who takes a payroll deduction for health insurance should not also be listing health insurance as an expense on Schedule J. Such double dipping is usually an innocent mistake, but it creates a false impression as to how little money the debtor has at the end of the month to pay creditors.

And once again, expenses that get your goat because they seem excessive for a bankrupt individual (like boats, spa memberships, and cosmetologists) may interest the court as well. However, the courts do try to refrain from telling debtors what kind of lifestyle they must live after filing for bankruptcy, so there are certain expenses that you may question but that many courts will allow. For example, private school tuition may be allowed if the local public schools do not provide a safe and adequate learning environment.

Courts won't make children suffer unnecessarily because of the financial mistakes made by their parents. Nevertheless, you may be able to point to some expenses that are out of line for a debtor who should be living on a tight budget. Summer camp is frequently a target of budget-crunching courts, and not necessarily because it involves overseas travel or luxury accommodations. People in bankruptcy are expected to let their kids spend the summer with relatives or at home. Other suspect expenses might include club fees and private instruction other than tutoring.

If the debtor is self-employed or works for a relative, you should question the accuracy of the income the debtor disclosed. You won't be the only one to ask this question, since self-employed persons have more opportunities to hide income and inflate their expenses than the salaried ones. You may want to leave this inquiry to the trustee, who will probably require that the debtor bring copies of pay stubs and tax returns to the creditors' meeting.

In a Chapter 7 bankruptcy, finding unreported income can impact the case in two ways:

- If there is enough income to fund a reorganization plan, the U.S. Trustee may challenge the debtor's ability to receive a Chapter 7 discharge. How much is considered "enough" varies from court to court.

- Failure to fully and accurately disclose income can be a reason to deny the debtor's discharge or dismiss the case.

In a Chapter 11, 12, or 13, the debtor's unreported income should be added to what is used to fund the plan. And, as with any type of bankruptcy, don't forget that the debtor's failure to fully and accurately disclose income can be a reason for the court to deny the discharge or dismiss the case.

8. Reviewing the Statement of Financial Affairs

The Statement of Financial Affairs is packed with information for you to sift through. Let's look at the key questions on this form.

Questions 1 and 2: Underreported Income. You'll find the debtor's income information in Questions 1 and 2 of the statement. Compare this information with what the debtor reported on Schedule I. If the debtor has received more income over the course of the year than you'd expect to see based on the Schedule I, it's possible that the debtor underreported his income on the Schedule I. Ask him about it at the creditors' meeting.

Questions 3, 5, 6, and 10: Property Transfers. These questions deal with property transferred by the debtor before the bankruptcy filing. Transferred property includes money spent by the debtor to pay an existing debt, gifts made to friends or relatives, bonuses paid to executives, and liens created to secure payment of an existing debt. Look for unusual payments made or liens created within the 90 days leading up to the filing. For example, lump sum payments to creditors, gifts to relatives, bonus payments, and liens given to secure an existing debt are considered unusual. These should be questioned to determine whether were preferential or fraudulent transfers, in which case the court may avoid (undo) them.

Property transferred by the debtor before filing for bankruptcy might be recoverable by the trustee for the benefit of creditors. If the trustee avoids (cancels) these transfers because they were fraudulent or preferential, the trustee can bring the property or its value back into the bankruptcy estate, where all creditors can share in the bounty. (A fraudulent transfer is one in which the debtor gave the creditor something of value and didn't receive something of reasonably equal value in return—see Chapter 15 for further discussion.)

You may have both an offensive and a defensive interest in the debtor's disclosure of transfers made within 90 days prior to filing for bankruptcy, depending on whether the debtor unfairly made payments to other creditors while ignoring you—or vice versa.

If the debtor made payments to other creditors while not paying you, you want the trustee to recover that money so that you can get a piece of it. Note, however, that the trustee is unlikely to use his avoidance power if the debtor can turn around and claim the property as exempt, which wouldn't help any creditors. Also understand that the placement of liens on property is treated the same as if the property had been transferred to the creditor with the lien. The trustee can avoid a lien created within 90 days of the bankruptcy if it secures more than $600. Furthermore, if the lien was created for the benefit of a relative or business insider, the trustee can avoid it if it took place anytime within the year leading up to the bankruptcy petition.

If the debtor made payments to you at the expense of the other creditors, you're going to want to begin preparing your defense. (See Chapter 15 for instructions.)

Question 4: Litigation. Believe it or not, litigation by the debtor—particularly if he was the plaintiff suing for damages—may be an indicator of unscheduled assets.

Check the status of any litigation that was pending when the debtor filed for bankruptcy or that ended during the year preceding the bankruptcy. Any ongoing lawsuit in which the debtor is a plaintiff may be as significant an asset as the debtor's house and car (assuming the debtor is suing for monetary damages). In fact, once the debtor files for bankruptcy, the trustee becomes the person responsible for prosecuting the action and deciding whether to settle it.

If the litigation was settled prior to the bankruptcy filing, ask what the debtor did with the money. If it was used to pay bills, the trustee may be able to recover the payments as preferential transfers. (Hopefully these payments were made to other creditors, not to you!)

If your efforts turn up any unscheduled assets, the trustee in a Chapter 7 case can sell these to pay creditors' claims. In a Chapter 11, the debtor will be unable to keep the assets unless the debtor's plan fully pays unsecured creditors. In a Chapter 12 or 13, the bankruptcy court will consider the value of any unscheduled assets when deciding whether to approve the debtor's proposed repayment plan. And, as always, debtors who fail to disclose all their assets may not be entitled to a bankruptcy discharge.

Question 5: Repossessions and Returns. The information in Question 5 helps you determine whether the debtor made any preferential transfers. Check to see whether the debtor gave property to any creditor prior to filing for bankruptcy. If the creditor's claim was not secured by that property, the trustee may be able to recover the property or its value. If the creditor's claim was secured by the property, check to make sure the creditor gave the debtor full credit for the value of the collateral surrendered. If the creditor gave the debtor less than full credit, the creditor may assert an unsecured (and undeserved) claim or the creditor may have received more than it was entitled to, in which case the creditor should return the extra value to the bankruptcy estate.

EXAMPLE 1: Dunham Machinery owed Curly's Heavy Equipment $40,000. Dunham's bankruptcy paperwork shows that Dunham surrendered a forklift truck worth $10,000 to Curly's. In reviewing this transaction, other creditors should first ask whether Curly's had a lien against the forklift truck. If not, then the trustee may be able to avoid the transfer. If so, the creditors should see whether Curly's reduced his claim against Dunham by the full $10,000. Note

that creditors might not even have Dunham's help in making sure that Curly's made an accurate claim, because if the forklift truck was Curly's only collateral then Dunham couldn't care less how much credit it received—it intends to discharge the rest of Curly's claim. (If, however, Curly's holds liens against Dunham's other property, Dunham will care how much credit it received, because Curly's claim against Dunham's other property will be reduced accordingly.)

EXAMPLE 2: Darby owes Colorado Finance $10,000. Colorado Finance is secured by a lien against Darby's riding lawnmower, which is worth $1,500. Darby surrenders the lawnmower before filing for Chapter 7 relief. Assuming the lawnmower is the only collateral for the loan, Darby doesn't care how much credit he receives for surrendering the lawnmower, since he's going to discharge the balance of the debt. Other creditors care, however, because any money available to pay unsecured claims (the balance owed to Colorado Finance being unsecured) will be divided, based on the amount of the claims.

Even if Darby had filed under Chapter 13, unsecured creditors would need to make sure that Colorado Finance reduced its claim by $1,500. Money would be distributed to unsecured creditors pro rata, based on the amount of their claims. (In other words, a creditor owed $1,000 would receive twice as much as a creditor who was owed $500.)

Question 7: Gifts. In Question 7, you can look for indications of fraudulent transfers or undisclosed assets. Keep an eye out for gifts that appear less than complete. For example, if a debtor gives her daughter a car, but the debtor makes the payments and maintains the insurance, was the car really a gift? The debtor can't have it both ways. If the car belongs to the daughter, then the daughter should be taking care of it—so make sure the debtor's Schedule J doesn't include expenses related to the car. The more you reduce the expenses that a Chapter 7 debtor claims to have, the more money you free up that the debtor could use to fund a reorganization plan. If the debtor has filed under one of the reorganization chapters, then showing that the expenses are overstated means the debtor can afford to pay more into the plan.

Also look for gifts that are potentially fraudulent—that is, were actually attempts to hide assets in anticipation of bankruptcy. Perhaps the debtor gave a golf cart to his brother with the idea that when the bankruptcy was over, the cart would be returned. If the transfer is sus-

picious, this information could form the basis for asking the court to dismiss the case or deny the debtor's discharge because the debtor did not act in good faith.

Gifts that don't fit the debtor's pattern of giving also raise red flags. The law allows debtors to give up to 15% of their income to charity. However, don't feel bad about second-guessing a debtor who suddenly finds God or becomes a model of philanthropy on the eve of the bankruptcy. You can challenge the legitimacy of the charitable deductions from the standpoint of the debtor's giving intent. However, the law regarding charitable donations by debtors is relatively new, so it hasn't been fully litigated. It's hard to say what the court will do with your challenge. You might also demand proof that the transfers were actually made.

Question 8: Losses. Look for evidence of losses that may have been compensated by the debtor's insurance. This would amount to another sort of undisclosed asset.

Review the insurance information provided regarding each reported loss. You want to know what happened to the proceeds from that insurance. Ask for proof regarding any uninsured losses. If the property was destroyed by fire or stolen, there should be a police report. If there isn't, find out why. A debtor who says valuable property was stolen or destroyed, but who can offer no proof for that statement, may be telling the truth—or may not be. Your pursuit of the truth may not only lead to an undisclosed asset, but may also convince the court to dismiss the debtor's case or deny the entry of the discharge.

If the debtor blames gambling for causing his bankruptcy, or says that money was lost gambling, these losses should be revealed here. Ask the debtor where he got the money to fund his gambling and how long he'd been gambling. You want to find out whether the debtor was borrowing money from you in order to gamble. If he was playing with your money, then you may be able to convince the court to except the debt from discharge—especially if he planned to repay you only if he won.

Question 9: Debt Counseling Payments. The debtor must report all payments made to debt counseling professionals within the 12 months leading up to the bankruptcy filing. Check to see whether your claim or any portion of your claim was incurred after the debtor's first payment to a debt counselor or bankruptcy professional. When a debtor files for bankruptcy within months of talking to a debt counselor, the law presumes that any action taken between the conversation and the filing was taken in contemplation of the filing. Consequently, there is a presumption that the debtor never intended to repay the debt—and

the court may therefore except it from discharge.

Question 11: Closed Financial Accounts. Here, the debtor lists financial accounts that were closed or financial instruments that were sold within the 12 months preceding the bankruptcy filing. Compare the dates of closure or sale with the date your claim was created. Did the debtor give you the impression that he still had these assets when he didn't? If so, the court may be willing to except your claim from discharge.

Question 13: Property Held for Another. The debtor must list here any property that she claims to be holding for someone else. The question for you to ask is whether the debtor's use of the property created the impression that the property belonged to the debtor. If it did, find out if the debtor ever owned the property and how long she used it without owning it. Also find out the terms of the debtor's arrangement with the property owner. Maybe the debtor acquired title to the property through its use or the rightful owner's neglect.

> **EXAMPLE:** The wooded area behind Denise's house looks like it belongs to her. She planted flowers there, and built a gazebo in the clearing. Denise borrowed the money to build the gazebo from Carl. At the time of filing for bankruptcy, she still owes Carl $500. Looking at Denise's bankruptcy

papers, Carl notices that Denise claims that she owns only the small strip of land on which her home, a double-wide trailer, sits. So, he wonders, what land is the gazebo sitting on? When Carl questions Denise about this at the Section 341 meeting, she says the wooded lot belongs to her sister. The trustee, alerted by Carl's questions, checks the land title records and discovers that Denise transferred the land to her sister for $1, five months prior to filing for bankruptcy. Based on this discovery, the trustee is able to avoid the land transfer as fraudulent. Moreover, the trustee convinces the court to deny Denise's discharge, based on her dishonesty in preparing her bankruptcy schedules.

Regardless of whether you knew about property that the debtor was holding for someone else, if it's valuable property, find out whether the debtor ever owned it, how long he's been using it without owning it and the terms governing its use. Your first two inquiries may help you prove that your claim should not be discharged. The final inquiry may help the trustee bring the asset into the estate, where it can be sold to pay your claim.

Question 15: Prior Addresses. The debtor must list her addresses for the past two years—a benign-sounding question that's ripe with opportunities for checking the consistency of her various answers. For starters, compare the addresses from the previous two years against the debtor's disclosures regarding legal actions and living expenses. If the debtor said she lost a home to foreclosure, there should be at least two addresses listed.

Conversely, if the debtor listed more than one address here, see if there's an explanation as to why she moved. If the debtor owned the first property, was it sold? If the debtor rented the first property, why was the lease ended? Find out how the debtor's current living arrangement compares with her previous situation. If it's more expensive, is the added living expense justified?

This inquiry is going to take you along two parallel paths. Inaccuracies and inconsistencies may pile up, showing that the debtor should be denied a discharge because she isn't being honest with the court. At the same time, to the extent that the errors show that the debtor has a higher income and/or lower expenses than reported on the schedules, you can show the court that a Chapter 7 debtor should not be allowed a discharge or that a Chapter 12 or 13 debtor should pay more money into the reorganization plan.

Question 17: Environmental Claims.
The debtor must list any real estate he owns that is subject to pollution claims. If you hold a claim secured by property that the debtor says is subject to an environmental claim, speak with an attorney. If the bankruptcy estate can't afford the clean-up cost, the government may look to you for payment. You'll want to make sure your loss doesn't exceed what you are owed on your claim. Liability for environmental claims is beyond the scope of this book.

Questions 18 through 25: Business Information. In Questions 18 through 25, the debtor must provide information about businesses in which she has been involved. This is another area where you may spot inconsistencies revealing undisclosed assets or bad faith by the debtor.

First, compare the information regarding the debtor's involvement in business enterprises with the descriptions of transfers in Questions 3 through 6 and 10. If the debtor has an interest in a business that appears to be a creditor, maybe that business is really just the debtor in disguise (the debtor's alter ego). If the other business is really the debtor in disguise, then money paid by the debtor to the other business, or assets transferred by the debtor to the other business, are still in the debtor's possession.

Or, perhaps the business is in a position to control, or at least influence, the debtor's decisions, meaning that transfers within

one year of the bankruptcy filing can be avoided. It is not unusual for an entrepreneur to have multiple ventures going at the same time. If one begins to falter, there is a temptation to transfer assets from the failing company to one of the viable companies. The transferred assets may be office furniture. They may be accounts receivable. Whatever they are, if they belonged to the bankrupt company, then they belong in the bankruptcy estate where they can be sold to pay creditors' claims. Look for clues, such as the debtor having a business but supposedly owning no office furniture and disclosing no lease of office furniture. You should ask what's up—and if things look fishy, the trustee may even decide that a site visit is in order.

Also compare the information regarding the debtor's business enterprises with the list of creditors in Schedules C, D, and E. The debtor may be creating the impression that there is greater creditor involvement than there really is. For example, if a creditor shown holding a secured claim is in truth just the debtor operating under another name, then the trustee may be able to avoid that creditor's lien as a fraudulent transfer. (A fraudulent transfer is one in which the debtor gave the creditor something of value and didn't receive something of reasonably equal value in return—see Chapter 15.)

If you received a financial statement from the debtor prior to bankruptcy, make sure that the person who prepared the financial information is listed as a bookkeeper or accountant. If not, question the veracity of the information provided to you on that statement. Find out why the financial disclosures made to you came from an undisclosed source. It could be that the debtor was trying to deceive you, in which case your claim may be excepted from discharge.

Check the list of partners, officers, directors, and shareholders for conflicts of interest and opportunities to exercise undue influence. Does a creditor hold a position of influence with the debtor? Was a member of the partnership or a member of the corporate board in a similar position with one of the debtor's creditors? Did one of your competitors hold a position of influence with the debtor? If so, question whether the creditor received preferential treatment from the debtor. Trustees can avoid preferential transfers as well as those that are fraudulent. (Again, Chapter 15 is the place to learn about the trustee's ability to avoid prepetition transfers.)

See if key executives left in the months preceding the bankruptcy. If they did, ask the debtor why. Find out what compensation was paid to them and when, and whether the debtor has any ongoing obligation to these departed chiefs. In fact, if

you're not satisfied with the debtor's answers, you can ask the court to subpoena the ex-executives to a Rule 2004 examination—unless they'll talk to you without a subpoena. Disgruntled ex-employees are a good source of information about what was going on inside the business in the days leading up to bankruptcy, and there's nothing to stop you from contacting them. This information could provide you with cause to challenge the discharge of your claim or the debtor's eligibility to receive a discharge.

Look for unusual withdrawals from partnership accounts or payments from corporate accounts. Did someone get paid outside the normal course of business? If so, for what? Was money withdrawn by partners in excess of their equity position? Did the withdrawal of funds render the partnership insolvent? If so, who benefited from the withdrawal and who was injured? All of these transfers may be recovered by the trustee if they were preferential or fraudulent.

9. Final Review

After you've gone over the bankruptcy statements and schedules and looked for the information suggested above, we recommend taking one last look over them. Your objective this time will be to compare the information in the documents with your real-world knowledge of the debtor. Let's look at the two possibilities, including whether you:

- voluntarily provided credit to the debtor (Subsection a), or
- hadn't intended to provide credit, but the debtor did something that gave rise to your claim (Subsection b).

a. If You Voluntarily Provided Credit

If you voluntarily entered into a debtor-creditor relationship with the debtor, (as opposed to merely providing goods or services with the expectation of getting paid immediately), you should have gathered some information about the debtor before extending the credit. Perhaps you got the information in a loan application, or perhaps it just came from your personal knowledge of the debtor. In either case, you can compare what you knew about the debtor at that time with what's now disclosed on the schedules. Discrepancies between what was said then and what is said now may determine whether your claim is paid.

If the debtor misrepresented himself when the credit was granted, you can challenge the debtor's ability to discharge your debt. If the debtor is now misrepresenting himself in the bankruptcy schedules, then you or the trustee can challenge the debtor's right to receive a discharge.

Here's what to look for in particular:

- Were assets listed on your loan application that aren't listed in the bankruptcy?
- Are debts listed in the bankruptcy that weren't mentioned in the loan application?
- Is the debtor's income lower than you were given the impression it was?
- Has the debtor's employment changed between when the debt was incurred and when the bankruptcy was filed? If so, what happened?
- Would you have given a loan to this person on the basis of the financial information being disclosed in the bankruptcy?
- Does the person described in the bankruptcy schedules and statements sound like the debtor you know?

The more recently you lent money to the debtor and the more detailed the financial disclosure you got before making the loan, the more likely it is that any inconsistencies will help you prove that the debtor lied to you when obtaining credit. That's one of the bases for having your claim excepted from discharge that we'll talk about in Chapter 9.

b. If You're an Involuntary Creditor

You may never have intended to become a creditor. Perhaps the debtor owes you money because of something he did (like hitting you with his car) or didn't do (like clearing the ice off his sidewalk). Perhaps the debtor was your employer, your former spouse, or your attorney.

There are plenty of ways that someone can end up owing you money without your consent or even your involvement. If the person who owes you money then files for bankruptcy, you are at a disadvantage. You didn't choose to be a creditor. You probably didn't find out much about the debtor before entering into your newfound creditor-debtor relationship. The bankruptcy law makes some attempt to protect you, however. You'll notice in Chapter 9 of this book that most of the obligations that debtors can't discharge (called discharge exceptions) are owed to involuntary creditors. Really, the only discharge exceptions that protect voluntary creditors are those based on fraud or that arose out of a domestic relationship.

You may have also noticed that the only discharge exception mentioned in this discussion of how to review the debtor's schedules and statements involves fraud by the debtor—yet the debtor couldn't have defrauded you, since you never actively agreed to become a creditor in the first place. Nevertheless, and despite your lack of knowledge about the debtor, you should review the schedules to look for reasons to challenge the debtor's right to receive a discharge or to uncover hidden assets. Compare whatever you know about the debtor with what's disclosed on the debtor's schedules and statements. You never know what you might uncover. You might even find evidence of fraud against all creditors, such as a failure to schedule all the debtor's assets.

How Would the Debtor Answer These Questions?

The following is a list of questions from which trustees routinely draw when examining debtors at the creditors' meeting. Although the trustee will normally choose only a few of these questions, the list itself is a valuable tool when you're reviewing the debtor's schedules and statements. If, after reviewing the debtor's bankruptcy paperwork, you remain unsure of the debtor's likely answer to any of these questions, you might want to ask about the issue during the meeting of creditors.

But remember, the trustee knows these questions and decided not to ask them. Make sure you have a reason to question the truthfulness of the information in the debtor's schedules before you start asking questions. For example, if the debtor said she doesn't own real estate and you have no reason to doubt that statement, don't ask questions regarding the debtor's real estate holdings. However, if you were led to believe that the debtor owned a home, but she didn't list it, then by all means speak up.

Here are the standard trustees' questions:

1. Do you own or have any interest whatsoever in any real estate?
   If owned: When did you purchase the property? How much did the property cost? What are the mortgages encumbering it? What do you estimate the present value of the property to be? Is that the whole value or your share? How did you arrive at that value?
   If renting: Have you ever owned the property in which you live and/or is its owner in any way related to you?

2. Have you made any transfers of any property or given any property away within the last one-year period (or such longer period as applicable under state law)?
   If yes: What did you transfer? To whom was it transferred? What did you receive in exchange? What did you do with the funds?

3. Does anyone hold property belonging to you?
   If yes: Who holds the property and what is it? What is its value?

4. Do you have a claim against anyone or any business?
   f there are large medical debts, are the medical bills from injury?
   Are you the plaintiff in any lawsuit?
   What is the status of each case and who is representing you?

How Would the Debtor Answer These Questions? (continued)

5. Are you entitled to life insurance proceeds or an inheritance as a result of someone's death?
   If yes: Please explain the details.

6. Does anyone owe you money? If yes: Is the money collectible? Why haven't you collected it? Who owes the money and where are they?

7. Have you made any large payments, over $600, to anyone in the past year?

8. Were federal income tax returns filed on a timely basis? When was the last return filed? Do you have copies of the federal income tax returns? At the time of the filing of your petition, were you entitled to a tax refund from the federal or state government?
   If yes: Inquire as to amounts.

9. Do you have a bank account, either checking or savings?
   If yes: In what banks and what were the balances as of the date you filed your petition?

10. When you filed your petition, did you have:
    a. any cash on hand?
    b. any U.S. Savings Bonds?
    c. any other stocks or bonds?
    d. any Certificates of Deposit?
    e. a safe deposit box in your name or in anyone else's name?

11. Do you own an automobile?
    If yes: What is the year, make, and value? Do you owe any money on it? Is it insured?

12. Are you the owner of any cash value life insurance policies?
    If yes: State the name of the company, face amount of the policy, cash surrender value, if any, and the beneficiaries.

13. Do you have any winning lottery tickets?

14. Do you anticipate that you might realize any property, cash or otherwise, as a result of a divorce or separation proceeding?

15. Regarding any consumer debts secured by your property, have you filed the required Statement of Intention with respect to the exemption, retention, or surrender of that secured property? Please provide a copy of the statement to the trustee. Have you performed that intention?

16. Have you been engaged in any business during the last six years?
    If yes: Where and when? What happened to the assets of the business? In cases where debtors are engaged in business, the following questions should be considered:
    a. Who was responsible for maintaining financial records?

How Would the Debtor Answer These Questions?, continued

b. Which of the following records were maintained?

1. Cash receipts journal

2. Cash disbursements journal

3. General journal

4. Accounts receivable ledger

5. Accounts payable ledger

6. Payroll ledger

7. Fixed asset ledger

8. Inventory ledger

9. General ledger

10. Balance sheet, income statement, and cash flow statements

c. Where are each of the foregoing records now located?

d. Who was responsible for preparing financial statements?

e. How often were financial statements prepared?

f. For what periods are financial statements available?

g. Where are such financial statements now located?

h. Was the business on a calendar year or a fiscal year?

i. Were federal income tax returns filed on a timely basis? When was the last return filed?

j. Do you have copies of the federal income tax returns? Who does have the copies?

k. What outside accountants were employed within the last three years?

l. Do you have copies of the reports of such accountants? Who does have copies?

m. What bank accounts were maintained within the last three years?

n. Where are the bank statements and cancelled checks now located?

o. What insurance policies were in effect within the last year? What kind, and why?

p. From whom can copies of such insurance policies be obtained?

q. If the business is incorporated, where are the corporate minutes?

r. Is the debtor owed any outstanding accounts receivable? From whom? Are they collectible?

s. Is there any inventory, property, or equipment remaining?

D. Using the Information You Find

As we've indicated in the sections above, your usual course of action upon finding an error or inconsistency in the debtor's paperwork is to question the debtor about it at the creditors' meeting (discussed in Chapter 6) and possibly bring up the matter with the trustee. Now let's dive a little deeper into what might happen next, in situations including:

- when income or assets are uncovered in a Chapter 7 case (Subsection 1)
- when income or assets are uncovered in a reorganization case (Subsection 2), and
- when the debtor's bad faith is established (Subsection 3).

1. Uncovered Income or Assets in a Chapter 7 Case

If your investigations turn up evidence that a Chapter 7 consumer debtor has more income or fewer expenses than were disclosed, the trustee may challenge the debtor's right to a Chapter 7 discharge. Only the trustee can bring this motion, but your findings can spur the trustee into action. The court will need to be convinced that the debtor would be substantially abusing the Bankruptcy Code by receiving a discharge. (11 U.S.C. § 707(b).) To determine "substantial abuse," the court will look for evidence that the debtor is attempting to obtain a Chapter 7

discharge even though he has the ability to repay some or all debts through a Chapter 13 reorganization. (Since this substantial abuse inquiry applies only to consumer debtors, Chapter 13 is the applicable reorganization chapter.)

If the court is convinced, it will either dismiss the debtor's bankruptcy or allow the debtor to convert to Chapter 13. Either alternative is better for you than having the debtor remain in Chapter 7 (unless your claim would be excepted from discharge based on the debtor's fraud—see Chapter 9, Section A). If the debtor converts to Chapter 13, your claim may be paid through the plan. If the case is dismissed, you're back to where you were before the debtor filed for bankruptcy.

If your investigations uncover assets that the debtor didn't disclose, or you are able to defeat a debtor's attempt to exempt certain assets, these assets may be sold by the trustee. The trustee may, however, choose not to sell the assets if he feels that the sale will not generate any money for the creditors. Assuming there is a sale, the proceeds, minus the trustee's commission and costs of the sale, will go to pay creditors' claims. The trustee may sell the assets by auction or by private sale, whichever generates the highest return for the estate. You will receive notice of any proposed sale of assets. If the case was previously listed as a no-asset case, you will also be told to file a proof of claim. The court must approve any final sale of the assets.

If none of the above remedies work, you may ask the court to dismiss the case based on the debtor's lack of good faith (see Subsection 3, below).

2. Uncovered Income or Assets in a Reorganization Case

If you are able to show that a debtor seeking reorganization has more income or fewer expenses than were disclosed, then the reorganization plan will have to account for this additional money. This will usually mean a greater distribution to creditors.

If you uncover hidden assets in a reorganization case, or you successfully challenge the debtor's claim to certain exemptions, then the value of these assets must be accounted for in the reorganization plan. For example, if you discover that a Chapter 12 or 13 debtor has real estate she didn't disclose, then her reorganization plan must include the value of her nonexempt equity in that real estate. That way, unsecured creditors will be assured of receiving at least as much through the debtor's plan as they would have in Chapter 7. If the debtor filed under Chapter 11, the debtor can't keep nonexempt property unless unsecured creditors are fully paid.

3. Bad Faith by the Debtor

When debtors don't fully disclose their financial information and prebankruptcy transactions, you have the right to question them about the missing information. When they fail to supply adequate explanations for their reporting errors and don't promptly correct those mistakes—or when they have clearly tried to hide their income or assets—you have a right to ask the bankruptcy court to deny them the benefits of a bankruptcy discharge. (11 U.S.C § 707(a).) The debtor's ability to receive a discharge is conditioned on being open and honest with the court, the trustee, and the creditors. If the debtor has hidden income or assets, that condition has not been met. (See Chapter 12 for more on challenging the debtor's right to a discharge.)

> **EXAMPLE 1:** A former member of Congress filed for bankruptcy. Two weeks after the filing, she submitted financial disclosure statements to the U.S. Senate showing that she owned securities and receivables worth $1.3 million. These assets had not been disclosed in her bankruptcy. She blamed her husband for the oversight. The court blamed her, and denied the discharge.

> **EXAMPLE 2:** A former securities dealer tried to hide more than $500,000 from his creditors when he filed for bankruptcy. It didn't work. He was sentenced to nine years and two months in federal prison. Eight of those years were for committing bankruptcy fraud. The remaining 14 months were added to his sentence for obstructing justice by presenting fake evidence during his trial.

Sample Objection to Debtor's Exemption Claim

IN THE UNITED STATES BANKRUPTCY COURT

FOR THE EASTERN DISTRICT OF PENNSYLVANIA

In re:

Harry Debtor

CASE NO.: 03-24561 JW

NOTICE OF OBJECTION TO CLAIM OF EXEMPTION AND HEARING DATE

Gary's Cleaners has filed an objection to your claim of exemption in this bankruptcy case.

Your claim of exemption may be eliminated or changed by the court because an objection has been filed. You should read these papers carefully and discuss them with your attorney, if you have one in this bankruptcy case. (If you do not have an attorney, you may wish to consult an attorney.)

If you do not want the court to eliminate or change your claim of exemption, or if you want the court to consider your views, you or your lawyer must attend the hearing on the objection, scheduled to be held before the Honorable Jeremy Wright on Dec. 12, 2003 at 9:30 a.m. in Courtroom 2, United States Bankruptcy Court, Robert N.C. Nix Sr. Federal Courthouse, 900 Market Street, Philadelphia, PA 19107

Date: Nov. 1, 2003

Larry Best

Larry Best, Esq.

Attorney for Gary's Cleaners

1212 Walnut Street

Philadelphia, PA 19107

215-567-4321

Sample Objection to Debtor's Exemption Claim

1	**IN THE UNITED STATES BANKRUPTCY COURT**
2	**FOR THE EASTERN DISTRICT OF PENNSYLVANIA**

3

4   )   **CASE NO.:** 03-24561 JW
)
5 **In re:**   )   **OBJECTION TO EXEMPTION OF**
)   **HOUSEHOLD GOODS**
6 Harry Debtor   )
)
7   )
)
8   )
)
9 _____)

10   Gary's Cleaners, by and through its attorney, Larry Best, respectfully moves the court to

11 deny Debtor's exemption to certain household goods because they exceed the available ex-

12 emption provided under 11 U.S.C. Section 522(d)(3). In support, Movant states as follows:

13   1. The Debtor, Harry Debtor, filed for bankruptcy under Chapter 7 of the U.S. Bank-

14 ruptcy Code on Jan. 2, 2003.

15   2. Movant is an unsecured creditor in this case.

16   3. Debtor is indebted to Movant in the amount of $300 for services provided to Debtor

17 as evidenced in the Proof of Claim filed by Movant.

18   4. Debtor owns a Sony 51-inch television set and a Hitachi surround-sound stereo sys-

19 tem. The debtor valued the television at $400 and the stereo system at $100. He claimed

20 both items as fully exempt under Section 522(d).

21   5. Movant understands that the television set and stereo system were purchased within

22 the past two years.

23   6. Television sets of age and quality similar to that owned by Debtor sell in excess of $1,000.

24   7. Stereo systems of age and quality similar to that owned by Debtor sell in excess of $700.

25   8. Section 522(d) allows debtors to exempt household goods up to $450 in value.

26   9. Because the television and stereo system claimed by Debtor as exempt exceed $450

27 in value, Debtor cannot claim these items as fully exempt.

28

Sample Objection to Debtor's Exemption Claim, continued

1	WHEREFORE, Movant requests this court to deny Debtor's exemption in the 51-inch
2	television and stereo system.
3	
4	
5	Date: Nov. 1, 2003
6	
7	
8	
9	
10	

Date: Nov. 1, 2003

Larry Best

Larry Best, Esq.

Attorney for Gary's Cleaners

1212 Walnut Street

Philadelphia, PA 19107

215-567-4321

Sample Objection to Debtor's Exemption Claim, continued

CERTIFICATE OF SERVICE

I hereby certify that on this 1st day of November 2003, I caused a true and correct copy of the foregoing objection to household goods exemption to be deposited in the U.S. mail with postage fully prepaid, to Harry Debtor, 220 W. Country Lane, Philadephia, PA 19111 and to Phyllis Trustee, 110 Main Street, Philadelphia, PA 19109.

Larry Best
_____

Larry Best

Attorney for Gary's Cleaners

1212 Walnut Street

Philadelphia, PA 19107

215-567-4321

The Meeting of Creditors and Other Communication With the Debtor

Although the debtor's bankruptcy will be handled by a court, you and the debtor will have a lot of communicating to do before any of you sets foot in the courtroom. Fortunately, not even the automatic stay prevents all communication with the debtor. In fact, certain contact either can't be avoided or has been worked into the legal process. In this chapter, we'll discuss:

- what you're allowed to discuss with the debtor in person or through an attorney (Section A)
- what questions you can raise at the meeting of creditors (Section B), and
- how to get a separate meeting with the debtor (Section C).

A. Permissible Contact Outside the First Creditors' Meeting

After the bankruptcy has been filed, but at any time or place other than in the room where the first creditors' meeting is being held, your communication with the debtor should be of the "name, rank, and serial number" variety. You are allowed to ask questions that basically confirm the bankruptcy and gather more information about it and your collateral. You must be careful that your conversations don't stray into any areas protected by the automatic stay—namely, anything that resembles an attempt to collect on your claim—or you will be in violation. You can't call or write the debtor to try to get paid, nor can someone working for you, like a collection agency.

1. Confirming that Bankruptcy Was Filed

If you haven't received a notice of filing from the bankruptcy court, but have heard via the grapevine that the debtor has filed for bankruptcy, it is perfectly acceptable to call the debtor and ask about it.

If the debtor confirms that a bankruptcy was filed, you may ask for particulars, such as the name of the court it was filed in and the docket number. As discussed in Chapter 3, you need to know this information in order to verify the bankruptcy filing. Therefore, asking these questions is not just something you may do—it's something you absolutely should do to protect your claim.

2. Getting the Attorney's Name

If you haven't yet received the notice from the bankruptcy court, you are also within your rights to ask whether the debtor is represented by legal counsel. If so, ask for the attorney's name and telephone number. After that point, it is safest for you to direct all your further communications to the attorney. For one thing, you're not going to violate the automatic stay by something you say to the attorney, but you may accidentally do so if you talk to the debtor. Also, it is accepted protocol that once a person with whom you're involved in litigation has hired an attorney, you stop communicating directly with that person.

3. Secured Creditors May Ask About the Collateral

If you provided credit to the debtor that was secured by collateral, you're probably curious about what the debtor plans to do with that collateral. How you approach this issue depends on what bankruptcy chapter the debtor filed under, as described below.

a. If the Debtor Filed Under Chapter 7

If the debtor is an individual who filed under Chapter 7, and your claim is secured, and your loan was for the debtor's household or served a household purpose, you may ask the debtor what she plans to do with your collateral. You can ask about this at any time, before or after receiving the bankruptcy notice. The law requires debtors to state in their bankruptcy papers whether they plan to keep or surrender collateral that secures consumer loans. (This law doesn't apply to business loans.)

During this initial contact with the debtor, it's okay to ask about the debtor's intentions. Don't press for an answer, however, or you could be accused of ha-

rassment. The law requires the debtor to send you a statement of her intentions within 45 days of filing for bankruptcy. Mark this date on your calendar. If you haven't received the information by then, you can ask the court to force the debtor to state her intentions. Alternately, you can ask for relief from the automatic stay in order to go after the collateral.

If the debtor plans to keep the collateral by paying you what it is worth, then you'll have to settle on a price. If the debtor plans to keep it by entering into a new obligation with you to replace the discharged claim, then you'll need to work out the terms of this so-called "reaffirmation agreement." If the debtor plans to let you take back the collateral, then you'll need to agree on a time and place for the property's surrender.

b. If the Debtor Filed Under Chapter 11, 12, or 13

Debtors who file under one of the reorganization chapters are not required to file a notice telling you what they plan to do with your collateral. You do have a right to ask, however—and you should exercise this right. If the debtor won't tell you, and is in default on his contractual obligations, ask the court for relief from the automatic stay. You don't want to play games with a debtor who is acting wishy-washy over whether he will keep or surrender the collateral. Here's why:

- If the debtor plans to surrender the property, then the sooner you get it, the more valuable it will be. Apart from red wine and coin collections, very few assets appreciate in value as time goes by. To maximize your recovery, get your hands on the collateral as quickly as possible.

- If the debtor plans to keep your collateral, then the debtor must cure— through the reorganization plan—any contractual defaults such as failure to maintain payments or insurance. You are also entitled to protection against any depreciation in the collateral's value. (See Chapter 4 for a discussion of adequate protection payments.)

4. Asking Chapter 7 Debtors About Reaffirmation of the Debt

If you hold a secured claim in a Chapter 7 case, you may contact the debtor or the debtor's attorney to work out a reaffirmation agreement. You're on especially solid ground if the debtor stated an intention to reaffirm the debt. Still, there's no harm in asking about reaffirmation even if the debtor expressed a contrary intention. The key is to ask but not to push.

Again, a written contact is preferred, especially given that your proposed reaffirmation agreement—which you may want to include with your letter—will need to be in writing. If the debtor is willing to negotiate directly with you, go ahead and hash out the agreement's modifications and details. (See Chapter 8 regarding how to work out a reaffirmation agreement.)

If you hold an unsecured claim, getting a debtor to reaffirm an unsecured debt is a tricky proposition. It involves proving why the reaffirmation would benefit the debtor. Trying to get the debtor to pay through reaffirmation a claim that the debtor can walk away from comes perilously close to violating the automatic stay, especially if the contact is directly with the debtor. Don't attempt it without the help of an attorney. Also, don't contact the debtor directly, but contact the debtor's attorney instead. When the contact is made through an attorney, it is sufficiently filtered that the stay won't be violated.

Summary of When You May Contact the Debtor Directly

By way of review, it's okay to contact the debtor under the circumstances listed below, but any other contact may be a violation of the automatic stay:

- to confirm the bankruptcy filing

- to learn the name of the debtor's attorney

- to ask about the debtor's intentions regarding your collateral, or

- to ask whether the debtor wants to enter into a reaffirmation agreement regarding your claim.

B. The Meeting of Creditors

The Bankruptcy Code requires all debtors to submit to a public examination by their creditors. (11 U.S.C. § 341(a).) This is known as the "meeting of creditors." The notice of the debtor's bankruptcy filing will tell you the time and place for the meeting. In some courts, it's held soon after the debtor files for bankruptcy, so you may get very little advance notice.

In this section, we'll cover:

- why it's worth attending the meeting (Subsection 1)
- what to expect at the meeting (Subsection 2), and
- questions to ask at the meeting (Subsection 3).

1. Reasons to Attend the Meeting of Creditors

Despite the fact that the debtor is compelled to attend and answer creditors' questions under oath, most creditors don't attend. However, attending the meeting of creditors is often a good idea.

a. Reasons to Attend in a Chapter 7 Case

Attending the meeting of creditors in a Chapter 7 case is a good idea if:

- you have questions about the information in the debtor's schedules and statements—particularly if you suspect that the debtor hid an asset, underreported income or overreported expenses
- you have reason to believe that the debtor was less than honest in his dealings with you. The meeting will give you an opportunity to see whether the trustee also has such concerns and how the debtor responds to those concerns.
- you'd like to ask the debtor about the events leading to the bankruptcy filing—while the debtor is under oath. If you have more than a few questions, the trustee may reschedule the hearing or require you to schedule a private examination of the debtor pursuant to Rule 2004 of the Federal Rules of Bankruptcy Procedure.
- you have a question about the debtor's stated intention regarding your collateral
- you don't know the debtor and want an opportunity for a face-to-face meeting, or
- you want to witness the trustee's examination of the debtor and publicly show the trustee that you are interested in the proceedings.

b. Reasons to Attend in a Reorganization Case

In a reorganization case, it's particularly useful to attend the meeting of creditors in order to show that the debtor under-stated his income or exaggerated his ex-penses. The emphasis in reorganization cases is on the debtor's ability to fund a plan out of future income, whether it be a Chapter 11 corporation's revenue stream, a Chapter 12 farmer's income from crop sales, or a Chapter 13 individual's salary. The higher the income or the lower the expenses, the more money is available to fund the plan.

2. Meeting Procedures

How the meeting of creditors will be con-ducted has a lot to do with the role the trustee plays, as detailed below. In Chap-ter 7 cases, the trustee is usually a mem-ber of a panel of trustees who are as-signed batches of cases on a rotating ba-sis. In Chapters 12 and 13 cases, you'll have a standing trustee, a person to whom all cases filed under that chapter in a given geographic area are assigned. In Chapter 11 cases, you'll have the U.S. Trustee, who works for the U.S. Depart-ment of Justice.

The Trustee's Handy Dandy Handbook

In order to guide bankruptcy trustees through their course of duties, the U.S. Trustee's office has written handbooks for each type of bankruptcy. The trust-ees use these handbooks as working manuals, consulting them to find out the policy for handling particular is-sues, and how to administer assets, conduct meetings, and more.

These handbooks can be excel-lent resources for you, too. If you're wondering how the trustee is ex-pected to handle a particular situa-tion that arises during the course of the bankruptcy, you may find the answer in the manual.

For a copy of the relevant hand-book, go to the U.S. Trustee's website at www.usdoj.gov/ust. Click the link for "private trustees listing and library."

---

a. Meeting Location and Scheduling

Trustees hold the meeting of creditors in a variety of places. Any room that can ac-commodate 50 people can host a meeting of creditors. Most meetings are held in an auxiliary court room or meeting room. If the court handles cases from a large geo-graphic area, the meeting of creditors

may be held at a satellite location somewhere within the district. In especially
large districts, the meeting may be conducted by videoconference.

In all cases except large Chapter 11s,
multiple meetings will be scheduled for
the same time slot. It's common to see a
trustee schedule as many as ten meetings
for a 30-minute slot. Impracticable though
this scheduling sounds, most meetings
take only a few minutes, and few creditors show up. If a creditor shows up or
there's another variation from the routine,
the trustee will pass over the case and
hear it after the routine cases on the list. If
the meeting looks like it will take an hour
or so to conclude, the trustee will reschedule it to another day. If your case is
at the top of the list and things are moving quickly, it might be heard on time.
But, if things are moving slowly or you're
at the bottom of the list, be prepared to sit
for an hour or two. The good news is that
all the meetings are open to the public, so
you can listen in on other cases before
the trustee gets to yours. That allows you
to get a feel for how the system works.

b. Routine Tasks of the Trustee

The trustee will call your case, and invite
any creditors present in the meeting room
to come forward. The trustee will be tape
recording the meeting, so everyone in attendance must state his or her name for
the record. Everyone must also sign a
form stating that they attended the meeting. Nowadays, the trustee may also ask
for proof of identification. Next, the
trustee will swear in the debtor. The
trustee will have the first opportunity to
question the debtor, after which you'll get
your chance.

The trustee will go through a routine
dictated in part by the U.S. Trustee. He'll
ask the debtor for proof of identification
and to produce any documents that he
requested in advance. Such documents
usually include tax returns and pay stubs.
Then he'll confirm that the debtor understood that she wasn't required to file for
bankruptcy and knew that she could have
filed under a different chapter of the
Bankruptcy Code.

In the course of the trustee's questions, the following information must be
solicited from every debtor:

- the debtor's name and current address
- whether the debtor read the Bankruptcy Information Sheet provided by
  the U.S. Trustee (made available at
  the meeting)
- whether the debtor personally signed
  the petition, schedules, statements,
  and related documents that were filed
  with the court
- whether the debtor read the petition,
  schedules, statements, and related
  documents before signing them

- whether the debtor was personally familiar with the information contained in the petition, schedules, statements and related documents
- whether the information in the petition, schedules, statements, and related documents is true and correct
- whether the debtor knows of any errors or omissions in the petition, schedules, and related documents
- whether all of the debtor's assets are identified on the schedules
- whether the debtor listed all of his or her creditors on the schedules, and
- whether the debtor has filed for bankruptcy before. If so, the trustee must obtain the case number and the discharge information to determine the debtor's discharge eligibility.

c. Nonroutine Questions by the Trustee

With the generic questions out of the way, the trustee will turn to asking questions specific to the debtor's case. Like you, the trustee has examined the debtor's schedules and statements. He should ask the debtor about any inconsistencies found there. Unlike you, the trustee doesn't know anything about the debtor except what's on the schedules and statements.

Listen closely to the trustee's questions, and take notes. For one thing, you don't want to embarrass yourself and waste time by asking the same questions. For another thing, the nature of the trustee's questions will tip you off to whether he believes there is something amiss with the debtor's paperwork. For example, if the trustee asks a lot of questions regarding the debtor's income and expenses, he may be considering challenging the debtor's right to receive a discharge. Also take accurate note of the debtor's answers.

When your turn comes, start by asking the debtor your most important question (assuming it wasn't covered by the trustee). You never know how much time the trustee will allow you, so planning a slow and dramatic build-up to your main point could lead to nothing but frustration.

d. Special Questions for Reorganization Cases

Up to this point, our discussion of creditors meetings applies (more or less) regardless of which chapter the debtor chose to file under. However, the trustee will need to adjust the usual script a bit in a reorganization case, since the main focus is on the future—namely on the debtor's plan for reorganizing and repaying creditors. You'll find trustees in reorganization cases don't ask many questions that aren't relevant to whether the debtor can fund a plan. The trustee will, however, spend a great deal of time on questions concerning the debtor's income and expenses.

3. Your Turn at Questioning the Debtor

Once the trustee has finished questioning the debtor, it's the creditors' turn. The trustee will determine the order in which the creditors proceed. The trustee's handbook gives creditors fairly free rein in examining the debtor—but the questioning must not rise to the level of harassment. This means you may ask the debtor for financial details about why he had to file for bankruptcy, but you may not ask why he chose to stiff his creditors. Try to be businesslike, and stick to questions to which you genuinely need the answer.

Trustees are instructed to balance your need for information with the time required to finish all the scheduled meetings. If you've prepared more than a few questions, the trustee will probably adjourn your meeting for a short while, in order to finish the rest of the routine cases. A "routine" case is one in which no creditors show up to question the debtor. The trustee may also adjourn the meeting until another day, when you can be allotted more time.

The trustee has the authority to cut you off if he feels that you've had a reasonable amount of time to get the information you need. Remember, the trustee will be listening to the debtor's answers,

too. Whether or not he cuts you off depends in part on whether you've piqued his interest with your line of questioning. The topics most likely to catch and hold the trustee's interest include:

- **Hidden assets.** Ask the debtor about any property listed on her loan application that doesn't appear on the bankruptcy schedules. Trustees get paid a percentage of any property they can seize from the debtor and sell for the benefit of the debtor's unsecured creditors.

- **Unreported income.** Ask the debtor about any extra income or overtime pay that the trustee isn't aware of. Perhaps this extra income was listed on your loan application. Perhaps you know that the debtor fixes cars in his driveway. Perhaps you've driven past the debtor's business and noticed somebody selling paintings in the parking lot. If you have any information that leads you to believe the debtor has more income than is being disclosed, you're free to ask about it at the meeting of creditors. The trustee is required to look for, and refer to the U.S. Trustee, all cases in which it appears the debtor has the ability to pay his bills and is trying to hide it. The trustee doesn't make any money on these referrals, but they do earn brownie points with the boss.

- **Fraud.** Ask the debtor about any discrepancies between what you know of the debtor and what the debtor said on the bankruptcy schedules. Here again, the trustee is supposed to look for fraudulent bankruptcy schedules and will be grateful for any help you can provide. (Guess who trustees say are the best source of hidden assets, unreported income, and exaggerated expenses: former spouses.)

The topics most likely to lose the trustees interest include those that concern only you, as an individual creditor. Questions related to whether your individual debt might be excepted from discharge lead the list. Also on this list are questions aimed at satisfying your curiosity about why the debtor filed for bankruptcy.

Don't Try Hallway Confrontations

Most meetings of creditors are held in office-like settings, not in courthouses. The hallways are quiet, with people moving from one place to another on business. Some creditors attend the meeting of creditors not to question debtors, but to ambush them on their way in or out of the meeting. They take advantage of the quiet hallways to intimidate and coerce the debtor into agreeing to repay their debts.

If you witness this conduct, don't take it as an example of a good business practice. It's not. In fact, blatant hallway confrontations can result in penalties for violating the automatic stay.

C. Requesting a Meeting to Finish Your Questions (Rule 2004)

If the trustee cuts you off before you're through questioning the debtor, the bankruptcy rules—namely, Rule 2004—let you force the debtor to submit to further questioning. You may also demand that the debtor provide you with copies of documents. In this section, we'll cover:

- when you might reasonably ask for a Rule 2004 examination (Subsection 1),
- arranging the meeting (Subsection 2), and
- how to conduct the Rule 2004 meeting (Subsection 3).

1. When to Use Rule 2004

Any request to further question the debtor or force him to produce documents must be reasonable. Rule 2004 examinations may not be used to annoy, harass, or embarrass the debtor. In particular, the questions you ask and the documents you request must either relate to the administration of the debtor's bankruptcy or to the debtor's:

- actions that led to the creation of your claim or to the debtor's attempt to discharge it through bankruptcy
- property as of the time your claim was created, the time the bankruptcy was filed, or any time in between

- debts as of the time your claim was created, the bankruptcy was filed, or any time in between
- financial condition as of the time your claim was created, the bankruptcy was filed, or any time in between
- entitlement to a bankruptcy discharge, or
- business operations, including where the money is coming from to keep the debtor in business and whether it's a good idea for the debtor to stay in business.

As you can see, your ability to question the debtor is fairly broad, but not unlimited. In fact, if you're suspicious about what the debtor did or didn't do, you can ask broad, general questions in the hope that you'll find something. This is what's known as a "fishing expedition." However, it's not cost effective to go fishing every time a debtor files for bankruptcy. Furthermore, if you cross the line and abuse your power to make debtors submit to questions, the court may impose penalties on you. An abusive inquiry is one in which you ask questions when you have no reason to be suspicious.

However, if you think the debtor did something wrong or may be hiding something, a Rule 2004 examination is a good place to start. Your other possible remedies include asking the court to dismiss the debtor's case, deny the debtor's discharge, or deny the dischargeability of your claim. But testing the waters with a

Rule 2004 examination will make you better able to decide whether one of these remedies is appropriate.

Suppose, for example, that you ask the court to deny the debtor's discharge based on your hunch that the debtor is hiding assets. After starting your case against the debtor, you hold a Rule 2004 examination at which you voice questions regarding your suspicions. At that time, you'll either find information to support your hunch or you won't. If you do, that's great. If you don't, then you'll need to dismiss the complaint—and the court may penalize you for filing an unwarranted action.

On the other hand, if you had asked for the Rule 2004 examination before filing your complaint, you might have found information to support your hunch and more. And, when you filed the complaint you could have asked for all the remedies available to you rather than just the one you had a hunch about. Or you might have found nothing—in which case you could have stopped right there.

Rule 2004 examinations are frequently used by creditors who believe—but are not sure—that their claims should be excepted from discharge (survive the bankruptcy), particularly based on the debtor's fraud in incurring the debt. (See Chapter 9.) If you think your claim might fit one of these categories, then use a Rule 2004 examination to make sure. For example, a spouse who believes that her ex-husband has the ability to make a property settlement payment despite his bankruptcy filing might conduct a Rule 2004 examination to investigate his current finances.

2. Arranging the Meeting

If the circumstances warrant a Rule 2004 examination, ask the debtor's attorney if his client will submit to one voluntarily. In many courts, the local version of Rule 2004 requires you to attempt to arrange a voluntary examination before you file a motion with the court seeking to compel the debtor's attendance. (See Chapter 10 regarding the procedures for filing motions—this may require an attorney's help.)

If the court grants your request, it will issue a subpoena directing the debtor to appear at a time and place of the court's choosing. You are not required to compensate the debtor for attending the meeting if it is held within 100 miles of the debtor's residence. See the sample blank subpoena form reprinted in this chapter (from Washington State; proof of service not shown).

You'll need to hire a stenographer to record the meeting. Don't skimp and go without one—the whole reason for this meeting is to get the debtor's answers in writing and under oath. This information can then be used to support any complaint you file against the debtor. It can be introduced into evidence in court to refute contrary statements made by the debtor ei-

ther on her bankruptcy schedules or in a subsequent trial. To locate stenography services, check your telephone directory or search the Internet under "stenographer" or "court reporter." Stenographer fees vary from one area of the country to another, but expect to spend between $100 and $200 for the stenographer's appearance, plus an additional amount for each transcript page produced. (That means that a longer examination will cost more than a shorter one.)

3. Conducting the Rule 2004 Meeting

If you're the person who requested the Rule 2004 examination, you're in charge of leading the meeting. There are no formal rules for opening it, other than to state for the record the time, place, and purpose of the examination, who is in attendance, and what their roles are. The trustee has no role at the examination. The debtor should have brought any documents listed in the subpoena issued by the court or in your agreement with the debtor's counsel.

You will be free to ask the debtor nearly any question, subject to the limitations we previously discussed. If the debtor or person being examined is uncooperative, the creditor may end the hearing and ask the court to impose sanctions.

Sample Rule 2004 Subpoena Form

UNITED STATES BANKRUPTCY COURT
WESTERN DISTRICT OF WASHINGTON

In re

SUBPOENA FOR RULE 2004 EXAMINATION

Debtor.

Case No.
Chapter

To:

( ) YOU ARE COMMANDED to appear pursuant to a court order issued under Rule 2004, Fed.R.Bankr.P., at the place, date, and time specified below to testify at the taking of a deposition in the above case.

PLACE	DATE AND TIME

( ) YOU ARE COMMANDED to produce and permit inspection and copying of the following documents or objects at the place, date, and time specified below (list documents or objects):

PLACE	DATE AND TIME

ISSUING OFFICER'S SIGNATURE AND TITLE	DATE

ISSUING OFFICER'S NAME, ADDRESS AND PHONE NUMBER

SUBPOENA FOR RULE 2004
EXAMINATION

Form No. B 254

Plan ahead for the examination. Know what you want to find out, and write down a list of questions that should elicit that information. For example, if you're suspicious about the fact that the debtor just bought a new car, start with that issue. Ask questions such as, "Did you buy a new car?" "Did you finance it?" "What are the payments?" "Are you making the payments?" and "How can you make the payments?"

Don't make the mistake that many people do of trying to act like a lawyer, and don't be antagonistic. It's far better to focus on the substance of your questions than on the image you're creating. If the debtor isn't cooperating, ask questions that seek short responses.

If the debtor is represented by an attorney, the attorney will attend the examination too. The attorney may object to your questions—and not always appropriately. Some attorneys use objections to try to intimidate you or disrupt your train of thought. If your questions relate to the circumstances surrounding the creation of your claim and the reasons for the debtor's bankruptcy filing, you will eliminate the source of many objections.

Luckily, objections by the debtor's attorney are not powerful enough to stop the debtor from answering the question.

Since there's no judge to rule on the objection, the attorney should simply state the objection out loud, which makes it part of the record, and allow the judge to rule on the matter later. (If the judge rules against you, the debtor's answer will be removed from the official record and the court will be unable to consider it.) If, however, the attorney believes that the debtor shouldn't answer the question, she can instruct her client not to answer until the bankruptcy judge rules on the objection. If this happens, you can still pursue other areas of inquiry. If you run into a truly recalcitrant attorney, don't hesitate to end the meeting and ask the court to sanction the attorney. This shouldn't happen, however, since most attorneys are well aware that the meeting is being recorded for transcription and that the judge could eventually read every word of what went on.

If you're going to ask for a Rule 2004 examination, pick up a copy of *Represent Yourself in Court,* by Paul Bergman and Sara J. Berman-Barrett (Nolo) or *Nolo's Deposition Handbook,* by Paul Bergman and Albert Moore. Both books provide tips and instructions on how to frame your questions so you'll get the information you're looking for. ■

Filing and Defending Your Proof of Claim

This chapter gets to the heart of how you, as a creditor, can assert your right to be paid what you're owed after a debtor's bankruptcy filing. Your right to payment is a "claim." In bankruptcy law terms, it doesn't matter whether you are a multi-national corporation or a single parent. No matter who you are, the focus of the proceedings is on giving you a right to state your claim, and then on adjusting your relationship with the debtor. In order to let the court, the trustee, and everyone else know about your claim against the debtor, you must file what's called a proof of claim.

A. Who Can File a Proof of Claim?

To know whether you're eligible to file a proof of claim, you need to first be sure that you have a legitimate claim, and then consider when it arose.

Any situation in which the debtor is supposed to pay you can give rise to a claim. Most claims result from credit transactions in which a creditor lent money to the debtor or provided goods or services on credit. But a claim can also arise as the result of a debtor's negligence, breach of contract, or other circumstances giving you the right to sue the debtor for money.

Ordinarily, you can file a proof of claim only for a right to payment that came into existence before the debtor filed for bankruptcy. However, there are exceptions. For example, if the debtor is leasing property from you and decides to terminate that lease during his bankruptcy, any claim you have against the debtor resulting from the lease termination will be treated as if it arose immediately before the debtor filed for bankruptcy—so you can file a proof of claim. Also, if the debtor made a payment to you before filing for bankruptcy and the trustee subsequently recovers that payment from you, your claim for the amount of the payment is treated as if the debtor never paid you. Again, you can file a proof of claim. (See Chapter 15 for more on the trustee's right to undo preferential transfers for the benefit of the unsecured creditors.)

B. The Benefits of Filing a Proof of Claim

There are numerous benefits to getting your claim on record. Even if the debtor is current with his payments to you, you should file a proof of claim (assuming you have been invited to do so, either by the court notice of the bankruptcy filing or by a separate notice from the trustee after the discovery of assets). The proof of claim form is fairly simple. It basically states that you have a right to payment from the debtor. Being unsure of the amount of your claim or its legal basis need not stop you from filing a proof of claim. It's fine to get your claim on the record and then amend it as you get more information.

In this section, we'll discuss:

- how filing helps you get paid (Subsection 1), and
- how filing helps you in other ways (Subsection 2).

No need to file a proof of claim in a Chapter 11, if your claim is accurately included in the debtor's list of liabilities. If, however, your claim is inaccurately listed, then you should file one anyway. In either event, if you file a proof of claim it will take precedence over the claim listed in the debtor's schedules—meaning yours will be the one that establishes the amount and nature of the claim.

1. How Filing Helps You Get Paid

If no one objects to your proof of claim, or if the court sustains your claim over someone's objection, having filed means you will eventually share in any distribution to creditors in your class. If you're an unsecured creditor with a priority claim, you will be paid in the order the Bankruptcy Code requires for this type of claim. (See Chapter 5 for a discussion of priority claims.)

If you're an unsecured creditor with a *non*priority claim, and it's a Chapter 7 bankruptcy, how much money you'll receive from what's left over at the end will depend on how much you are owed relative to other creditors and how much is available to pay claims. For example, if the debtor owes you $1,000 on an unsecured, nonpriority claim, and there's a total of $100,000 in unsecured nonpriority claims, you'll receive 1% of what's paid to unsecured creditors. If there were $60,000 available to pay this category of claims, you would receive $600.

Whether you're a secured or unsecured creditor, if the bankruptcy is under one of the reorganization chapters (11, 12, or 13), your claim will be paid according to the terms of the debtor's confirmed plan (see Chapter 13 of this book). In a Chapter 13 bankruptcy, priority claims must be paid in full over the life of the plan. Plans usually provide for full payment of secured claims and a stated percentage payment of nonpriority unsecured claims.

2. Nonmoney Reasons to File a Proof of Claim

In certain types of bankruptcies, various rights are reserved for creditors who have filed a proof of claim. For example, in a Chapter 11 bankruptcy, only holders of filed claims may vote on confirmation of the plan. (See Chapter 13 of this book for how the voting process works.)

In Chapters 12 and 13 bankruptcies, secured creditors may object to how the plan treats their claims only if they have filed a proof of claim. And, unsecured creditors must file a proof of claim in order to:

- object to the terms of the debtor's plan
- get paid under the plan, or
- ask the court to modify the debtor's plan after the court has approved it.

However, some courts have tried to expedite the Chapter 13 process by considering whether a debtor's plan should be approved before the deadline for filing claims. In these courts, creditors can object to confirmation without filing a claim.

Think Like an Unsecured Creditor

If your claim is secured, you may think you can ignore the debtor's bankruptcy filing and rely on your lien to collect your claim. You're correct if:

- your lien was recorded against the property earlier than any other liens against it
- the collateral's value is not depreciating, and
- the collateral is not likely to disappear before you're ready to foreclose or repossess.

However, if you hold a junior lien, or your collateral's value is depreciating or may disappear, it's better to think of yourself as holding an unsecured claim, because that's where you may end up. And you may end up there after the deadline has passed for:

- challenging the debtor's exemption
- contesting the discharge of your claim
- opposing the entry of a discharge, or
- objecting to the confirmation of the debtor's plan.

So, file a claim (unless the notice of filing tells you not to) and participate in the bankruptcy. Make sure that the collateral is valued properly. Challenge the discharge of your claim or the debtor's exemptions if there's a basis for doing so. Don't sit back and expect to get paid just because you have a secured claim.

C. Deadline for Filing a Proof of Claim

In most cases—including Chapter 7 "asset" cases and cases filed under Chapters 12 and 13—the deadline for filing proofs of claim is 90 days after the first scheduled day for the creditors' meeting. The bankruptcy notice will do these calculations for you, and tell you when the deadline is.

However, in Chapter 7 no-asset cases, there is no deadline for filing your proof of claim. In fact, the court notice will tell you not to file a proof of claim. Remember, however, that this notice is sent at the beginning of the bankruptcy, based on what the debtor says in his petition papers—not on what the court or the trustee later determine. Therefore, a supposed no-asset case can later turn into an asset case. If assets are eventually located, a new notice will be sent to you and you will have 90 days in which to file a proof of claim.

⚠️ **The debtor or the trustee may file a proof of claim for you.** They have this right in cases where a creditor can or should file a proof of claim, but doesn't do so before the meeting of creditors. The debtor's motive is to make sure a particular creditor is involved in the bankruptcy. For example, the debtor's Chapter 13 plan may allow the debtor to cure a mortgage arrearage by making payments over time. The debtor wants the mortgage company to file a claim, to avoid the possibility that it will simply seek stay relief and foreclose. If the mortgage company does nothing, the debtor would file a proof of claim for the creditor, because there may otherwise be no way to arrange for regular arrearage payments. (Trustees make payments only to creditors who have filed claims.)

D. If You Miss the Filing Deadline

The filing deadline may go by without your doing anything—perhaps because you consciously decided not to file a proof of claim, didn't realize you had a claim, or didn't know about the deadline.

If you didn't file a proof of claim on time but wish you had, you are still permitted to file the claim. However, your chances of being paid go way down, and you may be penalized, as we'll discuss further below.

Instead of simply filing late, you may instead ask the court to extend the deadline for you. However, the various bankruptcy courts disagree on whether they'll grant such extension requests. Most courts won't. A few courts will extend the deadline if there was a good reason why you missed it.

If the court refuses to extend the deadline to allow you to file a timely proof of claim, you may still be in luck if you filed any paper with the court that said you have a claim against the debtor. This might have been an objection to discharge or an objection to plan confirmation. Any document stating your claim that was filed before the deadline can be treated as an informal proof of claim, which can be amended after the deadline to correct any deficiencies.

Even if the court refuses to extend the deadline, you may still file a late claim. Again, however, the possibility that you will eventually get paid is remote, for the reasons described below.

1. Late Filings in Chapter 7 Asset Cases

In Chapter 7 asset cases, late-filed claims are paid only after—and if—timely filed claims have been paid in full. (Since there is no deadline for filing a proof of claim in a *no-asset* Chapter 7 case, there are no "late" filings in such cases—and no possibility of getting paid even if you were to file!)

2. Late Filings in Reorganization Cases

In a reorganization case (filed under bankruptcy Chapter 11, 12, or 13), the court will disallow any late-filed claim to which someone has objected. Many Chapter 13 trustees routinely object to any postdeadline attempts to file a claim—or even to amend a claim that has already been filed. Their purpose is to make sure they are paying only the claims entitled to payment under the terms of the confirmed plan.

The lesson is, if you think the debtor owes you money, and you are not dealing with a Chapter 7 no-asset case where claims need not be filed, file a proof of claim before the deadline passes.

EXAMPLE: A bumbling divorce attorney named Dale filed for bankruptcy. Among his many disgruntled clients was Chloe, whose divorce he had handled—or rather mishandled. Because of his lax efforts at valuing the assets in the divorce, Chloe had ended up with far less than her fair share of the property. Chloe hears about the bankruptcy, but doesn't file her malpractice claim against Dale until after the deadline for filing proofs of claim has passed. Chloe tells the court that she didn't file the proof of claim earlier because she was unsure whether she had a claim and didn't want to defame the attorney. The court ruled that the claim couldn't be treated as timely filed because Chloe knew when the deadline was and decided not to file the claim before it had passed.

E. How to File a Proof of Claim

The procedure for filing a proof of claim is to fill out a single-page form called Official Form B10 and file it with the bankruptcy court. Form B10 can be downloaded from most bankruptcy court websites or from the main federal courts' website at www.uscourts.gov/bankform/index.html. A copy of the form appears below.

In addition to providing the information requested on the form, which we'll review in the coming paragraphs, you must attach copies of all documents that prove and support your claim. Notes, mortgages, security agreements, judgments, and the like must be attached. If the documents are piling up and copying them would be a hassle for all concerned, attach a summary of the documents instead. Some courts may provide a summary form; see, for example, the one provided by the Western District of Pennsylvania, below. If any documents are not available, attach a statement explaining why you were unable to include them.

Here's how to fill out Form B10:

Caption Information. At the top of the form, fill in the name of the bankruptcy court, the name of the debtor, and the number of the debtor's bankruptcy case. Copy this information from the bankruptcy notice you received.

Name of Creditor. Fill in your name or the name of the business that is owed the money.

Name and address where notices should be sent. You could choose to have notices regarding the case sent directly to you. Or, if you have a lawyer and you want the notices sent to her, put the lawyer's name in this space. If you hired a bankruptcy assistance service, which is an enterprise that handles bankruptcy case management for creditors with a large number of claims, and you want the notices sent to this service, put its name in this space.

Warning boxes to the right of your name. The proof of claim has three boxes for you to check if you need to alert the court clerk that special attention needs to be paid to your proof of claim.

Box 1. Check the first box if someone else has filed a proof of claim relating to your claim. For example, you would check this box if you bought your claim from another creditor. You would also check this box if the debtor owes you and someone else money based on the same event. Let's say that you and a friend painted the debtor's house. The debtor owes $500 to both of you, together—there was no discussion about how the money would be split between you. You and your friend could file your claim either together or separately. If you decided to file separately, you would each claim $500, but you'd need to check this box to indicate that you're making separate claims for the same $500.

Proof of Claim Form

FORM B10 (Official Form 10) (4/01)

United States Bankruptcy Court _____ District of _____		PROOF OF CLAIM
Name of Debtor	Case Number	
NOTE: This form should not be used to make a claim for an administrative expense arising after the commencement of the case. A "request" for payment of an administrative expense may be filed pursuant to 11 U.S.C. § 503.		
Name of Creditor (The person or other entity to whom the debtor owes money or property): Name and address where notices should be sent: Telephone number:	☐ Check box if you are aware that anyone else has filed a proof of claim relating to your claim. Attach copy of statement giving particulars. ☐ Check box if you have never received any notices from the bankruptcy court in this case. ☐ Check box if the address differs from the address on the envelope sent to you by the court.	THIS SPACE IS FOR COURT USE ONLY
Account or other number by which creditor identifies debtor:	Check here if this claim ☐ replaces a previously filed claim, dated:_____ ☐ amends	

1. Basis for Claim

☐ Goods sold
☐ Services performed
☐ Money loaned
☐ Personal injury/wrongful death
☐ Taxes
☐ Other _____

☐ Retiree benefits as defined in 11 U.S.C. § 1114(a)
☐ Wages, salaries, and compensation (fill out below)

Your SS #: _____ _____ _____

Unpaid compensation for services performed

from _____ to_____
      (date)   (date)

2. Date debt was incurred:

3. If court judgment, date obtained:

4. Total Amount of Claim at Time Case Filed: $ _____

If all or part of your claim is secured or entitled to priority, also complete Item 5 or 6 below.
☐ Check this box if claim includes interest or other charges in addition to the principal amount of the claim. Attach itemized statement of all interest or additional charges.

5. Secured Claim.

☐ Check this box if your claim is secured by collateral (including a right of setoff).

Brief Description of Collateral:
☐ Real Estate   ☐ Motor Vehicle
☐ Other_____

Value of Collateral: $_____

Amount of arrearage and other charges at time case filed included in secured claim, if any: $_____

6. Unsecured Priority Claim.

☐ Check this box if you have an unsecured priority claim
Amount entitled to priority $_____
Specify the priority of the claim:

☐ Wages, salaries, or commissions (up to $4,650),* earned within 90 days before filing of the bankruptcy petition or cessation of the debtor's business, whichever is earlier - 11 U.S.C. § 507(a)(3).
☐ Contributions to an employee benefit plan - 11 U.S.C. § 507(a)(4).
☐ Up to $2,100* of deposits toward purchase, lease, or rental of property or services for personal, family, or household use - 11 U.S.C. § 507(a)(6).
☐ Alimony, maintenance, or support owed to a spouse, former spouse, or child - 11 U.S.C. § 507(a)(7).
☐ Taxes or penalties owed to governmental units - 11 U.S.C. § 507(a)(8).
☐ Other - Specify applicable paragraph of 11 U.S.C. § 507(a)(____).
*Amounts are subject to adjustment on 4/1/04 and every 3 years thereafter with respect to cases commenced on or after the date of adjustment.

7. Credits: The amount of all payments on this claim has been credited and deducted for the purpose of making this proof of claim.

8. Supporting Documents: *Attach copies of supporting documents,* such as promissory notes, purchase orders, invoices, itemized statements of running accounts, contracts, court judgments, mortgages, security agreements, and evidence of perfection of lien. DO NOT SEND ORIGINAL DOCUMENTS. If the documents are not available, explain. If the documents are voluminous, attach a summary.

9. Date-Stamped Copy: To receive an acknowledgment of the filing of your claim, enclose a stamped, self-addressed envelope and copy of this proof of claim.

THIS SPACE IS FOR COURT USE ONLY

Date	Sign and print the name and title, if any, of the creditor or other person authorized to file this claim (attach copy of power of attorney, if any):

Penalty for presenting fraudulent claim: Fine of up to $500,000 or imprisonment for up to 5 years, or both. 18 U.S.C. §§ 152 and 3571.

Proof of Claim Form, continued

FORM **B10** (Official Form 10) (9/97)

INSTRUCTIONS FOR PROOF OF CLAIM FORM

The instructions and definitions below are general explanations of the law. In particular types of cases or circumstances, such as bankruptcy cases that are not filed voluntarily by a debtor, there may be exceptions to these general rules.

—— DEFINITIONS ——

Debtor

The person, corporation, or other entity that has filed a bankruptcy case is called the debtor.

Creditor

A creditor is any person, corporation, or other entity to whom the debtor owed a debt on the date that the bankruptcy case was filed.

Proof of Claim

A form telling the bankruptcy court how much the debtor owed a creditor at the time the bankruptcy case was filed (the amount of the creditor's claim). This form must be filed with the clerk of the bankruptcy court where the bankruptcy case was filed.

Secured Claim

A claim is a secured claim to the extent that the creditor has a lien on property of the debtor (collateral) that gives the creditor the right to be paid from that property before creditors who do not have liens on the property.

Examples of liens are a mortgage on real estate and a security interest in a car, truck, boat, television set, or other item of property. A lien may have been obtained through a court proceeding before the bankruptcy case began; in some states a court judgment is a lien. In addition, to the extent a creditor also owes money to the debtor (has a right of setoff), the creditor's claim may be a secured claim. (See also *Unsecured Claim.*)

Unsecured Claim

If a claim is not a secured claim it is an unsecured claim. A claim may be partly secured and partly unsecured if the property on which a creditor has a lien is not worth enough to pay the creditor in full.

Unsecured Priority Claim

Certain types of unsecured claims are given priority, so they are to be paid in bankruptcy cases before most other unsecured claims (if there is sufficient money or property available to pay these claims). The most common types of priority claims are listed on the proof of claim form. Unsecured claims that are not specifically given priority status by the bankruptcy laws are classified as *Unsecured Nonpriority Claims.*

Items to be completed in Proof of Claim form (if not already filled in)

Court, Name of Debtor, and Case Number:
Fill in the name of the federal judicial district where the bankruptcy case was filed (for example, Central District of California), the name of the debtor in the bankruptcy case, and the bankruptcy case number. If you received a notice of the case from the court, all of this information is near the top of the notice.

Information about Creditor:
Complete the section giving the name, address, and telephone number of the creditor to whom the debtor owes money or property, and the debtor's account number, if any. If anyone else has already filed a proof of claim relating to this debt, if you never received notices from the bankruptcy court about this case, if your address differs from that to which the court sent notice, or if this proof of claim replaces or changes a proof of claim that was already filed, check the appropriate box on the form.

1. Basis for Claim:
Check the type of debt for which the proof of claim is being filed. If the type of debt is not listed, check "Other" and briefly describe the type of debt. If you were an employee of the debtor, fill in your social security number and the dates of work for which you were not paid.

2. Date Debt Incurred:
Fill in the date when the debt first was owed by the debtor.

3. Court Judgments:
If you have a court judgment for this debt, state the date the court entered the judgment.

4. Total Amount of Claim at Time Case Filed:
Fill in the total amount of the entire claim. If interest or other charges in addition to the principal amount of the claim are included, check the appropriate place on the form and attach an itemization of the interest and charges.

5. Secured Claim:
Check the appropriate place if the claim is a secured claim. You must state the type and value of property that is collateral for the claim, attach copies of the documentation of your lien, and state the amount past due on the claim as of the date the bankruptcy case was filed. A claim may be partly secured and partly unsecured. (See DEFINITIONS, above).

6. Unsecured Priority Claim:
Check the appropriate place if you have an unsecured priority claim, and state the amount entitled to priority. (See DEFINITIONS, above). A claim may be partly priority and partly nonpriority if, for example, the claim is for more than the amount given priority by the law. Check the appropriate place to specify the type of priority claim.

7. Credits:
By signing this proof of claim, you are stating under oath that in calculating the amount of your claim you have given the debtor credit for all payments received from the debtor.

8. Supporting Documents:
You must attach to this proof of claim form copies of documents that show the debtor owes the debt claimed or, if the documents are too lengthy, a summary of those documents. If documents are not available, you must attach an explanation of why they are not available.

Box 2. Check the second box if you have not received a notice from the bankruptcy court regarding this case. See Chapter 3 for a reminder of how you might learn about a bankruptcy without receiving an official notice from the court. Check this box if this is one of those cases.

Box 3. Check the third box if the address to which you want notices sent is different from the one at which you received the filing notice. This is a fairly common box to check. Debtors tell the court to send notices to creditors at the addresses where they paid their bills. Rarely is this the address to which creditors want the notice sent. Filing a proof of claim is a convenient way to correct the mailing address.

Account or other number by which creditor identifies debtor. If you identify the debtor by an account or service number, enter that number in this space.

Check here if this claim . . . . Check the appropriate box if your proof of claim replaces or amends a previously filed proof of claim (including by the debtor or trustee). You need to do this so that you don't have duplicate claims on the claims docket maintained by the clerk. If you don't make it clear that one proof of claim is amending an earlier proof of claim, the trustee may object to your claims—and both claims may be stricken. Save yourself time and trouble by checking the appropriate box.

Question 1: Basis for Claim. Check the box that best answers the question, "Why does the debtor owe you money?"

- Check "Goods sold" if the debtor bought something from you and hasn't fully paid for it.
- Check "Services performed" if you did work for the debtor, who hasn't fully paid for it.
- Check "Money loaned" if the debtor borrowed money from you and hasn't fully repaid it.
- Check "Personal injury/wrongful death" if your claim against the debtor arises out of an accident or assault.
- Check "Retiree benefits" if you are retired, the debtor has filed under Chapter 11, and the debtor was funding your or your family's medical care, disability, or death benefits. (Despite its name, this box doesn't refer to ordinary retirement cash benefits. See 11 U.S.C. § 1114(a).)
- Check "Wages, salaries and compensation" if you worked for the debtor and haven't been fully paid. You'll need to supply your Social Security number and the dates for which you were not paid.
- Check "Other" if your claim doesn't fit into any of the above categories. For example, let's say you cosigned for the debtor on a loan he took out, and the debtor defaulted so you had to pay. Your right to be reimbursed by the debtor should be listed under "other."

Sample Document Summary

LOCAL BANKRUPTCY FORM NO. 25
IN THE UNITED STATES BANKRUPTCY COURT
WESTERN DISTRICT OF PENNSYLVANIA

IN RE

                 :   Bankruptcy No. _____

                 :

                 :   Adversary No. _____

        Debtor(s)   :

DOCUMENT AND LOAN HISTORY ABSTRACT
(COMPLETE A SEPARATE ABSTRACT FOR
THE ORIGINAL TRANSACTION AND EACH ASSIGNMENT)

TYPE OF
INSTRUMENT
   ___ Mortgage   ___ Retail Installment Contract
   ___ Assignment   ___ UCC Financing Statement
   ___ Lease   ___ Promissory Note / Security Agreement
   ___ Other (describe) _____

PARTIES
   _____ Borrower / Lessee
   _____ Lender / Lessor

DATE OF INSTRUMENT _____ **# OF PAGES** _____

ESSENTIAL
TERMS
   _____ Original Principal Balance
   _____ Term
   _____ Interest Rate
   _____ First Payment Due
   _____ Payment Amount
   _____ Frequency of Payments(weekly, monthly, yearly, etc.)
   _____ First Payment Due Date
   Last Payment Applied to Installment due on _____
   _____ Amount in Arrears
   _____ Total Amount of Claim on Date of Filing of Petition
   _____ Total Amount of Claim on Date of Filing of Motion

SECURED (LEASED) PROPERTY DESCRIPTION

   ___ Real Property   ___ Motor Vehicle   ___ Other
   _____ Address / Description

Lien Recording
_____ Recorder of Deeds
_____ County / Commonwealth/State
_____ Secretary of State / Commonwealth/State
_____ Bureau of Motor Vehicles (Commonwealth/State _____)
_____ Other (Describe) _____
_____ Recording Date
_____ Book & Page/Instrument Number

OTHER ESSENTIAL INFORMATION:

PROOF OF CLAIM FILED WITH CLERK, U.S. BANKRUPTCY COURT _____ (Yes/No)

Question 2: Date debt was incurred.
When did the debtor first owe you
money? Usually this is easy to figure out:
It's when the debtor signed the note, or
you delivered the goods or did the work.
If the debtor's liability came into existence over a period of time, then enter the
date when you first had the right to sue
the debtor—that is, when the debtor defaulted on the obligation.

**Question 3: If court judgment, date
obtained.** If you sued the debtor and won,
when did the court rule in your favor?

**Question 4: Total Amount of Claim
at Time Case Filed.** How much money
does the debtor owe you? If you think the
debtor owes you interest or other charges
in addition to the principal amount of the
debt, include those charges as part of
your claim. Check the box on the form to
show that your claim has multiple compo-
nents and attach a statement itemizing
each component of your claim. You may
include interest as part of your claim if it
is called for in your agreement with the
debtor and it accrued before the bankruptcy was filed. This interest must also
be allowable under your state's law—in
particular, it mustn't violate any usury provisions. If your claim arose after the
debtor filed for bankruptcy, and the contract or your state's law allows you to collect interest, you may include interest in
your proof of claim only if your claim is
secured and the collateral is worth more
than your claim.

Question 5: Secured Claim. If your
claim is secured (see Chapter 2), you must:
- Check the box in part five of the
  proof of claim.
- Check the box that indicates the type
  of property that is collateral for your
  claim.
- Enter your estimate of the collateral's
  current fair market value. Base this
  on how much a willing buyer would
  spend to purchase the property from
  the debtor. If you haven't seen the
  collateral recently, or don't know
  what it's worth, state "unknown."
  Don't take a wild guess. If you're too
  low, you'll be stuck with that valuation. If you're too high, your credibility will be damaged.
- State whether any portion of your
  claim is due to payments missed by the
  debtor prior to filing for bankruptcy.

**Question 6: Unsecured Priority
Claim.** The order in which claims are paid
is not determined by the order in which
they are filed. Instead, the Bankruptcy
Code establishes categories of unsecured
claims that are entitled to be paid ahead
of other claims. These special claims are
called "priority" claims. If you have an unsecured priority claim, check the first box,
and then check the box that identifies
your type of claim. Your choices include:
- wages, salaries and commissions up
  to $4,650, earned within the 90 days
  before the debtor filed for bankruptcy
  or went out of business, whichever
  happened first

- contributions to an employee benefit plan. These are payments that an employer who filed for bankruptcy owed to the plan itself, not to individual beneficiaries of the plan. The administrator of a pension plan would be the type of creditor to check this box.

- deposits of up to $2,100 toward the purchase or rental of property or services for personal, family, or household use. This category includes deposits made for wedding dresses and family vacations. For example, if you gave a travel agent $400 towards your family's trip to Disneyworld and the travel agent filed for bankruptcy before your trip, your claim against the travel agent is entitled to priority.

- alimony, maintenance, or support that is owed to you as the debtor's spouse, former spouse, or child. In order to check this box, the obligation must have been created by a separation agreement, divorce decree, or other court order. However, the document need not specifically state that it is for alimony, maintenance, or support—the fact that it provides support for the debtor's spouse, former spouse, or child will be enough.

Date and signature line. Don't forget to sign and date the proof of claim. If you're filing for your corporation, include your title when you sign. If you're filing on behalf of another person or business, attach a copy of the document (power of attorney, assignment of claim, or something similar) that authorizes you to file the claim.

F. Where to File the Proof of Claim

Your proof of claim must be filed with the clerk of the bankruptcy court where the debtor's bankruptcy was filed. You may mail your claim to the court clerk, or deliver it in person. The address for your local bankruptcy court can be found by going to the website of the U.S. Court system, www.uscourts.gov, and following the links to your bankruptcy court. Include a stamped, self-addressed envelope and a copy of your proof of claim so that the clerk can return a time-stamped copy of your proof of claim for your records. It's also wise to include a cover letter requesting this service and letting the clerk know how to reach you with any questions about your filing.

Check with the clerk before you file your proof of claim to see how many copies you must send. Most courts require two copies so that one can be passed along to the trustee. Also, don't give your proof of claim to anyone other than the court clerk. Creditors frequently try to file their claims with trustees, debtors' attorneys and other court officials.

These people can't file your claim for you and will usually return it to you unfiled.

⚠️ **After filing, don't forget to inform the court of any changes to your proof of claim.** This includes minor changes, such as if you want the court to send notices to a new business address. By the time any payments are to be made on creditors' claims, months or years may have gone by. Be sure the court knows where to send your check.

G. How to Defend Your Claim

Once you file your proof of claim, the court will view it as legitimate unless the debtor or trustee objects and the court is convinced by that objection. However, making it over this first hurdle doesn't mean you can throw away your records and wait for the court to send you a check. Creditors have been known to inflate their claims, or simply to make errors about what they're owed. That's why the debtor, the trustee or another creditor may challenge your claim. Below, we'll talk about:

- how to avoid facing objections to your proof of claim in the first place (Subsection 1), and
- procedures for objecting to and defending a proof of claim (Subsection 2).

1. Avoiding Objections

Trustees routinely file certain objections, such as those challenging mathematical errors or duplicate claims. Here are some suggestions for avoiding these objections.

- **File one proof of claim per debt.** If the debtor has multiple accounts with you, file one proof of claim for each, to avoid confusion. Remember, it's called a proof of *claim*, not a proof of *claims*.
- **Don't file over the same debt more than once.** When the trustee reviews the claims docket, if one creditor is listed twice with claims for the same amount of money, the trustee will assume it's a duplicate claim, and object. This may result in both claims being stricken. Be sure to:
  ✔ Get the proof of claim right the first time, so you don't need to file an amendment.
  ✔ Limit the number of people authorized to file proofs of claim for you, so there's no possibility of duplicate filings.
- **Attach documents to support your claim.** Make sure to include any contracts, invoices, or other documents that prove the existence and amount of your claim. For example, if you say your claim is secured, but you don't attach a copy of the security agreement, the trustee will file an objection. The better you document your claim, the less likely anyone is to object.

- **Don't ask for postfiling interest payments.** You may ask for interest on your claim that came due before the debtor filed for bankruptcy, but not afterward (with rare exceptions). Any interest on your claim that arises after the bankruptcy filing is called "unmatured interest," meaning that it hasn't developed into an actual obligation to you. Your claim is set as of the day the bankruptcy petition was filed.

Secured creditors may receive interest. One of the benefits of being a secured creditor is that you may receive interest that has accrued after the filing of the petition (assuming the collateral is worth more than your claim). You may also be able to recover the cost of your attorney's fees if allowed by the contract you have with the debtor.

- **Don't claim priority status unless your claim merits it.** You may think that your claim should be paid ahead of other claims, but don't check it off as a priority claim unless it really fits into one of the given categories. (See Chapter 5 for a list of claims entitled to priority status.)
- **File prior to the deadline.** Remember, in many courts a late-filed claim in a Chapter 13 case is going to bring an automatic objection from the trustee. In a Chapter 7 case, it's rare

for the unsecured creditors to be paid in full—so that with a late-filed claim, you're likely to be paid last, if anything is leftover. In a Chapter 11 case, it's usually up to the debtor to decide whether to pay you or to object to your claim on the basis that it was filed late.

2. Procedures for Objections and Defenses

Any objections to your proof of claim must be in writing, filed with the court and served on you and the trustee. Most objections to proofs of claim are over minor enough issues to be handled as contested motions, which are like informal trials (see Subsection a). However, some objections go to the heart of whether you really have a claim, and are handled in adversarial proceedings (see Subsection b).

Regardless of the type of proceeding, you should understand whose responsibility it is to prove that your claim is proper or correct. If the objection makes a believable challenge to your claim's validity, you will have the burden of convincing the court that your claim is legitimate. Stated another way, your claim is assumed to be correct only as long as no one questions it. However, if someone raises a good question, the task of proving that you hold a bona fide claim falls back onto your shoulders.

a. Responding to Commonplace Objections

Some objections simply ask the bankruptcy court to adjust or correct your claim. (Bankruptcy Rule 9014.) For example, you might say that the debtor owes you $500, while the debtor says it's only $400. The two of you at least agree that the debtor owes you something. All the court needs to determine is the correct amount of the claim.

Such an objection would be handled as a contested motion, in which the regular rules of evidence and procedure would be relaxed. You should be able to defend your claim against such an objection on your own. See Chapters 10 and 11 for a discussion of bringing and responding to actions in bankruptcy court.

Some objections are so minor that they don't even require the filing of motions. For example, if someone challenges a clerical defect in your proof of claim, such as a mathematical error, you can agree with the objector that you'll correct the mistake.

b. Responding to Major Objections in Adversarial Proceedings

At the other end of the complexity spectrum, the debtor might say he owes you nothing at all. You would need to prove the debtor's liability before even arguing about how much your claim is worth.

EXAMPLE: Colin's Car Repair says Davey owes $1,000 for work it did to fix his engine. Davey says the car died before he got it home from the shop, and that he doesn't owe a penny. Colin's files a proof of claim for $1,000. Davey objects and says that Colin's breached the contract by failing to do a proper job.

When an objection to a proof of claim goes to the heart of your claim like this, it starts an adversarial proceeding. (Bankruptcy Rules 3007 and 7001.) This makes sense. Looking at the example above, it's a basic contract dispute being tried in the bankruptcy court. Instead of filing a complaint against the debtor in state court or small claims court, the creditor filed a proof of claim in bankruptcy court. The proof of claim probably set out all the points the creditor would have made in his complaint and attached all the documents that would have been included as exhibits. The debtor's objection is just like an answer to a state court complaint, so the bankruptcy judge will have to hear the case just like a state court judge would.

The bad news for you is that, since such proceedings will resemble a regular lawsuit, they'll follow strict rules of evidence and procedure. The objector will have to file a formal complaint against you and you will have to respond. If the debtor asserts defenses that would not only negate your claim but may end up costing you money, you ought to seek an attorney's assistance. For example, find legal counsel before defending any objection that asks the court to:

- order you to pay damages to the debtor
- order you to surrender property to the debtor
- determine the validity of your lien
- determine the dischargeability of your claim, or
- have your claim paid after all other claims in your class or after all other claims in a class or classes below yours.

⚠️ **Keep all the documents you need to prove your claim.**
Merely saying that the debtor owes you the money won't entitle you to payment in bankruptcy court any more than it does in state court. The more evidence you can show the court to support your claim, the better your chances of overcoming any objection.

H. How to Object to Another Creditor's Claim

In reviewing the debtor's schedules and statements, you might naturally get fixated on what the debtor owns. But there's another area that should interest

you: how much the debtor owes, and to whom. If the debtor seems to have any questionable obligations, you have a right to challenge them. You would do so by filing an objection, either to a proof of claim, if the other creditor has filed one, or to the scheduled debt in a Chapter 11 case. If no proof of claim has been filed and the debtor filed under any chapter other than Chapter 11, then you don't need to worry about questionable debts unless and until a proof of claim is filed.

A successful objection may increase the distribution on all legitimate claims. In particular, keep your eyes open for

- phony liens (Subsection 1), and
- phony creditors (Subsection 2).

1. Phony Liens

Debtors can hide equity in their property by granting liens to friends, relatives, and insiders. These are known as fraudulent transfers or preferential transfers, depending on the details. We'll discuss these concepts more fully in the next chapter. For now, know that a fraudulent transfer is one in which the debtor grants a lien for less than he should have gotten in return, while a preferential transfer is one in which the debtor gives a creditor more than the creditor would have received had the debtor filed for bankruptcy without making the transfer.

EXAMPLE: Dagmara has $100,000 in equity in her home but can exempt only $15,000. If she files for bankruptcy, her creditors will be able to get the $85,000 in unprotected equity. To cover that exposed equity, Dagmara grants her father a $90,000 lien against the property. Now, instead of having $85,000 in excess equity, she's got $10,000 in total equity, which is well below the amount she can exempt. The trustee or a vigilant creditor should challenge the lien given to Dagmara's father as being either fraudulent or preferential.

Getting phony liens avoided can transform a no-asset Chapter 7 case into an asset case or, in a reorganization case, increase the amount of money the debtor must pay to creditors in order to confirm the plan. You're more likely to encounter phony liens in cases involving businesses or individuals engaged in business, because this a somewhat sophisticated way to hide property. Also, businesses tend to have more secured creditors. The more creditors there are, the harder it is to separate real lienholders from fake ones.

Here are some tips for spotting phony liens:

- **Look at when the lien was created.** The closer to the bankruptcy filing, the more likely it is to be phony.

- **Look at who the lien was given to.** If the lienholder is a friend, relative or business associate, the lien may be phony.

- **Look at what sort of debt the lien secures.** It may not be an actual obligation of the debtor's. Look at the circumstances surrounding the creation of the lien to see if something seems off.

2. Phony Creditors

Some debtors try to diminish the return to unsecured creditors by claiming bogus unsecured debts owed to friends, relatives, and insiders. Remember that when debtors file for bankruptcy, they're told to list everyone to whom they owe money. Some of those obligations are better documented than others—or have a partial basis in reality. The debtor's family may have been subsidizing the debtor for years before he filed for bankruptcy, but can they prove they're owed the thousands of dollars scheduled by the debtor?

Challenging shaky unsecured debts is worthwhile only in reorganization cases in which the unsecured creditors are being paid a set amount of money that is insufficient to pay all the claims in full.

EXAMPLE: Damon's reorganization plan proposes paying $10,000 to unsecured creditors. These creditors are owed a total of $100,000, so each creditor would receive ten cents on the dollar. However, if half of this $100,000 represents phony claims held by the debtor's family, and the real creditors successfully object to these claims, their return would be doubled. The $10,000 would now be available to pay $50,000 in creditors' claims—that is, 20% instead of only 10% of what they're owed.

I. How to Sell Your Claim

Believe it or not, there are companies that buy bankruptcy claims. They're called "claims traders." They'll pay you their estimate of the current value of your claim, which usually means pennies on the dollar. It's up to you to decide whether getting a little money today is better than the hope—and effort—of getting more money later.

Be sure to decide whether to sell *before* the deadline for filing proofs of claim has passed, because you'll only be able to sell your claim if you timely filed a proof of claim. If you were not required to file a proof of claim, or if the deadline for doing so has not yet passed, you may be able to sell your claim without first filing a proof of claim. Of course, if you don't need to file a proof of claim because the debtor filed a no-asset Chapter 7 case, you'll be hard pressed to find a buyer anyway.

EXAMPLE: Chet has an unsecured $5,000 claim against Darla, a Chapter 13 debtor. Darla's confirmed plan promises to pay Chet 30% of what he's owed, or $1,500, to be paid at the rate of $100 per month. Here's the catch, though: Payment of Chet's claim will be deferred until near the end of Darla's five-year reorganization plan, so that these $100 checks won't start to appear until the final 15 months of the plan. Chet is approached by a claims buyer, who offers to pay the present value of Chet's claim. The question then becomes, how much is Darla's promise to pay Chet in the future worth to Chet today?

1. Whether Your Claim Will Tempt a Trader

If you've got a promising claim, you may not have to find the claims traders—they'll find you. For instance, assume you are a creditor who provided trade credit to a business that filed for Chapter 11 relief. The debtor says it will pay 100% of trade claims as soon as it can confirm its reorganization plan. It may take months for you to get paid, but the prospects for full payment look good. In this situation, a claims buyer may offer all trade creditors 50 cents on the dollar. It won't matter whether you're owed $500 or $500,000; the claims buyer will be interested in your claim. Depending on how good the prospects of payment are, you may even see claims buyers compete for your business.

Some companies specialize in buying delinquent receivables, otherwise known as bad debts. Generally, you'll need at least $1 million in claims before any of them will be interested in turning your bad debts into cash. But if you're holding a lot of IOUs, these companies will take them off your hands at a steep discount on the face value.

2. Negotiating the Claim Sales Contract

If you decide to sell your claim, be sure to carefully read the sales contract or assignment form. Realize that the claims buyer is taking a gamble on your claim, and may just try to protect himself by getting you to sign onto a bad deal. It may look like a fancy, preprinted form that you can't alter, but don't let that stop you from asking for rewrites or amendments. Here are some ways to make sure you're the one who gets the protection:

- **Don't limit your ability to sell your claim before the buyer commits to buying it.** Some claims buyers will ask you to sign a commitment letter, saying that you can't sell the claim to another buyer during the time that this buyer investigates the merits of your claim. You could be missing out

on opportunities while the buyer does its due diligence—only to have the buyer reject the deal. If the buyer won't deal with you without a commitment letter, set a deadline by which time she must complete review of your claim and give you an answer on the assignment.

EXAMPLE: Corey's Custom Parts provided custom-made parts to a telecommunications company that files under Chapter 11. A claims trader offers to pay Corey's 20% of its $48,000 claim. However, the trader wants to first make sure Corey's claim is legitimate. Because it's going to take some effort to determine whether Corey's claim is bona fide, the claims trader wants Corey's to sign a commitment letter. Corey's agrees to sign the letter, but only after negotiating an increase in its percentage—from 20% to 40%.

- **Don't give a money-back guarantee.** When the claims trader acquires the right to payment, she should also acquire all the risks that come with it. These include not only the risk of nonpayment, but also the risk that the debtor may have defenses to raise against your claim or have a claim of its own that would lower yours by way of a setoff. However, some claims buyers try to leave these risks with the sellers. Words like "indemnify" and phrases like "hold harmless" will warn you that the buyer is trying to acquire your claim but leave you with the risk. A buyer who is worried that your claim is risky has a simple remedy available—offer you less money for it. The riskier the investment, the less you'll get paid. If you want more money for your claim, however, you may decide to keep some of this risk.

EXAMPLE: After Really Big Trucking Co. filed for bankruptcy, its employees were approached by a claims trader with an offer to buy their claims for 35 cents on the dollar. However, there was a catch: If it turned out that the claim was not allowed by the court, the employee was responsible for repaying what he or she had received from Really Big Trucking, plus a 10% penalty. This repayment obligation and penalty was imposed regardless of the reason for the claim's disallowance.

- **Don't accidentally sell less than the full claim.** Sometimes the claims buyer will want to buy only as much of your claim as the debtor, in its schedules, admits you're owed. You might not even realize that this is what's happening, since the contract language will refer only to your "allowed claim." That would leave you

uncompensated for any of your claim that the debtor won't admit to. Before you sell your claim, make sure you know the amount of your allowed claim. It's either the amount listed in the Chapter 11 debtor's schedules or the amount listed on your uncontested proof of claim.

EXAMPLE: Chip's Painting repaints Daniel's office and sends a bill for $4,000. Daniel never pays Chip's bill, and Chip's receives notice that Daniel has filed for bankruptcy. A claims trader offers to pay Chip's 10% of its allowed claim. Chip's agrees to sell, believing it's going to receive $400. However, because Daniel's statements and schedules say Chip's is owed only $2,000 and because Chip's didn't file a claim contradicting this, Chip's receives only $200, which is 10% of the allowed claim.

- **Don't accidentally commit to selling more of your claim later.** If the claims trader insists that it will take only a portion of your claim, make sure the assignment doesn't commit you to sell the balance of the claim at a later time, at the buyer's option. Also, even if you sell the entire amount of the claim, make sure you're not committed to selling additional claims that you may have.

EXAMPLE: Clay invested in Delightful Ventures, which filed for bankruptcy amidst allegations of corporate mismanagement. Clay had a claim against Delightful for the $15,000 in his uninsured account. Clay was also a plaintiff in a class action suit against the company for violating federal security laws. Clay accepted a claims buyer's offer of $3,000 for his $15,000 against Delightful. Unfortunately, Clay didn't read the agreement, which said he agreed to sell any future claims against the company for 20 cents on the dollar. So, after the class action settled and Clay learned he'd been awarded $45,000, the claims buyer informed Clay that he could keep only $9,000. The rest went to the claims buyer.

- **Don't give the buyer your power of attorney.** It's alright to sell your claim, but don't authorize the buyer to act in your place. Whatever steps the buyer takes to collect the claim, it should take on its own, not as if it were acting on your behalf. If you grant a power of attorney along with

the claim transfer, you'll remain responsible for the buyer's actions in trying to collect on the claim. If the buyer violates the automatic stay, you'll pay the costs.

EXAMPLE: The Corny brothers sued the famous actress, Dolly Wood, for breach of contract after she backed out of a movie deal. A state court judge ordered Dolly to pay each of the brothers $200,000. She filed for bankruptcy instead. At the time of her bankruptcy filing, the brothers owed their lawyer $500,000. Each of the brothers assigned his claim against Dolly to the lawyer, in payment of his fee. They also granted him their power of attorney so he could sign any papers necessary to settle the claims against Dolly. Instead, he used the power of attorney to garnish her pay from her current movie. As a result, the brothers were liable for violating the automatic stay—even though they didn't know what the lawyer was doing and thought they were finished with the whole thing. ■

Getting Payment for Secured Claims

This chapter addresses the rights of secured creditors during a bankruptcy—that is, the rights of those creditors who loaned money or extended credit on the condition that they could reclaim or sell an item of the debtor's property ("collateral") if the loan wasn't repaid. This conditional right is known as having a "lien" on or a "security interest" in the collateral.

Under normal circumstances, and particularly in the eyes of the debtor, there would seem to be little difference between a creditor's demand for payment and her demand for the return of a refrigerator or other collateral. However, after the debtor has gone through bankruptcy, there will be a big difference between these two types of demands.

Simply put, a postbankruptcy demand for payment might violate the debtor's discharge rights—but a demand for return of the refrigerator probably wouldn't. This is because bankruptcy will usually wipe out the debtor's responsibility for the underlying debt without wiping out any liens on the property or collateral. But, if you are, in fact, a secured creditor, don't stop reading yet—you'll still need to take various steps during the bankruptcy proceedings to ensure that your rights against the collateral survive.

The steps you'll need to take may not happen in the exact order presented in this chapter, but they'll probably be chronologically pretty close. This chapter will help you:

- determine whether you have a valid lien. If you don't, then you don't have a secured claim, in which case nothing else in this chapter will be relevant (Section A).

- make sure your lien has been "perfected," meaning that you have taken all the necessary steps to make others aware of your lien (Section B). (If your lien isn't perfected, it can be avoided, as discussed in Section I.)

- determine how much your collateral is worth. If the collateral is worth less than what the debtor owes you, you're not likely to get paid the full amount owed to you (Section C)

- understand how the debtor's choice of bankruptcy chapter affects your rights (Section D)

- determine whether you can still foreclose on your collateral despite the debtor's bankruptcy filing (Section E)

- understand what to do if the debtor wants to keep your collateral by redeeming it (Section F)

- understand what to do if the debtor wants to reaffirm the debt (Section G)

- prepare for efforts to eliminate your lien (Section H)
- defend against any effort to eliminate your lien (Section I)
- combat serial bankruptcy filers (Section J), and
- take appropriate action following the bankruptcy if your lien survives (Section K).

A. Determining Whether You Have a Valid Lien

Knowing the legal basis for your lien is the first step toward knowing how to protect it. Liens ordinarily get created in one of three ways, either by:

- agreement with the debtor (Subsection 1)
- the law of your state (Subsection 2), or
- court judgment (Subsection 3).

⚠️ **Some creditors think they're secured when they're not.** As you read the coming sections, be alert to the possibility that, despite what you thought, no lien got created at all. This would put you into the category of an unsecured creditor.

1. Liens Created by Agreement

The most common way to get a lien is for the debtor to give it to you. Consensual or voluntary liens are typically created when people buy houses, cars, and expensive appliances on credit, pledging the property they bought as collateral. Many other liens are created when people pledge property they already own to secure a new loan that they take out.

Here are common types of consensual liens.

- **Dragnet clauses.** Some security agreements state that the collateral secures not only the current loan, but existing loans as well as all future loans to the debtor. This is a dragnet clause. It saves you from worrying about getting the debtor to grant you a new security interest for each new loan, and covers you for any old unsecured loans. The extent to which these clauses are enforceable varies from state to state. The Uniform Commercial Code (UCC), which has been adopted as law in every state except Louisiana, allows dragnet clauses as long as they apply only to future loans made for the same or a similar purpose as the original loan. So, a car loan with a dragnet clause could cause the car to be collateral for a later loan to buy a motorcycle or a boat, but wouldn't be enforceable to secure a credit card debt. (However, be aware that different states have adopted the UCC in slightly different forms or subjected it to differing interpretations.)

- **Floating liens.** If you loan money to a business, you might take a security interest in everything the business has—inventory, fixtures, accounts receivable, and the like. (Accounts receivable means money owed to the business.) If the business is doing well, the particular items securing your claim are likely to change on a regular basis. When the time comes for you to go after your collateral, you basically take whatever is available within the various categories of collateral.

- **Floor financing agreements.** If you provided inventory to a business on consignment, you continue to own that inventory until it is sold. At the time of sale, you have a lien against the sale proceeds.

  EXAMPLE: Catie is a quilter who supplies quilts to Duckworth's Craft Barn, on consigment. Duckworth's owes Catie $100 for each quilt sold. Until a quilt is sold, Catie has the right to recover the quilt or to be paid $100. After a quilt is sold, Catie has a right to be paid $100, and has a lien against the money Duckworth's received for selling the quilt.

- **Liens in household goods and furnishings.** When consumer finance companies loan money, they usually ask borrowers to pledge all their possessions as collateral. Toys, furniture, pots, and pans provide typical security. Usually the finance companies don't really want to repossess this type of property, but use these liens to pressure the borrowers into repayment. (Incidentally, this type of lien can usually be gotten rid of in bankruptcy.)

- **Primary real estate mortgages.** Real estate usually has sufficient value to secure more than one loan. As a general rule, when property (any property, not just real estate) serves as collateral for multiple loans, state law determines the order in which the liens are paid if the property is sold. In most states, it's a "first recorded, first paid" system. The first lien in line is called the "primary" lien. However, in the real estate context, the law steps in with some additional criteria: If money was borrowed to purchase the real estate, and the lender acquired a lien against it to secure repayment, that lien will always be the primary one (assuming the lender went through whatever hoops were required by state law). These real estate loans are usually made by banks or mortgage companies. Their liens attach to the property as soon as the debtor acquires it. Subsequent loans can also be turned into primary loans if the lender pays off the primary mortgage holder. If the original lender transfers its lien to you, you acquire the lien in the same priority position as the original lender—perhaps jumping over other lienholders who made loans to the debtor. You basically step into the original lender's shoes.

- **Secondary real estate mortgages.** These are loans that are secured by the property but that were not made for the purpose of buying the property. Home equity loans fit into this category.

- **Vehicle loans.** If you sold the debtor a car, truck, boat, or other motor vehicle on credit, you should have had the debtor sign a security agreement giving you the right to repossess this property if the debtor defaulted on payments. In order to enforce your lien against anyone else who might make a claim to the vehicle, you must have had your lien recorded on the vehicle's title. (See Section B, below, regarding perfection.)

- **Purchase-money security interests.** State law allows sellers of property to retain a lien in property they sold if they financed the sale. These liens do not need to be recorded in order to be enforceable against any outsider who claims an interest to the property (unless state law says so, which it usually does for sales of real estate and motor vehicles). All that's necessary to create the lien is for the seller to make the sale on credit, with the buyer's knowledge that the property sold is subject to the seller's lien, and with sufficient identification of the sold property on the receipt or other documentation that a stranger to the transaction can recognize the property subject to the lien.

- **Nonpurchase-money security interests.** Any lien you acquire in the debtor's property that is not the result of providing the financing for the purchase is a nonpurchase-money security interest. An example would be a pledge of household goods for a loan from Friendly Finance Company.

Mortgages Compared to Deeds of Trust

The terms "mortgages" and "deeds of trust" are used in different parts of the United States in regard to home sales. Their meanings are very similar, but not identical. Both refer in part to the security agreement that the buyer/borrower signs when borrowing money to buy a home, giving the lender the right to sell the house if the note isn't repaid according to its terms. This security agreement is usually called a mortgage in the eastern parts of the country and a deed of trust in the West. The differences between mortgages and deeds of trust, however, arise with respect to the legal definition of when the buyer acquires ownership of the property.

With a mortgage, the borrower is said to own the property, but subject to the lender's right to foreclose and become the owner. The lender's lien remains on the property until payments are completed.

With a deed of trust, the borrower doesn't actually own the property while the loan is outstanding. Instead, the borrower has the right to use the property as long as he keeps making payments. Ownership of the property is put into the hands of a neutral third party, usually a title company or an escrow agent, in trust. This ownership is shown on a document called the deed of trust, which is recorded just like any other deed. After the borrower finishes making payments, he can take title to the property. If the buyer fails to make payments, the property is returned to the lender.

2. Liens Created by Statute

The laws of your state may automatically entitle you to a lien against a debtor's property if you've done work for or provided services to the debtor. For example:

- Attorneys have a legal right to the proceeds from lawsuits they have successfully pursued—called "charging liens."

- Homeowners associations whose charges remain unpaid by member homeowners may impose liens against the homeowners' property.
- Providers of building supplies are given a legal right to collect against property created or improved with the use of their materials—called "materialman's liens."

- Contractors and repairmen who agree to be paid over time for their work may be given secondary real estate mortgages, in which the debtor allows them to take a lien against the real estate to secure payment. These are called "mechanic's liens."

3. Liens Created by Court Judgment

When a court rules that you have a right to seize the debtor's property to pay a claim, it creates a so-called judicial lien. As background, realize that if you were to sue the debtor—perhaps to collect on money owed to you, or to enforce a right against the debtor—and you won, the debtor probably wouldn't pull out a checkbook and pay you on the spot. To make sure the debtor gets around to paying you, the law may impose this lien against the debtor's property. In some states, the lien arises automatically with the court's judgment in your favor, and applies to any of the debtor's property located in the county where the judgment is entered. In addition, the creditor can record the judgment in the title records of other counties, thereby creating liens against any property located there. Not all states provide for automatic liens within the county, however. In some, the debtor must always record the judgment in the title records to create a lien.

There's also an issue regarding how much of the debtor's property will get pulled into the judgment lien's coverage. In many states, judicial liens can be recorded only against real estate. California is one of the exceptions to this rule, allowing judgment liens to be recorded against business property and bank accounts as well. In most states, instead of being given a lien against nonreal property, you must ask the sheriff or other designated government official to go ahead and levy on (sell) it.

B. Making Sure You've Advised the World About Your Lien ("Perfected" It)

You'll need to figure out if and when your lien was "perfected"—so let's start by reviewing what perfection means outside the bankruptcy context. As soon as the debtor gives you a lien or security interest in her property, you obtain certain conditional rights to sell it. However, in order for you to sell the property, it has to be in the debtor's possession. But what if the debtor has sold the property to an unsuspecting stranger? Then things get a little more complicated. The stranger certainly won't be happy if you try to repossess the property—but you can, if you've "perfected" your lien, do just that.

Perfection is a legal method by which creditors can put the world on notice that they have a right to property within the debtor's possession. It usually involves recording notice of the lien in some public place, so that purchasers of the property would naturally find out about the lien in the course of their transaction with the debtor.

> **EXAMPLE:** Wolfgang sees a car in Debbie the debtor's driveway. As the months go by, he notices Debbie wash, maintain, and drive the car. Wolfgang believes the car belongs to Debbie—and it does, but subject to the bank's lien. When Debbie puts a "For Sale" sign on the car, Wolfgang offers to buy it, knowing what great care she has lavished upon it. However, the bank has recorded its lien on the car's title. When it's time to complete the paperwork, Wolfgang sees the lien and backs out of the sale, since Debbie can't supply a clean title.

1. Perfecting Your Lien Prior to the Bankruptcy Filing

Assuming the bankruptcy hasn't yet been filed, the exact procedure you must follow to perfect a lien depends on the law of your state. It also depends on the nature of the collateral. With motor vehicles as well as mobile homes, liens are perfected by filing a form with, and paying a fee to, a designated state official. With

real estate, liens are usually perfected by recording the lien with the county recorder, registry of deeds, or similar public institution. With household items and other types of property, perfection usually requires filing a financing statement with the appropriate government office.

With this understanding, realize that whether and when you perfected your lien becomes doubly important when the debtor files for bankruptcy. If you have a lien but don't perfect it, you will not only lose your right to assert your claim against someone who buys the collateral from the debtor, you'll also lose any advantage you had by acquiring your lien earlier than another creditor. The lien that is perfected first will be paid first, the one perfected second will be paid second, and so on. That means that if the debtor goes bankrupt and the collateral is worth less than the total liens against it, some creditors will go unpaid.

2. Perfecting Your Lien After the Bankruptcy Filing

Normally, the automatic stay prevents you from acquiring an interest in the debtor's property after the bankruptcy filing. But what if the debtor's obligation to you was created before the bankruptcy filing, but your lien will be perfected only after the filing? Under the general bankruptcy rules, your lien would be void—meaning that debtors would be able to use bankruptcy to interrupt the perfection process. To combat this problem, however, state and federal laws have created a convenient legal fiction, treating some liens as having been perfected when the obligation was created. Though some actions may still need to be taken after the bankruptcy filing to truly complete the perfection process, these actions won't violate the automatic stay, since they are treated as if they took place when the lien was created.

The act of perfecting a lien won't violate the automatic stay in the following circumstances, in which the perfection act legally relates back to a prepetition event:

- **The lien secures the debtor's promise to repay a loan made for the purpose of purchasing property, and the lien was perfected within 20 days after the debtor took possession of the property.** In this case, the act of perfection relates back to when the debtor acquired the property.

- **The lien secures the debtor's promise to repay a debt, and was perfected within ten days after the lien was granted.** In this case, the act of perfection relates back to when the lien was granted.

- **The lien was created under a state or federal law that treats the perfection act as relating back to a prior act.** Take the case of a debtor who files for bankruptcy after his property was sold at foreclosure. The deed recording the involuntary transfer might not be filed until after the bankruptcy petition has already been filed. This act of perfecting the transfer doesn't violate the stay if state law treats the filing of the deed as having occurred when the property was sold.

Consult with your attorney before you take any action to create or perfect a lien if you know the debtor has filed for bankruptcy. You want to be entirely sure that your actions do not violate the stay.

C. What Your Collateral Is Worth

Once bankruptcy proceedings begin, many things that seemed like fixed business realities begin to shift. The value of your collateral—that is, the property securing your lien—is no exception. Its value will be estimated differently depending on when and why the estimate is being made.

If the collateral is being valued so as to calculate your secured claim for purposes of confirming a reorganization plan, the valuation will be made on the date the confirmation hearing is held. The value will be set at the amount it would cost the debtor to replace the collateral at that time.

EXAMPLE: Chrissy owns an antique shop. She sells Debbie a grandfather's clock for $2,000. Debbie pays $200, and agrees to pay $100 per month for the next 18 months. However, before completing her payments, Debbie files for Chapter 13 relief. Debbie can't bear to part with the clock, so she'll have to pay Chrissy the lesser of what the clock is worth or the unpaid balance of her debt, with interest. In order to determine what the clock is worth, it must be valued as of when Debbie's plan is considered for confirmation.

If the collateral is being valued so that the debtor can avoid (wipe out) your lien in a bankruptcy case, it will be assessed at its current value. (We'll discuss avoiding liens in Section H, below, but for now you should know that the Bankruptcy Code allows judicial liens to be removed when they reduce the amount of exempt equity a debtor would have if the liens were not there. Other liens can be treated as if they don't exist if the debtor has no equity in the property to which the lien can attach.) The court will determine what it would cost the debtor to replace the collateral on the day it considers the debtor's request.

EXAMPLE: Clarice sued Derek for not repaying the $1,000 she loaned to him. Clarice won the case, received a judgment in her favor, and recorded the judgment in the county courthouse. By recording the judgment she created a lien against Derek's home. Derek owes $100,000 on his mortgage, and in the state where he lives, he can claim a $50,000 homestead exemption. Derek can eliminate Clarice's judicial lien if his home is worth $150,000 or less but more than $100,000, because Clarice's lien reduces his exempt equity. If Derek's home is worth $150,001 to $150,999, then Clarice will retain her lien to the extent that Derek's home is worth more than $150,000. If Derek's home is worth $151,000 or more, then Clarice can keep her entire lien. If Derek's home is worth $100,000 or less, then some courts will also allow Clarice to keep her lien, because Derek has no equity in the property.

Then there's the situation where the collateral is being valued in order to determine the amount of the debtor's exemption in the collateral. In that situation, the valuation will be made as of the bankruptcy filing date. The value will be based on how much the debtor could get for the property from a willing buyer.

EXAMPLE: Dulcea files for bankruptcy under Chapter 7. She states that her house is worth $180,000. Dulcea owes $100,000 on the first mortgage and there's a $10,000 judicial lien recorded against the property. Her state's homestead exemption (see Chapter 6) is $100,000, so she believes that her equity in the property ($70,000) is fully exempt.

The Chapter 7 trustee keeps a sharp eye on the real estate market, and knows that real estate prices have been climbing dramatically. The trustee hires an appraiser, who confirms the trustee's instincts: The appraiser says the property is currently worth $220,000, and was worth $190,000 when Dulcea filed. That would raise Dulcea's equity to $110,000 now and $80,000 at the time she filed. Nevertheless, because Dulcea's ability to claim an exemption is determined as of the day she filed for bankruptcy ($100,000), her equity in her home ($80,000) is fully exempt even though the home is worth more than she said it was at the time of filing.

Dulcea also wants to avoid the $10,000 judicial lien, since it reduces the amount of her exempt equity. With the judicial lien, her exempt equity is reduced from $80,000 to $70,000. But when it comes to avoiding liens, remember that the court must determine the property's value on the date it considers Dulcea's request. Since her property is worth $220,000, she has more equity than she can claim as exempt. So Dulcea can't avoid the judicial lien, because it doesn't diminish her available exemption.

D. How Secured Creditors' Rights Are Affected by the Debtor's Choice of Chapter

Some debtors have a choice of which bankruptcy chapter they file under. This choice will affect what actions you, as a creditor, can or must take to protect your right to repayment. We'll discuss what happens if the debtor chooses Chapter 7 in Subsection 1, and what happens if the debtor chooses a reorganization chapter in Subsection 2.

1. When the Debtor Chooses Chapter 7

If the debtor files for Chapter 7 relief, you can choose to sit back and do nothing until after the debtor receives a discharge—at which time you will hopefully be able to sell your collateral. However, this approach means giving up on any chance to protect your claim from discharge. Also, it's a sensible strategy only if the collateral is of sufficient value to make it worth pursuing.

Even if you choose not to file and defend a proof of claim, don't ignore the bankruptcy. Make sure that:

- the bankruptcy schedules list your claim as "secured"
- your claim and the collateral are properly valued, and
- any exemption the debtor claims in the collateral is lawful.

Another feature of Chapter 7 bankruptcies is that the debtor can bring an action to avoid your lien at any time—even after the bankruptcy is over. That means the debtor can wait for months before asking the court to avoid your lien for any reason. That delay may prevent you from raising all the defenses available to you. For example, the debtor could ask the court to avoid your lien, because it impairs his exemption, even after the deadline has passed for you to challenge the validity of that exemption.

If your lien survives any efforts to avoid it, either during or after the bankruptcy, you can obtain your collateral or have your claim paid in any one of the following ways:

- You may have the automatic stay lifted so that you can proceed with reaffirmation or foreclosure.
- The trustee may sell the property to get at nonexempt equity in the property. In this event you'll get paid in the same manner as if the debtor had sold the property outside of bankruptcy.
- The trustee may abandon the property. This action rarely happens in routine consumer Chapter 7 cases because of their short duration. However, it may happen in protracted business cases, which means the collateral will no longer be property of the bankruptcy estate and you need not worry about the automatic stay.

- The debtor may redeem the property (discussed in Section F).
- The debtor may reaffirm the debt (discussed in Section G).

2. When the Debtor Chooses Chapter 11, 12, or 13

In each of the reorganization chapters—Chapters 11, 12, and 13—payments to creditors are governed by the terms of the confirmed plan. That means that your primary concerns as a creditor include how much input you'll have into the plan, how much interest the debtor's payments will include, how long the plan will last, and how your collateral will be handled along the way.

In a Chapter 11 bankruptcy, creditors will be given the opportunity to vote on the proposed plan. If you vote against a plan, the court may still confirm it—but only if the plan provides for payment of your secured claim. This means you would receive either a lump sum payment at the start of the plan consisting of the amount of your secured claim, or installment payments that include interest. (Most creditors would prefer—and vote for—a plan that surrenders their collateral instead of allowing the debtor to keep it by paying the secured claim. This is especially true if the creditor is undersecured.)

Creditors aren't allowed to vote for approval of Chapters 12, and 13 plans, but they may object to their confirmation. It's important to voice your objections, if any, because if you object to the plan, the court may only confirm it if your secured claim will be fully paid. Payment can be made either in a lump sum at the beginning, in installments with interest during the plan, or according to the schedule originally set in the loan agreement (but only if the last payment on the original loan is due after the last plan payment and any prepetition arrearage on the loan is full paid through the plan).

Setting the Interest Rate

The rate of interest paid to secured creditors is generally not the contract rate, because the contract rate normally includes profit on the loan. The purpose of paying interest in a bankruptcy case is to make sure you get the current value of your claim when it is paid over time. Courts try to create an interest rate that preserves the value of your claim and compensates you for the risk of non-payment. Rather than litigate the appropriate interest rate in every case, many courts have adopted, either by rule or by practice, a set rate of interest. Typically this is an easily determined rate, like the U.S. Treasury bill rate, plus a few points as a risk factor.

Chapters 12 and 13 plans present another concern for secured creditors because of the length of the plans. Sometimes debtors with confirmed plans calling for them to keep the collateral while paying the secured claim through the plan will come back to court asking to modify the plan to surrender the collateral or to replace it. Most courts will refuse such requests if they involve treating the unpaid balance of a secured claim as an unsecured claim. There's nothing to stop the debtor from giving you the collateral and subtracting the collateral's value from your secured claim. But the balance of your secured claim must be paid in full, with interest, according to the confirmed plan. The Bankruptcy Code does not allow plan modifications that alter the status of claims. (See 11 U.S.C. § 1329.)

EXAMPLE: U.S. CreditBank's claim is secured by Dominic the debtor's delivery truck. When Dominic's plan was confirmed, the truck was worth $10,000, so the creditor's claim was worth $10,000. One year into the plan, Dominic wants out of the delivery business. He asks the court to modify his plan in order to surrender the truck and deal with the balance of the claim in his Chapter 13 plan. Most courts will not allow this modification. Yes, the debtor can surrender the truck. No, the debtor can't say the balance of the claim should be treated like an unsecured claim.

If an important item of collateral, such as a car or truck, is worn out and needs to be replaced, the court will probably allow the debtor to swap it for a new one. The court will try to ensure that the replacement is truly necessary and that your claim is protected.

EXAMPLE: Donita's car is already several years old when she files for bankruptcy. Three years down the road, she still has two years to go on her plan and the car has stopped running. Charlie has a lien on her car. If Donita gets a new car, she must either pay off Charlie's secured claim or give him a lien in the new car to the extent of the secured claim.

What if the collateral is destroyed after the plan is confirmed, but before payments are completed? In that case, you are entitled to the insurance proceeds to the extent of the unpaid portion of your secured claim. If the proceeds exceed the value of your claim, the balance is paid into the bankruptcy estate for the benefit of all unsecured creditors (to the extent the debtor can't claim the money as exempt). So, if the unpaid balance of your secured claim is $2,000 and the insurance company pays you $3,000, then you keep $2,000 and turn $1,000 over to the trustee.

E. Finding Ways Around the Automatic Stay

The automatic stay protects not only the debtor, but the collateral as well. You are prohibited from taking any action against the collateral after the debtor files for bankruptcy without first receiving the bankruptcy court's permission. The automatic stay also prevents you from taking any action to create or perfect a lien after the debtor has filed for bankruptcy. However, there are some ways to get around these rules and foreclose on your property, including:

- asking the court to lift the stay (Subsection 1), or
- if you had a foreclosure sale pending, postponing rather than canceling it (Subsection 2).

1. Requesting Stay Relief to Allow Repossession or Foreclosure

The court may grant you relief from the automatic stay if you can show that repossession or foreclosure is justified. (See Chapter 4 on the procedures for this.) For example, you're likely to succeed at getting stay relief if the debtor has:

- failed to make payments on your claim (Subsection a)
- failed to perform a stated intention (Subsection b)

- failed to promptly confirm a reorganization plan (Subsection c), or
- shown a pattern of bad faith bankruptcy filings (Subsection d).

a. The Debtor's Failure to Make Payments

If the debtor has stopped making scheduled payments on your claim, the court may grant your request for stay relief. A debtor's failure to make payments after filing for bankruptcy is the most common reason why creditors seek stay relief. Sometimes the debtor stops paying because of confusion about the obligation to maintain payments. But usually it's an indication that the debtor can't maintain the payments even with the help of the bankruptcy.

b. The Debtor's Failure to Perform a Stated Intention

If the debtor files for Chapter 7 protection and your claim is for a consumer obligation, then, as you'll remember, the debtor must have filed a Statement of Intention with the court. (See Chapter 5, Section B2.) The Statement of Intention will tell you whether the debtor intends to surrender or keep your collateral and, if the debtor intends to keep it, how she intends to pay your secured claim.

The debtor has 45 days from when the Statement of Intention is filed to perform the stated intention. If the debtor fails to do so, most courts will lift the stay to allow you to proceed against the collateral. It doesn't matter what the debtor's stated intention was. Most courts find that the only appropriate way to punish the debtor for not doing what was promised in the Statement of Intention is to remove the collateral from the stay's protection.

c. The Debtor's Failure to Promptly Confirm a Reorganization Plan

If the debtor filed under Chapter 11, 12 or 13 but hasn't made a legitimate effort to confirm a reorganization plan, it's worth asking the court to lift the stay. Your first opportunity to ask for stay relief is when the debtor misses the deadline for filing the plan. (Chapter 13 plans must be filed within 15 days of the bankruptcy filing and Chapter 12 plans must be filed within 90 days. There is no deadline for filing Chapter 11 plans.) After that, repeated failures to propose a plan that can be confirmed, especially if it appears the debtor isn't making a good faith effort to get a plan together, would be a basis not only for stay relief but to have the debtor's case dismissed.

It's possible that the debtor filed for bankruptcy simply to stop your foreclosure, and isn't really interested in seeing the bankruptcy through. He'll drag the process out until something or someone brings it to a stop. By demanding stay relief to resume the foreclosure, you can thwart the debtor's unstated goal.

Don't let the fact that the debtor is making payments to the Chapter 13 trustee fool you into believing that he is sincere in his reorganization effort. You can't get any money from the debtor's plan until the court confirms it. If the case is dismissed without being confirmed, the money paid into the plan is returned to the debtor even if the debtor converts to Chapter 7. Let's say the debtor filed simply to stop your foreclosure. He'll stick with Chapter 13 until something or someone forces him out. The most likely force will be you. You'll demand stay relief to resume the foreclosure. Once you receive stay relief, the debtor will dismiss the bankruptcy because the stay—not the discharge—was all the debtor wanted.

d. The Debtor's History of Bad Faith Filings

If the debtor filed for bankruptcy for the sole purpose of preventing you from getting control of the collateral, you have a separate reason for asking the court to lift the stay. If the debtor is a serial filer, you should not only ask for stay relief but also ask the court to grant you prospective stay relief. Prospective relief says that even if the debtor files another bankruptcy, that new bankruptcy will have no effect on your ability to repossess or foreclose.

2. Postponing, Rather than Canceling a Foreclosure Sale

If the debtor filed for bankruptcy on the eve of a foreclosure sale, most courts say you may arrange to have the sale postponed without asking for stay relief. The purpose of the automatic stay is to preserve the status of the parties as it was when the petition was filed. If you had a foreclosure sale pending when the petition was filed, it's normally okay for you to keep it pending and avoid duplicative foreclosure costs. Once the stay is lifted you may proceed with the foreclosure as rescheduled.

Though this practice of postponing foreclosures is generally accepted, there's too much at risk not to double check the matter. Ask an attorney for the final word on what the courts in your state say.

F. How the Debtor May Redeem the Collateral

Chapter 7 consumer debtors have the right to redeem (reclaim) collateral that's their personal property (say, furniture or appliances), by paying the secured creditor the collateral's value. They can do this either as a forced redemption or by agreement with you, the creditor.

The Bankruptcy Code contemplates that debtors will choose to carry out a forced redemption. This involves the debtor making a lump sum payment to you in an amount equal to the collateral's value. You are forced to accept the cash value of your collateral in lieu of keeping your lien. Forced redemption is beneficial to the debtor, because he gets rid of your lien without necessarily paying the full amount owed on your claim.

However, redemption by agreement is also an option. It's a tradition that has grown between creditors and debtors. The Bankruptcy Code doesn't even cover this topic, and provides no guidance at all on what you and the debtor need to do to create a valid redemption agreement. That means that redemption agreements need not be filed with the court. Nor do they need court approval to be effective. To draft a contractually effective redemption agreement, however, the agreement must:

- identify the collateral being redeemed
- value the collateral

- specify the amount the debtor is going to pay and the terms of payment
- clearly state that the agreement is not a reaffirmation of the underlying debt
- clearly state that the creditor retains the right to foreclose on the collateral in the event the debtor defaults on the payments called for in the agreement
- acknowledge that the debtor is not required to redeem the collateral but has chosen to do so voluntarily, and
- be signed and dated by the debtor and the creditor.

A redemption agreement can be created at any time. After the debtor receives a bankruptcy discharge, if the debtor wishes to keep the property, you may agree to accept money instead of the collateral. The payment must be based on the collateral's value and not on the amount of the discharged debt. Many creditors make the mistake of filing a small claims action against the debtor and asking the court for the collateral's value instead of the collateral. Value means money and a money judgment violates the discharge injunction. You want the collateral—that is the refrigerator, the television, or whatever.

If the debtor wishes to redeem the collateral, but you can't agree on its value, either side may ask the court to value it for the purpose of redemption (whether it's a forced redemption or for purposes of a redemption agreement). The collateral would be valued as of the hearing date, probably at its replacement value. However, some courts have instead valued property at the amount it could be sold for at foreclosure.

Returning Collateral Repossessed Before Bankruptcy Was Filed

If the debtor files for bankruptcy after you have repossessed the collateral but while the debtor still has a chance to redeem it under state law, then you may be forced to return it to the debtor. Whether you must do so depends on how the bankruptcy court interprets your state's law. If the repossession ended all the debtor's interest in the collateral, then you may keep it. But if the debtor still has an interest in the collateral, it must be returned.

If you must return the collateral, you may condition return on the debtor having insurance to protect your interest. You may also (in the case of a car) demand proof that the debtor is a licensed driver. But if you're going to do more than that, like ask for adequate protection payments, then go to court. Using the self-help remedy of holding onto the collateral until you get what you want can result in a violation of the automatic stay.

G. How the Debtor May Reaffirm the Debt

Chapter 7 debtors have the right to reaffirm debts, meaning that they voluntarily agree to pay some or all of what they owe. Other than as an act of conscience, there are some practical reasons that debtors might agree to do this. For example, it may be in exchange for the creditor's promise to extend credit to the debtor after the bankruptcy. Or, the debtor may want to protect his co-signer from the creditor's collection efforts. But most commonly, it is so the debtor can keep your collateral without redeeming it or honoring the original contract. While the Bankruptcy Code doesn't tell us how to handle redemption agreements (discussed above), it provides very explicit rules on how to handle reaffirmation agreements. (See 11 U.S.C. § 524(c).) Your concerns if the debtor wishes to reaffirm the debt would include:

- ensuring that your reaffirmation agreement will hold up in court (Subsection 1)
- understanding what would happen if you failed to file the reaffirmation agreement (Subsection 2), and
- knowing when you don't need a reaffirmation agreement, because your state allows the debtor to make payments voluntarily (Subsection 3).

1. Requirements for a Valid Reaffirmation Agreement

The reaffirmation process is usually started by the creditor, who presents the debtor with a proposed reaffirmation agreement. To be valid, a reaffirmation agreement must:

- be in writing
- clearly and conspicuously tell the debtor that she may rescind the agreement at any time before she receives a discharge or 60 days after the agreement is filed, whichever occurs later
- clearly and conspicuously tell the debtor that the reaffirmation of the debt is not required by the Bankruptcy Code or under any other law
- be made before the debtor's discharge order is entered (courts will not withdraw the discharge order for the purpose of allowing a debtor to sign a reaffirmation agreement before the order is entered), and
- be filed with the court by the debtor.

In some courts, the reaffirmation agreement form is established by local rules. In that situation, either side can simply fill in the form. See, for example, the form used by the bankruptcy court in New Mexico, available online at www.nmcourt.fed.us/web/BCDOCS/Files/b240.pdf.

If the debtor is represented by an attorney, the attorney must submit an affidavit stating that the debtor fully understood the meaning of the reaffirmation agreement and signed it voluntarily. The attorney must also verify that the agreement does not impose an undue hardship on the debtor. Lastly, the attorney must confirm that she fully advised the debtor of the legal consequences of signing the reaffirmation agreement.

If the debtor is not represented by an attorney, the court must determine for itself whether the agreement imposes an undue hardship on the debtor and whether the agreement is in the debtor's best interests. When the subject of the agreement is a secured debt and the agreement allows the debtor to keep the collateral, most courts will okay the agreement if the debtor can afford the payments and needs the collateral to get a fresh start. Reaffirmation agreements for car loans are frequently approved. Reaffirmation agreements for big screen televisions don't fare as well.

⚠ Don't expect the court to rubber stamp the agreement just because the debtor has an attorney. Reaffirmation agreements have received a lot of scrutiny in recent years, mainly because several national creditors played fast and loose with the rules for making valid agreements. As a result, many bankruptcy courts are fully reviewing reaffirmation agreements even when they contain an affidavit from the debtor's attorney. To avoid such scrutiny, it's best if your agreement puts off your collection of payments until after the debtor receives a discharge.

Does Your State Allow Debtors to Make Voluntary Payments to Keep Secured Property?

If your state (or district) is not listed below, your bankruptcy court has not yet ruled on whether or not debtors can keep secured property by simply staying current on their payments.

State or District	Yes	No	Case
Alabama		✔	*Taylor v. AGE Federal Credit Union*, 3 F.3d 1512 (11th Cir. 1993)
Alaska	✔		*In re Parker*, 139 F.3d 668 (9th Cir. 1998)
Arizona	✔		*In re Parker*, 139 F.3d 668 (9th Cir. 1998)
Arkansas (Eastern District)		✔	*In re Kennedy*, 137 B.R. 302 (E.D. Ark, 1992)
Arkansas (Western District)	✔		*In re Parker*, 142 B.R. 327 (W.D. Ark. 1992)
California	✔		*In re Parker*, 139 F.3d 668 (9th Cir. 1998)
Colorado	✔		*Lowery Federal Credit Union v. West*, 882 F.2d 1543 (10th Cir. 1989)
Connecticut	✔		*In re Boodrow*, 126 F.3d 43 (2nd Cir. 1997)
Florida		✔	*Taylor v. AGE Federal Credit Union*, 3 F.3d 1512 (11th Cir. 1993)
Georgia		✔	*Taylor v. AGE Federal Credit Union*, 3 F.3d 1512 (11th Cir. 1993)
Hawaii	✔		*In re Parker*, 139 F.3d 668 (9th Cir. 1998)
Idaho	✔		*In re Parker*, 139 F.3d 668 (9th Cir. 1998)
Illinois		✔	*In re Edwards*, 901 F.2d 1383 (7th Cir. 1990)
Indiana		✔	*In re Edwards*, 901 F.2d 1383 (7th Cir. 1990)
Kansas	✔		*Lowery Federal Credit Union v. West*, 882 F.2d 1543 (10th Cir. 1989)
Louisiana		✔	*In re Johnson*, 89 F.3d 249 (5th Cir. 1996)
Maine		✔	*In re Burr*, 160 F.3d 843 (1st Cir. 1998)
Maryland	✔		*In re Belanger*, 962 F.2d 345 (4th Cir. 1992)
Massachusetts		✔	*In re Burr*, 160 F.3d 843 (1st Cir. 1998)
Michigan (Western District)		✔	*In re Schmidt*, 145 B.R. 543 (W.D. Mich. 1992)
Mississippi		✔	*In re Johnson*, 89 F.3d 249 (5th Cir. 1996)
Missouri (Western District)		✔	*In re Gerling*, 175 B.R. 295 (W.D. Mo. 1994)
Montana	✔		*In re Parker*, 139 F.3d 668 (9th Cir. 1998)

Does Your State Allow Debtors to Make Voluntary Payments to Keep Secured Property? (continued)			
State or District	**Yes**	**No**	**Case**
Nevada	✔		*In re Parker*, 139 F.3d 668 (9th Cir. 1998)
New Hampshire		✔	*In re Burr*, 160 F.3d 843 (1st Cir. 1998)
New Mexico	✔		*Lowery Federal Credit Union v. West*, 882 F.2d 1543 (10th Cir. 1989)
New York	✔		*In re Boodrow*, 126 F.3d 43 (2nd Cir. 1997)
North Carolina	✔		*In re Belanger*, 962 F.2d 345 (4th Cir. 1992)
Ohio (Northern District)	✔		*In re Laubacher*, 150 B.R. 200 (N.D. Ohio 1992)
Ohio (Southern District)		✔	*In re Lock*, 243 B.R. 332 (S.D. Ohio 1999)
Oklahoma	✔		*Lowery Federal Credit Union v. West*, 882 F.2d 1543 (10th Cir. 1989)
Oregon	✔		*In re Parker*, 139 F.3d 668 (9th Cir. 1998)
Pennsylvania (Eastern District)	✔		*In re McNeil*, 128 B.R. 603 (E.D. Penn. 1991)
Pennsylvania (Western District)	✔		*In re Stefano*, 134 B.R. 824 (W.D. Penn. 1991)
Rhode Island		✔	*In re Burr*, 160 F.3d 843 (1st Cir. 1998)
South Carolina	✔		*In re Belanger*, 962 F.2d 345 (4th Cir. 1992)
Tennessee (Eastern District)		✔	*In re Whitaker*, 85 B.R. 788 (E.D. Tenn. 1988)
Tennessee (Western District)	✔		*In re Barriger*, 61 B.R. 506 (W.D. Tenn. 1986)
Texas		✔	*In re Johnson*, 89 F.3d 249 (5th Cir. 1996)
Utah	✔		*Lowery Federal Credit Union v. West*, 882 F.2d 1543 (10th Cir. 1989)
Vermont	✔		*In re Boodrow*, 126 F.3d 43 (2nd Cir. 1997)
Virginia	✔		*In re Belanger*, 962 F.2d 345 (4th Cir. 1992)
Washington	✔		*In re Parker*, 139 F.3d 668 (9th Cir. 1998)
West Virginia	✔		*In re Belanger*, 962 F.2d 345 (4th Cir. 1992)
Wisconsin		✔	*In re Edwards*, 901 F.2d 1383 (7th Cir. 1990)
Wyoming	✔		*Lowery Federal Credit Union v. West*, 882 F.2d 1543 (10th Cir. 1989)

Source: *How to File for Chapter 7 Bankruptcy*, by Stephen Elias, Albin Renauer, Robin Leonard and Kathleen Michon (Nolo).

2. The Consequences of Failing to File Your Reaffirmation Agreement

Despite the voluntary nature of a reaffirmation agreement, they really do need to be filed with the court. A few years ago, major national creditors got into big trouble with bankruptcy courts by treating unfiled reaffirmation agreements as legitimate claims that could be collected after bankruptcy. Sears, Federated Department Stores (Macy's, Bloomingdale's, and others), Circuit City, May Department Stores (Lord & Taylor, Strawbridge's, and others), and General Electric Capital Corp. (Montgomery Ward) were among the first creditors to be hit with lawsuits by debtors who said they were being forced to pay discharged debts. These lawsuits eventually resulted in millions of dollars of damage payments.

The problem was, whether through ignorance or neglect, these creditors acted as if their reaffirmation agreements were valid even though they didn't comply with the Code's requirement that such agreements be filed with the court. And the problem wasn't limited to these high-profile creditors. Studies at the time showed that the filing and some other rules regarding reaffirmation agreements were routinely disregarded.

The lesson to be learned is that before you try to enforce a reaffirmation agreement, you should be sure it meets all the legal requirements—again, that it contains the required information, was signed by the debtor, and filed with the court.

3. When You Can Collect Voluntary Payments

Some courts allow the debtor to retain the collateral and continue making payments despite the absence of a reaffirmation agreement. (For a list of these states, see the chart below, "Does Your State Allow Debtors to Make Voluntary Payments to Keep Secured Property?") If you are in a state where this is allowed, and your debtor has chosen this course, (which you'll find out from the Statement of Intention) you may send advisory bills to the debtor without violating the automatic stay or the discharge injunction. These statements must, however, clearly state that they are not an attempt to collect the debt but are merely being sent as a courtesy to the debtor to advise him of the status of his voluntary payments. If the debtor fails to make payments, you may foreclose on your collateral.

For example, General Motors Acceptance Corp. sends statements to debtors making voluntary payments that look just like the billing statements they received prior to filing for bankruptcy—with two important exceptions. First, the statement bears the legend: "Transaction Summary of Voluntary Payments." Second, the statements include this warning: "Voluntary payments must be timely received by GMAC if you wish to retain possession of your vehicle."

The only court to review these statements found them to be fair and beneficial to debtors.

H. How Liens Can Be Eliminated During Bankruptcy

Your claim against the debtor's property—that is, your lien—will survive the bankruptcy unless the trustee or the debtor convinces the court that it should be reduced or eliminated. But bankruptcy provides several ways for a trustee or debtor to reduce or eliminate a lien. How and whether one of them will be able to do this depends on:

- whether the creditor has taken appropriate steps to perfect the lien (Subsection 1)
- the value of the property serving as collateral (Subsection 2)
- whether the property serving as collateral is exempt (Subsections 3 and 4), and
- the way in which the lien arose (Subsections 5 and 6).

1. The Trustee Can Avoid Unperfected Liens

After the debtor files for bankruptcy, the law gives an interesting status to the bankruptcy trustee—she'll be treated as if she had acquired a lien on all property owned by the debtor on the filing date. If your lien on the debtor's property was not perfected before the filing, the trustee may avoid it—that is, eliminate it entirely. For most creditors who hold secured claims in real estate, this will not be a problem, because of the almost universal practice of recording deeds (that is, perfecting the security interest) the instant they are executed by the old owner.

2. Your Lien May Be Reduced to the Value of the Collateral

Having a lien against the debtor's property doesn't mean your entire claim is secured by the lien. Your claim is secured only up to the amount you would be paid if the collateral were sold. So, if the debtor owes you $10,000 but the collateral is worth only $5,000, your secured claim is also worth only $5,000. The other $5,000 the debtor owes you is considered an unsecured claim. Claims that are worth more than the collateral are typically referred to as undersecured claims.

The fate of undersecured claims in bankruptcy depends on the nature of the collateral and the type of bankruptcy involved—see the appropriate section be-low, discussing cases where:

- the debtor filed under Chapter 7, and your claim arose in a consumer trans-action (Subsection a)
- the debtor filed under Chapter 7, and your claim did not arise in a con-sumer transaction, such as if you pro-vided inventory to the debtor's store on credit (Subsection b)
- the debtor filed under Chapter 11, 12 or 13, and your sole collateral is a home (Subsection c), and
- the debtor filed under Chapter 11, 12 or 13, and your lien is secured by some other form of collateral (Sub-section d).

a. Chapter 7 Consumer Transaction Liens

If the debtor filed under Chapter 7, he can either surrender the collateral to you or keep it. You'll find out what the debtor chooses to do by reading the debtor's Statement of Intention (discussed in Chapter 5). If the debtor surrenders the collateral to you, any balance left on the underlying debt after selling the collateral will be treated as an unsecured claim.

If, however, the debtor keeps the col-lateral, he again has two choices, if your collateral is personal property that the debtor uses for family, household, or per-sonal purposes. The first is to force you

to release your lien by paying you what the collateral is worth (called "redeeming" the debt). He'd have to redeem within 75 days of filing for bankruptcy (unless the court allows a longer time). The debtor's second choice is to "reaffirm" the debt (that is, agree to remain liable on the original contract after the bankruptcy).

Instead of the debtor specifically reaf-firming the debt, some courts allow debt-ors who are fully compliant with the terms of the security agreement to keep their collateral without reaffirming the un-derlying claim. The condition is that they continue to abide by the agreement's terms. That means they must make the monthly payments on time and they must obey all the other conditions of the loan, such as maintaining insurance on the col-lateral. (See Section F for more about re-demption and Section G for more about reaffirmation and the "maintain and re-tain" option.)

If the debtor wishes to keep real prop-erty that is collateral for your loan, the debtor must reaffirm the debt unless the court allows the debtor to keep the prop-erty by staying current on the original contract terms. Consumer debtors may not redeem real estate.

Regardless of the debtor's wishes, the trustee may elect to abandon the estate's interest in the collateral if it won't gener-ate enough money to pay unsecured creditor's claims. Many items owned by consumer debtors are worth too little to make them worth the trustee's time to administer. Also, any item that is fully encumbered by liens won't generate any money to pay unsecured creditors' claims.

Even if one lien is avoided, the remaining liens may equal or exceed the property's value, or the debtor may be able to claim any exposed equity as exempt. Either way, if the trustee sold the property, none of the proceeds would go to pay unsecured creditors' claims. In such a situation, the trustee would abandon the property without avoiding any of the liens. Once property is abandoned, it is removed from the bankruptcy estate and loses the protection of the automatic stay.

b. Chapter 7 Nonconsumer Transaction Liens

A slightly different set of rules applies if your claim against a Chapter 7 debtor did not arise in a consumer transaction—for example, if you provided inventory to the debtor's store on credit. The options of redeeming or reaffirming the debt are not normally available to nonconsumer debtors.

If the debtor keeps the property, you can ask the court to lift the automatic stay. That would either give you free access to recover your collateral or would force the debtor to bargain with you in good faith in order to keep the property.

Similar to consumer cases, the trustee may decide to abandon the debtor's property if selling it wouldn't clear enough money to make a significant payment to unsecured creditors.

EXAMPLE 1: Chic Clothesmakers, Inc. (CCI) has a lien against Damon's Duds' warehouse. The warehouse is worth $500,000 and CCI is owed $750,000. It costs the estate $1,000 per month to keep the warehouse open. The warehouse is empty, and there's no reason for the trustee to keep it. He abandons it to Damon's. (Most courts say the property must be abandoned to the debtor; however, the debtor will then either surrender it to the creditor or the creditor will immediately foreclose.)

EXAMPLE 2: Suppose the same facts as in the example above, but that the warehouse is filled with valuable inventory. In that case, even though the building itself is costing money, it is valuable to the estate because it is preserving other assets. The trustee chooses not to abandon the warehouse. CCI is forced to seek stay relief in order to foreclose on it. Whether CCI's action will be successful depends on whether its interest in the property was adequately protected and whether Damon's was in default on their agreement

c. Chapter 11, 12, or 13 Liens Secured Only by Homes

Normally, debtors who file under one of the reorganization chapters (11, 12, or 13) can modify the rights you received when you loaned them money. For example, debtors can pay you less than you're owed, extend the repayment period, or change the interest rate.

However, if your only security interest is the debtor's principal residence, and the debtor filed under Chapter 11 or 13, you are excepted from this rule. The purpose of this exception is to protect the mortgage lending market from the effects of bankruptcies, though if you're a creditor who accepts residential liens, you may also benefit.

Your claim qualifies for this protection if it is secured solely by the debtor's home—that is, the place where the debtor lives. It is also necessary that the debtor's home not be used to generate income. You may not qualify for the protection if the debtor works out of his home, and you probably won't qualify if the debtor lives in one part of the structure and rents out other parts. Also, the home must be worth at least $1 more than the total of all liens that are senior to your lien. If there is nothing of value left for your lien to attach to—that is, your lien is totally "underwater"—many courts allow the debtor to treat your claim as unsecured and to ask the court to avoid

the lien in its entirety. (However, a significant minority of courts do not allow debtors to modify residential mortgages even if they are completely unsecured. This minority position has not been adopted by any of the federal circuit courts of appeal.)

Let's consider some possible scenarios in which you might find yourself:

- You hold a second mortgage against the debtor's home and it is the only collateral for your loan. The debtor's home is worth $100,000 and the debtor owes $90,000 on the first mortgage—in other words, the debtor has $10,000 of equity in the property. Your right to receive the full amount of your claim, regardless of whether you're owed $5,000 or $50,000, can't be modified, because there is equity in the property to which some or all of your lien can attach.

- You hold a second mortgage against the debtor's home and it is the only collateral for your loan. The debtor's home is worth only $90,000 and the debtor owes $100,000 on the first mortgage. Your claim will be treated as unsecured, because there is no equity in the property to which some or all of your lien can attach.

- You hold a second mortgage against the debtor's home as well as a lien against the debtor's car. The debtor's home is worth $100,000 and the debtor owes $90,000 on the first mortgage. Your claim is not protected from modification because it is not secured solely by the debtor's home. Your claim will be treated as a secured claim only to a maximum amount of $10,000, because that's all the equity available to secure your claim.

- You hold a second mortgage against a duplex that the debtor owns. The debtor lives in one unit and rents the other. The duplex is worth $100,000 and the debtor owes $90,000 on the first mortgage. Your claim is not protected from modification because the property serves as more than just the debtor's residence. Your claim will be treated as a secured claim only to a maximum amount of $10,000 because that's all the equity available to secure your claim.

There are two exceptions to the rule that debtors may not modify the rights of creditors whose claims are secured only by a lien on the debtor's principal residence. They are:

- Debtors may cure a default in the mortgage and resume regular monthly mortgage payments.
- Chapter 13 debtors may extend their residential mortgage payments if the last payment on the mortgage was due prior to the last payment on their plan. This exception enables Chapter 13 debtors to pay off a balloon payment in installments.

While it is not an exception, also note that the antimodification rule discussed in this section does not apply to Chapter 12 debtors.

d. Chapter 11, 12, or 13 Liens Secured by Other Forms of Collateral

Now let's look at a situation where your claim is secured by something other than the debtor's home—or by a combination of the debtor's home and some other type of property—and the debtor files under Chapter 11, 12, or 13. In such a case, the bankruptcy court may confirm a plan that splits your claim into a secured portion and an unsecured portion. This is known as bifurcating the claim.

The secured portion will be treated as a fully secured claim. That means it must be paid in full with interest during the plan. A plan that fully pays only the secured portion of the claim is known as a "strip-down" or a "cram-down" plan. Loans secured by automobiles are commonly bifurcated in reorganization cases, because there is almost always more money owed on the loan than the collateral is worth. If the debtor owes $10,000 on a car that's worth $6,000, the debtor's plan pays the $6,000 secured claim with interest through the plan and treats the $4,000 claim as unsecured debt.

A debtor proposing a strip-down plan will often ask not only that the court bifurcate your claim, but that it eliminate your lien to the extent it secures the unsecured portion of your claim. (See 11 U.S.C. § 506(d).) The debtor wants your lien to be considered fully paid when the secured portion of your claim is paid. You'd have good reason to object to the debtor's plan if it calls for you to lose any portion of your lien before the debtor receives his discharge. After all, no one will know until the discharge is finally entered whether the debtor will succeed in meeting all the conditions warranting discharge of the unsecured portion of your lien. In fact, the debtor could convert to Chapter 7 after paying off the secured claims, in order to discharge the unpaid and unsecured balance of your claim.

EXAMPLE: Cassie sells her old Volvo to her neighbor, Dick, who likes to tinker with cars. Cassie's car isn't in particularly bad shape when she sells it to Dick. In fact, it is easily worth the $8,000 he agrees to pay. Dick gives Cassie $800 down and agrees to pay the balance at $200 per month. Unfortunately, Dick does more harm than good to the Volvo. When he files for bankruptcy he still owes $5,000 to Cassie—but her Volvo is worth only $3,000.

Dick's plan calls for the $3,000 secured claim to be paid in full with interest over the first 24 months of a 36-month plan. The plan says the lien will be extinguished as soon as Cassie receives the final installment payment on the secured claim.

If Dick's plan is confirmed, the car will remain as collateral for the loan for at least 24 months, but not until the end of the debtor's plan. Dick could—and many Chapter 13 debtors do—convert the case to Chapter 7 after paying off the secured debt and having the lien eliminated. Dick would then discharge the unsecured claim and all the other unsecured claims without making any payments. In essence, Dick would accomplish through conversion from Chapter 13 to Chapter 7 what he couldn't do if he filed for Chapter 7 initially—redeeming the collateral through installment payments over two years.

To prevent a lien from being stripped down as in the above example, you'll need to object to any plan that does not tie lien avoidance to a Chapter 13 discharge. Your objection should state that you would suffer irreparable harm if your lien were voided prior to the debtor's receipt of a discharge. This harm is based on your potential loss of a valuable property right without the debtor fulfilling his end of the bargain (the successful completion of the Chapter 13 plan).

3. The Debtor May Avoid Your Judicial Lien if the Property Is Exempt

If you obtained a court judgment against the debtor and took the steps necessary to impose a lien against the debtor's property, you acquired a judicial lien. The Bankruptcy Code allows debtors to avoid judicial liens if they impair the debtor's fresh start by diminishing the value of property that's on the exemption list. (See Chapter 5 for a discussion of which property can be claimed as exempt.) For example, a judicial lien against the debtor's home can be eliminated if the debtor's exemption is worth less because of the lien's existence. (See the sidebar below, "Determining Whether a Lien Impairs the Debtor's Exemption," for instructions.)

EXAMPLE 1: Charlie holds a $5,000 judgment against Daphne's home. Daphne's home is worth $100,000 and is subject to $90,000 in consensual liens. Daphne has a right to a $15,000 homestead exemption. Charlie's lien can therefore be avoided in full, since $100,000 minus $90,000 equals $10,000, which is less than the $15,000 exemption. If Charlie's lien were added to the $90,000 of consensual liens, then Daphne's exempt equity would drop to $5,000.

EXAMPLE 2: Let's alter the facts above, and assume that Daphne's house is subject to $82,000 in consensual liens and she has a $15,000 homestead exemption. In this case, Charlie's lien can be partially avoided, since $100,000 minus $82,000 equals $18,000, which is $3,000 more than the available homestead exemption. So Daphne's exempt equity would be $15,000 without considering Charlie's lien. If Charlie's lien were added to the $82,000, Daphne's exempt equity would drop to $13,000. Consequently, Charlie's lien can be reduced by $2,000.

EXAMPLE 3: If Daphne's house is subject to $75,000 in consensual liens and she has a $15,000 homestead exemption, then Charlie's lien cannot be avoided. This is because $100,000 minus $75,000 equals $25,000, which is $10,000 more than the available homestead exemption. So Daphne's exempt equity would be $15,000 with or without Charlie's lien.

The fact that the debtor's exemption is impaired doesn't mean your lien is worthless. First, the avoidance of liens doesn't happen automatically. The debtor must ask the court to avoid the lien. The debtor should do so while the case is open, but may do so after the case is closed, by getting the court's permission to reopen the case. The longer the debtor waits, the less sympathetic the court will be.

Second, only certain liens can be avoided. For example, where the collateral is the debtor's home, only judicial liens can be avoided. If the debtor's equity is fully impaired with consensual liens, she can avoid paying these loans in full only by filing under Chapter 13.

Third, if multiple liens impair the debtor's exemption, the court will void the liens in the reverse order that they were created. That is, the most recent lien will be voided first.

There are two exceptions to the rule that allows reduction of your judicial lien. First, debtors cannot avoid judicial liens held by a spouse, former spouse, or child of the debtor that were created as part of a divorce proceeding, separation agreement, or other domestic court proceeding and that secure alimony, maintenance, or support payments. Second, debtors cannot avoid judicial liens arising out of mortgage foreclosure proceedings.

A clever debtor can, with some advance planning, use the judicial lien avoidance rules to his advantage, by encumbering his property with the specific purpose of reducing his equity. In fact, there's no rule saying that consensual liens need to come into existence or be recorded prior to the judicial lien in order for the judicial lien to be avoided. That's what would happen in the last example, where Daphne couldn't avoid the judicial

lien, if she took out a second mortgage for at least $10,000. However, it's unlikely that the debtor would be able to obtain such a loan. Even if she does, you are not without recourse against both the lender and the debtor, for the following reasons:

- An uninterested lender is not going to loan money to a debtor on the eve of bankruptcy and is certainly not going to accept as collateral property that is encumbered by a judicial lien—and potentially other liens as well. Remember that, under state law, the judicial lien is going to be superior to the lender's consensual lien. It's only through bankruptcy that the creditor may be able to move to a higher priority through the elimination of the judicial lien—and bankruptcy is not an option that any lender is likely to view favorably. So, this lender may not be legitimate and you may be able to challenge the lien, as illustrated in the next point.

- The most likely funding source available to the debtor will be a friend or a relative. Such a lien can be avoided, either as a fraudulent transfer if the debtor gave the lien without receiving adequate consideration in return, or as a preferential transfer if the lien was given as compensation for an existing debt.

- If the debtor engages in this type of planning prebankruptcy, you have reason to question whether the bankruptcy was filed in good faith.

Determining Whether a Lien Impairs the Debtor's Exemption

The debtor may have any judicial lien and certain consensual liens avoided if the collateral's value is less than the combination of:

- the amount of the lien in question
- all other liens against the collateral, and
- the amount of the debtor's exemption.

In this manner, the Bankruptcy Code preserves the debtor's exemptions, by shielding them from these liens.

Let's assume the collateral is the debtor's home, which is worth $100,000, and the debtor is entitled to a $15,000 homestead exemption. Liens totaling as much as $85,000 would not impair the debtor's exemption, because that's how much equity the debtor has in the absence of any liens. If, however, the total value of the liens exceeded $85,000, the liens would impair the debtor's exemption. The reason is that if the property were sold and the liens paid in full, the debtor would receive less than the full amount of her exemption. The amount of the impairment is the amount by which the liens exceed $85,000.

Normally, challenges to exemptions must be made within 30 days after the first meeting of creditors. When debtors file lien avoidance actions more than 30 days after the meeting, some courts have applied this 30-day rule to prohibit creditors from challenging the legitimacy of a debtor's exemption when it is being asserted in a lien avoidance action. Other courts, however, have said that creditors may raise the issue in response to the debtor's lien avoidance action. Don't take any chances. If the debtor claims your collateral as exempt, you can bet there's a lien avoidance action coming. Be proactive and contest the exemption prior to the deadline. (See Chapter 5 for a full discussion of how to contest an exemption.)

Impairment Calculation	
A. Value of Collateral	**B. Value of Liens**
	Amount of your lien: $ _____
	+ amount of all other liens: $ _____
	+ amount of debtor's exemption: $ _____
A = $ _____	Total B = $ _____

Using the table above, if A is greater than B, the debtor can't complain of any impairment. If B is greater than A, however, then B minus A is the amount of the impairment.

4. The Debtor May Avoid Certain Liens on Exempt Household Goods

Next, let's consider a situation in which your claim is secured by certain household goods or personal possessions (listed below) that the debtor had before you loaned the money and still had when she filed for bankruptcy. In such a case, the debtor may avoid your lien to the extent it impairs her ability to exempt the property. (Again see the sidebar above, "Determining Whether a Lien Impairs the Debtor's Exemption.") As a practical matter, much of this property will be of little or no value and probably will be fully exempt. Therefore, you can bet that your lien won't survive the debtor's attempt to avoid it. But if by chance the debtor doesn't act, your lien will survive the bankruptcy.

The following items of property held for personal, family, or household use are subject to this rule. These come from 11 U.S.C. § 522(f)(1)(B). Note, however, that in order for the lien to be avoided, not only must the collateral be on the list within the federal code, but the debtor must also be able to claim it as exempt, which is determined by state law.

Household items, including:
- furniture
- goods (food, toiletries, and other sundries found in the debtor's home)
- clothing
- appliances
- books
- pets
- musical instruments
- jewelry, and
- professionally prescribed health aids.

Nonhousehold items, including:
- tools of the trade (instruments of manual operation that the debtor uses to create value or provide a service)
- professional books (manuals, reference works, and the like), and
- implements (small machines such as rototillers).

5. The Trustee, the Debtor or a Creditor May Avoid Liens That Are Preferential or Fraudulent

The court can avoid liens that were made preferentially or fraudulently, as elaborated on below. While you may benefit from this rule, by filing a complaint asking the court to avoid other creditors' liens, others may also use the same tactic against you. The trustee, the debtor, or, in some courts, another creditor could all file a similar complaint with the court. (Since the creation of a lien is considered a transfer, the discussion of defenses to preferential and fraudulent transfers in Chapter 15 applies to actions to avoid these liens.)

The adversary process that begins with the filing of a complaint can be complicated. You have a lot at stake, especially if the action has been filed against you. That's why we recommend that you hire an attorney to represent you in these proceedings. Also see Chapter 10 for details on the adversary process in bankruptcy, and Chapter 11 for information on how to respond to a complaint.

Look to the perfection date. The date that a lien is perfected governs whether the lien may be avoided under the rules for avoiding preferential and fraudulent transfers.

a.   Avoiding Preferential Liens

If a lien was created fewer than 90 days prior to the bankruptcy filing, and its purpose was to secure payment of an existing debt, the lien can be avoided as a preferential transfer if it improved the creditor's position. Your lien would fall into this category if your claim was unsecured and the collateral pledged had value that you could reach, so that you became better off after you received the lien than you were before.

> **EXAMPLE:** Dirk owes Candy $10,000. Dirk can't pay, so he gives Candy a lien against his garage in exchange for Candy's promise not to sue him.

Dirk files for bankruptcy a month later. This lien can be avoided as a preferential transfer because:

- Dirk was indebted to Candy before he gave her the lien,

- Dirk couldn't pay the debt to Candy, and

- Dirk filed for bankruptcy within 90 days of creating the lien (or within one year if Candy and Dirk had a close relationship).

This rule does not apply to liens that are created by law. So, a mechanic's lien that was created shortly before a bankruptcy filing can't be avoided even though it improved the mechanic's position relative to the bankruptcy.

Nor does this rule apply to certain purchase-money security interests (which, as you'll remember, are a type of lien that arise under state law when you sell the debtor property on credit). Because there's always a lag time between when the sale occurs and the minimum time by which the lien can be perfected (by recording it), the law gives creditors a break. Liens that are perfected within 20 days of the debtor taking possession of the collateral cannot be avoided if the loan enabled the debtor to purchase the collateral. This is what's known in the law as a legal fiction. Though the creation of the debt and the creation of the lien occur days apart, the law treats them as if they took place at the same time.

EXAMPLE: Chao-Yun sells a camera to Darla on credit. In order to protect his interest, Chao-Yun has Darla sign a security agreement, which he takes steps to record according to state law. As is inevitable, the recording process takes several days. Darla files for bankruptcy 15 days after picking up the camera, and the lien is perfected two days after that. Though Chao-Yun's security interest wasn't recorded before the bankruptcy, the law considers it to have been perfected on the day Darla got the camera—because Chao-Yun clearly has a purchase-money security interest in the camera, and because fewer than 20 days passed between Darla's taking possession of the camera and perfection of Chao-Yun's interest.

b. Avoiding Fraudulent Liens

Debtors have a couple of possible motives for granting liens without seeming to get much in return, or without any underlying debt, including to:
- hide the fact that they have valuable property by making the property appear to be collateral for a loan, or
- insulate debts owed to insiders from discharge.

Often these creditors are friends and family members. However, such liens may be avoided as fraudulent transfers, based on the fact that the debtor wasn't fairly compensated for the lien—in legalese, that there was inadequate consideration.

EXAMPLE: Delroy has $50,000 in equity in his home that he can't exempt. If he filed for bankruptcy right away, he would probably lose his home. So Delroy grants liens against the property to every friend and relative to whom he owes money. Although their claims will be discharged, the granting of the liens gives them a right against his property that Delroy intends to honor after bankruptcy. It also allows him to keep his house and keep peace in the family.

Delroy owes Carrie $300 for pet-sitting services. Carrie knows the family and recognizes several of their names when she reviews the list of creditors. She brings this fact to the trustee's attention, and the trustee files a complaint against Delroy to avoid the liens given to the relatives.

Not every lien granted to a friend or family member is fraudulent. In some cases, liens are granted in the amount of legitimate claims held by the debtor's friends and relatives. However, these liens can still be avoided as preferential, if the liens were created within one year prior to the bankruptcy filing. That's because they allowed these creditors to get more than they would have if the debtor had filed for bankruptcy instead of granting the liens.

Generally, preferential transfers are avoidable if they occurred within 90 days prior to the bankruptcy filing. However, a preferential transfer to an insider is avoidable if made within one year prepetition. So, if the relative is owed a legitimate debt but the creation of the lien improved the relative's chance of getting paid, then the lien is avoidable not as a fraudulent transfer, but as a preferential transfer.

What does all this mean to you? You're probably not the friend or relative of a generous debtor. (If you are, then be warned, the trustee is going to be looking to void your lien.) Most likely, you were on the sidelines when the liens were passed out. But your vigilance may still help the trustee identify which liens to ask the court to avoid.

6. A Statutory Lien Held by a Landlord Can Be Avoided

If you're a landlord whose bankrupt tenant has past rent due, you're in good shape if your lien against the debtor's property is based on your written agreement. A lease that creates a security interest is considered a consensual lien, and therefore cannot be avoided. However, if you're relying solely on state law to go after unpaid rent, don't count on your lien surviving the bankruptcy. Trustees may avoid statutory liens held by landlords for the payment of rent.

I. Defending Motions to Avoid Your Lien

Having a security interest is not as secure as it sounds. The trustee or the debtor may, under certain limited circumstances, ask the court to reduce or eliminate your lien. They would do this by filing a motion or complaint to avoid a lien.

The motion or complaint must state the legal basis for the action. The potential legal bases, as detailed in Section H, include:

- The lien was created by a judgment and impairs an exemption.
- The lien is secured by exempt property as set forth in 11 U.S.C.§ 522(f)(1)(B) that wasn't purchased with the money borrowed.
- The lien has not been perfected.
- The lien was created by a fraudulent transfer.
- The lien was created by a preferential transfer.

For example, a motion to avoid a judicial lien might state that you hold a judicial lien in the debtor's home, that the property is exempt and that your lien impairs that exemption. Similarly, a motion to avoid your security interest in household property might say that the debtor pledged property that he already owned as collateral for a loan, that he still has the property, has claimed it as exempt, and that your lien impairs that exemption.

Your possible defenses—which should be raised with a lawyer's help—include:

- showing that your lien doesn't fully cancel out the debtor's exemption (Subsection 1)
- challenging the legitimacy or value of the debtor's claimed exemption (Subsection 2), or
- showing that a particular consensual lien can't be avoided (Subsection 3).

1. Showing That the Debtor's Exemption Is Still Worth Something

Your lien may be avoided only to the extent that it impairs the debtor's exemption. Remember, an exemption becomes impaired when a lien reduces its value. If the collateral is worth more than the debtor says it is, it may be worth more than the exemption. Similarly, if the claims of other secured creditors are worth less than what the debtor says they are, there may be more equity available than originally thought. Any equity in excess of the exemption would preserve some, if not all, of your lien. (See Section H, above, for a full discussion.)

2. Challenging the Legitimacy or Value of the Claimed Exemption

You may also be able to challenge the legitimacy or the value of the exemption being claimed by the debtor. For ex-

ample, you may question the method by which the debtor calculated the available exemption, or the statutory support for the exemption.

3. Arguing Over Avoiding Liens on Household Goods

The debtor can ask the court to avoid liens that impair exemptions against certain types of property, such as household goods and tools of the trade. (See Section H4, above, for the types of property subject to lien avoidance.) However, the mere fact that your collateral is on that list and the debtor can claim it as exempt doesn't necessarily mean that the debtor can avoid your lien. If the collateral is a household item, it must also be primarily used by the debtor or the debtor's family for a household purpose. Some courts have read into this a requirement that the item be necessary for the debtor's fresh start.

For example, a television is an appliance used for household purposes. So, if your loan is secured by the debtor's TV, which you didn't sell to the debtor, and the debtor claims the TV as exempt, your lien is gone. But what if it's a big screen TV? What if the debtor has three TVs? At some point, items on the list will no longer be necessary for the fresh start.

Here are some household items that courts have said debtors may not avoid liens against, because they weren't necessary for a fresh start:

- **firearms** (when used for target practice or recreational hunting. However, some courts allow debtors to avoid liens against firearms used for personal protection.)
- **personal computers** (except as needed for educational purposes)
- **room air conditioners** (unless needed for medical reasons), and
- **jewelry.**

J. Combating Serial Bankruptcy Filings

Through serial bankruptcy filings, debtors are able to keep property that is subject to a valid security interest while making little if any payments to the creditor. Chapter 13 is the chapter of choice for serial filers, because debtors have an absolute right to dismiss their Chapter 13 case at any time. Here's the typical chronology of a serial filing.

Step One: The mortgage company schedules the foreclosure sale of the debtor's property.

Step Two: The debtor files for Chapter 13 relief to obtain the protection of the automatic stay and stop the foreclosure.

Step Three: The mortgage company asks the court to lift the automatic stay because the debtor has not made mortgage payments since filing for bankruptcy.

Step Four: The mortgage company receives stay relief.

Step Five: The debtor asks the court to dismiss the case.

Step Six: Go back to Step One.

In order to break this cycle and allow secured creditors a chance to sell their collateral after receiving relief from the automatic stay, the Bankruptcy Code (Section 109(g)) prohibits debtors from obtaining bankruptcy relief for 180 days after they voluntarily dismiss a case in which a creditor asked for stay relief. Debtors faced with the choice of losing their home or failing to disclose an earlier bankruptcy are tempted to opt for the latter course of action. Although the same trustee may have been involved in the earlier case, the second filing may slip by without detection. But you'll be on your guard and challenge the debtor's eligibility immediately.

What happens when ineligible serial filers file at the last minute? Let's start with the bad news. The automatic stay goes into effect as soon as a bankruptcy is filed regardless of the debtor's eligibility for relief. So what do you do if you have the bankruptcy court's permission to proceed against the collateral in one case, but the debtor files a second case just as you're about to sell the collateral to a third party?

You can always ask the court for a relief-of-stay order providing that any future bankruptcy filing by the debtor will not apply to your collateral. That would leave you free to disregard any new cases. Your chances of getting such an order are slim, however, unless the debtor has a history of serial filings.

Assuming you don't get this type of order, the next best advice is to be prepared for the debtor to file again—notwithstanding the fact that she's ineligible for relief. Find out how the bankruptcy judges in your district treat actions taken in violation of the automatic stay. Some courts treat them as voidable, that is, valid until the debtor obtains a court order saying that they aren't. Other courts say all actions taken in violation of the automatic stay are void—that is, courts have no authority to validate them.

If the court where the debtor has filed for bankruptcy considers actions taken in violation of the automatic stay to be voidable, you may want to let the sale go ahead and ask the court for retroactive relief or to nullify the stay. If they're void, then you're probably better off continuing the sale and getting stay relief before concluding the sale. However, even courts that treat stay violations as void may allow your sale to go ahead by finding that the filing of a bankruptcy petition by an ineligible debtor is a legal nullity. A nullity means something that, as a matter of law, didn't happen. If it didn't happen, there was no stay to violate.

The downside to ignoring the bankruptcy and proceeding with the sale can't be understated. If you're wrong about the bankruptcy's legitimacy and you proceed with the sale, your action is a willful violation of the automatic stay. Not only will the sale be set aside, but you'll be responsible for paying damages to the debtor. (See Chapter 4.)

Even if you're correct, the court may take a dim view of your unilateral decision that the bankruptcy filing violated the rules. Whether this exposes you to anything more than admonishment depends on how obviously improper the filing was.

K. Pursuing Your Rights After the Bankruptcy

Once the court enters the debtor's discharge order, the automatic stay ends as quickly as it began. State law now governs how you may proceed with the debtor, that is, assuming any matters remain legally unresolved between you. If your lien survived the bankruptcy, either in full or in part, then you may begin repossession or foreclosure proceedings as soon as state law allows you to.

If you obtained a reaffirmation agreement, then your postbankruptcy relationship with the debtor will be governed by that agreement. The old agreement is legally gone.

If your lien was eliminated in the bankruptcy, then whether you have any rights against the debtor will depend on whether your claim was discharged. If your lien was eliminated and your claim discharged, there's nothing left for you to do but to close the books and move on. If your claim was not discharged, then you may pursue the debtor for payment of the claim. ■

CHAPTER

9

Claims That Can't Be Wiped Out Through Bankruptcy

A lthough the debtor's goal in filing for bankruptcy is to get free of debts, not every debt can be wiped out, or "discharged," using bankruptcy. Some types of debts will survive the bankruptcy because the law specifically says so; others will survive if the creditor can prove that the debtor committed one of various types of misconduct. In fact, Congress has designated 18 types of obligations that cannot be discharged in bankruptcy. Some of these nondischargeable debts, like taxes and student loans, probably won't apply to you. Others may, such as losses caused by the debtor's fraud or actions meant to harm you. There's also an element of luck: Some exceptions apply only if the debtor filed under a particular bankruptcy chapter.

➡ **If your debtor is not an individual, you can skip this chapter.**

In this chapter, we'll focus on all of those claims that are or can be excepted from discharge—called nondischargeable debts. If your claim fits into one or more of these categories, you'll find out what—if anything—you can to do to prove that your claim should survive the bankruptcy.

This chapter will address:

- claims that survive bankruptcy only if you prove the debtor's misconduct to the judge (Section A)

- claims that survive bankruptcy as a matter of law, unless the debtor proves that the claim should be discharged (Section B), and

- special circumstances when the debtor has filed for Chapter 13 bankruptcy (Section C).

Challenging the debtor's ability to discharge your claim will require you to file a complaint in the bankruptcy court. This process is described in Chapter 10. However, we recommend that you seek an attorney's help if you decide to go forward with such a complaint.

A. Claims That Survive Bankruptcy If You Prove Certain Facts

Below are the five types of debtor misconduct with which you might convince the court that your claim should be excepted from discharge. These include:

- fraud (Subsection 1)

- fraud or defalcation where the debtor was acting in a fiduciary role (Subsection 2)

- larceny or embezzlement (Subsection 3)

- willful and malicious conduct (Subsection 4), and

- failure to pay marital obligations other than alimony, maintenance, or support (Subsection 5).

If your debtor engaged in any one of these, you'll need to alert the judge and prove that your claim should be excepted from discharge. How to do this is discussed in Subsection 6, below.

1. Nondischargeability Based on the Debtor's Fraud

If the debtor committed fraud in order to procure your loan or credit, you can argue that the debtor may not discharge your claim. Let's look first at what constitutes fraud (Subsection a), then at what you'd have to do to satisfy the court that fraud was, in fact, committed (Subsection b).

a.   What Is Fraud?

If the debtor engaged in deceitful conduct that resulted in you being deprived of property, that's fraud. Think about whether you would you have loaned money or provided credit to the debtor if you had known the true picture as later revealed in the bankruptcy schedules. Granted, if you had known that the debtor's future included filing for bankruptcy, you probably wouldn't have loaned the money. But focus on whether the debtor hid something from you that led you to overestimate the debtor's creditworthiness.

For example, did the debtor puff up her supposed income level or understate her expenses? Did the debtor lead you to believe that she owned property that wasn't actually hers? Did the debtor promise to pay you while already knowing that payment was going to be impossible? Did the debtor "forget" to tell you about other credit obligations? If the answer to any of these is "yes," you may be able to convince the bankruptcy court that your claim should be excepted from discharge based on the debtor's fraudulent activity.

⚠ You may need for the debtor's statement to have been in writing. If a debtor's statement was intended to give you a complete picture of his financial condition, the statement must have been made in writing for you to use it for a fraud challenge to the discharge of your claim. For example, if your lending decision was based on a summary of the debtor's income and expenses or a company balance sheet, that information must have been provided to you in writing. If it wasn't, then your claim can't be excepted from discharge—even if the debtor intentionally lied to you. Here are some additional examples:

• If you lent money to a debtor based on his oral statement that he had a job, when in fact he was unemployed, then his statement can be used to challenge the discharge of your claim. The reason is that the debtor's statement about his job wasn't intended to give you a complete picture of his financial condition.

• If you lent money to a debtor based on his oral statement that he earned $500 per week, when in fact he earned only $200, that statement can still probably be used to challenge the discharge of your claim. Again, the debtor wasn't giving you a complete picture of his financial condition.

• If, however, you lent money to a debtor based on his oral statement that he had about $100 left over at the end of the month when in fact he didn't earn enough to pay his bills, then you've got a problem. That statement cannot be used to challenge the discharge of your claim, because it apparently gave the debtor's complete financial picture.

To forestall such problems in the future, always have the debtor complete and sign a credit application. That way you'll have a written record of the debtor's financial position, and be in a better position to prove any fraud.

b.   How to Prove the Debtor's Fraud

There are six things, or "elements," you must prove before the court will except your claim from discharge based on fraud. These elements are:

1. The debtor said something that was false, or else actively led you to believe something that was false. The misrepresentation must have been about a fact that existed at or prior to

your decision to extend credit. Misrepresentations about the future don't count. For example, if the debtor said, "I expect to get a job that pays $500 per week," but the job never materializes, that's not a false statement. It was mere speculation.

2. The debtor must know or should have known that the statement was false. Although it's often hard to prove what a debtor actually "knew," it's much easier to prove what a debtor "should have known." For example, a New York court found that a debtor who wrote checks drawn on an empty bank account committed fraud—even though the debtor argued that he didn't know how much money he had in the bank due to his cocaine addiction. The court said that writing checks without knowing whether there was enough money in the bank was as good (or as bad) as knowing that the money wasn't there.

3. The false statement was intentionally made for the purpose of having you rely on it in making your decision to extend credit to the debtor. For many creditors, this is the toughest element to prove. You've got a debtor who lied about something important, but you don't have a case for fraud unless you can prove that he did so in order to mislead you. How do you do this?

- One way is to show that the misstatement was made at a time when the debtor knew you were considering extending credit to him. A false statement on a credit application will do this. The only reason the debtor completed the application was to get you to extend credit. The only reason to lie on a credit application is to mislead you.

- You can also prove intent to defraud by showing the significance of the misstatement. Overstating income, omitting obligations, and any other statements that give a false impression of the debtor's financial condition would be significant misstatements.

- Most creditors attempt to prove intent through circumstantial evidence. They tell the court everything that was going on at the time the decision to extend credit was made. While individual statements may seem minor taken out of context, when they're viewed as a whole it becomes obvious that the debtor intended to mislead the creditor.

4. **Your decision to extend credit must not have been based on old dealings with the debtor.** For example, you may have customers who maintain accounts with you. They probably submitted a credit application when the account was opened, at which time you made a credit check and approved the account. Over the years they incurred debt on their accounts and made payments according to your terms. However, if your current claim arose under such circumstances, it will not be excepted from discharge, even if the facts on the credit application have changed without your knowledge. Why? Because you were no longer extending credit based on the credit application but rather on the fact that the debtor owed you money before and paid it. (You can avoid this problem with established customers by periodically checking credit reports and asking for new financial statements.)

5. **You didn't ignore warning signs of trouble.**. It's not enough to have asked for credit information if you ignored signs that the information was false. For example, if the debtor said his business was doing fine but you read in the paper that he was laying off workers, then the court will find that you should have questioned whether the business was indeed in good shape.

6. Your reliance on the debtor's false statement or misleading conduct caused you to lose money. This may be the easiest element to prove. You have a claim that won't be paid if the debtor receives a discharge. That's an economic injury. So all you've got to do is show that the injury was the result of the debtor's action. Assuming your decision to extend credit was based on what the debtor said or did (or didn't say or do), you'll be able to prove this element.

The fact that a reasonable businessperson wouldn't have relied on the debtor's misrepresentation is irrelevant. All that matters is that you actually relied and were justified in doing so. For example, you might have loaned money to someone with whom you've done business, or been personal friends, for a long time. You accepted the debtor's statements at face value because you had no reason to doubt them. Under these circumstances your failure to do further investigation would not prevent you from challenging the discharge of your claim.

Certain Luxury Purchases Are Presumed Fraudulent

If a person's consumer debts totaled more than $1,150 and were incurred within 60 days before the person filed for bankruptcy, the person is presumed to have obtained the credit through fraud. This presumption means you wouldn't need to prove fraud unless the debtor can show the court a legitimate reason for having incurred the debt. The purpose of this rule is to make sure the debtor wasn't on a last-minute spree for luxury goods and services or cash advances under an open-ended credit plan. A luxury item is anything not reasonably necessary for the debtor or the debtor's home. The $1,150 aggregate figure applies separately to luxury items and cash advances.

Courts have found that vacations taken by debtors and paid for by their creditors are luxury items. But trips to visit family (especially in-laws) and to look for work are not luxury items. Also, jewelry purchased by a debtor on credit is not a luxury item if it was inexpensive and frequently worn by the debtor.

Despite this presumption, you will still need to file a complaint to challenge the dischargeability of your claim. The presumption simply makes your case easier to win by shifting the initial burden of proof to the debtor.

⚠ Don't mount a "fraud" challenge unless you are reasonably certain of winning. If you lose, the court will require you to prove that you were substantially justified in bringing the challenge. This means you'll need to prove that you investigated the legitimacy of your claim on both factual and legal grounds. If you didn't do so, you'll be ordered to pay the debtor's costs of defending your action—at a minimum, the debtor's attorney's fees and out-of-pocket expenses. If the court finds your action was particularly egregious, you may be ordered to pay thousands of dollars as a penalty. Seek an attorney's advice before filing a fraud complaint. Even if you then proceed on your own, having consulted the attorney should show the court that you acted in good faith.

Below are some examples of claims that may be excepted from discharge based on the debtor's fraudulent conduct.

EXAMPLE 1: You hire a contractor to renovate your house. You agree to pay him $50,000 in advance, because he says he'll need it to pay for supplies and labor. However, he ends up spending much of the money elsewhere. Any portion of the money that was used for a purpose other than the agreed-upon one may be excepted from discharge based on the debtor's misstatement. (Your claim may also be excepted from discharge based on fraud by a fiduciary or embezzlement, as discussed in Subsection 2, below.)

EXAMPLE 2: You go to a doctor, believing her to be a licensed physician. It turns out she was kicked out of med school. If you're injured as the result of the doctor's malpractice, your claim for compensation can be excepted from discharge because it flowed from the doctor's misrepresentation regarding her qualifications. You wouldn't have gone to the doctor if you'd known that she wasn't licensed. If you hadn't been treated by the doctor, you wouldn't have been injured. Therefore, your injuries would not have happened if the doctor had been honest, which is sufficient evidence to make your case for not discharging your claim.

EXAMPLE 3: The debtor tells you he owns a car, land, jewelry, or anything else of value, when he doesn't. Or, he tells you that certain property he owns isn't collateral for a loan, when the opposite is true. Remember that while these misrepresentations involve the debtor's financial condition, they don't need to be in writing in order for your claim to be excepted from discharge based on fraud, because they weren't intended to give you a complete view of the debtor's financial condition. If the debtor's false statement regards a single aspect of his financial condition, your objection may be based on the debtor's oral statement.

EXAMPLE 4: The debtor owes you $10,000 and wants you to provide additional services on credit. You refuse, because her account is delinquent. She gives you a check for $10,000, not mentioning that she doesn't have that much in the bank. You accept the check and provide $3,000 worth of requested services on credit. Of course, the check bounces. Your claim for the $3,000 can be excepted from discharge, since you did the work on credit in reliance on the debtor's fraudulent act of presenting the check to you. Your claim for the original $10,000 is a tougher case, however, since that underlying debt wasn't based on fraud—you'll have to look for other reasons that it should be excepted from discharge.

2. Nondischargeability Based on Fraud or Defalcation by a Debtor With Fiduciary Responsibilities

If the debtor commits fraud or "defalcation" while acting in a fiduciary role, then any resulting claims can be excepted from discharge. Let's start with some defi-nitions (Subsection a) and then discuss how you would prove that the discharge exception applies to you (Subsection b).

a. What Is Fraud or Defalcation by a Fiduciary?

We've already discussed the meaning of fraud, in Section A, above. Defalcation is simply a breach of trust or an abuse of someone's responsibilities. As for the fiduciary part of the exception: A fiduciary is someone with whom you have a relationship of trust. For example, your lawyer and your accountant are fiduciaries, because they are responsible for looking out for your best interests and preserving any assets you give them for safekeeping. Laws may also place someone in a fiduciary position. For example, the plan administrator of a retirement program has a fiduciary duty to all the plan participants.

Though this is a separate rule, chances are that most of the claims excepted under it could also be excepted from discharge based on fraud alone, as discussed in Section A1, above. However, the rule becomes especially fitting in cases where you didn't extend the debtor credit, but the debtor misappropriated your money outright while holding it in a fiduciary capacity. For example, if your lawyer steals money held in escrow for your benefit, then the lawyer cannot discharge your claim in bankruptcy.

b. How to Prove Fraud or Defalcation by a Fiduciary

In order to have your claim excepted from discharge, you'll need to prove all the following three elements:

1. **The debtor owed you a fiduciary duty.** In other words, he occupied a position of trust and confidence.
2. **The debtor committed fraud (as outlined in Section A1), or the debtor misappropriated your money or property.**
3. **Your claim is based on the loss of the money or property given to the debtor to be held in trust.**

Here are some examples of fraud or defalcation by a fiduciary:

EXAMPLE 1: In some states, landlords have a duty to hold security deposits in separate bank accounts for the benefit of the tenants. If your landlord didn't do this and then files a Chapter 7 bankruptcy, you may be able to show that the debt (your security deposit) qualifies to survive bankruptcy.

EXAMPLE 2: As a rule, attorneys who fail to deposit money that they're holding for their clients into a separate trust account have committed a "defal-cation" (breach of trust) while acting in a fiduciary capacity. If your attorney pulled this type of fast one, convincing the court that your claim should survive the bankruptcy should be easy.

EXAMPLE 3: You own a lumberyard and supplied materials to a builder who didn't pay you, even though he'd been paid on the project. You have a lien against the building for the cost of the material you supplied, but you also have a claim against the builder for payment. In many states, the money paid to the builder is held in trust for the payment of workers' and suppliers' claims. If the builder spent the money on something other than paying these claims, then he breached his fiduciary duty to you, and your claim may be excepted from discharge.

EXAMPLE 4: The debtor is the treasurer of a corporation, and arranges for the company to loan him money that he doesn't repay. The act of lending money to himself was a breach of his fiduciary duty to the corporation, which has a potentially nondischargeable claim against him.

3. Nondischargeability Based on the Debtor's Larceny or Embezzlement

If the debtor committed larceny or embezzlement in creating your claim, you can ask the court to except the claim from discharge. The definitions of larceny and embezzlement are discussed in Subsection a, and how you'd go about proving the debtor's guilt is discussed in Subsection b.

a. What Are Larceny and Embezzlement?

Larceny and embezzlement are crimes involving the theft of property. Larceny occurs when the criminal takes the property from its rightful owner. Embezzlement occurs when the criminal has lawful possession of the property but uses it for his own purposes rather than in a manner consistent with his permitted possession of the property. Yes, we're talking about old-fashioned crimes here—but in the event that the criminal files for bankruptcy, you want to make sure you still have a shot at getting your property back.

Actually, claims for larceny and embezzlement in bankruptcy proceedings are usually lodged against former employees and business associates. While you could pursue a larceny action against a burglar, chances are that a career criminal has no assets to protect. However, it's a different story when you're the victim

of white-collar crime. That perpetrator may have plenty to protect, which gives you a reason to preserve your claim.

The property involved must be tangible, which means it must be something that can be picked up. That doesn't mean it must have been physically taken in order for you to prove larceny or embezzlement. For example, money diverted electronically from a checking account isn't physically removed by the thief. But the fact remains that money—the object of the crime—is a tangible item. On the other hand, theft of services—such as not paying for parking—is neither larceny nor embezzlement because there is no physical manifestation of a service. (Theft of services may, however, be fraud and is treated as a crime under state law.)

b. How to Prove Larceny or Embezzlement

In order for your claim to be excepted from discharge based on larceny, you must prove the following four elements:

1. **The debtor took something that belonged to you.**
2. **The debtor did not have your permission to take the property**.
3. **The debtor took the property with the intent to deprive you of its use.** If the debtor merely intended to borrow the property or intended to pay you for it, no larceny took place.

4. Your claim is based on the loss of that property.

In order for your claim to be excepted from discharge based on embezzlement, you must prove these four elements:

1. **You allowed the debtor to use the property.**
2. **The debtor used the property in a way that wasn't in accordance with your agreement. For example, you might have let the debtor borrow your car, only to have him turn around and sell it.**
3. **The circumstances surrounding the debtor's misappropriation of your property indicate that the debtor acted fraudulently.**
4. **Your claim is based on your loss of the property as the result of the debtor's fraudulent misappropriation of it.**

Proving your case will be a cinch if the debtor has already been convicted of the crime. If you have a claim against a debtor for taking your property and the debtor was convicted of larceny or embezzlement, your claim will be excepted from discharge based on that conviction—assuming you file a complaint to challenge the discharge. Make sure to obtain a copy of the court record.

Let's look at some examples of larceny and embezzlement by debtors:

EXAMPLE 1: The debtor owns a jewelry store, and sells jewelry on consignment. You allow the debtor to sell your handcrafted jewelry after she tells you it will be insured against loss. If the debtor sells the jewelry but doesn't pay you, that's embezzlement. If the jewelry is stolen and there's no insurance to pay you, that's fraud. Either way, your claim should be excepted from discharge.

EXAMPLE 2: Your neighbor borrows your tools and never returns them—and then files bankruptcy. If the neighbor's intention all along was to make the tools his own without paying you, that's embezzlement. If the neighbor had instead broken into your garage and taken your tools without your permission, that would have been larceny. After the neighbor files bankruptcy, you should be able to convince the court that your claim for these tools should be excepted from discharge.

4. Nondischargeability Based on the Debtor's Willful and Malicious Conduct

If the debtor acted willfully and maliciously in incurring a debt to you, and thereby caused you economic harm, you could assert a nondischargeable claim against the debtor to the extent you were injured. Let's look at what willful and malicious means in Subsection a, and how you'd prove that the debtor's behavior rose to this level in Subsection b.

a. What Is Willful and Malicious Conduct?

Conduct is willful if it is intentional. Conduct is malicious if it does not serve a legitimate purpose. Taken together, conduct is willful and malicious if the conduct was intended and almost certain to cause harm. Very often, your claim against a debtor for a willful and malicious injury will be based on a state court judgment obtained before the debtor filed for bankruptcy. In fact, the entry of a judgment often precipitates the bankruptcy filing.

Negligent behavior is not considered willful or malicious. It's possible to bring a legal action against someone for negligence—that is, for having acted in a way that falls below the standard of care expected of a reasonable person. However, proving negligence won't help you prove a willful and malicious injury in bankruptcy court. The Supreme Court made this clear in *Kawaauhau v. Geiger*, 523 U.S. 57, 118 S.Ct. 974, 140 L.Ed.2d 90 (1988).

b. How to Prove Willful and Malicious Conduct

In order to have your claim excepted from discharge as the result of the debtor's willful and malicious actions, you must prove the following four elements:

1. **You were harmed as the result of something the debtor did.**
2. **The debtor intended to harm you.**
3. **The act was taken for a wrongful purpose or without regard for its consequences.**
4. **Your claim is for compensation based on the harm done to you by the debtor's willful and malicious act.**

EXAMPLE 1: Let's say the debtor's tractor is collateral for your loan. If the debtor sells the tractor without getting your permission and doesn't pay you the sale proceeds, you have been injured—you lost your collateral. The debtor's act of selling the tractor was willful. But was it malicious? The answer depends on the debtor's state of mind. If the debtor didn't realize the tractor was collateral for the loan, then the action wasn't malicious. But if the debtor knew you had a lien against the collateral and understood what that meant, then the action was malicious.

EXAMPLE 2: A person taps a loaded shotgun on a car window, intending to scare the driver so that he won't park on his property. The shotgun goes off, seriously injuring the driver. If the shooter files for bankruptcy, are the damages suffered by the driver excepted from discharge as being the result of the debtor's willful and malicious act? The act of tapping a loaded gun against the driver's window was malicious, because malicious acts are ones taken for an improper or wrongful purpose. Malice also exists if the act is taken without regard for the rights and safety of others. You can discourage drivers from parking on your property without sticking a loaded gun in their face. However, because the debtor intended only to scare the driver, not to shoot him, his action was not willful.

If you've already gotten a judgment against the debtor in state court, that should be helpful. However, whether the bankruptcy court follows the state court judgment will depend on whether the state court determined that the debtor's conduct was willful and malicious under the same standards used by the bankruptcy court.

Below are some real situations in which bankruptcy courts have found claims to be excepted from discharge based on willful and malicious conduct—in some cases, after a state court judgment.

- **Violence.** The debtor killed his ex-wife's lover in front of her in order to witness her anguish. A state court awarded her $400,000 in damages. The bankruptcy court held that the claim was excepted from discharge. (See *Maloney v. Converse (In re Maloney)*, 98 F.3d 1333 (1st Cir. 1996).)

- **Invasion of privacy.** The debtor secretly tape-recorded conversations with his neighbor in order to preserve an accurate record of the dispute between them. Although he didn't intend to harm the neighbor, the act of illegally tape-recording the conversation was willful and malicious. The bankruptcy court said "installing the device, recording the conversation, and sharing such recording with third parties was committed with an unjustifiable disregard of the debtor's duty to refrain from violating the plaintiff's right to privacy" as guaranteed under state law. (See *Mazurczyk v. O'Neil*, 268 B.R. 1 (Bankr. D. Mass. 2001).)

- **Sexual assault.** The debtor had sexual relationships with children. He agreed to pay $750,000 in damages. The bankruptcy court said this debt was excepted from discharge even though the debtor said he didn't intend to harm the children. (See *Pettey v. Belanger*, 232 B.R. 543 (D. Mass 1999).)

- **Sexual harassment.** A state court found that the debtor's actions created a hostile workplace for one of his female employees, who happened to be his former girlfriend. The debtor said his actions were those of a jealous lover. The bankruptcy court said he wanted to use economic pressure to convince the woman to resume their relationship. Her damages were excepted from discharge in bankruptcy court. (See *McDonough v. Smith (In re Smith)*, 270 B.R. 544 (Bankr. D. Mass. 2001).)

- **Unfair competition.** The debtor, an accountant, set up a business to compete with one of his former clients, using confidential information he obtained while working for the client. The former client's claim against the debtor was excepted from discharge. (See *Read v. Lundy (In re Brier)*, 274 B.R. 37 (Bankr. D. Mass. 2002).)

- **Vexatious litigation.** The debtor filed a citizen's complaint against a police officer, falsely accusing him of abuse. The bankruptcy court said that the police officer's claim for damages to his professional reputation and the stress caused by the charges was excepted from discharge. (See *Garcia v. Amaranto (In re Ameranto)*, 252 B.R. 595 (Bankr. D. Conn. 2000).)

The creditor doesn't always win, however. Here are some examples where the creditor was harmed by the debtor's conduct, but the bankruptcy court didn't find the debtor's action to be willful and malicious.

- **Breach of contract.** A landlord allowed a tenant to remain in her apartment because she promised to bring her rent payments current. The tenant didn't keep her promises, and filed for bankruptcy before the landlord could evict her. The landlord said he would have acted sooner if the tenant hadn't promised to pay. The court nevertheless said the unpaid rent could be discharged, because the debtor didn't intend to harm the landlord. (See *Kuan v. Lund (In re Lund)*, 202 B.R. 127 (Bankr. 9th Cir. 1996).)

- **Breach of contract.** Other bankruptcy courts have found claims to be dischargeable in situations where the debtor refused to pay a real estate agent's commission, where a bar owner showed a pay-per-view telecast without permission, and where a debtor refused to surrender collateral as promised in the Statement of Intention.

- **Failure to insure.** A debtor's failure to carry insurance for the benefit of others is not considered a willful and malicious act. Courts have allowed business owners to discharge liability based on their failure to maintain workers' compensation insurance. They have also allowed motorists to discharge liability based on their failure to have automobile insurance. In both cases, the court's reasoning was that operating without insurance was not certain to harm anyone.

- **Medical malpractice.** Damages resulting from a physician's professional errors can be discharged in bankruptcy unless the debtor-doctor intended to harm the patient. (But note that if the debtor was not qualified to perform the procedure, damages could be excepted from discharge based on the debtor's fraud.)

5. Nondischargeability of Marital Obligations Other Than Alimony, Maintenance, or Support

This section applies only to those readers whose debtors are their former spouses. If this description fits you, does the debtor owe you money that's not for alimony, maintenance, or support? Perhaps your ex promised to pay a marital debt that you are still on the hook for if the promise isn't kept. Perhaps your ex was ordered to pay your attorney's fee, and you'll otherwise have to pay it. Perhaps your ex still owes you money from the division of your marital property.

Let's look first at the real-world context and purpose of this exception (Subsection a) and then at what you'll need to prove to claim it (Subsection b).

Don't worry if your claim is for alimony, maintenance, or support—these are automatically nondischargeable. This means you don't have to go to court to have them survive the bankruptcy, as explained in Section B3.

a. The Purpose of This "Other" Category of Nondischargeable Marital Obligations

The most common situation in which these claims—that aren't alimony, maintenance, or support—arise is where the debtor promised to hold his or her former spouse harmless on a mutual debt incurred during the marriage. Both spouses are obligated to pay the debt, despite their agreement that one will do so. When the spouse who promised to pay files for bankruptcy, that spouse's obligation to pay the creditor is discharged. The other spouse, who wasn't supposed to pay, is left with the choice of paying the debt or filing for bankruptcy. This discharge exception gives the nonfiling spouse a chance to enforce the promise made by the spouse who filed for bankruptcy.

b. How to Prove Nondischargeable Marital Obligations

To enforce this promise and claim the discharge exception, you'll need to establish five things, including that:

1. **The debtor is your spouse, your former spouse, or your parent.**
2. **Your claim was created by separation agreement or court decree.** In order to be excepted from discharge, your "nonsupport" marital claim must have been created in a separation agreement, a divorce decree, or other

court order. If your spouse promised to pay a bill during the course of your marriage, that promise is not excepted from discharge. You can only use the discharge exception for obligations that arose from a documented break in the marital relationship.

3. **Your claim was not created as an alimony, maintenance, or support obligation.** If the purpose was to provide an economic benefit by relieving you of the burden of paying a debt, then the obligation is equivalent to alimony, maintenance, or support. That's true even if the separation agreement, divorce decree, or other court order labeled the obligation in some other way. If you're not sure what the claim is, you can leave it up to the bankruptcy court to decide. As we mentioned, obligations to pay alimony, maintenance, or support are automatically excepted from discharge, and different rules apply (discussed in Section B3).

For example, in most situations a spouse's obligation to pay all the marital debts would not be in the nature of alimony, maintenance, or support. However, if the spouse who is obligated to pay the bills is not required to pay spousal support in a context where spousal support would normally be expected (such as a long marriage, a disparate income, or a sacrifice of earning capacity by the creditor spouse to further the debtor spouse's career), the bankruptcy court may find that the obligation to pay the bills was really spousal support in disguise. Often a debtor's obligation to make mortgage payments on the marital residence is viewed as a support obligation if the debtor's former spouse and children are living there.

4. **Your former spouse is financially able to pay the debt.** This may seem like a strange issue to bring up, especially given that your former spouse has filed for bankruptcy and is therefore declaring to the world that he or she can't pay debts. Keep reading for an explanation of why this question is important.

5. **You are not better able than your spouse to pay the debt.** Or, to be more specific, the detriment to you of discharging the claim outweighs the benefit the debtor would receive from discharging the claim. When Congress added this discharge exception, it intended to close the loophole that existed when only marital obligations in the nature of alimony, maintenance, or support were excepted from discharge. Spouses would promise to pay anything to avoid having the obligation marked as alimony, maintenance, or support. Once the divorce was final, they'd file for bankruptcy and walk away from the obligations they created for their former spouse's benefit. Congress, however, didn't want to prevent the honest but unfortunate spouse

from being unable to discharge marital obligations that were created with a sincere intent to pay. Congress created a two-part test to distinguish between those debts that should be discharged and those that shouldn't. As we've seen, the first part asks if the bankrupt spouse can afford to pay the bill. If the answer is yes, then the second part asks the court to determine if the discharge of your claim will be more beneficial to your spouse than it is detrimental to you.

As awkward as it is to state this second part of the test, it has proven to be even more awkward to apply. In many situations, both the debtor-spouse and the creditor-spouse are in difficult financial circumstances. Neither former spouse can afford to pay the bill that the debtor promised to pay. In such situations, applying this test will require the bankruptcy court to determine whether you or your spouse is in a better position to pay this bill notwithstanding your spouse's promise to do so.

6. Action Needed to Protect Your Claim

If your claim fits into one of the qualifying categories described above, you must file—prior to the deadline set by the court—a complaint against the debtor objecting to the discharge of your claim. The last day for filing such a complaint comes 60 days after the original date set

for the meeting of creditors. This deadline is stated in the notice of bankruptcy filing you should have received at the start of the proceedings (discussed in Chapter 3).

B. Claims That Survive Bankruptcy Automatically

A separate set of discharge exceptions allows your claim to survive the bankruptcy automatically, unless the debtor convinces the court that the claim should nevertheless be discharged. The debtor would have to serve you with a court complaint laying out the reasons that the debt should be declared nondischargeable. Debtors may do this at any time. In fact, this issue may not come up until the bankruptcy is over. You, believing that your claim was automatically excepted from discharge, might attempt to collect your claim from the debtor, who believes that your action violates the automatic stay because your claim was discharged. The debtor would ask the bankruptcy court to reopen the case to determine whether your claim was, in fact, discharged and, if it was, whether your action violated the discharge injunction. If the debtor does nothing, the claim will survive the bankruptcy.

We're not, however, going to cover every possible automatic discharge exception here. Many of these exceptions are only usable by government institutions—for example, debtors' obligations to pay taxes, student loans, fines, penalties, and the like. Instead, we're going to focus our attention on the exceptions more likely to be useful to you and other readers, including where:

- you learned of the bankruptcy too late to file a proof of claim (Subsection 1)
- you learned of the bankruptcy too late to file a complaint alleging a discharge exception based on the debtor's misconduct (Subsection 2)
- you are owed alimony, maintenance or support (Subsection 3)
- you are owed damages for personal injury or wrongful death caused by the debtor's drunk driving (Subsection 4)
- you were awarded restitution for the debtor's criminal acts in federal proceedings (Subsection 5), or
- you represent a condominium association that is owed fees by resident debtors (Subsection 6).

➡ Interested in all the exceptions? For readers who are interested, a complete table of nondischargeable claims, including those owed to government units, is provided at the end of this chapter.

1. Nondischargeability Based on Your Learning of the Bankruptcy Too Late to File Your Proof of Claim

If you were not told and didn't learn of the bankruptcy until after the deadline for filing proofs of claim passed, your claim cannot be discharged. (The deadline for filing a proof of claim is 90 days after the first date set for the meeting of creditors—see Chapter 7.) However, if you learned about the bankruptcy even days before the deadline, and did nothing, your claim may not be excepted from discharge. You should have acted promptly to preserve your claim by asking the court to extend the filing deadline.

There is an important exception to this rule: If the debtor's case is a no-asset Chapter 7, you wouldn't have been asked to file a proof of claim at all, since there were no assets to collect from. That creates a potential problem for you, however. Since there was no deadline for filing claims, it's not too late for you to file one. Consequently, even though your claim was not scheduled, most bankruptcy courts will conclude that the debtor's failure to schedule a claim doesn't except the claim from discharge—since there is no harm to the creditor. No harm, that is, in terms of the ability to file a claim against an empty bankruptcy estate. Confused? So are many state courts judges, who conclude from the words of the bankruptcy statute that unscheduled claims are not discharged. Although this is an incorrect result under bankruptcy law—as you will learn—bankruptcy courts are powerless to correct it once it's made. What's the lesson for you if you hold an unscheduled claim? Take advantage of the error and try to collect on your claim in state court, not bankruptcy court.

2. Nondischargeability Based on Your Learning of the Bankruptcy Too Late to File a Discharge Challenge

As discussed in Section A of this chapter, if you believe your claim should be excepted from discharge for the debtor's fraud, defalcation, embezzlement, larceny or willful and malicious injury, or as a claim arising from certain marital debts, your deadline for filing a complaint was no later than 60 days after the first date set for the meeting of creditors. But what if you don't learn about the bankruptcy in time to file such a complaint? Then your claim is automatically excepted from discharge.

3. Nondischargeability of Claims for Alimony, Maintenance, or Support

If the debtor is your ex-spouse or the parent of your children, and is obliged to make periodic payments to you, were the payments labeled as support or maintenance in the divorce or separation agreement or court order? If not, was it your understanding that the payments were intended to help you adjust to living on your own or to provide financial assistance for your children? If the answer is

"yes" to either question, your claim will probably be excepted from discharge without your taking any action in the bankruptcy court. However, if you have any question about whether your claim is over alimony, maintenance, or support payments, review the discussion of non-support marital obligations in Section A5 and consider filing a complaint to determine the dischargeability of your claim, just to be safe.

The grayest area in limiting the discharge of alimony, maintenance, and support obligations is when the debtor is obligated to make a single payment rather than a series of periodic payments. If you're receiving monthly payments from the debtor, there's little doubt that those payments are intended to supplement your income or provide financial support for your children. But when the debtor is supposed to make one payment to you or to others on your behalf, then the reason for the payment may be something other than alimony, maintenance, or support. Most likely, such a lump sum payment would be made as part of an equitable division of marital property and obligations. Therefore, if you're entitled to receive a single payment from the debtor, you should file a complaint to determine whether the debtor's obligation will be discharged—even if you think the payment is most likely for alimony, maintenance, or support.

4. Nondischargeability of Claims for Personal Injury or Death Caused by the Debtor's Drunk Driving

If you have a claim for damages against the debtor for personal injury or the wrongful death of someone close to you or whose estate you manage, and the claim arose from the debtor's operation of a motor vehicle while intoxicated, that claim cannot be discharged.

However, this rule is not quite as broad as it first appears. First, note that only claims for physical injury or wrongful death fall under this rule—your claim for damage to your property is not excepted from discharge. (Nor can it be excepted from discharge as a willful and malicious injury, because the operation of a motor vehicle while intoxicated is not an act intended to harm you; see Section A4, above.)

Also, the debtor may have been behind the wheel of something that doesn't count as a "motor vehicle." Courts are divided as to what constitutes a motor vehicle. Cars, trucks, and other motorized landcraft are included. But several courts have said that airplanes, boats, and personal watercraft do not count as motor vehicles.

5. Nondischargeability of Claims for Criminal Restitution (Federal Proceedings Only)

Criminals are frequently ordered to compensate the victims of their crimes. This happens in state and federal courts. However, you can receive a discharge exception only for a restitution order that was entered in a federal criminal case.

6. Nondischargeability of Claims for Certain Condominium Association Fees

If the debtor owned a condominium, then she was probably responsible for paying regular fees to the association (for maintenance of common areas and the like). While any association fees that the debtor owed when she filed for bankruptcy are discharged, fees that came due after the bankruptcy filing may not always be discharged.

You're probably scratching your head about this one, knowing that only debts that came due *prior* to the bankruptcy filing can normally be discharged. So why it necessary to have a discharge exception for association fees arising *after* the bankruptcy filing? The reason is that, although condo fees are typically assessed on a monthly or quarterly basis, these fees are based on a contract—the condominium association agreement—signed prior to the bankruptcy. Therefore, the fees are treated as if they arose before the bankruptcy filing—and are therefore subject to discharge.

Now, for the terms of the discharge exception. Unpaid association fees that were assessed after the bankruptcy filing cannot be discharged if the debtor continues to live in the property or rent it to a tenant. The Bankruptcy Code won't let the debtor walk away from the responsibility of paying for the benefit of living on the property. If, however, the debtor has left the property vacant, the debtor's ongoing obligation to pay association fees is discharged.

A debate has arisen as to whether this exception applies to fees beyond those imposed by a condominium association or cooperative housing corporation. Because those are the only entities identified in the exception, some courts have ruled that the discharge exception does not apply to fees imposed by homeowners associations, despite their similar function. The distinction is based on state law.

C. Different Nondischargeability Rules When Debtors File Under Chapter 13

Individuals who successfully complete Chapter 13 plans are entitled to a broader discharge than they could receive under Chapter 7, 11, or 12. For instance, as we

mentioned earlier, the claims discussed in Part A can be discharged in Chapter 13. In other words, it won't do the creditor any good to file a complaint objecting to the discharge. But, you may have another avenue of relief: If the debtor's decision to file for Chapter 13 relief was for the sole purpose of avoiding one of the discharge exceptions in Chapter 7, you can ask the court to deny confirmation of the reorganization plan (see Chapter 13 of this book).

If the debtor files for Chapter 13 relief and completes her plan, the following claims are automatically excepted from discharge:

- **Claims not provided for by the plan.** If the debtor's plan doesn't include your claim by name or in a category of claims, then your claim survives bankruptcy.
- **A claim for which the last payment was due after the last plan payment.** For example, a mortgage or other long-term obligation would not be discharged.
- **Claims for alimony, maintenance, or support**
- **Claims for student loans**
- **Claims for death or personal injury arising from the debtor's intoxicated operation of a motor vehicle**
- **Claims for restitution or criminal fines entered by any court**

Complete Table of Nondischargeable Debts

The following table lists all the debts that may survive the bankruptcy, automatically or after a creditor's legal complaint, with references to who can make use of them, and any special eligibility criteria or other concerns, and what part of the Bankruptcy Code they're from.

Type of Debt	Type of Claimant	Necessary to File Complaint?	Special Criteria or Concerns	Bankruptcy Code Citation (11 U.S.C.)
Taxes	Governmental unit	No	None.	§ 523(a)(1)
Fraud	Anyone	Yes	False statements regarding the debtor's total financial condition must be in writing to be actionable. Claim can be discharged in Chapter 13.	§ 523(a)(2)
Unscheduled claims based on fraud, theft by a person in a position of trust, embezzlement, larceny, or intentional or malicious conduct	Anyone	No	May not apply in a no-asset Chapter 7 case.	§ 523(a)(3)
Theft by a person in a position of trust	Anyone	Yes	You must have had a fiduciary relationship with the debtor. Claim can be discharged in Chapter 13.	§ 523(a)(4)
Embezzlement	Anyone	Yes	Claim can be discharged in Chapter 13.	§ 523(a)(4)
Larceny	Anyone	Yes	Claim can be discharged in Chapter 13.	§ 523(a)(4)
Alimony, maintenance, or support	Must be spouse, former spouse, or child of the debtor	No	Claim must arise from a separation agreement, divorce decree, or other court order.	§ 523(a)(5)
Intentional injuries	Anyone	Yes	You must prove that the debtor intended to harm you. Claim can be discharged in Chapter 13.	§ 523(a)(6)
Fines and penalties	Government unit	No	None.	§ 523(a)(7)
Student loans	Anyone providing educational loans funded or guaranteed by a governmental unit or nonprofit institution.	No	None.	§ 523(a)(8)

Complete Table of Nondischargeable Debts (continued)				
Type of Type of Debt	**Necessary to File Claimant**	**Complaint?**	**Special Criteria or Concerns**	**Bankruptcy Code Citation (11 U.S.C.)**
Death or personal injury arising from operation of motor vehicle by an intoxicated person	Victim or victim's estate	No	Property damage not covered.	§ 523(a)(9)
Claims that were or could have been listed in an earlier bankruptcy in which the debtor was denied a discharge	Anyone	No	None.	§ 523(a)(10)
Fraud by an official of a bank or credit union	Anyone	No	You must have obtained a judgment or consent order against the debtor prior to bankruptcy.	§ 523(a)(11)
Malicious or reckless failure to fulfill duty to a bank or savings and loan	Government unit	No	None.	§ 523(a)(12)
Restitution owed for conviction of a federal crime	Anyone	No	None.	§ 523(a)(13)
Money borrowed to pay nondischargeable tax	Anyone	No	You must be able to prove that the debtor borrowed the money to pay the tax, that the money was used for that purpose, and that the tax would not have been discharged if it had not been paid.	§ 523(a)(14)
Marital obligations that are not alimony, maintenance, or support	Spouse, former spouse, or child of debtor	Yes	The obligation must arise out of a separation agreement, divorce decree, or other court order.	§ 523(a)(15)
Condominium association fees incurred after the bankruptcy filing	Condominium or cooperative housing association	No	The debtor must have lived in the unit or rented it after filing for bankruptcy. This exception may not apply to homeowners associations.	§ 523(a)(16)
Court fees	Courts	No	None.	§ 523(a)(17)
Reimbursement of aid provided to dependent children	State or municipality	No	Claim must be for support paid to debtor's child and assigned to government unit under the Social Security Act, Title IV Part D.	§ 523(a)(18)

Filing Motions and Complaints in Bankruptcy Court

I n a perfect world, bankruptcy trustees would administer cases in an orderly fashion without the court's involvement. But, in a perfect world, debtors would be able to pay their bills. Since we know this world is far from perfect, it should come as no surprise that you may, at times, need the bankruptcy court's involvement in resolving a particular dispute within the larger case. Not everyone will need the court to step in like this—it's perfectly possible to get through an entire bankruptcy proceeding without disputes arising between the parties. Whether or how often you'll need extra help from the court is usually governed by the following factors:

- The larger your claim, the more aggressively you may seek to preserve it.
- The more money the debtor has available to pay unsecured creditors' claims, the more reason you have to make sure you collect.
- The better a negotiator you are, the less likely you are to need the court's help.
- The less cooperative the debtor is with you and the trustee, the more likely you are to need the court's help.
- The more on the ball the trustee is, the less likely you are to need to approach the court on your own.

Usually, any beef you have that requires litigation will be with the debtor. The most likely possibilities include actions requesting that the automatic stay be lifted, that your claim be excepted from discharge, or that the debtor's discharge be denied or the case dismissed. It's rare, but not unheard of, for a creditor to sue a trustee. When it happens, it's to force the trustee to do something (abandon an asset, for example), or not do something (such as sell an asset). It would be rarer yet for you to have to sue another creditor.

In this chapter, you'll learn what types of issues must be dealt with using the Bankruptcy Code's system for dispute resolution, which is a dual system, including both "adversary" and "contested" proceedings. We'll give you an overview of what's involved in filing and responding to the most common court "pleadings," those being motions and complaints.

⚠️ **What's "adversarial" and what's "contested" isn't always clear.** Though these are supposedly distinct types of proceedings, the truth is that not even the courts can always agree on which is which. That means you'll need to not only review this chapter, but pay particular attention to local rules and customs.

The chapter is meant to round out your understanding of what is involved in adversary and contested bankruptcy court proceedings—but not to train you as a trial lawyer. There is not enough space in this book to prepare you for all the obstacles you'd face in preparing and arguing motions and complaints and otherwise representing yourself in bankruptcy court litigation.

If a dispute arises, ask yourself whether your interest in the matter is strictly for your own benefit. If it is, such as when you are the defendant in an action filed by the trustee or the debtor, then a lawyer's help is almost always worth the expense. If, however, you are interested in pursuing a matter that would benefit all creditors, such as challenging the debtor's right to receive a discharge, then talk to the trustee before you hire your own attorney. If you've got a good case, the trustee should pursue it. If the trustee isn't interested in pursuing it, then you should question whether it is really worth the expense of hiring an attorney to pursue on your own.

There are, depending on your abilities and experience, certain actions you could decide to handle on your own—for example, a motion requesting relief from the automatic stay would be the easiest one with which to start. As we go through this chapter, we'll point out which actions you can try to do by yourself and those for which you should look to either the trustee or your own attorney for help.

In this chapter, we'll cover:
- the risks associated with wading into a legal dispute without a lawyer (Section A)
- the court rules, briefly overviewed (Section B)

- rules for submitting complaints and handling adversary proceedings (Section C), and
- rules for submitting motions and handling contested proceedings (Section D).

A. What Could Go Wrong in Handling a Dispute on Your Own

The point of this book is to let you know your rights as a creditor. You want to maximize the recovery of your claims. The idea of getting this far only to hire an attorney may seem to conflict with that goal, but there are two good reasons why—especially in the prosecution of adversary proceedings—it can make good economic sense. These reasons include:
- to avoid making an irreversible mistake (Subsection 1), and
- to avoid making a mistake that could cost you actual money (in court-imposed penalties) (Subsection 2).

⚠️ **If your claim is held by your incorporated business, you must hire a lawyer to represent the business in any motion or adversary action filed with the court.** The reason is that the corporation—not you, individually—is the creditor. That makes you the representative of the corporation, a role you can't step into within the bankruptcy proceedings unless you're admitted to practice before the court.

1. To Avoid Irreparable Mistakes

When you file a complaint or a motion, you are asking the court to intervene in the bankruptcy on your behalf. If you draft and submit your request in the wrong way or at the wrong time, you may forfeit the opportunity to ask again— even if you would have received what you'd asked for had you done things right the first time. Judges hate placing form over substance, but sometimes they have no choice. The consensus is that justice is, in this litigation context, best served by sticking to hard and fast procedural rules.

Lawyers are responsible for knowing the deadlines for filing actions as well as all the other procedural rules applicable to your case. They know what kind of evidence you need to present to the court to support your case. They also know when the other side is doing something that is against the rules. So, unless you're planning to take a crash course on trial practice and procedure, they can be awfully handy to have around when things get litigious.

2. To Avoid Being Penalized for Your Mistakes

There's only one thing worse than a bankruptcy ending without your getting paid: it ending with your owing money to the debtor, the trustee, or someone else because you acted improperly in the course of the proceedings.

For example, you learned in Chapter 4 that you can be penalized for violating the automatic stay, and in Chapter 9 that you can be penalized for filing an unwarranted complaint challenging the discharge of your claim for fraud. In addition to these specific penalties, Bankruptcy Rule 9011 requires you to sign all papers filed with the court to affirm that you're acting properly, namely that:

- You made a reasonable inquiry into the accuracy of the information presented and the information is true to the best of your knowledge and belief.
- You didn't file the papers for an improper purpose such as to harass the defendant.
- There's a solid legal foundation for all your claims.
- There's a solid factual foundation for all your claims.
- Any responses you made to an earlier pleading (such as in an answer to a complaint) are warranted, based on the facts as you know them or, in cases where you made no response, you truly couldn't answer because you don't know the necessary facts.

Though you'll usually get a chance to fix something that doesn't meet the requirements on this list, if you fail at your second chance, the court can order you to pay a penalty.

⚠ Don't try to save money by hiring a nonlawyer. Though many nonlawyers offer services for less money than lawyers charge, only a lawyer can represent you in bankruptcy court. In addition, lawyers have gone through a fair amount of training and testing to get where they are, so—assuming you find a good one (as discussed in Chapter 19)—he or she will have far more knowledge and experience than a nonlawyer.

B. Strict Rules Governing Formatting and Paperwork

To give you an idea of what your lawyer will have to comply with—and to help you take an active role in reviewing or contributing to the paperwork—here are the basic formatting requirements for documents filed with the court. These rules apply in both adversarial and contested proceedings. All documents must:

- be typed or computer-generated and double-spaced. Handwritten documents are acceptable so long as they are legible.
- be printed on 8 1/2" by 11" white paper
- have a caption, at the top of the first page, with the name of the court, the names of the parties involved in the litigation, the name of the debtor, and the docket number of the bankruptcy case

- be headlined, immediately after the caption, to clearly state what the document is. For example, "Complaint to determine discharge of claim under Section 523(a)(2)."
- present information to the court in consecutively numbered paragraphs. Each paragraph makes a single statement or allegation.
- be signed by the person making the statements in the pleading, and
- be copied to everyone involved in the matter or their attorneys if they are represented.

In addition, each court has its own rules for handling the papers that flow through its clerk's office. Therefore, it's a good idea to check the court's local rules before filing anything. Most courts post their rules on their website. All courts make copies available at the clerk's office.

C. Adversary Proceedings

Filing an adversary proceeding is a lot like filing a lawsuit in regular state court. Each side files certain paperwork with the court, a trial may be held, and the court decides in favor of one side or the other. Let's look in more detail at:

- types of disputes that must be resolved through an adversarial proceeding (Subsection 1)
- the normal course of the adversarial process (Subsection 2)

- what happens after the complaint is filed (Subsection 3)
- what happens if the defendant doesn't answer your complaint (Subsection 4), and
- what happens when the defendant does answer your complaint (Subsection 5).

⚠ **Remember, this is an overview—we're anticipating that you'll hire a lawyer for much or all of this work.** Also, from here on in this chapter, when we refer to "you," we mean you and your lawyer, collectively.

1. Disputes That Must Be Addressed Through An Adversary Proceeding

An adversary proceeding must be initiated (by filing a complaint) whenever someone in the proceedings wishes to:

- **Recover money or property that was improperly transferred prior to the bankruptcy filing.** These actions are more likely to be filed against you than by you. For example, if the trustee believes you received money from the debtor prior to the bankruptcy filing that legally belongs to the bankruptcy estate, the trustee may file a complaint against you to recover that money. If you are the defendant in the action, then you'll need to hire an attorney. If you are considering bringing such an action, then talk to the trustee first. (See Chapter 15 for a discussion of avoiding prepetition transfers.)

- **Determine the validity, priority or extent of a lien.** You'll recall that a lien is an interest in the debtor's property that secures payment of your debt. Someone in the proceeding may wish to argue that a lien is invalid because it wasn't created in accordance with state laws, or ineffective because it wasn't perfected (see Chapter 8 for a discussion of lien avoidance). Someone might also argue about what priority (order) the liens should be paid off in if the property is sold. Arguments may also be made about the value of the lien.

  Here again, you are more likely to be on the receiving end of a complaint than you are to be the one initiating the action. However, if you believe there's a defect with a lien that would be paid ahead of yours, you have every right to bring an action challenging that lien. Even if you don't hold a lien against the property, you may wish to challenge somebody else's lien in order to free up equity that can be shared by unsecured creditors (including you). For example, you could ask the court to avoid a lien that was created to favor payment of a debt owed to one of the debtor's relatives.

Since the protection of your lien is personal to you, you will need an attorney to help you defend an action to avoid your lien or to challenge another creditor's lien.

⚠️ **To continue pursuing your lien rights, file a motion rather than a complaint.** In other words, if you want to repossess your collateral or begin foreclosure procedures, you'll need to file a motion for stay relief and go from there, as discussed in Section D, below.

• **Determine the dischargeability of a claim.** In Chapter 9 we discussed various types of claims that survive bankruptcy. For those nonautomatic situations where you must convince the court of the debtor's misconduct (such as fraud or embezzlement) you must file a complaint to show the court why the claim should not be discharged. Since this action will benefit only you, you will need to hire an attorney.

• **Object to or ask the court to revoke the debtor's discharge.** In Chapter 12 we discuss how to torpedo the entire bankruptcy by showing the court that the debtor isn't qualified to receive a discharge. As you'll see in that chapter, debtors may be denied a discharge for numerous reasons, such as lying to the court about what they own, or not cooperating with the trustee. If you believe the debtor should be denied a discharge or have his discharge revoked, you or the trustee will need to file a complaint.

EXAMPLE: Chapman sues Diane in state court, because she didn't pay him for his finishing work on a sculpture she created. The court awards Chapman $25,000. Diane files an appeal. While her appeal is pending, Diane files for Chapter 7 relief. On her bankruptcy schedules, Diane fails to disclose that she and her brother own a hunting cabin. Chapman knows about it, because he's been there with Diane's brother, who complained that he wanted to fix it up but that Diane wouldn't let him. Chapman asks Diane about this at the Section 341 meeting of creditors. Diane replies that she forgot to mention the cabin in her bankruptcy paperwork, and promises to correct the mistake. But the trustee notices that Diane also understated her income and overstated her expenses, leading the trustee to believe that the omission was intentional. For this reason, the trustee files a complaint with the court to have Diane denied a discharge.

- **In a reorganization case, ask the court to revoke confirmation of the debtor's plan.** If, after the reorganization plan has been confirmed, you learn that the debtor used fraud to bring about the confirmation, you may file a complaint asking the court to revoke the confirmation. Since this action will benefit all creditors, ask the trustee whether she is going to pursue the matter before hiring an attorney to do so on your own.

2. The Normal Course of an Adversary Proceeding

An adversary proceeding starts off when someone files what's called a complaint. The person filing the complaint becomes the plaintiff, and the person on the other side becomes the defendant. Except for the formatting required by the court (described in Section B, above), there's no "standard" complaint—whoever writes the complaint must set out facts and legal arguments to fit the particular situation.

After the plaintiff files the complaint, the defendant has a chance to tell his side of the story, responding to the allegations in the complaint. The defendant files what's called an answer. If the defendant fails to file an answer, the court may rule in the plaintiff's favor right then and there—so long as the plaintiff is legally entitled to receive what was requested.

The court may make the plaintiff prove its case even if no answer was filed. If your complaint proves your case, then there's no need for a hearing. But if there are holes in it, the fact that no answer was filed doesn't mean that you automatically win.

If the defendant does file an answer, the court will conduct a trial. But first, both sides have the right to ask the other side to provide documents and to submit to questioning. (In Chapter 6 we discuss Rule 2004 examinations, which you would use to force the debtor to answer questions.) Each side can also ask the other to agree to certain facts, in order to focus the litigation on only those facts and issues that are truly in dispute.

! Cooperation with the defendant is legally required. If you are involved in an adversary proceeding, don't ignore a request from the other side to produce documents, admit to facts, narrow the issues, or anything else. Your failure to cooperate with the other side's legitimate and reasonable requests could prevent you from winning. If you believe the request is unreasonable or you disagree with what's said, let the court know by filing an objection. The objection should carry the same caption as the request you're challenging, and be identified as a statement of your opposition to the request.

The bankruptcy judge will probably schedule at least one conference prior to the trial for the purpose of seeing how the pretrial process is moving and to determine if a trial is going to be necessary. This conference may be conducted over the telephone or in the judge's chambers, depending on which is more convenient.

The trial of an adversary action is a formal proceeding conducted under the Federal Rules of Bankruptcy Procedure and selected parts of the Federal Rules of Civil Procedure. (See Bankruptcy Rules 7001 to 7071.) Although there is no rule against representing yourself as an individual creditor, you'll be held to at least a basic understanding of these rules of procedure. Also, if you are incorporated or consist of another type of entity such as a partnership or limited liability company, you will need to be represented by an attorney because of rules against the unauthorized practice of law.

Whichever side loses may ask the court to reconsider its ruling or may file an appeal.

3. After a Complaint Is Filed

After a complaint is filed, the clerk will assign a hearing date and time for the court to address it. This information is presented to the defendant in a document called a subpoena or summons (the two terms are used interchangeably). In some places, the court's computer system automatically generates the subpoena for you. In others, you'll need to give the clerk a partially completed subpoena form that needs only the information regarding the hearing date and time to be filled in.

You must give copies of the subpoena as well as the complaint to each of the defendants named in the complaint. Giving out these copies is called "service of process." One way to accomplish this service is to mail a copy of the subpoena and complaint to the defendants by first class mail at the address listed in the petition. Another way is to have an adult who is not involved in the bankruptcy hand deliver a copy of the subpoena and complaint to the defendants (you can hire process servers for just this purpose).

There's a ten-day deadline for serving the subpoena and complaint. The clock starts ticking on the day the bankruptcy clerk issues the subpoena. If you miss the deadline, you'll need to start all over, by obtaining a fresh subpoena and taking the appropriate steps to serve it on everyone. The complaint that you'll attach to your subpoena doesn't go stale quite as fast—it can be as many as 120 days old (starting from the filing date) on the date you serve it on the other parties.

Once the subpoena and complaint have been served, you must create a short document called a "certificate of service," stating that service has been made and how it was done. This certificate of service must be filed with the court.

➡️ **You're as likely to be named as a defendant in a complaint as you are to initiate one as a plaintiff.** For more on responding to specific motions and complaints, see Chapter 11 of this book.

4. If the Defendant Doesn't File an Answer

If the defendant does not answer your complaint before the deadline, you may ask the court to enter what's called a "default judgment"—meaning that the court looks at your complaint to make sure it sets forth a valid and reasonable claim, then rules in your favor if it does. Requesting a default judgment requires filing the following documents with the bankruptcy clerk:

- **A motion for entry of default judgment.** This motion must tell the court when the summons was issued, when it was served, when the proof of service was filed, and when the answer was due. It must also state that no answer was filed and that the defendant is not in the military service.
- **A proposed order.** The proposed order should be ready for the judge's signature, and grant you the relief requested in your complaint.

You must let the defendant know, in writing, that you've asked the court to enter a default judgment. This notice warns the defendant that his or her rights may be lost if no action is taken, and provides the defendant with one last opportunity to act to preserve those rights.

5. After You or the Defendant Files an Answer

The filing of an answer tells everyone that the defendant is ready, willing, and able to oppose the complaint. It may say even more, if it asserts an affirmative defense or counterclaim.

The first thing the court will do is to try to help the parties settle their differences. If settlement is not possible, then the court will try to narrow the areas of disagreement. These settlement efforts are made through pretrial conferences, which may occur in the judge's chambers or over the telephone. A pretrial conference is not a hearing. It's an organizational meeting between the court and the parties.

Depending on the complexity of the litigation, the court may decide that legal briefs need to be filed to help the court understand the issues presented. The court may also recommend arbitration or suggest other ways for the parties to reconcile their differences out of court, such as mediation.

Once these preliminaries are dispensed with, the court will schedule the matter for trial. At the trial, you'll have a chance to present your case to the court. At this point, we'll stop our overview of adversary proceedings and reiterate our recommendation that you hire a lawyer. (And remember, if your business is a corporation or other entity, you have no choice but to hire a lawyer in bankruptcy court.)

Use of Motions in Adversary Proceedings

Though adversary proceedings are initiated by filing a complaint, there will probably be times during the proceedings when you or the other party will need to file the other common form of court pleading known as a motion. In particular, you may need to file a motion asking the court to enter an order. Motions made during a hearing may be made orally. All other motions must be made in writing. Typical procedural motions include requests to:

- dismiss the complaint
- extend the deadline for filing an answer
- extend the deadline for filing a complaint
- postpone a hearing
- enter a default judgment, or
- impose sanctions.

D. Contested Proceedings

Contested proceedings are less formal than adversary proceedings, though we usually feel they're also best done with a lawyer's help. In fact, the court can turn these proceedings formal with the swish of a pen: If circumstances warrant it, the court will inform the parties that certain rules applicable to adversary proceedings will apply to the contested proceeding.

There is an exception to our recommendation that you use a lawyer to prepare motions: If you're in an area where the bankruptcy court has created a standard motion form, you're pretty safe in filling it out on your own. For example, the bankruptcy court in Los Angeles has created standard forms for use in seeking relief from the automatic stay. Their forms include one to use if you're foreclosing on real estate and another for use in repossessing personal property. We've included copies of the stay relief form at the end of this chapter, for illustrative purposes. Of course, if you're anywhere but in the Central District of California, you should not rely on these forms.

Typical types of contested proceedings include motions requesting:
- relief from the automatic stay
- dismissal of the case, and
- examination of the debtor or the debtor's records.

To begin a contested proceeding, you would send a copy of your motion to any party who may oppose it, and file the motion with the court, together with a certificate stating that a copy was served on the opposition. As the person filing the motion, you are known as the movant. The person or persons who oppose the motion are respondents.

Whether a hearing will be scheduled on your motion depends on how your local bankruptcy court handles these proceedings. Many courts won't schedule a hearing unless the other side files a response. Other courts schedule a hearing for every motion, but cancel the hearing if the respondent doesn't file a response.

In some courts you'll be allowed to pick a hearing date from a list of available ones and send a notice of hearing along with the motion. In others, the clerk assigns a hearing date and sends out the notice or instructs you to do so.

If the other side doesn't file a response, you may file what's called a "certificate" of no response. Ask the court clerk what happens next. In most courts, you'll get the relief you requested (assuming you asked for something reasonable) without having to attend a hearing. Other courts require that you show up at a hearing to back up your motion.

If the other side does file a response, the court will hold a hearing on the motion. The rules of evidence and procedure are somewhat relaxed during a motion hearing. But rules still apply, and you'll need to be familiar with them.

For the relevant rules of evidence and procedure, see the Federal Rules of Bankruptcy Procedure (available on a handy Cornell website, www.law. cornell.edu/topics/bankruptcy.html, and at the Government Printing Office's website at www.access.gpo.gov/uscode/ title11a/11a_1_.html) as well as your local court's rules (available from the court clerk and usually online from your local court's website).

Getting What You Want From the Court

The following table sets forth the most common requests creditors present to the bankruptcy court and the laws and procedures that must be followed.

Type of action	Discussed in which chapter of this book?	Covered by which law or rule?	What to file with the court
Adequate protection for your interest in collateral	Chapter 4	11 U.S.C. § 361	Motion
Convert Chapter 11 case to Chapter 7	Chapter 14	11 U.S.C. § 1112(b)	Motion
Convert Chapter 12 case to Chapter 7	Chapter 14	11 U.S.C. § 1208(d)	Motion
Convert Chapter 13 case to Chapter 7	Chapter 14	11 U.S.C. § 1307(c)	Motion
Dismiss Chapter 7 case	Chapter 12	11 U.S.C. § 707(a)	Motion
Dismiss Chapter 11 case	Chapter 12	11 U.S.C. § 1112(b)	Motion
Dismiss Chapter 12 case	Chapter 12	11 U.S.C. § 1208(c)	Motion
Dismiss Chapter 13 case	Chapter 12	11 U.S.C. § 1307(c)	Motion
Examine the debtor or the debtor's financial records	Chapter 5	Bankruptcy Rule 2004	Motion
Extend deadline for objecting to claim's discharge	Chapter 9	11 U.S.C. § 523(c)	Motion
Extend deadline for objecting to debtor's discharge	Chapter 12	11 U.S.C. § 727	Motion
Object to confirmation of Chapter 12 plan	Chapter 13	11 U.S.C. § 1225	Motion
Object to confirmation of Chapter 13 plan	Chapter 13	11 U.S.C. § 1325	Motion
Object to discharge of debtor	Chapter 12	11 U.S.C. § 722	Adversary complaint
Object to discharge of your claim	Chapter 9	11 U.S.C. § 523	Adversary complaint
Object to exemptions claimed by debtor	Chapters 2,5	11 U.S.C. § 522	Motion
Prohibit the debtor's use of cash collateral	Chapter 4	11 U.S.C. § 363(c)	Motion
Relief from the automatic stay	Chapter 4	11 U.S.C. § 362(d)	Motion

Sample Local Form Motion for Stay Relief, page 1 of 8

Attorney or Party Name, Address, Telephone & FAX Numbers, and California State Bar Number	FOR COURT USE ONLY
☐ *Individual appearing without counsel* ☐ *Attorney for:*	

UNITED STATES BANKRUPTCY COURT **CENTRAL DISTRICT OF CALIFORNIA**	
In re: Debtor(s).	CHAPTER: CASE NO.: DATE: TIME: CTRM: FLOOR:

NOTICE OF MOTION AND MOTION FOR RELIEF FROM THE AUTOMATIC STAY
UNDER 11 U.S.C. § 362 (with supporting declarations)
(MOVANT: _____)
(Real Property)

1. NOTICE IS HEREBY GIVEN to the Debtor(s) and Trustee (if any)("Responding Parties"), their attorneys (if any), and other interested parties that on the above date and time and in the indicated courtroom, Movant in the above-captioned matter will move this Court for an Order granting relief from the automatic stay as to Debtor and Debtor's bankruptcy estate on the grounds set forth in the attached Motion.

2. **Hearing Location:**   ☐ **255 East Temple Street, Los Angeles**   ☐ **411 West Fourth Street, Santa Ana**
                    ☐ **21041 Burbank Boulevard, Woodland Hills**   ☐ **1415 State Street, Santa Barbara**
                    ☐ **3420 Twelfth Street, Riverside**

3. a. ☐ This Motion is being heard on REGULAR NOTICE pursuant to Local Bankruptcy Rule 9013-1. If you wish to oppose this Motion, you must file a written response to this Motion with the Bankruptcy Court and serve a copy of it upon the Movant's attorney (or upon Movant, if the motion was filed by an unrepresented individual) at the address set forth above no less than 14 days before the above hearing and appear at the hearing of this Motion.

   b. ☐ This Motion is being heard on SHORTENED NOTICE. If you wish to oppose this Motion, you must appear at the hearing. Any written response or evidence may be filed and served: ☐ at the hearing   ☐ at least _____ court days before the hearing.

        (1) ☐ An Application for Order Shortening Time was not required (according to the calendaring procedures of the assigned judge).

        (2) ☐ An Application for Order Shortening Time was filed per Local Bankruptcy Rule 9075-1(b) and was granted by the Court.

        (3) ☐ An Application for Order Shortening Time has been filed and remains pending.

4. You may contact the Bankruptcy Clerk's office to obtain a copy of an approved court form for use in preparing your response (*Optional Court Form 390*), or you may prepare your response using the format required by Local Bankruptcy Rule 1002-1.

5. If you fail to file a written response to the Motion or fail to appear at the hearing, the Court may treat such failure as a waiver of your right to oppose the Motion and may grant the requested relief.

Dated: _____

_____   _____
                                          Print Law Firm Name (if applicable)

_____   _____
Print Name of Individual Movant or Attorney for Movant   *Signature of Individual Movant or Attorney for Movant*

This form is mandatory by Order of the United States Bankruptcy Court for the Central District of California.

Revised January 2001   **350RP**

Sample Local Form Motion for Stay Relief, page 2 of 8

<table>
<tr><td colspan="2">Motion for Relief from Stay (Real Property) - *Page 2 of* ___</td><td>**350RP**</td></tr>
<tr><td>In re</td><td rowspan="2">(SHORT TITLE)</td><td>CHAPTER:</td></tr>
<tr><td>Debtor(s).</td><td>CASE NO.:</td></tr>
</table>

MOTION FOR RELIEF FROM THE AUTOMATIC STAY
(MOVANT: _____)

1. **The Property at issue:** Movant moves for relief from the automatic stay with respect to following real property (the "Property"):

   Street Address:
   Apartment/Suite no.:
   City, State, Zip Code:

   Legal description or document recording number (including county of recording):

   ☐ See attached continuation page.

2. **Case History:**
   a. ☐ A voluntary ☐ An involuntary petition under Chapter ☐ 7 ☐ 11 ☐ 12 ☐ 13 was filed on:
   b. ☐ An Order of Conversion to Chapter ☐ 7 ☐ 11 ☐ 12 ☐ 13 was entered on:
   c. ☐ Plan was confirmed on *(specify date)*:
   d. ☐ Other bankruptcy cases affecting this Property have been pending within the past two years. See Attached Declaration.

3. **Grounds for Relief from Stay:**
   a. ☐ Pursuant to 11 U.S.C. § 362(d)(1), cause exists to grant Movant the requested relief from stay as follows:
      (1) ☐ Movant's interest in the Property is not adequately protected.
         (a) ☐ Movant's interest in the collateral is not protected by an adequate equity cushion.
         (b) ☐ The fair market value of the Property is declining and payments are not being made to Movant sufficient to protect Movant's interest against that decline.
         (c) ☐ No proof of insurance re Movant's collateral has been provided to Movant, despite borrower(s)'s obligation to insure the collateral under the terms of Movant's contract with Debtor(s).
         (d) ☐ Payments have not been made as required by an Adequate Protection Order previously granted in this case.
      (2) ☐ *(Chapter 12 or 13 cases only)*
         (a) ☐ Post-confirmation plan payments have not been made to the Standing Trustee.
         (b) ☐ Post-confirmation payments required by the confirmed plan have not been made to Movant.
      (3) ☐ The bankruptcy case was filed in bad faith.
      (4) ☐ For other cause for relief from stay, see attached continuation page.

   b. ☐ Pursuant to 11 U.S.C. § 362(d)(2)(A), Debtor(s) has/have no equity in the Property; and pursuant to § 362(d)(2)(B), the Property is not necessary for an effective reorganization.

   c. ☐ Pursuant to 11 U.S.C. § 362(d)(3), Debtor(s) has/have not satisfied the requirements of this section because of a failure to:
      (1) ☐ Commence payments; or
      (2) ☐ File a reasonable Plan of Reorganization within 90 days of the petition date.

(Continued on next page)

This form is mandatory by Order of the United States Bankruptcy Court for the Central District of California.

Revised January 2001

350RP

Sample Local Form Motion for Stay Relief, page 3 of 8

Motion for Relief from Stay (Real Property) - *Page 3 of* ___		**350RP**
In re	(SHORT TITLE)	CHAPTER:
	Debtor(s).	CASE NO.:

4. ☐ Movant also seeks annulment of the stay to validate post-petition acts, as specified in the attached declaration(s).

5. **Evidence in Support of Motion:** *(Important Note: Declaration(s) in support of the Motion **MUST** be attached hereto.)*

   a. ☐ Movant submits the attached Declaration(s) on the Court's approved forms (if applicable) to provide evidence in support of the Stay Motion pursuant to Local Bankruptcy Rules.

   b. ☐ Movant submits the attached supplemental Declaration(s) under penalty of perjury, to provide additional admissible evidence in support of the Stay Motion.

   c. ☐ Movant requests that the Court consider as admissions the statements made by Debtor(s) under penalty of perjury concerning Movant's claims and the Property set forth in Debtor(s)'s Schedules. Authenticated copies of the relevant portions of the Schedules are attached as Exhibit _____.

   d. ☐ Other evidence *(specify)*:

6. ☐ **An optional Memorandum of Points and Authorities is attached to this Motion.**

WHEREFORE, Movant prays that this Court issue an Order terminating or modifying the stay and granting the following *(specify forms of relief requested)*:

1. Relief from the Stay allowing Movant (and any successors or assigns) to proceed under applicable non-bankruptcy law to enforce its remedies to foreclose upon and obtain possession of the Property.

2. ☐ Annulment of the stay to validate post-petition acts, as specified in the attached declarations.

3. ☐ Additional provisions requested:

   a. ☐ That the Order be binding and effective in any bankruptcy case commenced by or against the above-named Debtor(s) for a period of 180 days, so that no further automatic stay shall arise in that case as to the Property.

   b. ☐ That the 7-day waiting period prescribed by California Civil Code Section 2924g(d) be waived.

   c. ☐ That the 10-day stay described by Bankruptcy Rule 4001(a)(3) be waived.

   d. ☐ See Extraordinary Relief Attachment *(Use Optional Court Form 350ER)*.

   e. ☐ For additional relief requested, see attached continuation page.

4. If relief from stay is not granted, Movant respectfully requests the Court to order adequate protection.

Dated: Respectfully submitted,

_____
Movant Name

_____
Firm Name of Attorney for Movant (if applicable)

By: _____
      Signature

Name: _____
        Typed Name of Individual Movant or Attorney for Movant

This form is mandatory by Order of the United States Bankruptcy Court for the Central District of California.

Revised January 2001   **350RP**

Sample Local Form Motion for Stay Relief, page 4 of 8

Motion for Relief from Stay (Real Property) - *Page 4 of* ___		**350RP**
In re _____ (SHORT TITLE)	CHAPTER:	
Debtor(s).	CASE NO.:	

REAL PROPERTY DECLARATION
(MOVANT: _____)

I, _____, declare as follows:
(Print Name of Declarant)

1. I have personal knowledge of the matters set forth in this declaration and, if called upon to testify, I could and would competently testify thereto. I am over 18 years of age. I have knowledge regarding Movant's interest in the Property that is the subject of this Motion because *(state title and capacity)*:

□ I am the Movant and owner of the Property.

□ I manage the Property as the authorized agent for the Movant.

□ I am employed by Movant as *(state title and capacity)*:

□ Other *(specify)*:

2. I am one of the custodians of the books, records and files of Movant as to those books, records and files that pertain to loans and extensions of credit given to Debtor concerning the Property. I have personally worked on books, records and files, and as to the following facts, I know them to be true of my own knowledge or I have gained knowledge of them from the business records of Movant on behalf of Movant, which were made at or about the time of the events recorded, and which are maintained in the ordinary course of Movant's business at or near the time of the acts, conditions or events to which they relate. Any such document was prepared in the ordinary course of business of Movant by a person who had personal knowledge of the event being recorded and had or has a business duty to record accurately such event. The business records are available for inspection and copies can be submitted to the Court if required.

3. a. The address of the real property that is the subject of this Motion is:
   Street Address:
   Apartment/Suite no.:
   City, State, Zip Code:

   b. The legal description or document recording number (including county of recording) set forth in Movant's Deed of Trust is attached as Exhibit _____.

   □ See attached page.

4. Type of property: *(Check all applicable boxes)*

   a. □ Debtor's principal residence   b. □ Other single family residence

   c. □ Multi-unit residential   d. □ Commercial

   e. □ Industrial   f. □ Vacant land

   g. □ Other *(specify)*:

(Continued on next page)

This form is mandatory by Order of the United States Bankruptcy Court for the Central District of California.

Revised January 2001

350RP

Sample Local Form Motion for Stay Relief, page 5 of 8

Motion for Relief from Stay (Real Property) - Page 5 of ___   **350RP**

In re	(SHORT TITLE)	CHAPTER:
	Debtor(s).	CASE NO.:

5. Nature of Debtor's interest in the Property:

   a. ☐ Sole owner

   b. ☐ Co-owner(s) (specify):

   c. ☐ Lien holder (specify):

   d. ☐ Other (specify):

   e. ☐ Debtor(s) ☐ did ☐ did not list the Property in the Schedules filed in this case.

   f. ☐ Debtor(s) acquired the interest in the Property by ☐ grant deed ☐ quitclaim deed ☐ trust deed

        The deed was recorded on:

6. Amount of Movant's claim with respect to the Property:

   a. Principal: $

   b. Accrued PREPETITION Payment Arrearages: $

   c. Accrued POST-PETITION Payment Arrearages: $

   d. Costs (Attorney's Fees, Late Charges, Foreclosure Costs): $

   e. Advances (Property Taxes, Insurance): $

   f. TOTAL CLAIM as of _____, ____: $

   g. ☐ Loan is all due and payable because it matured on (specify date):

7. Movant holds a ☐ deed of trust ☐ judgment lien ☐ other (specify)
that encumbers the Property.

   a. A true and correct copy of the document as recorded is attached as Exhibit _____.

   b. A true and correct copy of the promissory note or other document that evidences the Movant's claim is attached as Exhibit _____.

   c. ☐ A true and correct copy of the assignment(s) transferring the beneficial interest under the note and deed of trust to Movant is attached as Exhibit _____.

8. Status of Movant's claim relating to the Property (fill in all applicable information requested below):

   a. Current interest rate:

   b. Contractual maturity date:

   c. Amount of current monthly payment: $

   d. Number of PREPETITION payments that have come due and were not made:

   e. Number of POST-PETITION payments that have come due and were not made:

   f. Date of POST-PETITION or Post-Confirmation default:

   g. Last payment received on the following date:

   h. Notice of default recorded on the following date:

   i. Notice of sale recorded on the following date:

   j. Foreclosure sale originally scheduled for the following date:

   k. Foreclosure sale currently scheduled for the following date:

   l. Foreclosure sale already held on the following date:

   m. Trustee's deed on sale already recorded on the following date:

   n. Future payments due by time of anticipated hearing date (if applicable):
An additional payment of $_____ will come due on _____, and on the _____ day of each month thereafter.
If the payment is not received by the _____ day of the month, a late charge of $_____ will be charged to the loan.

(Continued on next page)

This form is mandatory by Order of the United States Bankruptcy Court for the Central District of California.

Revised January 2001   **350RP**

Sample Local Form Motion for Stay Relief, page 6 of 8

Motion for Relief from Stay (Real Property) - *Page 6 of* ___	**350RP**

In re	(SHORT TITLE)	CHAPTER:
	Debtor(s).	CASE NO.:

9. ☐ *(Chapter 7 and 11 cases only):* The fair market value of the entire Property is $_____, established by:

   a. ☐ Appraiser's declaration with appraisal attached herewith as Exhibit _____.

   b. ☐ A real estate broker or other expert's declaration regarding value attached as Exhibit _____.

   c. ☐ A true and correct copy of relevant portion(s) of Debtor's Schedules attached as Exhibit _____.

   d. ☐ Other *(specify)*:

10. ☐ Calculation of equity in Property *(Chapter 7 and 11 cases only):*

   a. Based upon ☐ a preliminary title report ☐ Debtor's(s') admissions in the schedules filed in this case, the Property is subject to the following deed(s) of trust or lien(s) in the amounts specified securing the debt against the Property:

	Name of Holder	Amount as Scheduled by Debtor (if any)	Amount Known to Declarant and Source
1st Deed of Trust:			
2nd Deed of Trust:			
3rd Deed of Trust:			
Judgment Liens:			
Taxes:			
Other:			
TOTAL DEBT: $			

   b. Evidence establishing the existence of the above deed(s) of trust and lien(s) is attached as Exhibit _____, and consists of:

      ☐ Preliminary title report

      ☐ Relevant portions of Debtor(s)'s Schedules as filed in this case

      ☐ Other *(specify)*:

   c. Subtracting the deed(s) of trust and other lien(s) set forth above from the value of the Property as set forth in Paragraph 9 above, the Debtor(s)'s equity in the Property is $_____ (§ 362(d)(2)(A)).

   d. The value of the "equity cushion" in the Property exceeding Movant's debt and any lien(s) senior to Movant is $_____ (§ 362(d)(1)).

   e. Estimated costs of sale: $_____ (Estimate based upon _____% of estimated fair market value)

11. ☐ *(Chapter 12 and 13 cases only)* Chapter 12 or 13 case status information:

   a. 341(a) Meeting currently scheduled for the following date:
      Confirmation hearing currently scheduled for the following date:
      Plan confirmed on the following date:

   b. Post-petition payment history:
      (1) Post-petition payments due BUT REMAINING UNPAID since the filing of the case:

(Number of) _____ payment(s) due at $_____	each	=	$_____
(Number of) _____ payment(s) due at $_____	each	=	$_____
(Number of) _____ late charge(s) at $_____	each	=	$_____
(Number of) _____ late charge(s) at $_____	each	=	$_____

      (2) Advances or other charges due but unpaid: $_____
         (See attachment for details of types and amount)

             TOTAL POST-PETITION DELINQUENCY: $_____

(Continued on next page)

This form is mandatory by Order of the United States Bankruptcy Court for the Central District of California.

Sample Local Form Motion for Stay Relief, page 7 of 8

Motion for Relief from Stay (Real Property) - *Page 7 of* ___   **350RP**

In re	(SHORT TITLE)	CHAPTER:
	Debtor(s).	CASE NO.:

    c. ☐ The claim is provided for in the Chapter 12 or 13 Plan. Plan payment history is attached as Exhibit _____.

    d. ☐ See attached Declaration(s) of Chapter 12 or 13 Trustee regarding receipt of payments under the plan *(Attach Court Form 350.13).*

12. ☐ Movant has not been provided with evidence that the Property is currently insured, as required under the terms of the loan.

13. ☐ The Property qualifies as single asset real estate and

    a. ☐ More than 90 days has passed since the filing of the petition and Debtor(s) has/have not filed a plan of reorganization that has a reasonable possibility of being confirmed within a reasonable time; or

    b. ☐ Debtor(s) has/have not commenced the monthly payments to Movant as required by 11 U.S.C § 362(d)(3)(B).

14. ☐ Other bankruptcy cases that have prevented Movant from recovering possession of this Property include the following:

    a. Case Name:
              Case Number: Chapter:
              Date Filed: Date Dismissed:
              Relief from stay re this property ☐ was   ☐ was not granted.

    b. Case Name:
              Case Number: Chapter:
              Date Filed: Date Dismissed:
              Relief from stay re this property ☐ was   ☐ was not granted.

    c. ☐ See attached continuation page for more information about other cases.

15. ☐ Movant seeks annulment of the automatic stay and validation of any and all of the enforcement actions set forth in paragraph 8 above that were taken after the filing of the bankruptcy petition in this case.

    a. ☐ These actions were taken by Movant without knowledge of the bankruptcy filing, and Movant would have been entitled to relief from stay to proceed with these actions.

    b. ☐ Although Movant knew about the bankruptcy filing, Movant had previously obtained relief from stay to proceed with these enforcement actions in prior bankruptcy cases affecting this Property as set forth in paragraph 14 above.

    c. ☐ For other facts justifying annulment, see attached continuation page.

I declare under penalty of perjury under the laws of the United States of America that the foregoing is true and correct and that this Declaration was executed on _____, _____, **at** _____ *(city, state).*

_____   _____
Print Declarant's Name   *Signature of Declarant*

This form is mandatory by Order of the United States Bankruptcy Court for the Central District of California.

Revised January 2001   **350RP**

Sample Local Form Motion for Stay Relief, page 8 of 8

Motion for Relief from Stay (Real Property) - *Page 8 of* ___		**350RP**
In re	(SHORT TITLE)	CHAPTER:
	Debtor(s).	CASE NO.:

PROOF OF SERVICE

STATE OF CALIFORNIA
COUNTY OF _____

1. I am over the age of 18 and not a party to the within action. My business address is as follows:

2. **Regular Mail Service**: On _____, pursuant to Local Bankruptcy Rule 9013-1, I served the documents described as: NOTICE OF MOTION FOR RELIEF FROM THE AUTOMATIC STAY UNDER 11 U.S.C. § 362 and MOTION FOR RELIEF FROM THE AUTOMATIC STAY UNDER 11 U.S.C. § 362 (including supporting declarations) on the interested parties at their last known address in this action by placing a true and correct copy thereof in a sealed envelope with postage thereon fully prepaid in the United States Mail at _____, California, addressed as set forth on the attached list.

> **Note:** *If the Notice and Motion have been served pursuant to an Order Shortening Time ("Order"), you must file a Proof of Service that indicates that the notice and service requirements contained in the Order have been met.*

3. **See attached list for names and addresses of all parties and counsel that have been served** *(In the manner set forth in Local Bankruptcy Rule 7004-1(b), specify capacity in which service is made; e.g., Debtor, Debtor's Attorney, Trustee, Trustee's Attorney, Creditors Committee or 20 largest unsecured creditors, etc.)*

I declare under penalty of perjury under the laws of the United States of America that the foregoing is true and correct.

Dated:

_____
Typed Name

_____
Signature

This form is mandatory by Order of the United States Bankruptcy Court for the Central District of California.

Revised January 2001   **350RP**

Responding to Motions and Complaints

The discharge of your claim against the debtor may not be the only threat you face in bankruptcy. If your debt is secured by collateral, you may also lose your right to sell the collateral. You may even be forced to return money or property that the debtor transferred to you before going bankrupt. All of this will, of course, depend on what the debtor requests and what the court grants in the course of the proceedings. To obtain certain court decisions or orders, the debtor will have to file a motion or complaint—and you will then have to defend yourself.

Defending against this sort of maneuver is best done with a lawyer's help. Nevertheless, this chapter will give you a primer on opposing motions and defending against adversary actions. Our intention is that you decide how much you can handle on your own, and become better able to work with a lawyer in your defense and possibly save yourself legal fees as a result. We'll cover:

- responding to motions (Section A)
- typical motions and appropriate responses (Section B)
- responding to complaints (Section C), and
- typical complaints and appropriate responses (Section D).

A. How to Respond to a Motion

A motion is a request for the bankruptcy judge to enter an order. It's a document done in a specific court format (as described in Chapter 10), with numbered paragraphs containing alleged facts and arguments and concluding with a specific request.

You'll find out that a motion has been filed by receiving a copy in the mail from the person who prepared it. This person is usually the debtor or the trustee, but it could be another creditor. Once you receive the motion, you'll have a set amount of time within which to respond. How much time this is varies from court to court. The federal rules of bankruptcy procedure don't establish any standard deadline. Instead, they leave it to the court to set an appropriate response time based on the nature of the order requested. The more urgent the need for the order, the less time you will be given in which to respond. The notice you get with the motion will tell you how much time the court allowed you—usually no more than ten days.

When faced with a motion, some people instinctively respond with, "No I didn't!" to every allegation. Putting such knee-jerk responses into writing is counterproductive and can ruin your credibility with the court. Don't deny allegations that are true and don't oppose relief you know the other side is entitled to receive. At worst, either action might inspire the court to penalize you for acting in bad faith.

Instead, your response to the motion will tell the court where you disagree with the person who filed it (known as the "movant"). Maybe you'll dispute the facts upon which the motion is based. Maybe you feel the motion doesn't tell the judge everything she needs to know to make a ruling. Maybe you don't believe the movant is entitled to the requested relief. Whatever the reason for your objection, voice it in your response.

It's best to respond to each numbered paragraph in the motion and then state additional information as needed. Using this format ensures that you respond to everything in the motion without creating confusion as to the points of agreement and disagreement.

If you have nothing at all to say on your own behalf, you don't need to respond. If the judge doesn't receive a response from you, she'll only have one side of the story to go on—and may accordingly issue an order granting or denying what was requested. The judge is not required to hold a hearing to determine the merits of unopposed requests.

In addition to filing a response with the court, you must send a copy to the person who filed the motion. Always send a copy to the debtor and the trustee, even if they weren't the ones to file the motion.

B. Typical Motions and Responses

In this section, we'll describe a number of the motions you're likely to encounter in the course of bankruptcy proceedings. We'll also give some tips on how best to respond. You may be faced with a motion to:

- avoid your lien (Subsection 1)
- value the collateral (Subsection 2)
- allow use of the collateral by a business debtor (Subsection 3)
- assume or reject an executory contract or lease (Subsection 4)
- convert the case to another chapter (Subsection 5), or
- dismiss the case (Subsection 6).

1. Motion to Avoid a Lien

If you are an unsecured creditor, skip to Section B4, below.

If you are a secured creditor—meaning you have a lien against the debtor's property because of a contract or court judgment—the debtor may be legally allowed to eliminate or limit your lien. This could prevent you from selling the debtor's property for payment of your claim. The debtor knows that, under normal circumstances, any lien you have against the debtor's property will survive the bankruptcy, even if the underlying debt has been discharged. The debtor may prevent your lien's survival, however, by obtaining a court order that fully or partially avoids the lien. Two liens likely to be the subject of such a motion include voluntary liens on exempt household possessions and involuntary liens created by a court judgment.

a. Voluntary Liens on Exempt Household Possessions

Debtors may avoid liens on exempt items found around their homes that were pledged as security for loans, so long as they had the items before the loans were made and still have them in their possession. For example, if you took a security interest in the debtor's television, the court will probably allow the debtor to avoid your lien. Stated in more precise legal terminology, a debtor may legally avoid any nonpossessory, nonpurchase-money security interest on exempt household goods, clothing, appliances, books, animals, crops, musical instruments, jewelry, health aids, tools used in their trade, professional books, and implements. (This list of property types comes from the Bankruptcy Code, at 11 U.S.C. § 522(f).) To develop your argument against the lien avoidance, you'll need to start by figuring out whether the property does, in fact, meet every part of the definition of an exempt, "nonpossessory, nonpurchase-money security interest."

The issue of whether the debtor's items of property are exempt may have come up early on in the bankruptcy—you would have first had a chance to challenge the debtor's exemption claims at the meeting of creditors (discussed in Chapter 6 of this book). Hopefully you took advantage of that opportunity: If you did not challenge an exemption within 30 days after the meeting of creditors, some courts will refuse to allow you to question the debtor's entitlement to the exemption when it comes up in the context of a lien avoidance motion. The courts point to the Bankruptcy Code's statement that any exemption claimed by the debtor is allowed if there are no timely filed objections. However, many other courts say that this rule doesn't apply when a creditor questions the validity of a lien in response to the debtor's lien avoidance action.

Next, you need to figure out whether the lien is "possessory." This is not too hard. If you, as the secured creditor, have possession of the collateral, then the lien is possessory. If you don't have possession of the collateral, the lien is nonpossessory.

Moving right along, a "nonpurchase-money" lien is one where the debtor owned or possessed the collateral before the security interest was created. If you loaned the debtor the money to buy the collateral, then your right to sell the property if the debtor doesn't repay the loan is a purchase-money security interest. If the debtor pledged property she already had, then the loan is a nonpurchase-money one.

The categories of qualifying property—such as clothing and books—listed in the Bankruptcy Code don't seem to require extra definition. However, that doesn't necessarily mean you can't argue over them. Don't waste your breath (or paper) on items such as pots and pans, children's toys, and stereo equipment, which clearly fit within the household goods listing. But, realize that courts have disagreed as to whether debtors may avoid liens on computers, a second television, or a lawn tractor. If you see an item of property that doesn't seem like a neat fit, consult with a lawyer or try your own hand at legal research, as described in Chapter 19.

In order to avoid your lien, the debtor will have to break down the requirements described above into separate elements and prove each one, including that:

1. **The collateral is in the debtor's possession.**
2. **The debtor owned the property before the security interest attached to it.**
3. **The collateral fits into one of the property categories listed in the Bankruptcy Code.**
4. **The collateral is exempt under applicable state or federal law.**

If the debtor is unable to prove each of these elements, your lien can be saved. However, you'll need to point out the weaknesses in the debtor's assertions. You'll do this in your response to the debtor's motion, challenging one or more of the debtor's assertions. For example:

- If the property is in your possession, deny the debtor's allegation that the property is in his possession.
- If you loaned the debtor the money used to purchase the collateral, deny the debtor's allegation that she had the property before your lien attached to it.
- If the property does not clearly fit into one of the categories identified in the Bankruptcy Code (listed in the first paragraph of this section, above), deny the debtor's allegation that the property qualifies for lien avoidance. If the item isn't necessary for the maintenance of the debtor's household, you can usually convince the court to deny the debtor's motion to avoid the lien.
- If the debtor is unable to shield the property under applicable exemption laws, deny the debtor's allegation that the property is exempt.

See the end of this chapter for a sample response to a lien avoidance motion.

b. Involuntary Judgment Liens

Liens that are created as a part of a money judgment obtained in court (called judicial liens) give you the right to sell the debtor's property to collect on your judgment. Typically these liens are created as follows: You sued the debtor, a judgment was entered in your favor and you took whatever additional steps were necessary in your state to record that judgment against the debtor's property.

Your lien may be in danger, however. The Bankruptcy Code allows debtors to avoid judicial liens to the extent they reduce the debtor's ability to claim an item of property as exempt. (Debtors cannot, however, avoid judicial liens that cover the nonpayment of spousal or child support; see the sidebar below, "Important Exception for Child and Spousal Support.")

A lien impairs an exemption when it reduces the debtor's equity below the amount that can be claimed as exempt. If the debtor's home is worth $250,000 and the available homestead exemption is $100,000, then judicial liens can be avoided to the extent that the total of all liens against the property exceed $150,000. Why? Because once the liens exceed $150,000, the debtor's equity drops below the $100,000 that she can claim as exempt. (See Chapter 8, Section H for a complete discussion of avoiding judicial liens.)

Below are examples to help you get accustomed to doing this math. In each example, the debtor owns a house that is worth $250,000, and lives in a state where the homestead exemption is $100,000.

(Note: These examples follow a mathematical formula from Section 522(f) of the Bankruptcy Code.)

EXAMPLE 1: Dave and Dora didn't pay the orthodontist for their son's braces, so the orthodontist sued and received a $5,000 judgment against them. Dave and Dora own a home worth $250,000, and they owe $75,000 on their first mortgage. There are no other liens against the home. Dave and Dora can't avoid the orthodontist's lien because it does not impair their exemption. The total of the liens ($80,000) plus the exemption ($100,000) is less than the property is worth ($250,000).

EXAMPLE 2: Assume the same facts as in Example 1, above, but imagine that Dave and Dora had also taken out a second mortgage against their home in the amount of $100,000. Under these facts, the orthodontist's judgment lien can be completely avoided. Now the total liens ($180,000) plus the exemption ($100,000) exceed the property's value ($250,000) by $30,000. Hence, the liens impair the exemption by $30,000. If the exemption had been impaired by less than the $5,000 owed to the orthodontist, then the orthodontist's lien would have been reduced by the amount of the impairment. By avoiding such liens, the debtor can protect any and all potentially exempt property, including the debtor's home.

In order to successfully avoid your lien, the debtor will have to prove that the lien was both:

- created by a court judgment, and
- impairs the debtor's ability to exempt the property.

Check the debtor's motion carefully to see that these requirements have been met. If, for example, your right to place a lien on the debtor's property was created by law, not by a court decision, you will want to deny the debtor's allegation that the lien was created by a judgment.

You will want to deny any allegation that the lien impairs the debtor's exemption if the lien doesn't affect the exemption, or if the debtor is not entitled to an exemption. For example, you might show that the property is worth more than the debtor says it is (thereby increasing the debtor's equity in the property). Or, you could show that less money is owed on a consensual lien than the debtor claims, or that the property doesn't really fit within the exemption category.

Important Exception for Child and Spousal Support

If a court creates a lien against the property of a debtor because the debtor has failed to pay alimony, maintenance, child support, or spousal support, that lien cannot be avoided. In order for this exception to apply, the debtor's spouse, former spouse, or child must hold the lien.

For example, let's assume that when Delano and Carol divorced, Delano received possession of the marital residence and was ordered to pay Carol half its value. The court placed a lien against the property to secure payment of Delano's obligation to Carol. This lien cannot be avoided as long as Carol holds it. However, if Carol transfers the lien to someone else, Delano can avoid the lien even though it was created in the divorce proceeding.

Assume, also, that Delano was ordered to pay Carol's attorney's fees, and that the court imposed a lien against the property for payment of this obligation. This lien can be avoided because the lien was granted to Carol's attorney, not to Carol herself.

2. Motion to Value the Collateral

Bankrupt debtors may be able to avoid any portion of your lien that isn't backed up by the collateral's worth. Before doing this, however, they must ask the court to set a value on your collateral. The debtor may do this by filing a motion that alleges a value and asks for the court's agreement. (Recall that in most situations, your lien is secured only to the extent of the property's value, minus any liens that attached to the property before yours did. This can result in a wholly or partly unsecured lien.)

The exact mechanism by which the debtor can avoid your lien—and the circumstances under which he would ask the court for a valuation—depend on what chapter of the Bankruptcy Code the debtor filed under. Chapter 7 debtors filing as individuals may redeem personal property that is collateral for the secured value of your claim. Redemption has the practical effect of avoiding your lien to the extent it is unsecured. (Redemption is discussed in Chapter 8.)

EXAMPLE: Dard owes Caesar $5,000. The loan is secured by Dard's car, which is worth only $3,000—meaning that the loan is only partially secured. Dard files for Chapter 7 bankruptcy. If Dard wants to keep the car and pay Caesar only the secured value of the claim, Dard must make a lump sum payment to Caesar equal to the car's value. Dard will, therefore, start by submitting a Motion to Value the Collateral to the bankruptcy court.

Chapters 11, 12, and 13 debtors may avoid the unsecured portion of liens through their confirmed plans. Before doing so, they must prove that the collateral is worth less than what they owe on the debt. They would do this by filing a motion to value collateral, which the court will consider at the same time as the confirmation of their reorganization plans.

EXAMPLE: Davina, an aspiring concert pianist, buys a grand piano for $15,000 from Clive. She still owes $13,0000 when she files for Chapter 13 protection. The piano, which endured spilled coffee and a cat's claw sharpening while in Davina's home, was by now worth only $8,000. Davina wants to keep the piano and pay Clive what it's worth through her plan. To do so, she must have the court value the piano. She could accomplish this by filing a Motion to Value the Collateral, which the court would consider along with the confirmation of her plan.

Wholly secured, partially secured, and wholly unsecured liens arise most frequently when real estate is the collateral. In fact, real estate tends to be the only asset a debtor has that can secure more than one lien.

The only fact at issue in this motion will be the property's value. If you have reason to believe that the collateral is worth more than the debtor says it is, you should deny the debtor's allegation as to value. In a reorganization case, you may also want to object to confirmation of the debtor's plan. Also object to the plan if it calls for you to lose the unsecured portion of your lien before the debtor receives a discharge. (Plan confirmation is discussed in Chapter 13.)

3. Motion to Allow Use of Collateral by Business Debtor

The Bankruptcy Code allows business debtors to continue to use property that has been pledged as collateral without getting the court's permission. The main conditions are that the property be something other than cash, and that the debtor will use, sell, or lease it in the ordinary course of the debtor's business. However, the debtor will have to file a motion asking the court's permission if the debtor wishes to use cash collateral (Subsection a), or to use the collateral for a nonbusiness purpose (Subsection b).

In cases where the debtor doesn't need to file a motion asking permission to use the collateral, you may still have some recourse. If you think the collateral's use will harm you by lessening its value, then you may file a motion seeking adequate protection (see Chapter 8).

a. Use of Cash Collateral

Cash collateral is an exception to the general rule that debtors may continue to use, sell, or lease collateral. Bank accounts, checks, and securities are all considered cash collateral. Therefore, debtors may not withdraw money from a bank account that serves as collateral for a loan without first asking the court's permission. Nor may debtors use money that comes from the sale of goods that were subject to a lien, because the lien attaches to the sale proceeds, which is cash collateral.

Because debtors need to be able to use their cash to survive, expect the debtor to file a motion seeking permission to use cash collateral shortly after the bankruptcy petition is filed. In fact, this is so customary in Chapter 11 cases that the motion seeking permission to use cash collateral is part of a package of documents filed by business debtors known as "first day" orders.

While creditors are rarely able to defeat a motion for cash collateral, because denying a debtor the use of the cash means the debtor will go out of business, courts will condition the debtor's use of cash collateral when there is creditor opposition to the motion. Typical conditions require debtors to submit periodic reports to creditors showing how the money is being used, place a limit on the amount of money the debtor may use, and create an alternative security interest to protect the creditor who is secured by the debtor's cash.

b. Use of Collateral Outside the Debtor's Business

If the debtor wishes to use your collateral for a purpose outside the ordinary course of business, then the debtor must file a motion and obtain the court's permission. You may oppose this motion by arguing that the debtor really doesn't need to use your collateral to accomplish her purpose or that she's not minimizing her use of your collateral. Even if you concede that the debtor must use your collateral in the manner she wants to, you may ask the court for compensation or protection against the reduction of the collateral's value as a result of its use.

> **EXAMPLE 1:** Denver Dry Goods, a store, files for bankruptcy under Chapter 7. Denver's still has a good deal of inventory on its shelves, and hopes to hold a "going out of business" sale. However, the store's inventory is collateral for a loan. That means that Denver Dry Goods will need to get the court's permission before proceeding with such a special sale, which is outside its usual course of business. The creditor might oppose Denver's motion by showing that the goods could be sold at a higher price on another market. Even if the court denies the motion, however, the store may remain open and sell the inventory in the normal course of its business.

> **EXAMPLE 2:** Delilah, a farmer, files for bankruptcy under Chapter 12. Delilah can continue to sell crops in the same manner as before she filed for bankruptcy even if those crops are collateral for a loan. However, she would also like to sell off some of her land. Because this is outside the ordinary course of her business, she will need to first file a motion to allow this use of the collateral. A creditor might oppose this motion based on the qualifications of the buyer or the areas selected for sale.

4. Motion to Assume or Reject an Executory Contract or Lease

The Bankruptcy Code allows trustees and debtors to assume (recommit to) or reject executory contracts and leases. By way of reminder, an executory contract is one in which you, the debtor or both of you have a substantial obligation yet to perform. A lease, for example, is an executory contract because the tenant has a continuing substantial obligation to pay the rent. If the trustee or the debtor wishes to assume the lease, they would file a Motion to Assume an Executory Contract. If they don't take steps to assume the lease or other contract, it is automatically rejected—in other words, the lease is cancelled and the agreement is treated as if it was breached when the bankruptcy was filed.

If the contract's terms are favorable to the debtor, the trustee will want to assume the agreement in order to take advantage of the payment stream, and will file a motion accordingly. For example, if the debtor's business is located in rented space, then the trustee will keep the lease if the business is going to stay open and the rent is fair. If, however, the trustee plans to close the business or move it to a cheaper location, then the trustee will want to reject the lease because its terms are unfavorable. The trustee's action doesn't mean the lease was unfair or inappropriate. It just means the agreement's terms are not consistent with the debtor's current situation.

The trustee may assume an executory contract only if the debtor is current on all obligations under the contract. If the debtor is in default, the court will grant a motion to assume only if the debtor's obligations are brought current, the creditor is compensated for any harm caused by the default, and the debtor provides adequate assurance of future performance.

As a creditor, you may or may not want to oppose a motion to assume the contract—it depends on whether or not you want out of the contract. If, for example, you'd be just as happy continuing under the contract, then don't file an objection to the motion. If, on the other hand, you'd rather that the debtor move out of your rental or cut whatever other contractual ties he has with you, oppose

the motion. Your opposition to the motion is particularly appropriate if the debtor:

- is not current with all of his duties under your agreement
- has not paid damages for a previous breach, or
- appears incapable of meeting the obligations called for in the agreement.

Note regarding Chapter 7 cases: Leases of residential real estate and personal property must be assumed within 60 days after the bankruptcy is filed. If they are not assumed by this deadline they are automatically rejected—that is, there is no longer any agreement between you and the debtor. If 60 days is not enough time for the trustee to decide what to do with the contract, the trustee should file a motion to extend this deadline. If you favor rejection of the contract—that is, you want the contract to end—oppose the extension by telling the court that the extension imposes a hardship on you, unfairly prejudices your position, and is not needed by the trustee.

Note regarding Chapters 11, 12, and 13 cases: Residential real estate and personal property leases may be assumed at any time prior to plan confirmation. The court may extend this deadline.

Trustees' attempts to reject executory contracts tend to create more opposition than motions to assume do. However, there are times when you may be better off with the rejection of a contract that the trustee wants to assume. Here are two examples:

EXAMPLE 1: Carlton Properties has leased property along a swank commercial street to Dan's Cup-O-Yogurt. Unfortunately, after a particularly cold summer, Dan's ends up filing for Chapter 7 bankruptcy. Because the rental value of commercial space has appreciated in the last year, Carlton believes it could get more rent by putting the space on the market. However, the trustee wants to assume the lease, because its terms are favorable. Unfortunately for Carlton, it will need to find some ground of opposition that is based on the merits of the debtor's ability to meet the agreement's terms rather than on its desire to find a higher rate of return.

EXAMPLE 2: Dip-In-Road Communications files for Chapter 11. The company's board of directors decides it needs its founder and CEO, Mr. Dip, to stay with the company if it has any chance of reorganizing. Mr. Dip says he'll do it, but only if his team of assistants stays on as well. The company agrees. However, Cooley's Pipes and Wires—which provided the cables for Dip-In-Road Communications' expansion project and is still owed $1.5 million—objects.

According to Cooley's, it was Mr. Dip and his crew that wrecked the company. Cooley's also says that these people are so overpaid that with them, reorganization is impossible. And, Cooley's argues that Mr. Dip improperly influenced the board while it was considering whether to keep him around. For all these reasons, Cooley's objects to Dip-In-Road's motion to assume the contracts of Mr. Dip and his aides.

5. Motion to Convert to Another Bankruptcy Chapter

Debtors don't necessarily have to stick with the bankruptcy chapter under which they filed. They may switch their cases from a liquidation proceeding under Chapter 7 to a reorganization proceeding under Chapter 11, 12 or 13—or vice versa. Debtors can also slide from one type of reorganization to another. If you are opposed to the debtor's conversion, you may need to file a motion saying so.

Because conversion is such a significant topic, we've devoted a whole separate chapter to it. In Chapter 14 of this book, you'll learn about the nuances of bankruptcy chapter changes and how they affect you. You'll also learn whether and how you should file a motion opposing the debtor's conversion.

6. Motion to Dismiss

If the debtor files a motion to dismiss the entire bankruptcy case, your first instinct may be to say, "Sure, go right ahead." You may have been wishing the case would return to its prebankruptcy status. However, there are several situations in which a dismissal can actually hurt your interests, and in which you would want to oppose the motion to dismiss. These include:

- when assets have been discovered in a Chapter 7 case (Subsection a), and
- when the debtor has acquired property after the filing and you want the court's assistance in ensuring that some of it is used to pay you (Subsection b).

But first, you might be wondering why the debtor needs to file a motion to dismiss his own case. The answer is that Section 707(a) and Section 1112(b) of the Bankruptcy Code say that Chapter 7 and Chapter 11 cases can only be dismissed "for cause." A debtor who says, "I changed my mind" has not shown sufficient cause for dismissal. If the debtor asks the court to dismiss the bankruptcy and you'd rather have the debtor remain in bankruptcy because you think you have a better shot at getting paid with a trustee handling the debtor's affairs, then oppose the motion.

Debtors who file under Chapter 12 or Chapter 13 do not need to show cause to have their cases dismissed, provided that they have never converted their cases to or from Chapter 7 or Chapter 11. The Bankruptcy Code gives them an absolute right to dismiss their cases. However, if you filed a motion to convert their case to Chapter 7 or Chapter 11 before they asked the court to dismiss their case, some courts—though not all—will consider whether it would be better for creditors if the case were converted or dismissed.

a. Discovered Assets in a Chapter 7 Case

If the debtor's change of heart is motivated by the trustee's discovery of hidden assets or by a successful objection to an exemption, you should oppose the debtor's motion to dismiss. It's better to have the trustee administer those assets than to trust the debtor to use them to pay your claim. After all, the debtor's attempt to hide the assets or to claim an unwarranted exemption indicates that the debtor can't be trusted to use the assets to pay creditors' claims. This concern would be the basis of your opposition to the debtor's motion.

b. Property Acquired by the Debtor Postfiling

As you've learned, the bankruptcy estate includes not only everything the debtor owned or had a legal right to when the petition was filed, but also certain property acquired after the bankruptcy. The debtor may feel that this new property can save him from bankruptcy, but you may prefer that the bankruptcy court be the one to ensure that some of this property comes your way. The mere fact that the debtor now has enough money to pay creditors' claims doesn't mean that he actually will pay, if he's allowed to exit from bankruptcy.

What kind of property are we talking about? In Chapter 7 and Chapter 11 cases, property the debtor acquires within 180 days after filing for bankruptcy will be added to the bankruptcy estate, and may include inheritances, insurance proceeds, and marital property settlements.

The debtor's acquisition of postpetition property may be sufficient to give the debtor a fresh start without a bankruptcy discharge. If, however, the debtor's windfall has become property of the bankruptcy estate, you may be better off if the debtor stays in bankruptcy. You can argue that the conduct of the debtor that led to the bankruptcy should prevent the dis-

missal of the case. For example, if the debtor filed for bankruptcy after losing substantial sums of money gambling, it may be more prudent to have the trustee use the postpetition assets to pay creditors' claims than to allow the debtor to spend the money after the case is dismissed.

In Chapter 12 and Chapter 13 cases, postpetition property that will be made part of the bankruptcy estate at confirmation includes the debtor's future earnings and all property acquired by the debtor after filing for bankruptcy and before the plan is confirmed. If the debtor acquires unexpected property after the plan is confirmed, however, its status is less clear—some courts will add it to the bankruptcy estate, others not.

Oddly enough, you can oppose a debtor's motion to dismiss a Chapter 12 or 13 case only if the case has been converted from another bankruptcy chapter. If it has not been converted, then you have no basis upon which to oppose the debtor's motion to dismiss. If the case has been converted, you can oppose dismissal for the same reasons mentioned for opposing dismissal under Chapters 7 and 11, above. However, you can't force the debtor to remain in Chapter 12 or 13. (See Chapter 14 of this book for a complete discussion of how and when to oppose motions to convert or dismiss.)

C. How to Respond to a Complaint

Certain issues that arise in bankruptcy proceedings cannot be dealt with using a motion, but will require the debtor to file a more formal court pleading known as a complaint. The filing of a complaint starts an adversary action. (See Chapter 10 for a discussion of complaints and adversary actions.)

If you receive a complaint from the debtor, you will have 30 days in which to file an answer. If you need more time, file a motion to extend the deadline.

Your answer should mirror the complaint, admitting or denying the statements made in each paragraph. If you don't know the answer, it's alright to say that you neither admit nor deny the statement but that you demand proof at trial. Whatever you say, be sure it's accurate. If you don't answer accurately or in good faith, the court may penalize you for violating Bankruptcy Rule 9011.

After you've responded to everything in the complaint, you may feel that the court still needs more information. You may add statements at the end of your answer, following the rules stated above for filing a complaint. Begin numbering these paragraphs where the complaint ended. So, if the complaint has 27 paragraphs, your additional material begins at paragraph 28.

There are two types of additional information that you must add to your answer or risk forever losing the opportunity to raise the underlying issues. These are known as affirmative defenses and counterclaims (including crossclaims).

a. Affirmative Defenses

An affirmative defense says to the court that even if everything the plaintiff says is true, there are reasons why the plaintiff should not win. In the answer that you file, all affirmative defenses should be listed separately and identified as such.

For example, there are deadlines for filing various types of complaints. If the deadline has passed, you need to raise the debtor's failure to timely file the complaint as an affirmative defense. (You'd also want to ask the court to dismiss the complaint, because the court does not have authority to hear it after the deadline has passed.)

b. Counterclaims and Crossclaims

A counterclaim is an action you have against the plaintiff based on the same facts that support the plaintiff's action. You could have sued the plaintiff, but the plaintiff beat you to it. For example, if the debtor sued you for violating a consumer protection law, you could countersue for damages based on the debtor's breach of contract. Now you're prevented from filing a separate suit against the plaintiff, since this would result in piecemeal litigation. Instead, you must include a counterclaim in your answer to the debtor's complaint so that the court can hear everybody's claims at the same time.

If your counterclaim is against someone other than the debtor, you may still raise it as part of your answer. This action is known as bringing a crossclaim. Let's say the debtor sues you to recover a payment made to you, but you passed the money along to someone else. The debtor sues you, but you don't have the money, so you sue the person who has the money. This example involves both an affirmative defense ("Yes, I got the money but it wasn't for me it was for Mr. X") and a crossclaim ("Mr. X, whatever money I owe to the plaintiff, you owe to me.")

D. Typical Complaints and Answers

Certain types of complaints appear in bankruptcy cases with predictable regularity. You are most likely to be served with a complaint in which the debtor or trustee is either trying to recover property from you or to get assurance that your claim has been discharged. Below, we'll discuss what these complaints mean and your most effective means of convincing the court to see things your way, including complaints:

- over prepetition property transfers (Subsection 1)
- over postpetition transfers (Subsection 2), and
- requesting a discharge determination (Subsection 3).

1. Complaint to Avoid Prepetition Transfers and Liens

You may receive a complaint from the trustee that seeks to recover property that was transferred to you before the bankruptcy was filed. As discussed at length in Chapter 16, trustees have broad powers to recover property transferred prebankruptcy. Such property might include tangible items like cash and possessions, as well as intangible property interests such as liens. In particular, the trustee is likely to allege either that:

- you received the property as a preferential transfer (Subsection a)
- you don't really have a lien because its perfection was defective (Subsection b) or done too late (Subsection c)
- the lien was for unpaid rent (Subsection d), or
- the property was transferred fraudulently (Subsection e).

a. Preferential Transfers

Trustees may file a complaint to avoid any transfer that the law says favored one creditor over the rest. For example, the trustee will look for payments made on existing claims by debtors who couldn't afford to pay all their bills. These payments are frequently made to people who are friends or relatives of the debtor or whose cooperation the debtor needs in order to stay in business.

Your response to such a complaint needs to focus on the factual allegations and present any evidence you have that the trustee is wrong. You might also find a loophole among the rules and exceptions governing the avoidance of preferential transfers, which we'll consider in Chapter 16.

For the format and "look" of an answer to such a complaint, see the second sample at the end of this chapter. Paragraphs that are marked as "admitted" refer to general statements identifying the debtor and creditor, describing when and how the debt arose and when the debtor filed for bankruptcy. This sample includes two affirmative defenses based on exceptions to the trustee's ability to avoid preferential transfers.

b. Defective Liens

The trustee may file a complaint asking to avoid any lien that was not properly per-fected. You'll recall from Chapter 8 that perfection of a lien makes it enforceable against anyone who may subsequently claim an interest or title to the collateral. When a lien is not properly perfected, a person who does not know about the lien's existence can acquire the collateral without paying off the lien. The trustee, who has a right to all of the debtor's property as of the petition date, is one of those people who can come along later and acquire the property without paying off the lien.

A trustee's complaint to avoid your lien because it was improperly perfected is going to state the nature of the defect. For example, information may be missing from the document you filed to perfect your lien. The trustee will claim that the missing information negates your lien. Your response would be either that the information was included or that it didn't need to be included for the lien to be perfected.

c. Untimely Perfection

The trustee may file a complaint to avoid any lien that you did not perfect quickly enough or at all. Failure to timely perfect the lien does not make it defective, but it does make perfection of the lien a preferential transfer. The reason is that the perfection does not relate back to the creation of the debt. Therefore, the lien is a transfer on account of an antecedent debt.

A trustee's complaint to avoid your lien because it was untimely perfected is going to state when your claim was created and when it was perfected. Your response should dispute either the dates asserted by the trustee or the application of the law governing the timeliness of perfection. For example, the Bankruptcy Code says that, in order to be treated as a purchase-money lien, a security interest must be perfected within 20 days of when the debtor takes possession of the collateral. The trustee's complaint might allege that more than 20 days went by between these events. You might argue the opposite.

d. Lien for Unpaid Rent

The trustee may file a complaint to avoid any statutory liens on the debtor's property that were imposed for unpaid rent. (Recall that statutory liens are ones imposed automatically by law.) Your best response to the trustee's complaint would be that the lien was based on a security provision in your lease and not merely on the statute. Check the terms of your lease.

e. Fraudulent Transfer

Trustees may file a complaint to recover property that the debtor transferred fraudulently. As a creditor, the type of fraud complaint you're most likely to encounter is one alleging that the debtor, who was insolvent, made the transfer for little or nothing in return (by way of so-called "consideration"). If faced with such a complaint, you might respond that the transfer was, in fact, made for fair consideration or that the debtor was solvent at the time of the transfer.

2. Complaint to Avoid a Postpetition Transfer

Another type of complaint that might arrive from the trustee is one asking the court to void a property transfer the debtor made after filing for bankruptcy. As you've learned, all the property that the debtor owns or has an interest in as of the date of the bankruptcy filing becomes property of the debtor's bankruptcy estate—and is therefore under the power of the trustee. If the debtor transfers this property without the court's permission, the trustee can ask the court to void the transfer and recover the property.

In your answer to the trustee's complaint, you might argue that the transfer occurred before the bankruptcy was filed, or that it was authorized by the court. You also have two potential affirmative defenses, depending on when and how your lien in the property was perfected.

Your first potential defense applies to cases where the so-called transfer targeted by the trustee was not of actual property, but was the perfection of your security interest. The trustee will probably allege that perfection didn't happen by the time it should have. In such cases, you would defend yourself by looking at the law, in hopes that it treats the date of perfection as earlier than the trustee is claiming. For example, the federal Bankruptcy Code says that you have 20 days from the date when the debtor takes possession of collateral to perfect a purchase-money security interest. The automatic stay doesn't prevent you from perfecting your lien if the debtor files for bankruptcy during those 20 days. So, even though your lien was a created postpetition, it is treated as if it was created prepetition.

You can also put forth a defense any time the property transferred was real estate. (See 11 U.S.C. § 549(c).) In order to benefit from this broad defense, you must have recorded your claim to the property before the bankruptcy was recorded, you must not have known of the bankruptcy and you must have paid fair value for the property.

3. Complaint to Determine Whether a Debt Has Been Discharged

There are times when the debtor may wish to clarify whether a creditor's claim will be discharged. The debtor would accomplish this by filing a complaint asking the bankruptcy court to decide the mat-

ter—and usually alleging, of course, that your claim should be discharged.

If you believe that your claim should be excepted from discharge, but the debtor doesn't file a complaint seeking to discharge your claim, see Chapter 10 for a discussion of how to proceed.

As an individual creditor, the only discharge challenge that you're likely to face is one based on alimony, maintenance, or support. The debtor may feel the obligation isn't for alimony, maintenance, or support and try to have it discharged. (See Chapter 9 for details.) If you're faced with one of these complaints, try to show, through denials of the debtor's assertions, that the claim arose in a divorce or separation and is in the nature of alimony, maintenance, or support. (See 11 U.S.C. § 523(a)(5).)

It's best not to wait for the debtor's complaint. If the debtor owes you money based on an obligation created in a separation agreement or divorce decree and you're not sure whether it constitutes support or not, file a complaint to determine dischargeability under Sections 523(a)(5) and (a)(15) of the Code before the deadline, which is 60 days after the creditors' meeting. Don't sit back and wait for the debtor to ask the court for a ruling. The debtor probably won't ask until it's too late for you to challenge the discharge of a nonsupport obligation.

Sample Response to Debtor's Motion to Avoid Lien

1

2

3

4

5

6

7

8

9

10

11

12

13

14

15

16

17

18

19

20

21

22

23

24

25

26

27

28

IN THE UNITED STATES BANKRUPTCY COURT
FOR THE DISTRICT OF MARYLAND

In re:)

Juanita Gomez   )

)

)

)

)

)

_____)

CASE NO.: 03-23415

OPPOSITION TO DEBTOR'S
REQUEST TO AVOID LIEN

1. It is admitted that the debtor filed for Chapter 7 relief on October 13, 2002.

2. It is admitted that the debtor borrowed $500 from the creditor.

3. It is admitted that the debtor pledged a stereo as security for repayment of the loan referenced in paragraph 2.

4. It is denied that the debtor is entitled to claim the property pledged as security as exempt.

WHEREFORE, the creditor prays this court to deny the debtors' request to avoid its security interest.

Dated February 22, 2004

John Fundy

John Fundy

Creditor

123 Main Street

Baltimore, MD

Sample Response to Complaint Over Prepition Transfer

1	**UNITED STATES BANKRUPTCY COURT**
2	**FOR THE WESTERN DISTRICT OF MISSISSIPPI**
3	

4   **In re:**   )

5   Harley Bloke   )   Bky. No. 111098

6   John Jones, Trustee   )   Adv. No. 02-0191

7   v.   )   **ANSWER TO TRUSTEE'S COMPLAINT**

8   Hyram Wallpaper and Paint   )   **TO AVOID PREFERENTIAL TRANSFER**

9   _____)

10   1. Admitted.

11   2. Admitted.

12   3. Admitted.

13   4. Admitted.

14   5. Denied. On the contrary, the payment made by the debtor was on account of a

15 current obligation.

16   6. Neither admitted nor denied because the Defendant does not have sufficient

17 knowledge or information to properly respond.

18   Affirmative Defenses

19   7. The debtor's payment was made within 30 days after the creditor provided ser-

20 vices to the debtor.

21   8. The debtor always paid his bills late and his payments were always accepted. Fur-

22 ther, late payments are customary in this industry. Consequently, the payment was not late

23 but was made in the ordinary course of the debtor's business relationship with the creditor.

24   WHEREFORE, the creditor prays the court to dismiss the trustee's complaint.

25

26

27

28

Sample Response to Complaint Over Prepition Transfer, continued

1	Dated February 22, 2004
2	
3	
4	
5	

Dated February 22, 2004

Amy Cratowski

Amy Cratowski, Esq.

Attorney for Some Creditor, Inc.

12 Potage Street

Imlostin, MS

How To Torpedo an Undeserving Bankruptcy

Not every person or business that files for bankruptcy succeeds in having all its debts discharged. As discussed in Chapter 9, certain types of debts cannot be discharged in bankruptcy. In addition, however, there are times when a debtor is ineligible to discharge any debts—not one, period. Such cases are the subject of this chapter.

You may be able to take an active role in denying the debtor a bankruptcy discharge. There are two ways that a bankruptcy case can be derailed, including convincing the court to dismiss the case, or deny the discharge.

Dismissal means the bankruptcy case is ended without a ruling on the discharge. The court may dismiss the case at any time between its opening and its conclusion. While you might expect dismissal requests to come earlier in a case, the circumstances that give rise to dismissal can occur at any time while the case is open. For example, a motion to dismiss a Chapter 13 case based on the debtor's failure to make plan payments could come years after the case was filed.

The effect of a dismissal is to nullify all orders entered during the case and to return everything and everyone to the positions they held when the debtor originally filed for bankruptcy. While a dismissal order may restrict the debtor's ability to file another bankruptcy petition for a few months, it usually doesn't permanently bar the debtor from returning to

bankruptcy court. If the debtor refiles for bankruptcy, your claim will again be subject to discharge.

Denial of discharge means the case is ended without the debtor being excused from paying any of his debts. It's as if the court were to say that each creditor's claim is excepted from discharge. Only Chapter 7 debtors, and debtors using Chapter 11 to liquidate rather than reorganize, face the possibility of having their entire discharge denied. For them, the main effect of the denial would kick in only if they once again filed for Chapter 7, in which case they would not be allowed to discharge any claim that was owed when the first case was filed. Even if the claim wasn't listed in the initial case, it would be forever protected from a Chapter 7 discharge. And, if the debtor is an individual, these claims could not be discharged in a subsequently filed Chapter 11. However, they could be discharged through Chapter 12 or 13.

While both dismissal and discharge denial end the debtor's bankruptcy, only the discharge denial gives creditors any form of permanent relief.

In this chapter, we'll discuss certain grounds for dismissal or denial of the discharge, including:

- dismissal of the case based on the debtor's ineligibility (Section A)
- dismissal of the case based on the debtor's behavior, or "for cause" (Section B)
- denial of the discharge (Section C), and

- revocation of an earlier-granted discharge (Section D).

This chapter discusses the grounds upon which you can request a stop to the bankruptcy, not the procedures for approaching the court with this request. Requesting a dismissal is done by filing a motion. Requesting a denial of discharge is done by filing a complaint. Both procedures are discussed in Chapter 10 of this book, and may require the help of an attorney.

A. Dismissal Based on Debtor's Ineligibility

If you're hoping to have the bankruptcy court dismiss a case because the debtor is not eligible for the relief sought, you'll have to go back and review the rules for the particular bankruptcy chapter under which the debtor filed. (See Chapter 2 of this book; we'll also give you a quick review in the subsections that follow.) And, you'll have to act quickly—a motion to dismiss based on the debtor's ineligibility must be brought extremely early in the case. This stands to reason: The more court decisions that must be undone if the case is dismissed because the debtor is ineligible for relief, the less likely the court is to dismiss the case. In reorganization cases, courts will not, as a rule, consider this type of a motion to dismiss after the reorganization plan has been confirmed. Therefore, if you have a reason to doubt the debtor's eligibility, get your motion in early.

Fortunately, you may get some free help with your efforts. The bankruptcy trustee—who is the first to see the debtor's paperwork—often takes on the task of examining the debtor's eligibility for bankruptcy. Making a preliminary determination of eligibility, based on the information in the debtor's schedules and statements, is one of the first things the trustee does with a new file.

The trustee will certainly check the paperwork to see whether the debtor has, as required, disclosed any previous bankruptcy filings. If one or more previous filings are disclosed, the trustee will find out the circumstances under which the last one was concluded. If the case was dismissed, the trustee will see if there were any restrictions on refiling. Or, if the previous case was successfully concluded, the trustee will determine whether a new filing is precluded for a particular period of time under the bankruptcy laws.

However, not all debtors disclose everything they're required to—especially when they're feeling desperate and have filed for bankruptcy in order to save their homes. The trustee may not have time to look beyond the paperwork, so if you know something about a previous filing that the debtor didn't reveal, bring it to the trustee's attention right away.

1. Review of Eligibility for Chapter 7 Bankruptcy

The eligibility grounds for Chapter 7 bankruptcy are pretty broad, so you're unlikely to have a case dismissed for the debtor's ineligibility. For example, all individuals may file for Chapter 7 relief, and all corporations and partnerships may file for Chapter 7 relief except railroads, banks, and insurance companies.

However, even if the debtor meets the basic eligibility grounds for a Chapter 7 bankruptcy, you shouldn't forget one rule that knocks many debtors out of the running: Debtors may be rendered ineligible for a discharge on the basis of previous bankruptcy filings. It may seem odd that ineligible debtors aren't barred at the courthouse door from refiling, but that's the way the system works.

More specifically, Chapter 7 debtors cannot receive a discharge if they received a Chapter 7 or Chapter 11 discharge in a case filed within the six years prior to filing the current case. Nor can Chapter 7 debtors obtain a discharge if they received a Chapter 12 or Chapter 13 discharge in a case filed within the six years prior to the filing of the current case, unless 100% of allowed unsecured claims were paid or the debtor paid at least 70% of allowed unsecured claims and that was the best the debtor could do.

2. Review of Eligibility for Chapter 11 Bankruptcy

Eligibility for filing a Chapter 11 bankruptcy is the same as it is for Chapter 7, with two exceptions:

- Railroads may file for Chapter 11 (but not Chapter 7) relief.
- Individuals who are stockbrokers or commodity brokers may not file for Chapter 11 relief.

3. Review of Eligibility for Chapter 12 Bankruptcy

Only individuals, partnerships, or corporations that are "family farmers" with stable income may file under Chapter 12. An individual is a family farmer if her debts don't exceed $1.5 million, at least 80% of the debts are attributable to the farm, and at least 50% of her income comes from farming.

A partnership or corporation is eligible for Chapter 12 relief if at least half the business is owned by the family that runs the farm, there is no publicly traded stock, and the debt and income eligibility requirements for an individual family farmer are met.

4. Review of Eligibility for Chapter 13 Bankruptcy

Only individuals with regular income, unsecured debts not exceeding $290,525, and secured debts not exceeding $871,550 are eligible for Chapter 13 bankruptcy.

⚠️ **The debt ceilings for Chapter 13 eligibility are adjusted every three years.** The amounts just quoted are as of April 1, 2001. The next adjustment will occur on April 1, 2004.

The amount of debt and whether it is classified as secured or unsecured is determined as of the date the debtor files the bankruptcy petition. However, the court may not necessarily rely on how the debtor classified the debt when making its determination. For example, if a judgment was entered against the debtor for $300,000, and that judgment was recorded against the debtor's property so that it created a judgment lien, the debtor may schedule the claim as secured. However, the court may treat this debt as unsecured for purposes of determining Chapter 13 eligibility. Why? Because the debtor clearly can avoid the lien, making the debt unsecured. (See Chapter 8, Section B.)

B. Dismissal Based on Debtor's Behavior ("For Cause")

Any bankruptcy case can be dismissed "for cause." Every chapter of the Bankruptcy Code has its own set of examples of what constitutes cause for dismissal, as discussed in the subsections below. In addition to the examples given in each chapter, courts wrestle with what other forms of debtor misconduct can constitute cause. Chief among these is "bad faith," which generally means having filed for bankruptcy to achieve a goal that is contrary to the letter or the spirit of the Bankruptcy Code.

A common example of bad faith is when a person files for bankruptcy only to obtain the benefit of the automatic stay. This person may have no intention of fulfilling the duties of a debtor (including making complete financial disclosures, attending the meeting of creditors, and cooperating with the trustee). The courts see a lot of bad faith filings from tenants who file for bankruptcy to slow down an eviction. Often, these tenants will submit only the minimum number of documents necessary to start their case and to receive the benefits of the automatic stay. Because they're not interested in receiving a discharge, they never complete their paperwork and their cases are dismissed—but not before the eviction process has been stopped in its tracks, if only temporarily.

Requests to dismiss a debtor's bankruptcy case for cause may be brought by creditors and trustees at any time prior to the entry of a discharge order. The court can also dismiss a case for cause on its own, without anyone asking for it.

1. Dismissal for Cause under Chapter 7

The following acts or omissions by debtors are cause for dismissal of a Chapter 7 case (see 11 U.S.C. § 707(a)):

- **Causing an unreasonable delay in the proceedings that is harmful to creditors.** A debtor who doesn't respond promptly to a trustee's request to produce documents, asks for a continuance of the meeting of creditors without an adequate reason, or otherwise drags out the case may be more interested in keeping the automatic stay in place than in receiving a discharge.
- **Not paying court fees.** Debtors can sometimes pay the filing fee in installments, but they must eventually pay the fees in full. Bankruptcy court filing fees cannot be waived. If the fee isn't paid, the case should be dismissed for cause.
- **Not completing the bankruptcy paperwork within 15 days of filing.** Debtors will sometimes file a "bare bones" petition in order to kick the automatic stay into effect. (The Bankruptcy Code allows a case to be started by merely filing the bankruptcy petition and a list of creditors.) However, the balance of the documents must be filed within 15 days. U.S. Trustees are the only ones empowered by the Code to ask for a case to be dismissed for failure to complete the paperwork, and they tend to be very vigilant in carrying out this duty.

In addition to these examples from the Bankruptcy Code, some courts have dismissed Chapter 7 bankruptcy cases they found to have been filed in bad faith. Here are some actual case examples:

EXAMPLE 1: A debtor filed for bankruptcy just before a divorce that was soon to terminate his marital property rights in his home. The court said that the timing of the filing was motivated by a desire to discharge debts while he could claim the marital residence as exempt. If he had waited to file for bankruptcy until after the divorce was final, the property would no longer have been protected from his creditors' claims. While some bankruptcy judges are more sympathetic to debtors than this judge was, the important point is that the timing of the bankruptcy filing can be an indication of bad faith.

EXAMPLE 2: A debtor filed for bankruptcy for the sole purpose of resolving an honest dispute with a single creditor. The court found that using bankruptcy just for dispute resolution constituted bad faith.

Other courts have found that good faith is not a requirement for seeking Chapter 7 relief. These courts narrowly interpret the examples given in Section 707(a) and are reluctant to dismiss a case for cause unless it fits into one of the specified categories.

⚠ Ability to pay unsecured creditors isn't bad faith. As a creditor, you may view the debtor's bankruptcy with doubt and frustration, especially if you believe the debtor to be perfectly capable of paying the bills. Nevertheless, most courts don't view a debtor's ability to repay debts as sign of bad faith or a reason to dismiss a bankruptcy case. But don't give up: A debtor's ability to repay debts is commonly considered a valid basis for dismissing a bankruptcy case under another part of the Bankruptcy Code, Section 707(b). The catch is that only the U.S. Trustee has the power to raise a challenge under Section 707(b)—but you can certainly mention the issue to the trustee.

2. Dismissal for Cause Under Chapter 11

The following acts or omissions by debtors are cause for dismissal of a Chapter 11 bankruptcy case (see 11 U.S.C. § 1112(b)):

- **The debtor is losing money or value with no hope of rehabilitation.** Businesses sometimes file for Chapter 11 hoping that someone with money will arrive on the scene and save the company. It rarely happens. So they sit in bankruptcy until someone—usually a creditor or a group of creditors—asks that the case be converted to Chapter 7 or dismissed.
- **The debtor can't propose a confirmable plan.** This is similar to the previous example, except that the debtor may not be losing money or value. The problem for this debtor is a lack of viable restructuring alternatives. The assets may be strong but overencumbered. Cash flow may be positive while the debtor is in bankruptcy, but not strong enough to sustain a plan.
- **The debtor is unreasonably delaying the bankruptcy, to the detriment of creditors.** This reason is the closest one to bad faith. The debtor appears to have filed for bankruptcy for a purpose other than restructuring the business.

- **The debtor has not proposed a plan.** Unlike bankruptcy chapters 12 and 13, which set deadlines for the filing of plans in every case, there is ordinarily no deadline for filing a Chapter 11 plan. (The exception is if the debtor has elected to proceed as a small business, in which case a plan must be filed within 160 days of the petition date.) In an ordinary Chapter 11 case, if a plan is not filed within 120 days after the case is filed, any interested party may file a plan—but this is the only incentive written into the Code for getting the debtor to file a plan. It is possible to ask the court to cut short the 120-day exclusivity period if circumstances warrant it. Otherwise, a creditor should seek dismissal after the 120-day period and as soon as it appears that the debtor isn't making progress toward confirming a plan.

- **The court has denied confirmation of every proposed plan and refuses to allow any more attempts.** After creditors, equity holders, and anyone else with an interest in the debtor's reorganization have had a chance to present a confirmable plan and all the proposed plans have failed, the court may dismiss the case for cause.

- **The confirmation order has been revoked and confirmation of a modified or new plan has been denied.** Sometimes a plan with hidden flaws will be confirmed—perhaps based on a faulty premise, an inaccurate disclosure, or intentional falsehoods. Whatever the reason, the court may dismiss a Chapter 11 case for cause after revoking confirmation of the plan and denying confirmation of substitute plans.

- **The debtor is unable to substantially consummate its reorganization plan.** "Substantial consummation" is a defined term in Chapter 11 bankruptcy. It means the point in time when the plan is not quite complete, but is almost there. If the debtor's plan includes turning the business over to a new entity, or the debtor resuming control of the business, this switch must have already occurred for the plan to be considered "substantially consummated." If the plan calls for payments to be made to creditors, these payments must have been started. If the plan calls for some or all of the debtor's property to be transferred, all or nearly all of these transfers must have been made. If the debtor can't reach the point where its plan is substantially consummated, then cause exists to dismiss the case.

- **The confirmed plan is ended by its own terms.** Cause also exists to end a case when the plan has run its intended course. Given that this sounds like the successful end of the bankruptcy, you might expect it to result in a discharge rather than a dismissal.

However, it applies only to cases that weren't such great successes, namely ones where:

- the plan called for the liquidation of the debtor's assets
- the debtor goes out of business (regardless of whether this outcome was contemplated by the plan), or
- the debtor would have been denied a discharge under Chapter 7, most commonly because the debtor is not an individual.

So, once such a plan is completed, there's nothing left to do but dismiss the case, which does not affect the discharge of debts that was accomplished when the debtor's plan was confirmed (see Chapter 13 of this book for a discussion of the effect of confirmation of a Chapter 11 plan). The motion is most likely to be brought by the U.S. Trustee.

- **The debtor has not paid the filing fee or the quarterly fees owed to the U.S. Trustee.** Again, this motion is most likely to be brought by the U.S. Trustee.

In addition to the examples of cause found in the statute, courts have found cause to dismiss cases where solvent debtors have filed for bankruptcy in order to delay a state court lawsuit, to avoid paying taxes or to recover property that had been transferred by the order of a state court judge to a receiver.

3. Dismissal for Cause Under Chapters 12 and 13

For reasons having to do with their drafting history, Chapters 12 and 13 are written and interpreted almost identically on some topics, including the grounds for dismissing a case. The following acts or omissions by debtors are cause for dismissal of a Chapter 12 or 13 case (see 11 U.S.C. §§ 1208(c), 1307(c)):

- **The debtor has unreasonably delayed confirming a plan, to the detriment of creditors.** Since it's hard to imagine a scenario where unreasonable delay would be helpful to creditors, a creditor will be able to seek dismissal pretty much any time the debtor is procrastinating. Creditors in Chapter 12 cases may also ask the court to dismiss the case for cause when the debtor is mismanaging the farm.
- **The debtor has not paid the bankruptcy court fees and costs.** This motion would be brought by the trustee.
- **The debtor has not filed a plan by the deadline for doing so.** In Chapter 12 cases, debtors have 90 days after they file the bankruptcy petition to file a reorganization plan. In Chapter 13 cases, the plan is due at the same time as the initial filing.

- **The debtor is late making the initial payment under the plan.** The time for debtors to begin making payments in Chapter 12 cases is governed by the plan. In Chapter 13 cases, debtors must begin making payments within 30 days after filing for bankruptcy. This motion would likely be brought by the trustee.

- **The court has denied confirmation of a plan and won't allow more time to draft an alternative plan.** When the court says that the current plan won't work and the court won't allow the debtor to draft a new plan, the case clearly has no future in Chapter 13.

- **The debtor has materially defaulted on the terms of a confirmed plan.** This usually means the debtor has failed to make payments to the trustee, but it can also mean the debtor failed to surrender property as promised in the plan or to obtain insurance against the loss of collateral.

- **The court revokes confirmation and denies confirmation of a modified or replacement plan.** The only way a court may revoke confirmation is if the debtor obtained confirmation of the plan through fraud. This means that the debtor misrepresented an important part of the plan or lied, either to the court in order to get its approval, or to the trustee and creditors to get their acceptance. The law allows the debtor to propose a new plan after the court revokes confirmation, but as a practical matter, it's hard for a debtor to propose a confirmable plan after a confirmation order has been revoked.

- **The plan ends by its own terms without the debtor being eligible for a discharge.** This is a rare situation in which the debtor's plan would include a provision calling for the debtor to stop making payments before the plan was completed. For example, the debtor could file to save his home and include a provision in his plan that if he sold his home during the plan the plan would come to an immediate stop. In essence, the plan would ask the court to dismiss the case based on the occurrence of this condition. The trustee will file a motion in such a case, because she doesn't want an open, dormant case in her files.

Some differences between Chapters 12 and 13 grounds for dismissal for cause also exist. Chapter 12 cases may be dismissed if the farm is losing money or value and if it's not reasonably likely that the debtor will be able to confirm a plan. Chapter 13 cases may be dismissed at the request of the U.S. Trustee if the debtor has not filed all the paperwork.

Courts have also found cause for dismissing Chapter 12 and Chapter 13 cases when the debtors have filed multiple bankruptcy cases for the sole purpose of preventing foreclosure. This is known as serial bankruptcy filing. (See Chapters 4 and 8 for further discussion of serial filing.)

C. Denial of Discharge

From the debtor's perspective, the worst possible outcome of the bankruptcy case is for the court to deny the discharge. Discharge denial is an extreme remedy, available only in Chapter 7 and certain Chapter 11 cases, and reserved for the worst offenders. A denial ends the bankruptcy without relieving the debtor of his debt burden. And it doesn't even bring the proceedings to an immediate halt: The case remains open for as much time as the trustee needs to gather, sell, and distribute the debtor's nonexempt, unencumbered assets to pay allowed unsecured claims. The debtor's future use of bankruptcy becomes bleak as well: The debtor will not be allowed to discharge debts that were part of the discharged case in a subsequent case filed under Chapter 7, or under Chapter 11 if the debtor is an individual. A request to the court to deny the discharge can be made by the creditors or the trustee.

Because the relief requested in these actions is broad—it applies to all claims, not just yours—undertaking a discharge challenge requires representing not just your claim, but all claims. This means, for instance, that you can't settle the case in exchange for something that benefits only you. In fact, you may not be able to settle the case at all. Don't challenge the debtor's ability to receive a discharge if all you really want is for your claim to be paid.

Since the relief benefits all creditors, the trustee is the best person to file these actions. But the trustee knows only as much about the debtor as he or she can learn from the papers the debtor filed with the court and the answers to the questions asked by the trustee. So, if you know of any reason why the debtor should be denied a discharge, it's imperative that you bring it to the trustee's attention. This will not only save you the expense of suing the debtor on your own, it will allow you to pursue your own interests in the bankruptcy free from worry about how your actions may affect other creditors.

In reorganization cases, try objecting to confirmation of the debtor's plan and seeking conversion to Chapter 7. (See Chapters 13 and 14.) None of the reorganization chapters provides for denying discharge as Chapter 7 does. Only Chapter 11 talks about denying discharge, and it references the Chapter 7 rules when doing so. That's because in reorganization cases, discharge of debts is conditioned upon confirmation of the debtor's plan. So, instead of challenging a debtor's eligibility to receive a discharge, you challenge the debtor's ability to confirm a plan. If the reasons for your challenge are of a type that would cause a court to deny a discharge to a Chapter 7 debtor, then, in addition to arguing that the debtor's plan shouldn't be confirmed, you should ask the court to convert the case to Chapter 7. After the conversion, you can challenge the debtor's eligibility for a discharge.

Don't confuse a challenge to the debtor's discharge with a challenge to the discharge of your claim. The latter (called a "dischargeability action") merely separates your claim out of the rest of the action. A discharge challenge alleges that the debtor should not receive a discharge at all, based on grounds discussed below. (You may, however, need to include any challenge to the dischargeability of particular claims within a complaint alleging that the debtor's discharge should be denied, but as a separate count. Such procedures are discussed in Chapter 10 of this book.)

There is a deadline for filing complaints challenging a debtor's entitlement to receive a discharge. In Chapter 7 cases, these complaints must be filed no later than 60 days after the first date set for the meeting of creditors. In Chapter 11 cases, they must be filed no later than the first date set for the hearing on confirmation.

The Code provides nine situations in which Chapter 7 debtors cannot obtain a discharge. (See 11 U.S.C. § 727(a).) In this section, we'll cover these reasons, including when the debtor:

- is not an individual (Subsection 1)
- is misusing property (Subsection 2)
- has concealed, destroyed, mutilated, falsified, or failed to keep financial records (Subsection 3)
- has made false statements (Subsection 4)
- cannot satisfactorily explain the loss of assets (Subsection 5)
- refuses to obey a court order (Subsection 6)
- has engaged in misconduct to help another bankrupt debtor (Subsection 7)
- has already received a bankruptcy discharge, within the last six years (Subsection 8), or
- has waived his right to receive a discharge (Subsection 9).

1. The Debtor Is Not an Individual

Real live human beings are the only entities who can receive a Chapter 7 discharge. Corporations can't, although they can receive a discharge under one of the reorganization chapters. Partnerships can't, although their individual partners can. It's unlikely that you will encounter a situation in which a nonindividual seeks a Chapter 7 discharge.

⚠ **You're unlikely to see a corporation or partnership attempt to receive a Chapter 7 discharge.** However, you may encounter a corporation or partnership that tries to get around the rules by confirming a Chapter 11 plan that is a Chapter 7 liquidation disguised as a Chapter 11 reorganization. Because this is a possibility, the Bankruptcy Code says that when a Chapter 11 plan calls for the debtor to sell all or most of its assets and go out of business, the plan will result in a discharge of debts only to the extent that the debtor could have received a discharge under Chapter 7. So, any corporation or partnership that uses Chapter 11 to go out of business is denied a discharge of debts just as if it had filed under Chapter 7.

2. The Debtor Misuses or Fraudulently Transfers Property

Sometimes when their financial matters are going poorly, debtors will transfer valuable property to friends or relatives for "safekeeping." They're not really afraid that the property will be stolen—they're just afraid that creditors will take it. Similarly, a business in dire straits may spin off its moneymaking sectors while bankrupting the rest. The Code allows discharge to be denied if the debtor has transferred, mutilated, or destroyed property within one year prior to filing for bankruptcy with an intent to make it difficult or impossible for creditors to get paid. The same rule applies to property of the estate that the debtor transfers, mutilates, or destroys after filing for bankruptcy.

Any time you see that property has been transferred for less than full value less than one year before the bankruptcy was filed, ask the trustee if she is going to try to recover the property and get the court to deny the discharge. The same goes for property that has been damaged or hidden by the debtor. Courts don't look kindly on debtors who misuse property—they have even been known to deny discharge to debtors who voluntarily returned property after having transferred it to hide it from creditors. Discharge denial under these circumstances is intended to be punitive and to reinforce the message that a discharge is available only for honest debtors.

3. The Debtor Has Concealed, Destroyed, Mutilated, Falsified, or Failed to Keep Financial Records

Debtors must keep and preserve their financial records. The more sophisticated the debtor or the more complex the debtor's business, the more elaborate the debtor's recordkeeping must be. In all situations, debtors are expected to maintain and preserve their financial records with sufficient organization and detail that the trustee and creditors can review the events leading up to the bankruptcy. For consumers, a checkbook and pay stubs may be enough. Businesses will likely have to provide ledger books, computer files, and whatever else would be appropriate for the operation of the particular business.

As a creditor, you don't care why the debtor's financial records are unavailable or incomplete. You just care that they are. The same is true for the court. It doesn't matter whether the debtor hides, destroys, mutilates, or falsifies the records; all that matters is that the debtor prevented the records from being reviewed. It doesn't even matter if the debtor has no records to produce. It's the debtor's obligation to present her complete financial records in a reasonable manner. If part of the record is missing, the debtor must provide a reasonable explanation and assist the trustee in filling in the gaps. If the records are badly organized, it is the debtor's responsibility to put them in order.

4. The Debtor Has Made False Statements

A debtor who knowing and fraudulently makes a false statement in order to gain an advantage in the bankruptcy can be denied a discharge. Likely examples of false statements include failing to disclose assets, or misstating income and expenses. The false statement could be made orally or in writing, for example:

- on the bankruptcy petition, schedules, or statements
- at the creditors' meeting
- at a hearing, or
- in response to a letter from the trustee.

This basis for denying discharge is often used as a catch-all for bad acts by debtors. For example, a debtor who does not keep accurate records is likely to make a false statement about his finances. Since these false statements are usually made to the trustee, the trustee is in the best position to catch the debtor's misconduct and to challenge the debtor's ability to receive a discharge based on this misconduct.

5. The Debtor Cannot Satisfactorily Explain the Loss of Assets

In some bankruptcy cases, it becomes clear that the debtor had certain assets at one time—such as a piece of property or cash from a sale—but the assets have disappeared. It is up to the debtor to satisfactorily explain what happened to missing assets. An inability to do so is cause for the court to deny the discharge.

> **EXAMPLE:** Darryl receives $57,000 when he sold his house. Two months later, he files for Chapter 7 bankruptcy. By that time, however, he is unable to give a good explanation of what happened to the money. In response to a creditor's questions, he says that he

used $17,000 to pay bills and buy a pickup truck; lost $15,000 gambling; misplaced $20,000; and spent $5,000 on repairs. However, he produces no receipts or other evidence to support his unlikely story. The trustee files a complaint against the debtor and the court denies the discharge.

How to discover hidden or missing assets was discussed in Chapter 5 of this book. By way of a quick review, consider what assets the debtor said he owned when you agreed to lend him money, what property the debtor bought from you and, if you lent the debtor money, what was bought with the money.

You won't be the only with questions about what happened to the debtor's assets. If the reason the debtor filed for bankruptcy is not obvious from reviewing the debtor's bankruptcy schedules and statements, the trustee will question him about the events leading up to the bankruptcy. The trustee will also ask the debtor what happened to the proceeds from property sold during the year preceding the bankruptcy and what was done with money borrowed during this time. The purpose of the trustee's inquiry, like yours, is to determine whether the debtor is seeking a discharge in good faith. If not, the trustee will request that the court deny the debtor's discharge.

6. The Debtor Refuses to Obey a Court Order

The bankruptcy court will issue several orders during the course of a routine bankruptcy. The debtor's failure to obey any of these orders—routine or otherwise—is grounds to deny the debtor's discharge.

The orders most commonly disobeyed by debtors are the ones forcing them to cooperate with the trustee. There are times when the trustee must get a court order to force their cooperation. That order may require the surrender of property or business records. Whatever the order requires, if the debtor doesn't do it, the trustee will go back to court to ask for the debtor's discharge to be denied. In this way, the debtor will lose the benefit of bankruptcy, while the creditors retain the trustee's assistance in liquidation of the debtor's estate.

7. The Debtor Has Engaged in Misconduct to Help Another Bankrupt Debtor

The misconduct described in Subsections 2 through 6, above, isn't only prohibited in a debtor's own bankruptcy case. If a debtor commits any of these acts in a bankruptcy filed by a relative, a partner, or another person with intimate, inside information about the debtor within one year prior to the bankruptcy filing, the debtor's discharge can be denied.

EXAMPLE 1: Danica files for bankruptcy by herself. Danica's husband Dashiell lies to the bankruptcy court during Danica's case. He pretends to own a business that Danica actually inherited from her mother and owns by herself. A few months later, Dashiell files his own Chapter 7 bankruptcy. However, the trustee learns of Dashiell's earlier lie. Dashiell will now be unable to get a Chapter 7 discharge, since his case was filed within one year after making the false statement in Danica's case. Danica, too, will be denied a discharge because of the false statement.

EXAMPLE 2: Don was Chief Financial Officer for Endotheworld.com, which filed for bankruptcy after disclosing it had misstated its corporate earnings. In order to cover up the corporation's deceit, Don ordered many of the company's financial records to be destroyed. Don's actions on behalf of the corporation could cost him a personal discharge if he files for bankruptcy within 12 months of destroying the records.

8. The Debtor Has Received a Discharge Within the Last Six Years

If the debtor is an individual who has received a Chapter 7 or 11 discharge within the six years before filing the current case, the court will deny the discharge. If the debtor filed under Chapter 12 or Chapter 13 within six years of filing under Chapter 7, and the debtor didn't fully pay allowed unsecured claims or at least 70% of those claims (provided that was the debtor's best effort), the court will deny the discharge. The trustee will raise these issues with the court.

The fact that the debtor isn't eligible to receive a Chapter 7 discharge doesn't mean the debtor isn't eligible to file for bankruptcy at all. There's no rule that requires or even allows the bankruptcy clerk to refuse to accept a bankruptcy petition from a debtor who is ineligible to receive a discharge. The primary reason a person files for bankruptcy when in such circumstances is to get the protection of the automatic stay. But even if the debtor files with the mistaken belief that she is entitled to receive a discharge, the ultimate conclusion of the case will be the denial of the discharge and dismissal of the case.

9. The Debtor Waives the Right to a Discharge

In very rare cases, the debtor, in order to avoid continued litigation over her eligibility to receive a discharge, agrees to waive the discharge. The debtor may decide it's not worth the continued legal expenses because she has a losing position, or as part of a compromise of other claims against her. A discharge waiver is effective only if it is made in writing, after the debtor filed for bankruptcy. (Debtors cannot waive their right to receive a discharge before filing for bankruptcy.) The waiver must also be approved by the court.

D. Revocation of an Earlier-Granted Discharge

Under certain circumstances, the court can revoke—that is, cancel or undo—a bankruptcy discharge that has already been granted. The grounds for revoking a discharge vary among the different bankruptcy chapters, so we'll discuss each one separately.

1. Revocation of a Chapter 7 Discharge

You may ask the court to revoke a Chapter 7 discharge within one year after it was entered if you learn that the discharge was fraudulently obtained or if the debtor does not obey a court order.

If you believe that the discharge was fraudulently obtained, that is, that the debtor misrepresented a material fact that caused the court to grant a discharge that should have been denied, you may ask the court to revoke the discharge. However, you must show that you learned of the fraud after the discharge was entered. If you had discovered the fraud during the case, then you should have challenged the entry of the discharge before the discharge order was entered. You can't, in these circumstances, wait until after the discharge is entered and then ask the court to revoke it. If you discover the fraud more than one year after the discharge was entered, it's too late to do anything.

You might gain some time if the debtor's fraud involved a failure to disclose property. In such cases, you are allowed up to one year after the case has been closed to ask the court to revoke the discharge. The reason this might give you more time is that, when the debtor's case has assets that the trustee is going to collect and sell, the case will be kept open until after all the proceeds are distributed. The debtor's discharge is usually granted at some time during this process. Consequently, the debtor can receive a discharge months or years before the case is closed.

If you're going to ask the court to revoke the debtor's discharge based on the debtor's failure to obey a court order, you have up until the later of one year after the entry of the discharge or the closing of the case. This provision enables trustees to coerce the debtor's cooperation with the liquidation of assets after the debtor has received a discharge.

2. Revocation of a Chapter 11 Discharge

In a Chapter 11 case, the only grounds for revocation of the discharge is that the confirmation order was obtained by fraud. As a technical matter, you wouldn't ask the court to revoke the debtor's discharge, but instead to revoke confirmation of the debtor's plan. That's because it is the confirmation of the plan that triggers the discharge of debts in a Chapter 11 case. You've got up to 180 days after the plan has been confirmed to request that the confirmation be revoked.

3. Revocation of a Chapter 12 or 13 Discharge

Chapter 12 and Chapter 13 discharges can be revoked if they were obtained by fraud and the fraud was discovered after the discharge. Complaints asking the court to revoke the discharge must be filed within one year of when the discharge order was entered.

Debtors don't receive a discharge under Chapter 12 and Chapter 13 until they complete their plan payments (or the court grants them a hardship discharge). However, you can still ask the court to revoke confirmation of the debtor's plan within 180 days after the confirmation order was entered if confirmation was obtained by fraud. ■

CHAPTER

13

The Creditor's Role in a Reorganization Case

C hapters 11, 12, and 13 of the Bankruptcy Code are the reorganization chapters. They allow debtors to discharge their debt burdens in exchange for repaying some or all of these debts through a reorganization plan.

The "plan" forms the heart of the reorganization process. It allows debtors to custom-design relief for their particular situation—unlike in a Chapter 7, where all debtors are treated the same. There are legal limits, however on what a reorganization plan may do. The court, through the plan confirmation process, must determine whether a proposed plan follows the rules and stays within these limits.

The purpose of this chapter is to acquaint you with where you, as a creditor, fit into the process of developing and confirming the reorganization plan, and how you can act to protect your interests. There is some variation in the rules regarding the different bankruptcy chapters, though for Chapters 12 and 13 they overlap a good bit. We'll talk about:

- common features among and comparisons between the reorganization chapters (Section A)
- particular features of Chapter 13 plans (Section B)
- particular features of Chapter 12 plans (Section C), and
- particular features of Chapter 11 plans (Section D).

⚠️ **We're going in reverse numerical order for a reason. Chapter 13** cases comprise the overwhelming majority of reorganization cases. In fact, for every 940 Chapter 13 cases filed in 2002, there were 23 Chapter 11 cases and 1 Chapter 12 case filed.

A. Overview of Reorganization Case Rules

When you think about a reorganization bankruptcy case, think "plan." The plan is the key to the debtor's reorganization, because it spells out the timetable, amounts, and other details of how the debtor will repay you and the other creditors. Consequently, all the activity of reorganization cases moves according to the life cycle of this plan—its proposal, its confirmation, its execution, and its completion.

One of the first concerns for you as a creditor is who gets to come up with the plan. In a Chapter 12 or 13 bankruptcy, only the debtor may propose the plan. Your participation is limited to pointing out defects, whether in the plan as a whole or in your own claim's treatment within the plan. In a Chapter 11 bankruptcy, the debtor has the first shot at proposing a plan, but creditors may vote on it and offer their own plans if the debtor's plan is voted down or the court denies its confirmation.

After a proposed plan has been put forth and the objections heard and considered (and, in a Chapter 11 case, the creditors have voted to approve the plan) the bankruptcy court will review the plan to make sure it meets the various legal requirements. If the court is satisfied, it will confirm the plan. Once a plan is confirmed, it is binding on the debtor and all creditors who are included in the plan. That makes it very important that you raise any objections to the plan's provisions prior to its confirmation—otherwise, you'll have to live with the consequences.

After a Chapter 12 or Chapter 13 plan has been confirmed, the trustee will follow the plan's terms for distributing payments by the debtor to the creditors. In a Chapter 11 case, the debtor (who is technically the trustee) will be responsible for taking whatever action is called for in the plan.

If circumstances change while the plan is in effect—for example, the debtor changes jobs—there's some room for plan modification. In a Chapter 12 or 13 bankruptcy, creditors holding allowed unsecured claims may file a motion asking the court to modify the terms of the plan—most likely to have their payments increased. Chapter 11 plans can also be modified after they are confirmed, but only at the request of the debtor or the person who proposed the plan.

Though all plans lead to a bankruptcy discharge, the timing of the discharge varies. Chapter 12 and 13 debtors do not re-ceive a discharge of their obligation to pay debts until their plans are completed (or the court grants them a hardship discharge). However, Chapter 11 debtors receive a discharge—assuming they're eligible for one—when the plan is confirmed.

B. Chapter 13 Reorganization Plans

Things move fast at the start of a Chapter 13 case. The debtor must file a proposed reorganization plan within the first 15 days, on pain of dismissal by the court. The meeting of creditors will be held within the first few weeks and the confirmation hearing may be held at the same time. The deadline for objecting to exemptions comes 30 days after the meeting of creditors is concluded, and the deadline for filing proofs of claim comes 90 days after the meeting of creditors was originally scheduled. Within a few months of the bankruptcy filing, the typical Chapter 13 plan is confirmed and creditors begin receiving payments.

In this section, we'll discuss:
- the importance of filing your Chapter 13 proof of claim (Subsection 1)
- the standard contents of a Chapter 13 plan (Subsection 2)
- optional provisions in a Chapter 13 plan (Subsection 3)
- how the confirmation process will begin (Subsection 4)

- how to evaluate the proposed plan (Subsection 5)
- how to prepare and present your objections (Subsection 6)
- what happens at the confirmation hearing (Subsection 7)
- issuance of the judge's confirmation decision (Subsection 8)
- what to expect when the plan gets underway (Subsection 9), and
- what happens after the debtor completes all obligations under the plan (Subsection 10).

1. Importance of Having Filed Your Proof of Claim

Apart from your participation in creation and confirmation of the plan (discussed in Section A, above), one of your first tasks as a creditor in a Chapter 13 case will be to file a proof of claim. (See Chapter 7 of this book for a full discussion of filing proofs of claim.)

By way of reminder, if you don't file a proof of claim, you have no hope of getting paid. At a more technical level, you also need to file a proof of claim in order to speak up about the treatment of your claim during the confirmation process. In the language of the Code, your claim is "allowed"—that is, considered legitimate and entitled to payment—when it is filed, and will stay allowed unless the court disallows it in response to an objection filed

by the debtor or the trustee. (See 11 U.S.C. § 502.) Note, however, that some bankruptcy courts temporarily overlook whether you've filed a proof of claim and assume that all claims listed on the debtor's schedules will be filed and allowed. This allows the court to forge ahead with confirmation of the debtor's plan without waiting for the deadline for filing proofs of claim and for filing objections to those proofs of claim.

In most courts, you will receive a blank proof of claim form along with the notice of bankruptcy filing. Follow the instructions in Chapter 7 of this book for completing this form and filing it with the court.

2. What's in a Standard Chapter 13 Plan

While only the debtor can propose a plan, many Chapter 13 trustees have adopted standardized plans for debtors to use. A sample plan from the San Francisco bankruptcy court is reproduced below.

Although plans vary in length and complexity, they all answer these two questions:

- What are the terms of the debtor's payments to the trustee? (Subsection a), and
- What are the terms of the trustee's payments to the creditors? (Subsection b).

Model Chapter 13 Plan

UNITED STATES BANKRUPTCY COURT
NORTHERN DISTRICT OF CALIFORNIA

In re:	Case No.
_____	**Chapter 13 Plan**
Debtor(s).

1. The future earnings of the debtor(s) are submitted to the supervision and control of the trustee, and the debtor(s) will pay to the Trustee the sum of $ _____ each month for _____ months. Unless all allowed claims are paid in full, this Plan shall not be completed in fewer than 36 months from the first payment date. Debtor(s) elect a voluntary wage order. _____.

2. From the payments received, the Trustee will make disbursements in accordance with the Distribution Guidelines as follows:
   (a) On allowed claims for expenses of administration required by 11 USC §507 (a)(1) in deferred payments.
   (b) On allowed secured claims, which shall be treated and valued as follows:

Name	Value of Collateral	Estimated Mortgage/Lease Arrears	Minimum Monthly Payments (If specified)	Interest Rate (If Specified)

   [The valuations shown above will be binding unless a timely objection to confirmation is filed. Secured claims will be allowed for the value of the collateral or the amount of the claim, whichever is less, and will be paid the monthly installments and the interest rates shown above. If the monthly payment is not specified, secured creditors will share pro rata. If an interest rate is not specified, 5/6% per month (10% per annum) will be paid. Secured creditors will retain their liens until their allowed secured claims have been paid. The remainder of the amount owing, if any, will be allowed as a general unsecured claim paid under the provisions of paragraph 2(d).]

   (c) On allowed priority unsecured claims in the order prescribed by 11 USC § 507.
   (d) On allowed general unsecured claims the debtor(s) estimate(s) the general unsecured claims will be paid _____%.

3. The following executory contracts are rejected. The debtor(s) waive the protections of the automatic stay provided in 11 U.S.C. § 362 to enable the affected creditor to obtain possession and dispose of its collateral without further order of the court. Any allowed unsecured claim for damages resulting from rejection will be paid under paragraph 2(d).

4. The debtor(s) will pay directly the following fully secured creditors and lessors:

Name	Monthly Payment	Name	Monthly Payment

5. The date this case was filed will be the effective date of the plan as well as the date when interest ceases accruing on unsecured claims against the estate.

6. The debtor(s) elect to have property of the estate revest in the debtor(s) upon plan confirmation. Once the property revests, the debtor(s) may sell or refinance real or personal property without further order of the court, upon approval of the Chapter 13 Trustee.

7. The debtor(s) further propose pursuant to 11 USC § 1322(b):

Dated: _____   _____   _____
                                         (Debtor)   (Debtor)

San Francisco & Oakland Divisions, Chapter 13 Plan
(October, 2001)

a. The Debtor's Payments to the Trustee

The debtor's plan must state:

- how frequently payments will be made to the trustee
- the amount of the payments, and
- the duration of the payments.

Payments to the trustee are usually made monthly, unless they are tied to the timing of the debtor's paychecks. In that case they might be made weekly, bi-weekly or semimonthly.

To determine the minimum amount that a debtor must pay into the plan, the court and trustee will add up the following:

$_____ **The amount of any arrearage owed on a residential mortgage.** If the debtor filed for bankruptcy in order to stop a foreclosure sale, then the debtor will have to pay off the amount of the missed mortgage payments plus interest and costs through the plan.

$_____ **The secured value of any undersecured claim that the debtor wants to pay off through the plan.** Claims are secured only to the extent of the collateral's value. If you are owed $8,000, but the collateral is worth $5,000, then you have a $5,000 secured claim and a $3,000 unsecured claim. If the debtor wants to keep the collateral, he can do so by paying off your secured claim ($5,000) in full through the plan, with interest.

$_____ **The replacement value of any property the debtor wishes to keep but can't exempt.** If the debtor has property that would be sold by the trustee in a Chapter 7 case, the debtor must pay the value of this property into the plan. (In this manner, the debtor can use a Chapter 13 filing to protect nonexempt property.)

$_____ **The amount of any priority claims.** Priority claims must be paid in full through the plan. These include claims for alimony, maintenance, and child support.

$_____ **TOTAL**

The sum of the above items is the amount that the debtor must pay over the life of the plan. The Bankruptcy Code allows plans to be of any length up to 60 months. However, if the plan is going to be fewer than 36 months in length, it must provide for full payment to unsecured creditors. If the plan is going to be longer than 36 months in length, the court must find a reason to extend payments beyond 36 months. The most likely reason is the debtor can't afford to pay what the law requires within 36 months.

Assuming the plan isn't paying 100% of unsecured claims—and it is the rare plan that does—the amount of the debtor's monthly payments is calculated by dividing the total amount to be paid by 36. This figure will then be compared to the amount of the debtor's disposable income, that is, the debtor's take-home pay minus those expenses that are reasonably necessary for the support of the debtor and the debtor's family. If the debtor's monthly disposable income exceeds the amount that must be paid into the plan, then the debtor must commit all his monthly disposable income into the plan. If doing so enables unsecured creditors to be paid in full, then the plan may be for less than 36 months. However, it cannot end until unsecured creditors are fully paid.

More often than not, the amount that the debtor would have to pay into a 36-month plan is higher than the debtor's monthly disposable income. Consequently, the plan will need to last longer than 36 months—but no more than 60 months. Debtors determine how long the plan must last by dividing the total amount that must be paid into the plan by their disposable income. If the result of this division is greater than 60, then the debtor would need more than 60 months to complete the minimum payments. Since the Code prohibits this, debtors can propose a plan calling for monthly payments in excess of their disposable income. Alternately, they can propose a plan with graduated payments, in which the payments are equal to the disposable income at the beginning but increase over time.

b.   The Trustee's Payments to Creditors

The trustee acts as the intermediary in administering the reorganization plan. If your claim is to be paid through the plan, then your payment will come from the trustee, not directly from the debtor. Under the plan, the debtor will have to make regular payments to the trustee in amounts sufficient to allow the trustee to turn around and make the appropriate payments to the creditors. The plan will contain specific instructions to the trustee on how much to pay each creditor. These payment instructions will divide the creditors into classes based on the type of claims they hold.

Creditors holding secured claims are usually identified by name. If the creditor's collateral is the debtor's home, then the plan will say whether the debtor is going to pay off a prepetition delinquency, as well as how much interest the debtor will pay. The plan will also state whether the regular mortgage payments are going to be made by the trustee or by the debtor outside of the plan (see sidebar, "When Payments Are Allowed Outside the Plan.") If the collateral is something other than the debtor's home, then the plan will state how much the debtor will pay for each secured claim.

Creditors holding priority unsecured claims may or may not be identified by name. If they're not identified by name, the plan will have a general provision stating that creditors holding priority claims are to be paid in full.

Creditors holding general unsecured claims, which include the unsecured portion of undersecured claims (see Chapter 8), are usually not identified by name. Instead, the plan will state that general unsecured claimholders will receive a certain percentage of their claims or will share in a certain amount of money, usually the amount that's left over after paying secured and priority claims in full.

When Payments Are Allowed Outside the Plan

In certain situations, debtors may be allowed to make payments directly to certain creditors, without going through the trustee. Unfortunately, the bankruptcy courts are not in full agreement on when such direct payments should be allowed. At a minimum, however, the Code allows debtors to continue making regular payments to creditors if the last payment on the debt is due after the last payment on the plan. For example, most mortgages are longer term than the normal Chapter 13 plan. So, most Chapter 13 plans provide for direct payment of the mortgage outside of the plan.

Car loans might also seem like good candidates for being paid outside the plan. However, the issue tends not to arise with car loans, because most debtors want to modify the loan's terms and not maintain regular payments. And, for long-term unsecured claims such as student loans, most courts deny confirmation if debtors seek to pay them outside the plan. Why? Because such a provision would unfairly discriminate in favor of the creditor being paid outside the plan.

Another consideration that stops some courts from allowing payments outside the plan is the funding of the Chapter 13 trustees—you may recall that they get paid with a percentage of the money that is administered through the plan. When payments are made outside of the plan, the trustee loses out. Because mortgage payments tend to be significant, debtors save a lot on making their payments outside of the plan, while trustees lose a lot.

3. Optional Provisions in Chapter 13 Plans

The Bankruptcy Code also allows debtors to include certain optional provisions in their plans in order to accomplish specific goals. These optional provisions carry with them their own confirmation requirements. The most common of these optional provisions include ones that:

- modify the creditors' rights (Subsection a)
- modify the order in which debtors pay secured and unsecured claims (Subsection b)
- provide for payment of claims that arose postbankruptcy (Subsection c)
- allow assumption or rejection of executory contracts (Subsection d), and
- maintain the bankruptcy estate or provide for estate property to be transferred to someone other than the debtor (Subsection e).

a. Modifying Secured Creditors' Rights

You're probably all too aware that the plan may modify your rights by discharging some or all of the debtor's obligation to pay you. However, the plan may also modify any other right you have as a result of extending credit to the debtor. For example:

- You will lose the right to repossess collateral if the debtor repays the secured portion of an undersecured debt. Your claim is secured only to the extent of the property's value. Once you receive that money, your lien is satisfied even though your claim isn't.
- You may lose the right to accelerate the debt based on nonpayment. When the debtor defaulted on his payments to you, your loan contract probably said you could sue him for the entire amount due. When the debtor filed for Chapter 13 he gained the ability to cancel your acceleration rights by paying off the defaulted amount (referred to as a "prepetition arrearage"). If the last payment on your claim is due after the last payment on the debtor's plan, then the debtor may resume making regular payments to you outside the plan if the court allows it. Otherwise, the debtor may resume making the full contractual payment to you through the trustee.

Since it seems like every secured creditor loses these rights, you might ask why they are treated as optional provisions. The fact is that the loss of these rights is not an automatic outcome of the bankruptcy filing. Instead, they're the result of the debtor's use of optional relief allowed under the law. This means if the plan doesn't say your lien is satisfied when the secured portion of your claim is paid or doesn't provide for the debtor's resumption of payments, then these events don't happen. It also means that if the debtor attempts to alter your rights, you have the right to object, as we'll discuss in Section 5, below.

b. When Unsecured Claims May Be Paid

Debtors are relatively free to structure the order in which claims are paid. Although Section 1322(b)(4) of the Code says unsecured claims may be paid concurrently with secured claims, some courts require priority unsecured claims to be paid first. In fact, debtors normally prefer to pay secured creditors ahead of all unsecured ones, because secured creditors' claims are entitled to interest. That order of payment is not a bad deal for unsecured creditors, either—the less money the debtor uses up paying interest on the secured claims, the more that is left over to pay the unsecured claims.

c. Payment of Claims That Arose Postbankruptcy Filing

Two types of claims that arise after the debtor filed for bankruptcy may be paid through Chapter 13 plans:

- taxes that become due during the course of the bankruptcy, and
- money owed by consumer debtors to creditors who didn't know about the bankruptcy.

Chapter 13 bankruptcies can last up to five years. While most Chapter 13 debtors have employers who withhold income taxes, debtors who will be responsible for the direct payment of any tax can provide for future tax payments through their plan. The most typical example is for the payment of real estate taxes during the life of the plan.

Creditors who lent money or provided a service to a Chapter 13 consumer debtor without knowing about the bankruptcy may also get paid from the plan if they wish. Why would they want to? Because the plan is likely to eat up all the debtor's available cash. If the plan provides for payment of postpetition claims, you may want to file a proof of claim and have your claim treated as if it arose before the bankruptcy filing.

On the other hand, accepting payment under the plan may mean accepting less than full payment of your claim. The balance will be discharged. If you see that the plan won't be providing you much of a return, you could still choose not to file a claim and try to collect your claim directly from the debtor. The automatic stay won't apply, because your claim arose postpetition and your claim won't be discharged. But, you may have trouble getting paid.

d. Assumption or Rejection of Executory Contracts

An executory contract is one in which you or the debtor or both of you have a substantial obligation yet to perform. Options to buy real estate and leases are examples of executory contracts that can be assumed or rejected by the debtor.

Chapter 13 debtors may keep these agreements as part of their plans or reject them prior to plan confirmation. The rules for doing so are the same as applied to Chapter 7 debtors. (See Chapter 11 for a discussion of motions to assume or reject executory contracts.)

e. Who Controls the Debtor's Property?

Whenever a debtor files for bankruptcy, all the debtor's property becomes property of the bankruptcy estate. While the debtor's property is in the bankruptcy estate, she can't sell it, trade it, or give it away without the bankruptcy court's permission. In cases where the debtor filed under Chapter 13, her future income stream also becomes part of the estate—and in fact becomes the focal point of how creditors will be compensated.

In Chapter 13 cases, property only remains in the bankruptcy estate until the reorganization plan is confirmed. At that time, the property "revests" in the Chapter 13 debtor—in other words, the debtor regains full control over her property, free and clear of the interests of all creditors whose claims are provided for in the debtor's plan, unless the plan says that the property is to stay in the estate or be turned over to someone other than the debtor.

The distinction between property that is still in the estate and property that has revested in the debtor also affects what property you can get at without violating the automatic stay. For the most part, the automatic stay protects only property that is within the bankruptcy estate. The only exception is that property that the debtor acquires postpetition, and that remains outside the bankruptcy estate, cannot be touched by creditors collecting prepetition claims or establishing liens on account of prepetition claims.

> **EXAMPLE:** Darryl owns a $1,000 certificate of deposit when he files for Chapter 13 relief. The CD becomes part of Darryl's bankruptcy estate, and is still part of the estate when his plan is confirmed. Because Darryl's plan doesn't mention what will happen to the CD, he regains control over it when his plan is confirmed. Corey, who is owed $300 for work done on Darryl's car after Darryl filed for bankruptcy, sues Darryl for payment and receives a judgment against him. Corey could have the sheriff seize the CD for payment of the claim, since it was no longer protected by the automatic stay.

4. Starting the Confirmation Process

The process of confirming the debtor's Chapter 13 plan begins when you learn how the debtor intends to treat your claim. It ends when the court decides whether the debtor's plan meets the confirmation requirements.

The bankruptcy court must give you at least 25 days' notice of the date that it sets for the confirmation hearing. However, the Bankruptcy Rules don't give the court any guidance on when to set this date for. Some courts schedule the hearing for the same day as the Section 341 creditors' meeting, which means it comes 90 days before the deadline for filing claims. In those courts you must act quickly to protect your rights.

The court's hearing notice will include either a copy of the debtor's plan or a summary of what's in it. In many courts, the notice of the confirmation hearing is combined with the notice of the first meeting of creditors. These all-purpose notices tell you that the debtor filed for Chapter 13 relief, when the meeting of creditors will be held, when the confirmation hearing will be held, and what's in the plan for you.

Beware, however: The debtor may modify the plan at any time prior to the confirmation hearing. Debtors are supposed to tell you about changes to their proposed plans, but sometimes they don't. Fortunately, there are ways that you can be proactive.

Start by calling the debtor's attorney a few days before the confirmation hearing and asking for a fax of the current copy of the plan—unless the plan has not been amended and you received it with the notice of the confirmation hearing. Also, prior to the meeting of creditors, obtain the debtor's schedules and statements from the court clerk. (See Chapter 5 for a discussion of how to access the debtor's file.) Then, attend the meeting of creditors. You'll also have a chance to question the debtor about the documents' contents and hear whether the trustee instructs the debtor to change the plan.

If the confirmation hearing is set for a different day than the creditors' meeting, call the debtor's attorney the day before the hearing to find out whether a modified plan has been filed. If one has, ask that it be faxed to you.

5. Evaluating the Proposed Chapter 13 Plan

As you review the proposed plan, you should be alert for reasons to object to its confirmation. Check to see:

- how your claim is being treated (Subsection a)
- how similar claims are being treated (Subsection b)
- how your lien is being treated (Subsection c)

- whether the plan was proposed in good faith (Subsection d)
- whether your claim would have fared better in a Chapter 7 bankruptcy (Subsection e), and
- whether the debtor is likely to be able to pay the amounts called for in the plan (Subsection f).

You won't be the only one taking a close look at the plan. Checking to see if the plan meets the Bankruptcy Code's requirements for confirmation is one of the trustee's jobs. You can count on the trustee to thoroughly review the debtor's plan, because the court will ask the trustee for a recommendation on whether the plan should be confirmed. That shouldn't stop you from doing your own independent review, however.

a. How Your Claim Is Being Treated

The most important question is how much of your claim will be paid through the plan. The more money you stand to receive, and the sooner you'll receive it, the better. If the debtor intends to fully pay your claim with interest, then you can probably relax. If the plan gets confirmed and your proof of claim has been filed, you'll get your money.

But what if the plan doesn't provide for full payment of all claims and you're not sure how much the debtor plans to pay you? For example, creditors holding general unsecured claims often feel mystified, because the plan says only that they'll get what's left over after the payment of secured and priority unsecured claims. Payment of your claim will depend on what the collateral is, whether your claim is given legal priority, how much of your claim the collateral secures, and to what extent your claim is unsecured.

i. Secured claims where the debtor's home is the only collateral

The court will not approve a plan that modifies the rights of creditors whose liens are secured only by the debtor's primary residence. If you hold a secured claim and your only collateral is the debtor's home, then you have an unassailable right to the full payment of your claim.

For your claim to meet the standard of being secured only by the debtor's residence, you must have no claim against any of the debtor's other property. While this may seem clear enough, debtors' lawyers have uncovered plenty of gray areas. Early on, interests in mineral rights, easements, and other boilerplate provisions in residential mortgages were treated as "additional collateral." These interests and provisions were often just boilerplate language in the standard forms everybody used, but they cost creditors protection just the same. The current view is that any rights that are routinely transferred along with the land do not constitute additional collateral.

The determination of whether the sole collateral is the debtor's residence is made by many courts either as of the day the debtor filed for bankruptcy or the day the court considers confirmation of the plan. If the collateral was the debtor's residence when the mortgage was signed but the debtor had turned it into rental property by the time of filing for bankruptcy, then the mortgage would not be protected from modification in these courts. There are, however, a good number of courts that say the creditor's rights remain protected even if the debtor decides to turn his home into a bed and breakfast or use it for some purpose other than, or in addition to, his residence.

The exception to the antimodification rule is that Chapter 13 debtors may cure a mortgage default through their plans and resume making regular mortgage payments either through the plan or directly to the creditor. The cure must be made within a reasonable amount of time. How much time is "reasonable" seems to be in-terpreted differently in every court, however. Even the same court sometimes gives seemingly inconsistent rulings on how much time is reasonable. Some courts say that the cure must be accomplished within months of confirmation, while other courts have allowed the cure to extend over the entire life of the plan.

While we can't tell you definitively how much time the debtor will be given to cure the arrearage, the amount of the arrearage is easier to calculate. It's the amount of the payments that were missed prior to the bankruptcy filing, plus any additional charges (attorneys fees, interest, and the like) that were provided for in the contract and are permissible under state law.

What happens if you don't fit the category being described here—that is, your loan is secured by property that undeniably includes more property than just the debtor's residence? In that case, the debtor may have your loan modified. For example, the loan may be modified if the collateral is a duplex with the debtor living in one unit and renting the other. The most likely modification you face is being paid only what the collateral is worth. If the collateral is worth more than what you are owed, your claim could still be modified by a change in the interest rate being paid or in the repayment term.

Even a Home Mortgage Can Leave Some Creditors in the Cold

The Bankruptcy Code says creditors are secured only to the extent of the collateral's value. When the collateral is the debtor's home, it is common for more than one creditor to claim the property as collateral. If the property is sold, state law determines the order in which the competing claims will be paid from the proceeds. This payment order also applies in bankruptcy, to determine which claims are fully secured by the collateral, which are partially secured and which are wholly unsecured. In every bankruptcy case, no more than one claim will ever be partially secured, because only one claim can ride the cusp between entirely secured and wholly unsecured.

EXAMPLE: Dorinda's home is worth $200,000. She owes $125,000 on a first mortgage. This mortgage is fully secured. She owes $50,000 on a second mortgage. This mortgage is also fully secured because the total of the first two mortgages ($175,000) is less than the home's value ($200,000). She owes $40,000 on a third mortgage. This mortgage is partially secured, because there's only $25,000 in equity left in the property to secure the claim. There-fore, the third mortgage is secured for $25,000 and unsecured for the balance. If Dorinda has any more mortgages against her home, they are fully unsecured because the first three mortgages on the property exhausted the property's value.

If you're one of the unlucky creditors whose claim would remain unpaid even after a sale of the property, because the sale proceeds would be eaten up by more senior lienholders, there's more bad news coming your way: The debtor can probably modify your claim even though the debtor's home is your only collateral. Why? Because your claim is not secured for bankruptcy purposes if there is no equity available to which your lien can attach. How will your claim be modified? By being treated as if it was not secured at all.

Although some bankruptcy courts forbid debtors from modifying the rights of holders of residential mortgages regardless of the amount of available equity, these courts are distinctly in the minority. So far, no appellate court has agreed with this position, while several courts have found that wholly unsecured mortgage holders have no protection from modification.

ii. Secured claims where the collateral is something other than the debtor's home

If your claim is secured by some form of collateral other than the debtor's home, the debtor's plan must fully pay the present value of your secured claim and allow you to keep your security interests. There are two exceptions to this rule. One of the exceptions is of your own choosing: Secured creditors may consent to plans that don't pay their claims in full or that don't allow them to retain their liens. The other exception is of the debtor's choosing: The debtor may opt to surrender the collateral rather than repay the secured debt.

Assuming the debtor sticks with the standard route of paying your secured claim through the plan, the debtor must pay the present value of the claim. That normally means that the claim must be paid with interest, in order to preserve the claim's current value. Determining how much interest should be paid on these claims has proven a difficult challenge for the courts. Some courts allow secured creditors to receive the contract rate of interest, while other courts allow the current market rate of interest for similar loans. Still other courts criticize these two approaches because they include a profit component. After all, interest is supposed to be paid on secured claims in order to preserve their value, not to preserve the creditors' intended profit. In these courts, you'll receive an interest rate that's equal to or a little higher than the prime rate or the federal Treasury bill rate.

We recommend you file an objection to the plan in any of the following circumstances:

- **The plan undervalues the collateral.** If the debtor says the collateral is worth less than it really is, then your secured claim will be valued lower than it should be.

- **The plan pays a lower rate of interest on your secured claim than allowed by the court.** The allowed interest varies from one court to the next, so you'll need to check with the court or research this issue.

- **The plan voids your lien prior to the entry of the discharge.** You want your lien to remain throughout the bankruptcy even if the secured portion of your claim is paid early.

- **The plan does not fully pay your claim or does not call for the debtor to resume making regular payments, and your only collateral is the debtor's home.** Section 1322(b)(2) of the Code prohibits debtors from modifying your rights when the debtor's home is your sole collateral.

iii. Priority creditors

If your claim is entitled to a priority (see Chapter 5, Section B2 for a list of priority claims) then your claim must be paid in full. For example, if the debtor owes you child or spousal support, the debtor must pay this claim in full.

If the plan does not identify priority creditors by name, then check to see whether your claim is listed on Schedule E (which the debtor filed with the bankruptcy petition). Even if your claim is not listed on Schedule E, you will still be paid as a priority creditor if your proof of claim says that you are the holder of a priority claim and if no one objects. File an objection if the plan identifies priority creditors by name, but doesn't mention you and your claim.

iv. Unsecured creditors

If your claim is unsecured and is not paid in full, then you'll want to make sure that the plan requires the debtor to pay all projected disposable income into the plan. If it doesn't, you should object.

⚠ You're among the few who have the power to make this objection. Only the Chapter 13 trustee and holders of unsecured claims may object to confirmation of the debtor's plan based on its failure to include all the debtor's projected disposable income.

However, you'll first need to understand the meaning of the phrase "projected disposable income." Let's start with the "disposable income" part of it. This means the amount that the debtor earns, minus a few items. The debtor can subtract out the amounts needed to support herself and her dependents; keep a business going; and donate to charity (though charitable gifts are limited to 15% of the debtor's gross income).

The amount that's supposedly needed by the debtor for support must be reasonable. However, courts are reluctant to impose their values on debtors. Instead, many courts look at the total amount that the debtor is spending (shown on the debtor's Schedule J) and compare it with the debtor's total income (shown on Schedule I). The court then decides whether the debtor's expenses are, on the whole, reasonably necessary. Items that are inconsistent with bankruptcy will be singled out for exclusion. For example, boats are red flags. Debtors who are not fishermen and are not repaying all their creditors in full should not be able to spend the money necessary to keep boats. The same is true for expenses related to personal services, such as house cleaning, yard maintenance and pool service.

"Projected" is another key word in this requirement—it basically means "predicted." In considering the plan, the court will not only look at the debtor's current situation, but at how that situation can be predicted to fluctuate over the life of the plan. However, the true importance of this projection comes up after confirmation, particularly when the debtor's disposable income increases after confirmation of the plan. We'll talk more about such changes in the section on postconfirmation issues. For the moment, however, realize that it's not unusual for a debtor to get a pay raise during the course of the bankruptcy. Whether the plan should be modified to include this extra money (say, for example, to pay a higher percentage of unsecured debt) depends on whether the court says this disposable income was or should have been anticipated at the time of confirmation. If it was or should have been, then the change was already figured into the plan, and no modification is necessary.

Summary of Rules Regarding Treatment of Your Claim in Chapter 13	
Nature of Claim	**Creditors' Rights**
Claim is secured only by an interest in the debtor's home.	Claim may not be modified except that the debtor may cure any default through the plan—by paying the arrearage during the course of the plan—and then resume making regular mortgage payments.
Claim is secured by an interest in something other than, or in addition to, the debtor's home.	The value of the secured claim as of the date when the debtor filed for bankruptcy must be paid in full with interest. The interest will have two parts, one for interest accruing prior to confirmation and one for interest accruing after confirmation. Rather than repay the claim, the debtor may choose to surrender the collateral to the creditor. If the creditor is owed more than the collateral is worth, then the amount by which the claim exceeds the collateral's value will be paid along with the unsecured claims.
Claim is entitled to a priority as identified in Chapter 5.	Claim must be paid in full.
Claim is unsecured.	Creditor is entitled to receive at least as much as if the debtor had filed under Chapter 7. Creditor is also entitled to demand that the debtor propose a plan that makes a good faith effort to repay the claim and commit all projected disposable income toward that goal.

b. How Similar Claims Are Being Treated

The Bankruptcy Code allows debtors to divide creditors into classes and provide differing treatment to those classes. Generally, the dividing lines will be drawn between secured, priority unsecured, and general unsecured creditors. Sometimes, however, debtors will use a classification scheme to pay one creditor more than similar creditors are being paid. The Code allows this practice so long as the different treatment doesn't unfairly discriminate against the payment of certain claims. "Unfair discrimination" sounds like an oxymoron and, in practice, it can be. Here are examples of how it does—and sometimes doesn't work:

- Most courts won't allow debtors to discriminate in favor of the payment of nondischargeable debts such as student loans. Courts reason that Congress excepted these obligations from discharge so that debtors would pay them notwithstanding filing for bankruptcy. Congress's goal would be defeated if debtors could pay these claims with money that could have been used to pay other, dischargeable claims.
- Courts will allow debtors to pay more on one claim than is paid on similar claims if the discrimination is justified and minimized. Discrimination is justified if it serves a purpose the court

deems to be legitimate, like paying back rent so the debtor can stay in subsidized housing. Discrimination is minimized if the favored creditor receives the least amount necessary to accomplish the debtor's goal.

As a general rule, you should file an objection if you hold an unsecured claim and the plan calls for you to receive less money than the holder of another unsecured claim.

c. How Your Lien Is Being Treated

If your claim is secured by the debtor's property, pay careful attention to how the plan treats your lien. You want to be sure you keep your lien as long as possible, particularly if the collateral is worth less than what you are owed. If the plan pays the secured portion of your claim but says nothing about your lien, ownership of the collateral will be returned to the debtor once the plan is confirmed—free from your claim but subject to your lien. That's okay, because you'll keep your lien until the debtor receives a discharge or the court orders your lien removed.

What you need to guard against, and object to, is a plan that says you retain your lien only until the secured claim is fully paid—instead of until the debtor receives a discharge. Why? If your lien lasts only until your secured claim is fully paid, then you'll lose your lien before the debtor completes his plan and receives a discharge. As that time the debtor is free to convert his case to Chapter 7 and discharge the unsecured portion of your claim without paying you anything, despite the promise he made in his plan to pay some or all of your unsecured claim. He can also have his case dismissed, in which case the law says you are entitled to reacquire your lien, but that's an empty promise if the debtor has already gotten rid of your collateral. So, the only way you can make sure you get what you were promised by the debtor and the Bankruptcy Code is to insist that your lien survive until the debtor receives a Chapter 13 discharge.

If your claim is not included in the debtor's plan, either by a specific reference or as part of a class, then any claim you have against the debtor's property will survive confirmation intact.

d. Whether the Plan Was Proposed in Good Faith

The Bankruptcy Code doesn't define "good faith," but it clearly means that the plan is an honest and sincere attempt by the debtor to repay all debts to the best of the debtor's ability. Courts consider the following factors when determining whether a plan was filed in good faith.

- **Whether the debtor has filed for bankruptcy before.** The more times the debtor has had cases dismissed and then refiled, the less likely it is that the current plan was filed in good faith. This is especially true if there has been no change in the debtor's circumstances that would warrant a new bankruptcy filing or suggest that the current case will have a more positive outcome than the last one.
- **Whether the debtor has been honest with the court.** If the debtor's schedules and statements include a number of errors, then the court has good reason to question the debtor's good faith.
- **Why the debtor filed for bankruptcy.** The court may cotton onto the debtor's hidden motivations. For example, the debtor may have filed for bankruptcy merely to stop a foreclosure on the debtor's home. Such a debtor might exhibit a distinct lack of interest in curing the arrearage and resuming regular mortgage payments.
- **What caused the debtor's financial trouble.** The more unexpected the circumstances leading to the debtor's financial demise, the more likely it is that the plan was filed in good faith. Loss of one's job and uninsured medical expenses are examples of financial problems that force otherwise responsible people into bankruptcy. Gambling and credit card abuse also lead to bankruptcy, but are viewed less sympathetically by the courts.

Lay the Groundwork for Challenging Exemptions in Chapter 13

Some people say objecting to a debtor's exemptions in Chapter 13 is a waste of time, because the debtor retains possession of everything regardless of whether the property is exempt. While it's true that debtors keep all their property in Chapter 13 (that's one reason debtors choose to file Chapter 13 instead of Chapter 7), the value of their nonexempt property helps set the minimum amount that must be paid to unsecured creditor0s. That's because the Bankruptcy Code requires unsecured creditors to be paid at least as much through a Chapter 13 plan as they would have received if the debtor had filed under Chapter 7. Well, if the debtor had filed under Chapter 7, the trustee would have sold the debtor's nonexempt property and distributed the proceeds, minus his commission and expenses, to the unsecured creditors. If the debtor—in Chapter 7—claimed an exemption to which he wasn't entitled, or undervalued an asset to make it appear that it was exempt, then you or the trustee would have objected in order to bring more money into the estate. The same is true in Chapter 13. Even though the improperly exempted property won't be sold, its value will set the minimum amount that unsecured creditors must receive through the debtor's plan. Therefore, objecting to the legitimacy of an exemption as well as challenging undervalued assets is as important in a Chapter 13 case as it is in Chapter 7 case.

Let's imagine, for example, that the debtor has $2,000 available in a wildcard exemption to protect whatever property he wants. He says his stock is worth $2,000, and claims the shares as fully exempt. But what if the stock is really worth $20,000—or $200,000? If the stock is worth $20,000, then the plan must commit at least $18,000 to the payment of unsecured claims. If the stock is worth $200,000, then the plan must commit $198,000 to the payment of unsecured claims. But if no objection is made to the exemption, then no objection can be made to confirmation of the debtor's plan based on the incorrect exemption.

The same is true if the debtor claimed an exemption to which she was not entitled. Once the opportunity for objecting to the exemption is past, the error cannot be the basis for challenging confirmation.

However, while you may be unable to challenge confirmation directly based on the debtor's improperly claimed exemption, you can challenge confirmation based on the debtor's bad faith. (See Chapter 5 for a discussion of what property the debtor may claim as exempt.)

e. Whether the Plan Treats Your Claim Worse Than It Would Be Treated Under Chapter 7

In bankruptcy circles this is known as the "best interests of creditors" test. In general, it means that you must fare at least as well under Chapter 13 as you would have under Chapter 7. More particularly, it means that if there would have been assets available for a Chapter 7 trustee to use to pay unsecured creditors' claims, then you must receive at least as much as you would have under that distribution.

f. Whether the Debtor Is Unlikely to Be Able to Make the Planned-For Payments

This is the "feasibility" test. Some debtor's plans call for monthly payments in excess of the debtor's disposable income. That doesn't necessarily mean the plan isn't feasible. For example, many debtors file for Chapter 13 protection in order to save their homes from foreclosure. To accomplish this goal, they must repay the mortgage arrearage within a reasonable period of time and resume making regular mortgage payments. Desperate or ambitious debtors will commit to plan payments that are higher than their projected disposable income. If the debtor tries to commit to something that is completely beyond his ability, the plan will be denied confirmation because it's not feasible. The same is true if the debtor has a history of confirming plans and not making payments. But if it's the debtor's first bankruptcy, the court will probably confirm the plan, even though the debtor has to stretch his budget to make it work. It's better to have the plan fail because the debtor couldn't make the payments than to deny confirmation and have the debtor lose his home.

The greater the gap between what the debtor says he can afford to pay and what the plan says he will pay, the less feasible the plan is. A plan also fails the feasibility test if payment is contingent on an unlikely event, such as winning the lottery.

6. Preparing Your Objections

As mentioned, the Code allows creditors to object to the plan. So, let's say you've reviewed the debtor's plan and you've got problems with it. What to do next is covered in the following subsections.

a. Talking to the Trustee

Because of the fast pace of Chapter 13 cases, there may not be time to get the information you need from the debtor. Don't panic. The trustee will share whatever information she has gathered about the debtor with you. Talking to the trustee isn't the same as questioning the debtor, but the trustee is a reliable source of information about the current bankruptcy and any previous filings by the debtor.

Some trustees are more accessible than others. However, you don't actually need to speak with "the" trustee. Many trustees delegate confirmation questions to a paralegal or a staff attorney. What's important is talking to the person who is going decide whether the trustee recommends confirmation. Simply ask the person, "Is this your call, or is the trustee going to rely on your recommendation?"

b. Talking to the Debtor's Attorney

If you find something troubling about the plan, call the debtor's attorney or talk to the attorney at the creditors' meeting. Of course, if the confirmation hearing is scheduled for the same day as the creditors' meeting, then waiting until the creditors' meeting to talk to the debtor's attorney (or to question the debtor for that matter) may be too late. Better to pick up the phone and discuss your concerns with the attorney before the meeting.

Attorneys representing Chapter 13 debtors are quite willing to work with creditors to present confirmable plans. This isn't so surprising, when you think about it: Getting creditor input works to everyone's advantage. The debtor benefits by getting the plan confirmed. You benefit by having the trustee start making plan payments. Even the debtor's attorney is happy—the accepted practice across the country is for a significant portion of the debtor's attorney's fee to be paid after the plan is confirmed, as a priority claim.

c. Complaining to the Trustee

If you've had no luck convincing the debtor's attorney to change the plan, see what the trustee thinks about it. If the trustee agrees with you, she can ask the debtor to amend the plan. Her request will carry much more weight than yours, because she's a neutral party. Also, most bankruptcy judges value the trustee's opinion. If the trustee joins your objection and the matter goes to court, you have a greater chance of success than if you go it alone. Conversely, if the trustee thinks you're way off base, then you should seriously reconsider what you're asking for.

d. Filing and Presenting Your Objection

Objections to confirmation are made by motion, a sample of which appears below. The court will set a deadline for filing objections. You'll find this deadline in the information disclosed on the notices for the meeting of creditors and the confirmation hearing. Your objection must be filed with the court by the deadline, sent to the U.S. Trustee, and served on the debtor, the debtor's attorney, and the Chapter 13 trustee.

Filing objections to confirmation is a procedure you can undertake on your own. (See Chapter 10 for the procedures for filing objections.) However, if you've followed our advice and discussed your objection with the debtor's attorney and the trustee and you still need to file an objection, then you should give serious thought to hiring an attorney. The first reason is that at least two attorneys (the one working for the debtor and the trustee) have already disagreed with you. The second is that you can expect opposition from at least one of those two attorneys.

In addition to filing your motion, however, you'll need to be at the confirmation hearing (described in Subsection 7, below) to back up your objection. Be prepared to present evidence to the court that supports your objection. Expect the court to rule on your motion as soon as both sides have completed presenting their evidence.

Sample Objection to Confirmation of Debtor's Plan

IN THE UNITED STATES BANKRUPTCY COURT
FOR THE NORTHERN DISTRICT OF IOWA

In re:)
)
Maria Sue Martinez   )   **CASE NO.** 03-19837
)
)   **OBJECTION TO CONFIRMATION**
_____   )   **OF DEBTOR'S PLAN**

Harriet Creditor, respectfully moves the court to deny confirmation of Debtor's plan pursuant to 11 U.S.C. Section 1325 because Debtor's plan fails to preserve the present value of Movant's allowed secured claim. In support, Movant states as follows:

1. The Debtor, Maria Sue Martinez, filed for bankruptcy under Chapter 13 of the Bankruptcy Code on October 16, 2003.

2. Movant is a secured creditor in this case.

3. Debtor is indebted to Movant in the principal amount of $4,509 plus attorney's fees and costs as evidenced in the Proof of Claim filed by Movant.

4. Debtor's plan treats Movant's claim as fully secured.

5. Debtor's plan proposes to pay Movant's secured claim over the life of the plan with interest at 8% per year.

6. The contract signed by Debtor and attached to Movant's Proof of Claim requires Debtor to pay interest at 24% per year.

7. The market rate of interest for loans similar to that made to Debtor is 24% per year.

8. 11 U.S.C. Section 1325(a)(5)(B)(ii) mandates that holders of allowed secured claims receive the present value of their secured claim through the plan. This provision requires Movant to receive interest on its allowed secured claim at an annual rate of interest of 24%.

9. Because Debtor's plan fails to preserve the present value of Movant's claim, Debtor's plan should be denied confirmation.

WHEREFORE, the moving party requests the court to deny confirmation of Debtor's plan.

Dated: January 20, 2004

Harriet Creditor

Harriet Creditor

Sample Objection to Confirmation of Debtor's Plan (continued)

1
2
3   **CERTIFICATE OF SERVICE**

    I hereby certify that on this 20th day of January, 2004, I caused a true and correct copy
4 of the foregoing motion with postage fully prepaid to Maria Sue Martinez at 213 High
5 Street, Somewhere, Iowa, and to Bob Mortan, Chapter 13 Trustee, at 6535 Office Building,
6 23 First Street, Big City, Iowa.
7
8   *Harriet Creditor*
9   Harriet Creditor
10
11
12
13
14
15
16
17
18
19
20
21
22
23
24
25
26
27
28

Sample Objection to Confirmation of Debtor's Plan (continued)

1
2

IN THE UNITED STATES BANKRUPTCY COURT
FOR THE NORTHERN DISTRICT OF IOWA

3)   **CASE NO.** 03-19837
)
4 **In re:**   )   **ORDER DENYING CONFIRMATION OF**
)   **DEBTOR'S PLAN**
5 Maria Sue Martinez   )
)   **CH. 13**
6)
7)
)
8)

9 ─────────────────────────────

10

11   AND NOW, this 20th day of February 2004, the Court having found that:

12   1. Movant is the holder of an allowed secured claim.

13   2. Debtor's plan proposes to pay Movant's allowed secured claim in installments

14 through the plan.

15   3. Movant is entitled to receive interest an annual rate of 24% in order to preserve the

16 present value of Movant's allowed secured claim.

17   IT IS HEREBY ORDERED THAT

18 Debtor's plan is denied confirmation pursuant to 11 U.S.C. Section 1325.

19
20
21 Dated: Feb. 20, 2004   *Ima Judge*

22   U.S. Bankruptcy Judge

23
24
25
26
27
28

7. The Confirmation Hearing

Chapter 13 plans are not effective until they receive a judge's approval. Normally, this is given at a confirmation hearing. In some courts, however, the hearing is held only if the trustee or a creditor objects to confirmation. If no objections are filed, the plan is confirmed without a hearing.

Assuming the hearing is held, expect it to be jammed in with a bunch of other court business. Most courts set aside a few days per week to hear motions. Confirmation of Chapter 13 plans are included in a lineup that may include motions for stay relief, motions to dismiss, and assorted other requests. The court may try to attend to more than 100 matters, which the judge will quickly run down in an attempt to see which ones can be dispensed with in short order and which ones will take some time.

If you have filed an objection to the debtor's plan with the court, you'll need to make your presence known. The best practice is to arrive early and check with the court clerk or courtroom deputy to find out if you need to sign an appearance sheet and how to respond when the case is called. When the debtor's case is called, let the judge know you're there and ready to proceed.

Last-minute objections may be heard in some courts. If you didn't realize until the day of the confirmation hearing that you wanted to raise an objection, some (but not all) courts will allow you to raise it at the hearing itself. You should definitely be allowed to raise a last-minute objection if the debtor only recently amended the proposed plan. A trustee may be available to give you feedback about the merits of your objection just before the hearing. Still, the best practice is to file your objection and contact the trustee as early in the process as possible.

Also, check in with the trustee before the hearing begins. You'll learn whether the trustee is going to raise the same objection. If so, the debtor will be hard-pressed to convince the court to confirm the plan. If not, the trustee will tell you whether he thinks your objection has merit and, if not, why not. You can then rethink whether you want to raise the objection when the time comes.

When it's time to present your objection, you'll need to show the court that there's a legitimate basis for your complaint. If you succeed, then the debtor has the burden of convincing the court that the plan should be confirmed over your objection.

EXAMPLE: Carruthers the creditor objects that Derwood the debtor's plan was filed in bad faith, based on Derwood having filed for bankruptcy four other times in the last three years. The court finds that Carruthers' objection is legitimate. Now it's up to Derwood to convince the judge that the current filing was done in good faith. Derwood argues that previous circumstances were beyond his control, and that his bankruptcy filings were caused by a string of lousy employers who underpaid him and then laid him off without warning. Derwood has an uphill battle, however, given that the court threw out (dismissed) his four previous cases.

After hearing your position and the debtor's counterposition, the court will ask the trustee if she has anything to add or would care to offer a recommendation. Many judges rely on the trustee's recommendation.

Keep in mind that arriving at a confirmed plan is in the trustee's best interest. The trustee doesn't get paid until she starts making distributions to creditors pursuant to the confirmed plan. Plan confirmation is also favored by creditors and the debtor's attorney, who will be getting paid through the plan.

8. The Judge's Decision on Confirmation

If the judge finds that the plan should be confirmed, then the plan goes into effect right away. The plan's terms are immediately binding on the debtor and all creditors who received notice of the confirmation hearing and the terms of the proposed plan. The plan becomes a binding contract between these parties.

If, on the other hand, the judge finds that the plan should not be confirmed, then the judge must decide what happens next. The judge may either give the debtor an opportunity to file an amended plan, order that the case be converted to a Chapter 7, or dismiss the case altogether.

If the judge confirms the plan, but you don't agree with the judge's decision, you have three options:

- appeal the ruling (Subsection a)
- ask for a revocation of the plan (Subsection b), or
- live with the decision (Subsection 9).

a. Filing an Appeal

If you think the judge's decision was out of line, you may appeal the order to the district court or bankruptcy appellate panel. Requests for reconsideration and appeals must be made within ten days of the entry of the confirmation order. Hiring an attorney would be a good idea at this point, because filing a frivolous appeal could expose you to penalties.

Of course, you must have a good reason to challenge the judge's decision. For example, the debtor may not be committing all her disposable income to the plan.

b. Asking for Revocation of the Plan

Even if you miss the deadline to ask for reconsideration or to appeal the judge's decision, you may be able to later ask that the plan be revoked if the debtor deceived the court. For example, if you discover that the debtor misrepresented material information that was relevant to the court's decision to confirm the plan, this would be a good basis upon which to ask the court to revoke confirmation. Or, if the debtor understated her income or overstated her expenses so as to minimize her disposable income, this would also form the basis for asking the court to revoke confirmation.

A request for revocation is made by filing a motion within 180 days of the entry of the confirmation order. Your motion should allege that the plan confirmation was obtained by fraud. You might be more comfortable in having an attorney help you meet the challenges of proving a fraud allegation.

9. Living With the Plan

If the plan calls for you to receive payments, those payments should start coming sometime after confirmation of the plan. The exact schedule depends on the nature of your claim and the terms of the plan. If you're holding a secured or priority unsecured claim, your payments may start coming right away, or they may be deferred until later. If you have any questions about when you should expect to see your first payment, talk to the trustee.

If the plan calls for property to be sold or collateral surrendered, these transfers will take place as provided for in the plan. As long as the debtor keeps making payments to the trustee and nothing particularly good or bad happens to the debtor, the plan will continue until completion, with no more court appearances. However, such smooth sailing is rare. According to statistics maintained by the U.S. Trustee's office in Washington, DC, 22.2% of all Chapter 13 cases were either dismissed or converted during the year 2002. That must mean that creditors in more than 22.2% of the cases asked for dismissal or conversion, since it's safe to assume that some of their motions were denied. So you can see the frequency with which these motions arise in typical cases. Usually one or more of the following has occurred:

The debtor failed to make payments to the trustee. Chapter 13 plans can be dismissed if the debtor doesn't live up to the promises made in the plan. Usually, this means the debtor doesn't make the required payments. It can also mean that the planned-for payments aren't adequate to make the distributions to creditors. This can happen if the plan was confirmed before the deadline for filing proofs of claim, and the total claims filed exceed the amount anticipated in the confirmed plan. When this happens, the trustee will ask the debtor to modify the plan to correct the problem and ask the court to dismiss or convert the case if the debtor doesn't do so.

Debtors can keep their plans alive by modifying the plan in order to extend its life, increasing the amount of their payments, or reducing the payments to unsecured creditors.

The debtor failed to make payments to a secured creditor. Given a choice between making a mortgage payment outside the plan and making a Chapter 13 plan payment, most debtors will make the mortgage payment. As we've just discussed, however, if debtors fall behind on their plan payments, their cases can be converted to Chapter 7 or dismissed. So, some debtors will make their plan payments and skip their mortgage payment instead. When this happens, the secured creditor who is supposed to be receiving the payment should file a motion asking the court to convert or dismiss the debtor's case because the debtor has not made the payments as promised in the plan. If the plan promises that the debtor will make payments directly to you and the payments stop coming, you can ask the court to lift the stay so you can foreclose on the collateral just like you'd do under Chapter 7. (See Chapter 4.)

The debtor damaged the collateral. The collateral is normally something the debtor is using, such as a car, so damage is always a possibility.

EXAMPLE: Chuck's Autos' loan to Dudley is secured by Dudley's car. The plan says Chuck's is to be paid the secured value of its claim plus interest. The plan allows Chuck's to retain its lien until Dudley receives a discharge, and orders Dudley to keep the car insured. Six months after the plan is confirmed, the car is wrecked. What happens?

Dudley needs a car, so he's going to ask the court to modify the plan to surrender the car to Chuck's and use the insurance proceeds to buy a new one. Dudley may or may not also ask to modify the plan to reduce the secured claim to the scrap value of the car and to add the unpaid balance of the secured claim to your unsecured claim.

Chuck's will oppose Dudley's request, arguing that the insurance proceeds belong to Chuck's and that Chuck's should be allowed to apply them against the total amount Dudley owes rather than just against the amount of the secured claim. After all, the collateral was the insured car, so Chuck's should be entitled to the insurance if the car is no longer available.

The bankruptcy courts have developed two equally popular resolutions to the scenario in the example above. Both solutions treat the creditor's secured claim based on its confirmation value. In one solution, the insurance proceeds pay off the balance of the allowed secured claim, and anything that's left over goes to the trustee. The other solution allows the debtor to use the insurance proceeds to buy a replacement car and gives the creditor a lien on the new car.

But what if the collateral just wears out? Most courts say the obsolescence of the debtor's vehicle or other collateral has no effect on the value of the creditor's secured claim. If the car is no good, then the debtor must ask the court to modify the plan so that the car may be traded in on a new one. If this isn't possible, the debtor may ask the court to dismiss the case to resolve the problem and then refile after it's solved.

The debtor experiences an unexpected change in financial circumstances. If the debtor's financial situation improves unexpectedly, you may well want to ask the court to modify the debtor's plan. The debtor's plan will already include "projected" disposable income, so don't get excited if you hear about a routine pay increase—this does not qualify as an event necessitating plan modification. However, a change of jobs to a higher-paying position would warrant modification of the debtor's plan. Less likely but much more favorable events, such as the debtor's receiving an inheritance or winning the lottery, would also be fine reasons to ask for modification.

If the debtor's plan calls for the full payment of unsecured claims, the debtor's extra cash might enable the debtor to complete the plan early. However, the Bankruptcy Code does not insist that the debtor to do so.

If the plan calls for less than the full payment of unsecured claims, then any unsecured creditor may ask the court to modify the debtor's plan to include the unaccounted-for money by increasing the payments made on unsecured claims.

If the debtor's financial situation takes an unexpected turn for the worse, the debtor can also ask the court to modify the plan.

When considering modification requests, courts use the same criteria as they do for confirmation of the original plan, with one major exception—the plan does not need to commit all the debtor's *projected* disposable income. Instead, the court limits its concern to the debtor's *current* financial situation.

10. Completion of the Plan

After the debtor has made the last payment called for in the plan, the trustee will inform the court and recommend that the debtor receive a discharge. This is the broadest discharge available under the Bankruptcy Code, covering all claims provided for in the plan except those:

- on which the last payment is still due
- for alimony, maintenance, and support
- for student loans
- arising out of injury or death caused by the debtor's intoxicated operation of a motor vehicle, and
- for restitution in a federal court or a fine imposed as part of a criminal sentence.

If you believe that your claim fits one of these discharge exceptions, you may file a complaint challenging its discharge as soon as the debtor completes the plan. (See Chapter 10 regarding filing complaints—in this instance, we recommend getting a lawyer's help.) Though you can ask the court to rule on your claim before the case has been discharged, the court

may decide that the issue isn't ready to be heard until the debtor is actually eligible for the discharge.

If the debtor is unable to complete the planned-for payments, he may still receive a discharge by converting the case to Chapter 7 or by asking the court for a hardship discharge. Hardship discharges are available to debtors after confirmation of their plans if:

- the debtor is unable to complete payments due to circumstances beyond his control
- unsecured creditors have received at least much through the plan as they would have received had the debtor filed for Chapter 7, or
- modification of the plan is not practical.

The exceptions to discharge applicable in Chapter 7 cases also apply to a hardship discharge under Chapter 13. So if you receive a notice that the debtor is asking for a hardship discharge and you believe your claim would be nondischargeable in a Chapter 7 case, file a complaint objecting to the discharge of your claim prior to the deadline for doing so that will be stated in the notice you received.

C. Chapter 12 Reorganization Plans

We don't have a lot to say about Chapter 12—as far as the reorganization plan goes, the law for Chapter 12 is nearly identical to that for Chapter 13 (covered above). Chapter 12 cases also happen to be very rare. In fact, they're totally unheard of in many parts of the United States.

Here are the few notable differences between Chapter 12 and Chapter 13:

- Chapter 12 debtors have 90 days after they file for bankruptcy to file their plans, while Chapter 13 debtors have 15 days.
- Chapter 12 debtors may modify the rights of secured creditors regardless of the nature of their collateral. This means there's no protection from modification for creditors who are secured only by a mortgage on the family farmer's homestead. (Contrast this with Chapter 13, where creditors who are secured only by the debtor's home must have their claims fully paid pursuant to the contract terms.)

D. Chapter 11 Reorganization Plans

Companies file for Chapter 11 because they wish to stay in business while working out a plan to repay their creditors. For a corporation that wants to reorganize, Chapter 11 is the only choice. Individuals can also file under Chapter 11, although it was not written with them in mind.

The number of Chapter 11 cases filed each year pales in comparison to the number of Chapter 13 cases. Of course, that doesn't mean the impact of Chapter 11 cases is limited. A casual glance at the companies that have recently sought Chapter 11 relief—WorldCom, Enron, and Kmart, to name but a few—shows how a single Chapter 11 case can affect thousands of creditors, employees, and stockholders. If you are named as a creditor in a large Chapter 11 case, you'll probably have very little say about the outcome. That's the reality of Chapter 11. Nevertheless, we think it's worth learning what your rights are and following what's going on.

Also, these megacases that attract national headlines are a tiny fraction of all the Chapter 11 cases filed every year. The more typical Chapter 11 cases are filed by struggling smaller companies. The smaller cases follow the same rules as the larger ones. However, you have a much better chance of being an active participant, since such cases involve fewer creditors.

To better understand your potential role as a Chapter 11 creditor, lets look at:

- the formation of committees to represent your interests (Subsection 1)
- how the Chapter 11 plan is developed (Subsection 2)
- your opportunity to vote on the plan (Subsection 3)
- deciding how to cast your vote (Subsection 4), and
- what happens when the plan is confirmed (Subsection 5).

1. The Role of Committees in Speaking for Creditors

After the debtor files for bankruptcy, the U.S. Trustee will appoint one or more committees to represent everyone holding claims against the debtor. At a minimum, one of these committees will represent the interests of unsecured creditors. This committee must be made up of the holders of the seven largest unsecured claims who are willing to serve. Upon request, the bankruptcy court may also create additional committees to represent the interests of other groups of creditors such as stockholders and employees.

Creditors' committees perform all the functions that individual creditors would in a case filed under another bankruptcy chapter. First, the committees play a key role in enabling debtors to successfully reorganize, by participating in the formulation of the debtor's reorganization plan (as described in Subsections 2 through 5, below). Even after that, the committees are expected to play an active role in the bankruptcy. They are specifically authorized to investigate how the debtor is conducting its business. If a committee believes the debtor is mismanaging the company or mishandling its assets, the committee may ask the court to either appoint a trustee to run the company while it's in bankruptcy or appoint an examiner to conduct a thorough examination of the debtor's operations.

2. Development of the Chapter 11 Plan

Chapter 11 plans are frequently the product of negotiations between the debtor, the creditors, and others who have an interest in the bankruptcy, such as employees. Only the debtor can propose a plan during the first 120 days of the bankruptcy. If the debtor does so, then no creditor can offer a competing plan during the first 180 days of the bankruptcy. This extra 60 days gives the debtor an opportunity to solicit acceptance of the plan without competition. However, the bankruptcy court may extend or reduce these time periods, (known as the "exclusivity period") if requested by the debtor, any creditor or the trustee. It is more common for courts to extend the exclusivity period than to cut short the time for filing plans. However, either result is possible if the court believes it is in the best interests of all parties.

Once the exclusivity period is over, and if no plan has been adopted, creditors may offer their own plans. Most creditors' plans call for the company to be sold.

At least you're permitted to propose a plan! In the other reorganization chapters, creditors have no opportunity to offer up their own prospective plans, with or without an exclusivity period.

The best situation from the standpoint of the bankruptcy court is where the debtor and the creditors' committee(s) agree on a plan. This is known as a consensual plan.

The worst situation for the bankruptcy court is where the debtor is unable to get a plan confirmed and one or more competing plans are offered. The court must then review all the plans and decide which one is in the best interests of all creditors. As a creditor, however, you'll probably benefit from this plethora of plans: Competition among plan proponents tends to drive up the return to unsecured creditors.

3. Opportunity to Vote on the Chapter 11 Plan

Even if you don't propose your own plan, you may be given an important right as a Chapter 11 creditor: to vote on the other plans on the table (including the debtor's initial plan during the exclusivity period). Creditors in Chapters 12 and 13 aren't given any such right. There are exceptions, however: Any Chapter 11 creditor whose claim is paid in full is considered to accept the plan. And on the other side of the coin, any creditor whose claim is not paid at all is considered to reject the plan. That leaves those creditors whose claims are paid something—but not everything—in the pool of eligible voters. Their claims or interests are referred to as being "impaired."

Whoever puts forth the plan must provide you with a copy or a summary of it, plus a disclosure statement containing any information that you might reasonably need to make up your mind. The court must approve the adequacy of the disclosure statement.

Votes are counted by class of claims, with class divisions created by the plan. In order for a class of claims to accept the plan, more than half the creditors in the class must vote in favor. In addition, those voting in favor must represent at least two-thirds of the dollar amount of claims in the class. For example, if the class of unsecured creditors consists of 100 creditors owed $100,000, then 51 creditors would need to vote for it and those creditors would need to be owed at least $66,667.

4. Evaluating the Proposed Chapter 11 Plan

How will you choose to vote? You may be thinking it makes sense to reject any plan that pays you less than 100% of your claim—hoping for better luck under the next proposed plan. However, the plan you're voting on may be the only plan you see for a while. In fact, there may not be another plan at all. You're being asked to vote on a bird in the hand when you're not sure there's a bush out there with more birds in it. If the plan is rejected, the debtor may offer another plan, other creditors may offer competing plans or the case may be converted to Chapter 7, in which case you might receive nothing. If multiple plans are under consideration, then obviously you should vote for the one under which you fare best.

Which plan offers you the best deal may depend on several factors. One factor worth considering is what's happening to the company's current owners. The Bankruptcy Code says that if the current owners are allowed to keep any interest in the company, then either your claim must be paid in full or you must accept how your claim is being paid. This is known as the "absolute priority" rule. Like any rule, however, it was made to be broken.

The common way that debtors get around the rule is by having the old company's owners contribute new value to the debtor in exchange for a continued equity interest in the reorganized debtor. Creditors should question the validity and necessity of the contribution. Is it really new? Is it really valuable? For example, the owner of a privately held corporation that files bankruptcy may claim that she contributed new value to the debtor in possession (DIP) by continuing to work without receiving adequate compensation.

Many plans ask you to accept something other than full cash payment of your claim. Usually you'll be offered an ownership interest in the reorganized debtor or a new claim to replace your discharged one. Under such circumstances, you must decide whether having an interest in or a claim against the reorganized debtor is a good investment.

5. Confirmation of the Plan

After the votes are all in, the court must confirm the Chapter 11 plan if every class has voted for it and:

- the plan complies with the law
- the plan proponent properly disclosed the plan's terms in soliciting votes
- the plan was proposed in good faith
- payments to professionals in the case are reasonable
- the plan proponent has disclosed who is going to run the business after confirmation
- the appropriate regulatory body has approved any proposed rate change
- each holder of a claim that is partially secured will receive the current value of its secured claim
- each holder of an administrative expense claim (typically, professionals who helped in the case) will be paid as of the plan's effective date

- employees' claims for wages and benefits will paid in full on the plan's effective date, or paid over time if this class of priority claims accepts the plan
- plan confirmation is not likely to immediately result in the debtor's liquidation or in any need for financial reorganization except as called for in the plan
- all administrative fees have been paid, and
- the plan calls for the continuation of all retiree benefits.

If the plan is not accepted by every class of claims, it may still be confirmed if at least one class of impaired claims has accepted the plan, holders of impaired claims will be paid at least as much as they would have received in a Chapter 7 case (this is called the "best interests of creditors" test), and the plan does not unfairly discriminate in favor of a class of creditors and is fair and equitable. If you hold a partially secured claim, the plan will be considered fair and equitable if you keep your lien and are paid the current value of your secured claim.

If you hold an unsecured claim, the plan will be considered fair and equitable if you receive at least as much as you would have received under Chapter 7 and stockholders get nothing. This is the "absolute priority" rule at work. If your claim is unsecured and you get less than full payment, then the holders of equity in the debtor must receive nothing.

Confirmation of the plan changes the debtor's relationships with creditors and employees. Everyone covered by the plan, including those who voted against it, are governed by its terms.

Confirmation of the plan also results in the discharge of claims as provided for in the plan. If, however, the plan calls for the debtor to sell all or most of its assets and go out of business, then the discharge is limited to whatever the debtor could have received in Chapter 7. That means that if you hold a claim that would have been excepted from discharge in Chapter 7, you may file a complaint to challenge its discharge. You can also challenge the debtor's right to receive a discharge if the plan calls for the debtor to liquidate or go out of business. You won't be able to collect your claim from the corporation because it is out of business. However, the judgment may help you in the event that one of the debtor's principals files for bankruptcy.

If Your Employer Files for Chapter 11 Bankruptcy

When companies file for bankruptcy, their employees are left wondering what will happen to their jobs, benefits, and pensions. If you're in this situation, here are the key things to understand.

First, your job is as safe after the filing as it was before. That news may not seem very comforting. However, the fact that your employer is taking steps to correct its financial problems—instead of just closing its doors and issuing pink slips—is reason for hope. If you are a key employee, such as a corporate officer or department head, you may be approached about signing a retention agreement. Such an agreement would contain your promise to stay with the company through the bankruptcy. The bankruptcy court must approve any such agreement for it to become effective.

Any wages that you earned but weren't actually paid prior to the bankruptcy filing become an unsecured claim. However, wages earned during the last 90 days prior to the bankruptcy filing are treated as a priority claim, up to $4,650.

Now, about your pension. If your employer was following the rules, your pension should be safe. The federal government requires pension contributions to be kept separate from a company's operating funds. This money should have been held in trust by your employer or turned over to an insurance company for safekeeping. In addition, if you participate in a traditional benefit plan with defined benefits, the plan is insured by the federal government. Nontraditional retirement plans, such as supplement plans for executives and early retirement packages, are more vulnerable in bankruptcy, since they may depend on continued payments from the bankrupt company.

If, however, your employer violated the pension rules or your plan isn't insured, then the money may not be there. The Bankruptcy Code provides a priority for unpaid contributions to pension plans of up to $4,650 per employee for payments missed within 180 days prior to the bankruptcy filing. Any claim against the company for unpaid contributions must be made by the pension plan's administrator.

Health benefits are another important concern. Federal law requires that you receive 60 days' notice if your employer wishes to decrease or eliminate your health benefits. If your employer maintained several health plan options,

If Your Employer Files for Chapter 11 Bankruptcy (continued)

you may be forced to switch to the one option your employer continues to offer. If all options are eliminated, you'll need to find health insurance elsewhere.

If you have retired from the bankrupt company, but continue to receive health and life insurance benefits, then the continuation of those benefits depends on how much they're fed by contributions from the company. Many companies that file for bankruptcy are unable to afford paying the insurance premium for retired workers—and there's nothing in the Bankruptcy Code to force them to do so. Developing some solidarity among

your fellow retirees may be key to protecting your interests. After some 6,000 retirees from Polaroid learned that their bankrupt former employer had terminated their health and life insurance benefits, they convinced the bankruptcy court to recognize them as a creditors' committee. They then challenged the company's plan to pay $19 million in bonuses to 45 top executives. Polaroid later withdrew that proposal. This is how Chapter 11 is supposed to work—a creditor constituency organizes a committee to protect the collective interest of its members. ■

CHAPTER

14

Conversions Between Bankruptcy Chapters

Don't get too attached to the bankruptcy chapter under which the debtor filed—it may be changed midstream. In fact, you may be the one to request the change. The procedure of switching chapters is known as conversion. Regardless of whether the request for conversion comes from the debtor, a creditor, or the trustee, the motive is usually the same: a belief that current or changed circumstances make another type of bankruptcy better than the current one.

For example, debtors who started under Chapter 7 may switch to a reorganization chapter because they misjudged their ability to keep certain property items under Chapter 7 or their eligibility to receive a Chapter 7 discharge. Or, they may simply become able to propose a viable Chapter 13 reorganization plan after the initial bankruptcy filing date.

Then there are the debtors who start under one of the reorganization chapters, but later wish to switch to Chapter 7. They may be unable to propose a plan that the court will confirm, or perhaps they decide that a Chapter 7 discharge would offer certain advantages they can't get with a discharge under Chapter 11, 12 or 13.

You or another creditor may also ask the court to convert the case. For example, perhaps the debtor is a business filing under Chapter 11, but you believe you'd get more money if the case went forth under Chapter 7. Some businesses file under Chapter 11 in the mistaken belief that they can resuscitate their dying venture in bankruptcy when you, as a creditor, know that all they're doing is wasting assets. Or, perhaps the debtor is an individual who filed under Chapter 13, owing you a debt that can be discharged in Chapter 13 but not in Chapter 7. Debts incurred by fraud are the most common example (see Chapter 9 for a list of the discharges available under each type of bankruptcy).

You need not read this chapter if:

- The debtor, an individual, filed under Chapter 7 and has not filed a motion to convert. Though you can ask the court to convert the case to Chapter 11, it's doubtful you would want to.

- The debtor filed under one of the reorganization chapters and has proposed a plan that will pay you more than you would receive if the case were converted to Chapter 7.

- The debtor filed under one of the reorganization chapters and the case is progressing toward plan confirmation. If the debtor appears to be acting in good faith, there's no reason to ask for a conversion.

Each type of conversion has its own rules and idiosyncrasies. In this chapter, we'll look at:

- what types of cases can be converted (Section A)
- rules for conversion from Chapter 7 to a reorganization chapter (Section B)
- rules for conversion from Chapter 11 to Chapter 7 (Section C)
- rules for conversion from Chapters 12 and 13 to Chapter 7 (Section D)
- how creditors are affected by conversions to Chapter 7 (Section E), and
- conversions between reorganization chapters (Section F).

A. Cases Eligible for Conversion

Conversion isn't a free pass. A debtor's case can be converted only to a bankruptcy chapter under which the debtor could have filed originally.

> **EXAMPLE:** Dante has $1 million in unsecured debt. This debt level makes him ineligible to file under Chapter 13, so he files under Chapter 7 instead. Later, however, he attempts to convert the case to Chapter 13. His conversion request is denied, since he was originally ineligible to use Chapter 13.

This eligibility rule applies even if the debtor's circumstances change during the bankruptcy. If Dante, in the example above, owned valuable, nonexempt property that the Chapter 7 trustee sold to reduce his unsecured creditors' claims below Chapter 13's statutory maximum, Dante would still be stuck with Chapter 7—his subsequent request to convert to Chapter 13 would be denied.

You can oppose any request for conversion to a chapter that the debtor wasn't eligible to file under initially, but the trustee will usually step in and do this without your taking the initiative. Other reasons for objecting to a conversion—or asking the court to dismiss a converted case when you can't oppose conversion—are specific to the bankruptcy chapter involved and are more likely to be raised by the affected creditors, as discussed in the coming sections.

B. Conversions from Chapter 7 to a Reorganization Chapter

This section will focus on cases where the debtor has requested conversion from Chapter 7 to a reorganization chapter. (As a creditor, you have no legal right to request a conversion to Chapter 12 or 13, and probably wouldn't want to request conversion to Chapter 11.) We'll discuss:

- when and why the conversion may happen (Subsection 1)
- how to deal with a bad faith conversion (Subsection 2), and
- what happens after a conversion out of Chapter 7 (Subsection 3).

⚠ **Don't rely on debtors' promises to convert to Chapter 12 or 13.** Such promises cannot be enforced. Why? Because it's unconstitutional to force debtors to work to repay their debts. Since Chapters 12 and 13 plans are funded by the debtor's future income, the courts say that requiring a debtor to convert to or stay in these chapters against his will amounts to involuntary servitude—which was outlawed by the 13th Amendment to the U.S. Constitution.

1. When and Why Conversion May Happen

A debtor may, according to the law, convert a Chapter 7 case to a Chapter 11, 12, or 13 "at any time," so long as the case was not already converted from one of those chapters to Chapter 7. (See 11 U.S.C. § 706.) Most courts—but not all—interpret this provision as giving debtors an absolute right to convert their cases, at any time and for any or no reason. Some debtors have even been known to convert from Chapter 7 to Chapter 13 after receiving a discharge but before the clo-

sure of their cases. You're not likely to face such a scenario, because it doesn't gain the debtor much, but it illustrates how far courts will go to give meaning to the statute.

The few remaining courts, however, say they have a duty to review the motives behind the debtor's conversion request. They reason that the judge can order a case converted from any of the reorganization chapters to Chapter 7 if the judge believes the debtor is abusing the Bankruptcy Code or otherwise acting in bad faith. Why should the court allow the debtor to convert a case out of Chapter 7 if the judge can immediately send it back to Chapter 7?

You should be skeptical of any debtor's request to convert a case out of Chapter 7: The usual motive is to avoid losing property the debtor thought he'd be allowed to keep, or to get out a debt the debtor mistakenly thought he could discharge. If, for example, you successfully increase the size of the debtor's bankruptcy estate by discovering hidden assets or challenging the debtor's exemptions, your "reward" may be the debtor's request to convert his case to one of the reorganization chapters.

You'll also find that debtors are eager to convert their Chapter 7 cases to Chapter 13 after creditors have proven that their claims are excepted from discharge based on the debtor's fraud. This is because claims based on fraud can be discharged under Chapter 13 but not under Chapter 7.

2. Dealing With Bad Faith Conversions

You or the trustee may oppose conversion out of Chapter 7 if the debtor's action was motivated by bad faith. Normally, you would welcome a conversion out of Chapter 7 with open arms. In legal terms, your chances of getting partial or full payment of your claim improve greatly under a reorganization chapter. But what if the debtor's motive for converting is to escape an aggressive trustee who is hot on the trail of nonexempt assets that could be seized and sold for your benefit as an unsecured creditor?

Debtors often choose Chapter 7 because they believe they'll get to keep the property that's valuable to them, leaving creditors with a few crumbs. However, an aggressive trustee can interfere with this scheme. The debtor, faced with the prospect of losing property he intended to keep, may cast a fond eye on a different chapter. By switching to Chapter 12 or 13, he would get a different trustee. By switching to Chapter 11, he would lose the trustee altogether and be in charge of disbursing his own assets.

In such a situation, it may be in your best interests to have the debtor stay in Chapter 7. You'll want to hang on to any trustee who will see to it that the debtor's assets are gathered and sold and the proceeds distributed among the creditors.

If your court takes the position that debtors do not have an absolute right to convert their cases out of Chapter 7, your first step is to ask the trustee if she's going to oppose conversion (which the trustee has the power to do). If not, or if the court does not consider opposition to conversion requests, you should—at your earliest opportunity—file a motion asking the court to reconvert the case to Chapter 7.

If there's a chance that the debtor will dispose of newly found assets, then move quickly. If not, you may wait to see what kind of plan the debtor proposes before acting. If the plan is not favorable to you, then file a motion objecting to confirmation and asking the court to reconvert the case.

Be aware, however, that many courts believe debtors have an absolute right to convert their cases out of Chapter 7 into Chapter 13. If that's the position of your court, you're out of luck on the conversion motion—but you can still file a motion to reconvert the case or dismiss it. (See Chapter 10 for more on what's involved in filing motions.)

3. Effect of Conversion Out of Chapter 7

When a case is converted out of Chapter 7, the Chapter 7 trustee is immediately out of work. If the trustee discovered hidden assets, the debtor will request conversion to a chapter where he can keep the property while repaying some or all of his debts. (If you're worried about how the trustee gets paid, he will file a proof of claim in the reorganization case for services rendered. The Chapter 7 trustee's claim will be given priority status, which means it will probably be paid ahead of your claim out of the debtor's plan.)

The conversion does not change any relevant court orders previously entered in the case. Also, if the debtor surrendered collateral to you during the Chapter 7 case, you don't need to give it back following the conversion. However, if you obtained relief from the automatic stay during the Chapter 7 case, you may need to return to court if anyone other than the debtor is responsible for paying your claim. Under Chapter 7, the automatic stay applies only to the debtor. Under Chapter 13, the automatic stay is extended to prevent collection actions taken against anyone who is liable on a debt with the debtor. (See Chapter 4.)

If you didn't file a proof of claim in the Chapter 7 case, you'll need to file one to share in any distribution in the reorganization case. If you did file a proof of claim, then you don't need to file another one in the reorganization case.

C. Conversions from Chapter 11 to Chapter 7

Very few Chapter 11 cases make it all to way to confirmation—they're usually either dismissed or converted. The law says that Chapter 11 cases can be converted or dismissed "for cause." (See 11 U.S.C. § 1112(b).) To help us understand what "cause" is, the statute also lists examples of actions or inactions justifying conversion. Among the examples are the debtor's inability to propose a confirmable plan and inability to abide by the terms of a confirmed plan. Continuing losses of income and reduction in the value of the debtor's assets are also reasons to convert a case from Chapter 11 to Chapter 7. Because the items on this list are merely examples, you may ask the court to convert a case for a reason not on the list if you believe the debtor is not making a good faith attempt to reorganize.

As a practical matter, however, you probably don't need to jump into action. While you are entitled to file a motion asking the court to dismiss or convert a Chapter 11 case, such motions are generally brought by either:

- the U.S. Trustee, whose job it is to supervise these cases
- a large creditor, whose goal is to quickly move against collateral, or
- the debtor, whose original incentive for filing Chapter 11 has disappeared.

Be on the lookout for indications that the debtor isn't going to be able to reorganize. For example, if the debtor doesn't show signs of turning things around after filing for bankruptcy, ask the U.S. Trustee if there are any plans to move for the case's conversion or dismissal. Your interest in the matter will keep the trustee alert to the situation and may save you the expense of seeking dismissal or conversion on your own.

D. Conversions from Chapters 12 and 13 to Chapter 7

Next, let's look at conversions from Chapter 12 or 13 (reorganization chapters) to Chapter 7. Chapter 12 or 13 debtors can exercise their right to conversion at any time and for any or no reason, even if the case was previously converted. (See 11 U.S.C. §§ 1208 and 1307.) (Reorganization debtors can also request dismissal of their cases at any time, though this right is limited to debtors who have not previously converted from another chapter. (See 11 U.S.C. §§ 1208 and 1307.)) As a creditor, you may ask the court to convert a debtor's case to Chapter 7 for "cause"—

namely for certain reasons discussed in the subsections below. See the end of this section for a sample motion to convert.

You couldn't oppose a debtor's request to convert from Chapter 12 or Chapter 13 to Chapter 7 even if you wanted to. Procedurally, all the debtor needs to do is to file a notice of conversion. Unlike a motion, such a notice doesn't make a request of the court— thereby giving you a chance to object— the notice just announces that the case has been converted. However, if you feel that the debtor has not acted in good faith or that the conversion is going to harm you, ask the court to dismiss the case. (For this, you'll need to file a motion to dismiss, probably with the help of a lawyer, as discussed in Chapter 10.)

The usual reasons that the debtor or you might request a conversion include:

- plan failure (Subsection 1), and
- strategic planning by the debtor (Subsection 2).

1. Plan Failure as a Reason for Conversion

When debtors abandon their reorganization attempts, it's usually because things aren't working out as planned. For instance, a debtor who filed for Chapter 13 to save his home, but ends up losing the home to foreclosure after the filing, may ask to convert to Chapter 7. If the debtor decides to give up on his reorganization bankruptcy, you can't force him to stick with it.

You may, however, be the one who wants the debtor's case converted to Chapter 7. You can do this on your own or with the help of an attorney, by filing a motion with the court. But the better choice is to ask the trustee whether she is going to ask the court to convert or dismiss the debtor's case. Section 1307 lists ten reasons why a court may convert or dismiss a case. Keep in mind that the items on this list are just examples of which debtor activities justify dismissal. As a creditor, you can file a motion with the court requesting conversion or dismissal for any of the ten reasons listed in the law. (See 11 U.S.C. § 1307.) Among these reasons, the most likely ones for your use include the debtor's failure to file a confirmable plan, failure to file any plan at all, or failure to abide by the terms of the confirmed plan. In the first situation, where the debtor has repeatedly failed to propose a confirmable plan, you'll especially want to consider requesting conversion or dismissal if:

- your claim is secured by an asset with depreciating value
- your claim would be excepted from discharge under Chapter 7, or
- the debtor is trying to protect an asset that a Chapter 7 trustee could sell.

In the situation where the debtor is unable to maintain plan payments, you

probably won't need to act—the trustee will beat you to it.

If none of the reasons in the law seems to fit your situation, you have another option: You can request dismissal by simply showing that the debtor is abusing Chapter 13.

2. The Debtor's Financial Strategy Motivating Conversion

Not all conversions are the result of an inability to propose or sustain a reorganization plan. In rarer cases, the debtor reaches a point where "what's in it for him" has run out. The beneficial aspects of the reorganization have been exhausted, leaving only the burden of making payments under the plan. Of course, receiving the final discharge remains a worthwhile benefit—but debtors quickly realize that they can do that under another chapter. For example, debtors commonly seek conversion to Chapter 7 after they've successfully cured their mortgage arrearages (Subsection a, below) or paid off their automobiles (Subsection b, below).

a. Cured Mortgage Arrearages

Bankruptcy Chapters 12 and 13 are great for debtors who want to save their residential and agricultural property. Debtors who are delinquent on their payments to secured creditors can resume making regular payments while paying off the default through their plans. Once the default is cured, their secured debts are treated as if there had never been a default. Attaining that return to normal may be the debtor's goal rather than attaining a full bankruptcy discharge. If so, the debtor will ask the court to dismiss the case once the arrearage is paid.

However, in some cases the debtor may ultimately want a discharge, but decide to convert to Chapter 7 after the arrearage is paid. For example, if only unsecured creditors are getting paid from the plan and the debtor would lose no property by converting to Chapter 7, then the decision to convert is a no-brainer, because in Chapter 7 the unsecured debts can be discharged without payment. The closer the debtor is to reaching the end of the plan, the less likely the debtor is to go for a conversion. But remember, the Code says the debtor may convert "at any time."

If the debtor elects to have the case dismissed after paying the mortgage arrearage, you probably won't care. Any rights you had against the debtor that were stayed by the bankruptcy filing can be asserted again after the case is dismissed. If, however, the debtor decides to convert to Chapter 7, you'll want to take some action if:

- your claim is secured by an asset whose value depreciated during the Chapter 13 case

- your claim can be discharged in Chapter 7, or
- you believe the conversion was proposed in bad faith.

Remember, you can't force the debtor to stay in Chapter 13, but you may be able to frustrate the purpose behind the conversion by having the case dismissed.

b. Discharging Undersecured Liens

If you are a secured creditor whose collateral isn't worth enough to fully cover your lien, you probably already realize what a lousy position you're in—but we'll revisit the issue here, for good measure. The debtor can pay off the value of your secured claim with interest through the reorganization plan, then convert the case to Chapter 7 and discharge the unsecured portion of your claim.

Your best opportunity to deal with this possibility was during the confirmation of the reorganization plan. (See Chapter 13, Section B5ii for a discussion of what to look for in the debtor's plan and when to object.) At that time you should have opposed any arrangement under which you would lose your lien when the secured portion of your claim is paid in full. If the plan says nothing about what happens to your lien, or conditions the avoidance of your lien on the debtor completing plan payments and receiving a discharge, you're protected.

Sample Motion to Convert or Dismiss Debtor's Case

1 **IN THE UNITED STATES BANKRUPTCY COURT**

2 **FOR THE WESTERN DISTRICT OF OKLAHOMA**

3

4 **In re:**

5 Dorian Delmont

6

7

8

CASE NO.: WOK-03-2348-bk

MOTION TO CONVERT OR DISMISS DEBTOR'S CASE

9   Movant, Lawrence Lawful, respectfully moves the court to dismiss debtor's Chapter 13

10 case or convert it to Chapter 7 pursuant to 11 U.S.C. Section 1307(c) because Debtor has

11 failed to propose a confirmable plan within a reasonable period of time. In support Movant

12 states as follows:

13   1. The Debtor, Dorian Delmont, filed for bankruptcy under Chapter 13 of the Bank-

14 ruptcy Code on June 14, 2003.

15   2. Movant is an unsecured creditor in this case.

16   3. Debtor is indebted to Movant in the principal amount of $1,283 plus attorneys fees

17 and costs as evidenced in the Proof of Claim filed by Movant.

18

19   4. Movant has reason to believe that its claim would be excepted from discharge

20 under 11 U.S.C. Section 523(a)(2).

21   5. As of the date of this motion, Debtor has failed to propose a plan that meets the

22 qualifications for confirmation.

23   6. Movant is harmed by the continuation of Debtor's Chapter 13 case because the

24 automatic stay of Section 362 prevents Movant from pursuing its claim against Debtor in state

25 court.

26   7. 11 U.S.C. Section 1307(c) allows the bankruptcy court to dismiss a Chapter 13

27 case or convert it to Chapter 7 when the debtor engages in unreasonable delay that is preju-

28 dicial to creditors.

Sample Motion to Convert or Dismiss Debtor's Case (continued)

1	8. Debtor's failure to propose a plan that could be confirmed by the court is an unreason-
2	able delay.
3	9. Movant's inability to pursue its claim against Debtor in state court is prejudicial to Movant.
4	10. Movant's inability to challenge Debtor's ability to discharge its claim under Chapter 7 is
5	prejudicial to Movant.
6	WHEREFORE, Movant requests the court to dismiss Debtor's Chapter 13 case or con-
7	vert it to Chapter 7.
8	
9	Dated: Oct. 2, 2004 *Lawrence Lawful*
10	
11	
12	
13	
14	
15	
16	
17	
18	
19	
20	
21	
22	
23	
24	
25	
26	
27	
28	

Sample Motion to Convert or Dismiss Debtor's Case (continued)

1	**CERTIFICATE OF SERVICE**
2	
3	I hereby certify that on this 2nd day of October, 2003, I caused a true and correct copy of
4	the foregoing motion by facsimile to Dorian Delmont at 333-333-3333 and to Chapter 13
5	Trustee Amy Whorten at 333-444-4444.
6	
7	
8	*Lawrence Lawful*
9	
10	
11	
12	
13	
14	
15	
16	
17	
18	
19	
20	
21	
22	
23	
24	
25	
26	
27	
28	

Sample Motion to Convert or Dismiss Debtor's Case, continued

1	**IN THE UNITED STATES BANKRUPTCY COURT**
2	**FOR THE WESTERN DISTRICT OF OKLAHOMA**
3	) **CASE NO.:** WOK-03-2348-bk
4	**In re:**) **ORDER CONVERTING DEBTOR'S CASE**
5	Dorian Delmont) **TO CHAPTER 7**
6	) **CH. 13**
7	)
8	)

AND NOW, this 13th day of November, 2004, the Court having found that:

Movant is the holder of an allowed unsecured claim.

Debtor has failed to propose a plan that can be confirmed within a reasonable period of time.

Movant is harmed by Debtor's failure to propose a confirmable plan.

IT IS HEREBY ORDERED THAT

Debtor's case is converted to Chapter 7 pursuant to 11 U.S.C. Section 1307.

Dated: Nov. 13, 2004

Gary K. Stringent, U.S.B.J.

U.S. Bankruptcy Judge

However, if the plan says your lien is extinguished when the secured portion of your claim is paid, and the debtor converts to Chapter 7 after paying the secured portion of your claim, the only way you can preserve your lien is to file a motion asking the court to dismiss the debtor's case. The dismissal of the case will negate the order avoiding your lien. Remember, you can't force a debtor to stay in Chapter 13, but you can ask the court to consider the circumstances surrounding the conversion when deciding whether the debtor should be allowed to stay in Chapter 7. You can file a motion seeking dismissal on your own or with the help of an attorney. If you are successful in having the debtor's case dismissed, your resurrected lien attaches to the property, as long as the debtor still has it.

You can base your motion on the debtor's bad faith in seeking the conversion without fully paying unsecured creditors. You'll usually be better off with your lien and what's left of your claim outside of bankruptcy than you would be as the holder of a wholly unsecured claim in a Chapter 7 case.

EXAMPLE: Dina files for Chapter 13 bankruptcy owing $15,000 to Carlota's Used Cars. Dina's 1999 Toyota, which is pledged as collateral for Carlota's loan, is worth $10,000. Her confirmed plan requires her to make payments for five years, but fully pays Carlota's $10,000 secured claim with interest in three years. The plan also provides that Carlota's loses its lien in Dina's car as soon as the secured claim is fully paid. During the final two years of Dina's plan, her payments were to be used to pay unsecured creditors' claims, including Carlota's $5,000. However, as soon as Dina made the last payment on Carlota's secured claim she told the court that she was converting to Chapter 7 where she could discharge her unsecured debts without paying anything to them. Carlota's can't oppose Dina's decision to convert, but it can—and does—ask the bankruptcy court to dismiss Dina's Chapter 7 case because she didn't act in good faith. She promised to pay a portion of Carlota's unsecured claim through Chapter 13 but didn't do so. She wants the benefit of being rid of Carlota's lien without the cost of completing her confirmed plan. The bankruptcy court, when ruling on Carlota's motion, will decide whether Dina abused the bankruptcy process by converting her case when she did.

E. What Happens After a Conversion to Chapter 7

What happens after a debtor converts to Chapter 7 depends on what chapter the case came from and whether the conversion was requested in good faith. The answers to these questions will determine the amount of your Chapter 7 claim, what property is in the debtor's bankruptcy estate, and what property the debtor may claim as exempt. Let's look in particular at:

- the effect of a good faith conversion from Chapter 13 (Subsection 1)
- the effect of a conversion from Chapter 11, or a bad faith conversion from Chapter 13 (Subsection 2)
- how conversion impacts your claim (Subsection 3), and
- how conversion impacts postpetition, preconversion claims (Subsection 4).

1. Effect of Good Faith Conversions from Chapter 13

If the debtor converted his case to Chapter 7 from Chapter 13, the first question becomes whether he did so in good faith. It's easiest to define good faith by comparing it to bad faith: A bad faith conversion is one that attempts to unfairly manipulate the Code to provide a benefit to the debtor that wasn't intended. For example, one debtor was found to have acted in bad faith when he converted his case to Chapter 7 on the eve of a hearing on whether he was eligible for Chapter 13 relief. This good faith determination establishes what is included in the bankruptcy estate in the converted case.

If the conversion from Chapter 13 was, in fact, made in good faith, then property the debtor owned on the original petition date and still has in his possession becomes property of the Chapter 7 estate. If the conversion was not made in good faith—or if the conversion was from Chapter 11 or 12—then the property of the debtor's Chapter 7 estate includes all the property the debtor had at the time of conversion as well as at the time of the original filing (see Subsection 2, below). Since bankruptcy courts can't force a debtor to stay in Chapter 13, this provision dissuades debtors from converting to Chapter 7 in an attempt to receive the benefits of a Chapter 7 discharge without living up to the promises made in confirming the Chapter 13 plan.

If the court valued the debtor's property during the Chapter 13 phase of the bankruptcy, the property retains this value in the Chapter 7 bankruptcy. Even if the court did not hold a formal valuation hearing, the value of the property may have been established by the debtor's confirmed reorganization plan.

Any money the debtor paid to the trustee in a Chapter 13 case that hasn't been disbursed to creditors is returned to the debtor—minus the trustee's expenses—if the debtor's case is converted to Chapter 7 prior to confirmation (regardless of whether or not it's a good faith conversion.) If the case is converted to Chapter 7 after confirmation, then the courts disagree as to whether or not this money should be returned to the debtor, turned over to the trustee, or paid out to creditors pursuant to the plan. You'll need to research what courts in your area say.

Courts also disagree on whether the debtor's ability to exempt property is determined as of the filing date or the conversion date. Since the property in the debtor's bankruptcy estate is determined at least as early as the original filing date, many courts say that the filing date should also be the date for determining the debtor's exemptions. But this can create problems, especially if the debtor's circumstances have changed since the filing.

EXAMPLE: Derwood the debtor owns two houses. He lives in one and rents the other. Derwood files for Chapter 13 bankruptcy. During the Chapter 13 case, he kicks out his tenant and moves from the one house into the former rental, then rents the other house out. Soon after, he converts the case to Chapter 7. Derwood is now at risk of losing his homestead exemption. Why? Because the house he was living in at the time of conversion, which is now his home, was not his homestead when he first filed for bankruptcy. The courts in Derwin's area say that the availability of exemptions is determined as of the day Derwin filed for bankruptcy. The net result is that the property that Derwin claimed as exempt on the petition date must be the same property that he claims as exempt on the conversion date in order to use the exemption. But, because the house Derwin declared to be his homestead is being used as rental property at the time of conversion, it is therefore not exempt in Derwin's state.

However, if courts determine exemptions as of the conversion date, then changes in the exemption laws that occur after a debtor has filed for Chapter 13 protection create an incentive to convert.

EXAMPLE: Dierdre files for Chapter 13, because she has $50,000 in equity in her home that she can't exempt. After filing, the state legislature increases the homestead exemption by $100,000. In the state where Dierdre lives, the bankruptcy courts say that exemptions are determined as of the conversion date. That means that Dierdre has no incentive to stay in Chapter 13. She'll convert and grab the modified exemption.

If the debtor will be claiming new exemptions after the conversion to Chapter 7, you may have an opportunity to object to the new exemptions. However, in most courts, your ability to object depends on whether the debtor files an amended schedule of exemptions in the Chapter 7 case. If the debtor does file an amended schedule, you are automatically given 30 days to object to any amendment. This procedural rule holds true whether the case has been converted or not. But if the debtor doesn't amend his schedule of exemptions, many courts refuse to allow objections, on the ground that you had your chance during the Chapter 13 case. Courts are more divided over whether the newly appointed Chapter 7 trustee should be given a chance to object.

2. Effect of Conversions from Chapter 11 or 12 or Bad Faith Conversions from Chapter 13

Converting to Chapter 7 can significantly impact what property is included in the bankruptcy estate—and what is therefore potentially available to pay creditors' claims. With the notable exception of a good faith conversion from Chapter 13, property the debtor acquired during the reorganization phase becomes property of the estate in the converted Chapter 7 case. This rule covers not only conver-

sions from Chapters 11 and 12, but also bad faith conversions from Chapter 13 (see Subsection 1, above, for a definition of bad faith).

When the case is converted, ownership of the debtor's property is transferred to the bankruptcy estate under the trustee's control, just as if the debtor had originally filed under Chapter 7. Property that the debtor cannot claim as exempt must be surrendered to the Chapter 7 trustee. The debtor must also file a list of debts incurred after the bankruptcy was filed, along with a list of how much was paid to creditors holding prepetition claims.

3. Effect of Conversion on Your Claim

A conversion to Chapter 7 may raise various questions about your claim, such as "What happens to the previous court rulings about my claim?" "How much is my claim worth after the debtor has made some payments?" and "Do I need to file a new proof of claim?" This section attempts to answer those questions.

Any rulings the court previously made regarding the amount of your claim or the value of your collateral are unaffected by a good-faith conversion from Chapter 13 to Chapter 7. In all other conversions, these issues can be revisited by the court in light of the conversion.

To calculate the worth of your claim after a good faith conversion from Chapter 13, take the amount of your allowed reorganization claim and subtract any payments you received under the plan. For example, if your reorganization claim was for $5,000 and you received ten payments of $100, your claim would now be for $4,000.

If the debtor's case was converted from Chapter 12 or 13, you do not need to file another proof of claim following the conversion. If, however, you didn't file a claim during the reorganization case, you can file one in the Chapter 7 case. Don't worry if the deadline that applied in the Chapter 13 case has passed— the conversion allows you to file a proof of claim in the new case without regard for the old deadline.

If the debtor's case was converted from Chapter 11, and you were not initially required to file a claim because your claim was properly scheduled, you'll need to file a claim in the Chapter 7 case in order to share in any distribution.

If you believe your claim can be excepted from discharge or that the debtor is not entitled to receive a Chapter 7 discharge, you'll need to file a complaint no later than 60 days after the meeting of creditors in the converted case. At this point, you'll be proceeding as if the case started under Chapter 7. Follow the instructions for challenging the discharge of your claim that are covered in Chapter 9 of this book.

4. Effect of Conversion on Postpetition, Preconversion Claims

A special situation is created where a debtor attempts reorganization but converts to Chapter 7 without having a plan confirmed. In such cases, any debts incurred during the reorganization case are treated as if they were incurred before the bankruptcy was filed. This rule applies regardless of whether the debtor originally filed under Chapter 11, 12, or 13. That means that if you provided credit to the debtor after the original filing and before the conversion, you may now be forced to participate in the bankruptcy.

EXAMPLE: Drusilla, who lives in an apartment, files for bankruptcy under Chapter 13. Before her plan is confirmed, she misses a rent payment. Drusilla tries to confirm a plan but can't, so she converts the case to Chapter 7. The rent payment Drusilla missed is discharged in Chapter 7 even though it was incurred after she filed for bankruptcy.

You might at least be able to improve your position in the bankruptcy if your claim is for a service you provided that was beneficial to the bankruptcy estate—

that is, you helped preserve an asset of the estate. If so, your claim will treated as an administrative expense, which will be paid ahead of general unsecured claims. For example, if you provided emergency road service for the debtor's car, and that car was part of the bankruptcy estate, your claim should be treated as an administrative expense because your work extended the car's useful life. Administrative claims are just as dischargeable as general unsecured claims, but if there's not enough money in the pot to pay everyone, you're better off at the head of the line.

⚠ **In a Chapter 13 case, the debtor's threats to convert may be a bluff.** Claims of postpetition creditors can't ordinarily be discharged through Chapter 13 unless the creditors agree to participate in the plan. A viable threat from the debtor that if they don't participate in the plan he'll convert to Chapter 7—where these claims may be discharged without receiving any money—might convince creditors that they'd be better off sharing in a distribution in the reorganization case than having their claim discharged in Chapter 7.

If the debtor owes you money for a debt incurred after the bankruptcy was filed but before it was converted, you'll need to follow the rules for filing proofs of claim in Chapter 7 cases. (See Chapter 7 of this book.)

F. Conversions Between Reorganization Chapters

Because the reorganization chapters are fairly similar, debtors face only a few restrictions in converting between them. The greatest restriction is imposed on debtors who filed under Chapter 12: They cannot convert their cases to Chapter 11 or Chapter 13.

Despite the similarities between the reorganization-based chapters, conversions between chapters are sometimes requested by either the debtor or a creditor. We'll look at all the possible (and some impossible) permutations, including:

- conversions away from Chapter 11 (Subsection 1)
- conversions away from Chapter 12 (Subsection 2)
- conversions from Chapter 13 to Chapter 11 (Subsection 3), and
- conversions from Chapter 13 to Chapter 12 (Subsection 4).

1. From Chapter 11 to Chapter 12 or 13

Only the debtor may ask for a conversion from Chapter 11 to Chapter 12 or 13—you, as a creditor, cannot. The usual reason for requesting conversion is to take advantage of easier confirmation requirements.

The basic eligibility requirements of the various chapters may stop some debtors from converting. Only individuals may convert from Chapter 11 to Chapter 13, since only individuals may file under Chapter 13. And only corporations, partnerships, and individuals who also happen to be family farmers may convert from Chapter 11 to Chapter 12, since only family farmers may file under Chapter 12.

Assuming, however, that the debtor is an individual or a family farmer, she may request conversion from Chapter 11 to either Chapter 12 or 13. If you believe the confirmation request is abusive or unwarranted, file a motion asking the court to either reconvert the case or dismiss it. You can take this action with or without an attorney's assistance.

⚠ Have you filed a proof of claim? If you were not required to file a proof of claim in the Chapter 11 case, you'll need to file one now, in the converted case, in order to protect your right to payment.

2. From Chapter 12 to Chapter 11 or 13

Chapter 12 cases can be converted only to Chapter 7 and only at the debtor's request. The Bankruptcy Code makes no provision for converting cases from Chapter 12 to Chapter 11 or 13. It is possible, however, that a court could be convinced to use its equitable power to order a conversion from Chapter 12 to one of the other two reorganization chapters.

3. From Chapter 13 to Chapter 11

As a creditor, you cannot ask the court to convert the case of a debtor who is a farmer. If the debtor is not a farmer, you can ask the court to convert the debtor's case from Chapter 13 to Chapter 11 at any time prior to confirmation. For example, you may want to move the debtor into Chapter 11 in order to ask the court to appoint a trustee to manage the debtor's business or to prevent the debtor from dismissing the bankruptcy.

4. From Chapter 13 to Chapter 12

Up until the confirmation of the Chapter 13 plan, the debtor can ask for conversion to Chapter 12 at any time. (This assumes, of course, that the debtor is eligible for Chapter 12 bankruptcy.) As a creditor, however, you cannot ask the court to convert the case from Chapter 13 to Chapter 12. ■

15

Prepetition Transfers: How to Keep Payments You've Already Received

L et's say you have a customer who is in financial trouble. You've done your best to collect on the customer's past-due account, but so far with no luck. You know that every day that you don't get paid brings you one day closer to never getting paid. Then a check arrives from the customer. Payment in full! Hallelujah!

Okay, not so fast. For one thing, there's no point in celebrating until after the customer's bank honors the check. For another—and more pertinent to the subject of this chapter—that money can be taken right back if the person files for bankruptcy within the next 90 days. It's okay to deposit the check, but you're better off not spending it, just in case the bankruptcy trustee shows up with a demand for its return.

Unfair as it might seem to give back money that was rightfully paid to you, this is all part of the bigger picture of trying to treat all creditors evenhandedly. The bankruptcy court, at the request of the bankruptcy trustee (or the debtor in Chapter 11 cases), will review all transfers of property that the debtor made during the months preceding the bankruptcy filing. In certain situations, the court will re-

quire creditors to return money and other property interests received from the debtor. This money and property will be turned over to the trustee, for distribution to the creditors.

In this chapter we'll describe the types of transfers that may be cancelled by the court and tell you how to defend yourself. (For details on what types of transfers are safe from retroactive cancellation, see the sidebar, below, "Transfers That Cannot Be Undone.") We'll also explain how you can help the trustee look for transfers made to other creditors that may be avoided. We'll cover:

- what types of transfers can be avoided (Section A)
- how to defend yourself against an avoidance action (Section B), and
- when and how to participate in avoidance actions against other creditors (Section C).

In a situation where the trustee— who is an expert on bankruptcy law and procedure—is looking to get money from you, it may be a good time to hire an attorney. Read this chapter, however, to understand your rights and how to assist in your defense.

Transfers That Cannot Be Undone

Certain transfers may not be retroactively cancelled, including:

- **Payments on past due child or spousal support made to the debtor's spouse or former spouse.** If the debtor owed you alimony, maintenance, or support and paid it just before filing for bankruptcy, you won't be required to give the money back.

- **Consumer payments of less than $600.** If you provided household goods or services to someone on credit and received payment of less than $600, then you won't be asked to give the money back.

- **Payments made to buy something if the money paid was what the item purchased was worth.** You don't need to get a credit report from everybody you sell stuff to for cash.

- **Wages received just before filing for bankruptcy if they were paid in the regular work cycle.** Was your employer able to maintain its payroll schedule during the days leading up to the bankruptcy filing? If you got paid on time, then you can keep the money. However, you may be asked to return any wages that were paid late. You may also lose any bonuses paid to you within three months of filing (one year if you're an officer or director of the company).

- **Loans received from a lender that filed for bankruptcy.** Your obligation to repay a loan is not affected by the lender's bankruptcy.

A. Transfers Subject to Recapture (Avoidance)

One of the jobs of the bankruptcy trustee is to identify transfers that are vulnerable to cancellation by the court. A transfer becomes vulnerable if it:

- favored one creditor over others (a "preferential transfer," discussed in Subsection 1), or

- allowed the recipient to receive more value from the debtor than it gave to the debtor (a "fraudulent transfer," discussed in Subsection 2).

The same rules for avoiding transfers apply regardless of whether the transfer was a payment or the granting of a lien. If the debtor gave you cash, the court can order it returned. If the debtor gave you a security interest in property, the court can erase it. Nor does it matter whether the transfer was made voluntarily, as with a cash payment, or involuntarily, as with a payment obtained by a creditor through attachment of the debtor's wages.

1. Preferential Transfers

A preferential transfer is one in which one creditor was given preference over others. This rule applies only to transfers made within 90 days prior to the bankruptcy filing, unless the transfer was made to an insider (close relatives and business associates). In an insider case, the court will scrutinize the transfer if it occurred within one year of the bankruptcy filing. You may be the target of a preferential transfer action if you convinced the debtor to pay you shortly before the debtor filed for bankruptcy and at a time when the debtor was not paying other creditors.

In order to have the court avoid a preferential transfer, the trustee must prove a long list of things, including that the transfer:

- was made to you or for your benefit (Subsection a)
- was made because the debtor owed you money (Subsection b)
- was made at a time when the debtor was insolvent (Subsection c)

- was made within the appropriate time prior to the bankruptcy filing (Subsection d), and
- caused you to receive more than you stood to receive once the debtor filed for bankruptcy (Subsection e).

a. The Transfer Was Made to You or for Your Benefit

Payments made to you can be avoided, as can payments made to someone else for your benefit. So, you can't get around this issue by having the transfer made to someone other than you if you're the one who benefits, as shown in the following example.

EXAMPLE: Damara owes Carlton's Classic Cars $10,000 for a shiny restored vehicle. Carlton's happens to owe Damara's father $10,000 for accounting services. Although Damara does not owe any money to her father, she pays him the $10,000 she owes to Carlton's. Damara's father marks Carlton's debt as paid, and Carlton's does the same for Damara's debt. If Damara files for bankruptcy within 90 days, the trustee may demand that Carlton's pay $10,000 into the bankruptcy estate, because this was a preferential transfer.

Think of it this way: If the transfer had been made step by step,

Carlton's would have gotten its $10,000 from Damara, then turned around and paid the $10,000 it owed to Damara's father. Even though the father is now in possession of the $10,000, Carlton's got the benefit of that money, and got it at a time when other creditors were waiting in line.

Understand also that the payment from Damara to her father would not be viewed a preferential transfer, because she didn't owe him anything. There must be an existing debt for a payment to be a preferential transfer.

b. The Transfer Was Made Because the Debtor Owed You Money

The transfer needs to have been made based on an existing debt for the trustee to avoid it as preferential. If no debt existed at the time of the transfer, it would be classified in some other way: perhaps as a gift, which may be subject to possible avoidance as a fraudulent transfer; a loan that you must repay; or a simultaneous exchange between you and the debtor, where both of you gave up something of value at the same time.

EXAMPLE 1: Dwight owes his interior designer, Carolina, $10,000. Dwight doesn't have the money to repay her, but gives Carolina his car, instead. A month later, Dwight files for bank-ruptcy. The bankruptcy court may order Carolina to return the car or the value of the car. This is because the car was transferred to Carolina as a payment on a debt, while other creditors were left hanging.

EXAMPLE 2: Now let's say that Dwight didn't owe Carolina anything. The transfer was a gift, given with no thought of getting something in return. Dwight had a crush on Carolina, wasn't using the car, and knew that Carolina was taking the bus everywhere she went. This wouldn't be considered a preferential transfer.

EXAMPLE 3: Another possibility is that Carolina was expected to eventually give the car back to Dwight and to pay rent for its use in the meantime. In such a case, the transfer might be considered a loan, instead of a preferential transfer.

c. The Debtor Was Insolvent When the Transfer Was Made

Debtors are presumed to be insolvent within 90 days of filing for bankruptcy. This presumption puts the burden on you to prove otherwise. Insolvency is shown by looking at the debtor's balance sheet, but with a bankruptcy twist: The Bankruptcy Code says debtors are insolvent when their liabilities exceed their *nonexempt* assets. Assets considered exempt (under state and federal bankruptcy laws) aren't part of this calculation. So, in states with liberal exemptions, insolvency is easier for the trustee to prove (and harder for you to disprove).

d. The Transfer Was Made Within the Appropriate Time Prior to the Bankruptcy Filing

To be considered preferential, a transfer must have taken place within the 90 days prior to the bankruptcy filing, unless it was between "insiders." In insider cases, the entire year before the bankruptcy filing will be looked at by the court.

When counting the 90 days, you start on the day the transfer became effective under state law (day zero), then count to 90. Counting up to a year (365 days) works the same way.

Insiders are people whose close relationship to the debtor puts them in a position where they should have known about the debtor's tenuous financial situation. This knowledge, coupled with their influence over the debtor, enables them to get paid ahead of other creditors. Spouses and children are insiders of individual debtors. Officers and directors are insiders of corporate debtors. Partners are insiders of partnerships. Professionals working for a business and spouses of insiders may be insiders, depending on how involved they are with the debtor.

e. You Received More Than You Would Have in Bankruptcy

How would you have fared if, on the day that the debtor transferred the property to you, the debtor had filed for Chapter 7 bankruptcy instead? Nearly every payment made by an insolvent debtor to an unsecured creditor enables that creditor to receive more than the creditor would have received if the debtor had filed for bankruptcy first. Therefore, as a practical matter, this requirement is relevant only for payments made to secured creditors. In secured creditor cases, the court will compare what the creditor received from the debtor with the amount the creditor would have received from their collateral.

2. Fraudulent Transfers

There are two types of transfers that the bankruptcy court may view as fraudulent and therefore avoid, resulting in your having to surrender property to the bankruptcy trustee:

- transfers in which the debtor got rid of money or property in order to keep these assets away from creditors, and

- transfers in which the debtor received less than reasonably equivalent value in exchange for the property that was given up.

The first type of transfer rarely involves a transfer to a creditor. These fraudulent transfers are usually made to insiders, who agree to hold the debtor's property until after the bankruptcy is concluded and then return the property to the debtor. While these recipients may try to pass themselves off as creditors in an attempt to give legitimacy to the transfer, these people rarely had an arm's-length relationship with the debtor.

Because we assume you are not in cahoots with the debtor, we're going to focus our discussion on the second type of fraudulent transfer, that is, transfers in which the trustee believes the debtor got less than a fair deal.

Bankruptcy courts can avoid all fraudulent transfers that occurred within the year leading up to the bankruptcy filing. (See 11 U.S.C. § 548.) But the Code also allows bankruptcy courts to avoid fraudulent transfers that could be avoided under state fraudulent transfer laws by a creditor holding an allowed unsecured claim against the debtor. (11 U.S.C. § 544(b).) Since state fraudulent transfer laws are very similar to Section 548, what needs to be proven in order to avoid the transfers is usually the same regardless of whether the avoidance action is based on

federal or state law. The biggest difference between the laws is that some state laws provide a longer time period for avoiding fraudulent transfers.

To satisfy the court, the trustee will need to prove each of the following three elements:

1. **The transfer was made within the year prior to the bankruptcy filing, unless the trustee is relying on a state fraudulent transfer law that allows for a longer time period.** Let's imagine that a debtor, facing financial problems, gives a $5,000 ring to a friend. If the debtor files for bankruptcy within one year, the trustee can ask the court to avoid this transfer as fraudulent. If the debtor files for bankruptcy more than one year later, the only way the trustee can challenge this transfer is if state law allows a longer time period for challenging fraudulent transfers and if there is a creditor holding an allowed unsecured claim who could have challenged the transfer.

2. **The debtor received less than reasonably equivalent value in exchange for the transfer.** Just because you may have given something to the debtor in return for what you got doesn't mean the transfer passes muster. The debtor must receive something of comparable value to whatever the debtor gave to you—

otherwise the transfer can still be avoided as fraudulent. The court determines comparable value by looking at all the circumstances surrounding the transaction.

Take another look at the example involving the three-way transfer between Damara, Carlton's, and Damara's father, above. We explained that the trustee could look to Carlton's to recover the benefit received as a preferential transfer but that the transfer to Damara's father wasn't a preference because Damara didn't owe him any money (remember, transfers can be avoided as preferences only if they are made on account of an existing debt). The transfer to the debtor's father also wouldn't be considered fraudulent, because the debtor received reasonably equivalent value in the form of a cancelled debt.

But what if Carlton's hadn't owed any money to the debtor's father? Suppose that Carlton's instead accepted an offer from Damara's father to take a lien against his home in exchange for not suing Damara. Despite Carlton's indulgence, Damara files for bankruptcy. The transfer of an interest in the father's property is not subject to avoidance in bankruptcy, because it wasn't a transfer of Damara's property. However, if Damara's father files for bankruptcy within one year of granting the security interest, this lien can be avoided as a fraudulent transfer because the father didn't receive fair value in exchange for granting the lien. Damara received the lien's benefit, her father didn't.

3. **The debtor was insolvent at the time of the transfer or became insolvent as a result of the transfer.** There is no presumption of insolvency for fraudulent transfers unlike preferential transfers which, you'll remember, have a 90-day presumed insolvency period). Instead, the trustee must prove that the debtor's liabilities exceeded her assets, either when the transfer was made or as a result of the transfer.

B. Defending Yourself Against Avoidance Actions

If the bankruptcy trustee brings an action against you to recover a transfer that was allegedly fraudulent or preferential, you'll need to defend yourself by refuting any of the elements presented by the trustee that you honestly believe to be in dispute. For example, if you believe you the transfer was not fraudulent because you received fair value, then deny the trustee's allegation regarding value and show the court why you're right.

But even if everything the trustee says is correct, there are exceptional situations when the bankruptcy court won't avoid the transfer. The law provides exceptions to the rules governing preferential transfers (see Subsection 1) and fraudulent transfers (see Subsection 2).

1. Preferential Transfer Exceptions

There are certain transfers that can't be avoided even though they benefit one creditor over another. These include:

- transfers that were substantially contemporaneous exchanges of new value (Subsection a)
- transfers made in the ordinary course of business (Subsection b)
- transfers made to enable a debtor to buy an asset (Subsection c)
- transfers followed by the creditor giving something of value to the debtor (Subsection d)
- transfers attached to floating liens (Subsection e)
- transfers creating statutory liens (Subsection f)
- payments of alimony, maintenance, or support (Subsection g), and
- transfers of less than $600 when paid by a consumer (Subsection h).

a. Transfers That Were Substantially Contemporaneous Exchanges of New Value

If the debtor gave you something of value in exchange for something of value from you, the transfer is not considered preferential. The exchanges need not have happened simultaneously, but they must have happened close enough together in time that the debtor never became obligated to you.

This fact pattern usually arises in one of two situations. The first is when an exchange was intended to be simultaneous, but instead a brief interlude took place between the transfer and the payment. Someone who goes through a store's checkout line, then realizes he left his wallet in the car, would be the most everyday example. If the clerk lets the person take his groceries to the car when he goes to retrieve the wallet, then the exchange isn't simultaneous but the interval was not enough time to create a debt. The second likely situation is where the law allows a subsequent action to be treated as if it occurred earlier than it actually did. For example, state law may give lenders 20 days in which to perfect liens on automobile titles. If they do, then the perfection of the lien is treated as if it happened at the same time as the creation of the debt. If they don't, then the creation of the debt and the creation of the lien are treated as separate events.

If you sold the debtor a television on credit, keeping a security interest in the television, and then you gave the debtor something of value (the television) in exchange for the debtor's promise to pay, a security interest has been created. In this example, the transfer can't be avoided, because it was created as part of a simultaneous exchange in which both sides gave up and received something of value. Preferential transfers are not concerned with whether the exchange was for equal value. Instead they examine whether creditors received more than they would have if the debtor had filed for bankruptcy instead of making the payment. So, if you received more than you gave, the extra benefit you received can be avoided.

EXAMPLE: Crate-O-Goods delivers several boxes of organic fruits and vegetables to Devon's store. Because Devon doesn't have any cash on hand, he gives Crate-O-Goods his fancy Swiss wristwatch. The fruits and vegetables were worth $800. The watch is worth $1,800. Although there was a simultaneous exchange of value, Devon received only $800 while Crate-O-Goods received $1,800. The trustee can't recover the extra $1,000 from Crate-O-Goods as a preferential transfer because both sides

received something of value. The fact that the values were not the same is irrelevant.

It's not enough that both sides gave up something of value and received something of value at about the same time. It is also necessary that the transaction was intended to be a substantially contemporaneous exchange.

EXAMPLE: Dexter is having financial problems. Trying to help, Clara lends him $4,000. Dexter signs a promissory note that obligates him to repay Clara over five years. Almost immediately, Dexter has a change of heart, gives Clara back the $4,000 and files for bankruptcy a few days later. The trustee can avoid the early repayment of the note if Dexter intended to keep the money when he signed the note.

b. Transfers Made in the Ordinary Course of Business

Transfers that were made as part of the ordinary course of business cannot be avoided as preferential. In order to qualify for this exception, the debt must have been incurred and the payment made in accordance with both the custom of the creditor's relationship with the debtor and with generally accepted business practice.

EXAMPLE: Duffy's Developing has an ongoing business arrangement with Capitol Artframes, selling the frames in its photo printing shop. Duffy's usually pays its invoices within 30 days (in accordance with the usual trade practice). However, Duffy's falls into financial trouble. It receives two invoices from Capitol in the 90 days before it files for bankruptcy. Duffy's pays the first one within 30 days. The second one, however, it waits 75 days to pay. The first transfer is not avoidable, because it was made in the ordinary course of business and in accordance with customary trade practices. The second transfer, however, can be avoided and the amount of the invoice collected from Capitol.

c. Transfers Made to Enable a Debtor to Buy an Asset

A particular type of loan known as an enabling loan cannot be avoided as a preferential transfer. An enabling loan is one that finances the debtor's purchase of an asset. Any time a debtor borrows money to buy something—a home, a combine, an oil field, whatever—that loan is an "enabling" or "purchase-money" loan. This exception also protects any lien you received to secure repayment of the en-

abling loan. There is one catch to protecting your lien—all the paperwork must have been completed and filed within 20 days of the debtor's receipt of the collateral. If you dawdle and don't complete things until 21 days have passed, your security interest can be avoided as a preferential transfer. This is true even if state law gives you more than 20 days to complete the process.

d. Transfers Followed by the Creditor Giving Something of Value to the Debtor

An otherwise avoidable preferential transfer can be saved if you give something of value to the debtor sometime after receiving the transfer. The preferential transfer is saved only to the extent of the new value received by the debtor. This exception is usually used by insiders who say that their continued support of the debtor supports the transfer they previously received. While preferential transfers are not concerned with whether there is an even exchange of value, just with whether the creditor received more than it would have if the debtor had filed for bankruptcy instead of making the transfer, this exception is limited to the amount of new value received by the debtor.

EXAMPLE: Darleen's pottery business is in financial trouble. Darleen owes $10,000 to her supplier of clay and glazes. She agrees to give the supplier a security interest of $10,000 in her company's inventory. Subsequently, her all-too-trusting supplier sends her another $2,000 worth of materials. The granting of the $10,000 security interest would have been a preferential transfer if nothing else had happened afterward. But the supplier's new loan provides new value to Darleen's business. That means that the lien is excepted from avoidance to the extent of $2,000, the amount of new value given to the business after the lien was created.

e. Transfers Attached to Floating Liens

A transfer that took place under the terms of a floating lien is not subject to avoidance based on each transfer, but based on the creditor's secured position when the debtor filed for bankruptcy and 90 days prior to the bankruptcy filing. Retail businesses frequently use so-called floating liens in order to finance their operations. Floating liens allow the retailer's bank to take security interests in their current assets as well as in assets that are subsequently acquired, along with the proceeds from the sale of current inventory. The term "floating lien" arose because the lien hovers over the debtor's assets, always there but never impeding transactions. As the inventory and accounts receivable change, the assets subject to these liens also change. Each time an item is sold, the lien detaches from that item and reattaches to the payment. When the cash received is used to buy replacement inventory, the lien detaches from the cash and attaches to the new inventory.

Although the debtor may have signed only one security agreement creating the floating lien, thousands and thousands of transfers may be subject to that lien. Rather than trying to dissect each transfer looking for preferences, the Bankruptcy Code created the following test for whether the creditor received the benefit of a preferential transfer:

1. Compare the collateral's value with the amount owed on the debt as of the day the debtor filed for bankruptcy.

2. Make the same comparison for a date 90 days prior to the bankruptcy.

3. If the creditor attained a better financial position by the filing date than it held 90 days prior, then the creditor received a preference to the extent that its position improved.

EXAMPLE: First Solvent Bank lends $10,000 to Dapper's Collectibles with which to buy antique hats. The bank holds a lien in all the hats Dapper's buys. When Dapper's sells a hat, the bank has a lien against the money paid for it. If Dapper's uses the money to buy a new hat, the bank's lien attaches to the new hat. As a result, all the hats in Dapper's store, plus all the money in Dapper's bank account that come from the sale of the hats are collateral for the bank's loan. On August 1, 2003, Dapper's has $5,000 in hats and $2,000 in the bank. On November 1, 2003, when Dapper's files for bankruptcy, it has $3,000 in hats and $3,000 the bank. The bank's lien in the hats and money cannot be avoided, because the bank's secured position on August 1 was worse than it is on November 1. If the numbers had been reversed, then the bank's lien could have been avoided to the extent of $1,000.

f. Transfers Creating Statutory Liens

The trustee cannot avoid a lien acquired on the debtor's property if state law gives the creditor the right to claim that lien. A mechanic's lien would be a likely example. The key element of this exception

is that the lien owes its existence entirely to the law. If the law is fuzzy on whether a lien has been created—for example, the law requires you to go to court to acquire the lien and gives the court discretion as to whether to impose the lien—then the lien is one that's created by the court and not by the law, and is therefore not protected.

g. Payments of Alimony, Maintenance, or Support

A transfer made to pay a legitimate debt for alimony, maintenance, or support owed to the debtor's spouse, former spouse, or child is not considered preferential. This is consistent with the Bankruptcy Code's efforts to hold the debtor to such important obligations. If, however, you're someone other than the debtor's spouse, former spouse, or child, the transfer can be avoided. The transfer can also be avoided if it was not made under the terms of a divorce decree, separation agreement, or court order.

The biggest issue in transfers involving matrimonial obligations is whether non-support payments can be avoided. When spouses separate or divorce, it can be difficult to determine whether each spouse received reasonably equivalent value in exchange for what was given up to the other spouse. Courts don't like to undo property settlements, but they will if the circumstances point to a collusive divorce.

EXAMPLE: When Donald divorces Claudia, he signs over the house to her and assumes responsibility for paying all the marital debts. However, Donald stays in the house and files for bankruptcy. If a bankruptcy court views this arrangement as an attempt to defraud creditors rather than an equitable end to Donald and Claudia's marriage, the court may set aside the transfer of Donald's interest in the home.

h. Transfers of Less Than $600 Paid on a Consumer Debt

A consumer payment—or a series of payments to the same creditor during the preference period—of under $600 will not be avoided as preferential. Consumer debts are those owed by individuals primarily for personal or household goods or services. If, however, the transfer or transfers total $600 or more, they can be cancelled in their entirety. This exception wasn't meant to create a $599.99 exception for consumer payments. It's goal is to create a threshold below which the court doesn't have to be troubled with avoidance actions.

EXAMPLE: In an effort to avoid bankruptcy, Deacon stops using his credit cards and adopts a budget that calls for him to make the minimum monthly payment on each card. After one year, Deacon notices that he still owes as much to the credit card companies as he did when he cut up his cards. Frustrated and seeing no alternative, Deacon files for bankruptcy. During the 90 days prior to filing, he makes three monthly payments on a Visa card and a MasterCard. The monthly payments to Visa were $230. The monthly payments to MasterCard were $195. The trustee can avoid the payments to Visa because they totaled $690, but not the payments to MasterCard, because they totaled $585.

2. Fraudulent Transfer Exceptions

For some transfers made by debtors, it can be argued that the debtor didn't receive equal value. Nevertheless, certain of these transfers cannot be avoided because they were not contrary to bankruptcy purposes. They include:

- certain transfers to religious or charitable institutions, and
- transfers accepted in good faith for reasonably equivalent value.

a. Transfers to Religious or Charitable Institutions

Until recently, courts struggled with the question of whether religious and charitable contributions should be treated as fraudulent transfers. Should a debtor who can't pay her bills be allowed to give money away, even if it's to a worthy cause? Many courts said no and forced churches, particularly Protestant churches whose debtor-members contributed a tenth of their salaries, to surrender payments made to them. Congress changed the law in 1998 to protect these payments, up to 15% of the debtor's gross pay or more if the debtor has a history of donating a greater percentage of his income to charity. The institution must also be a legitimate charity and the payment must have been made consistent with the debtor's pattern of charitable donations.

b. Transfers Accepted in Good Faith for Reasonably Equivalent Value

If you received property from the debtor in an arm's-length transaction and gave fair value in exchange for what you received, then the transfer was not fraudulent. If you gave less than reasonably equivalent value, but otherwise acted in good faith, then you'll be protected to the extent of the value of what you gave up.

EXAMPLE: Facing the prospect of bankruptcy, Darcy starts selling off family heirlooms. Catherine pays $100 for an oak table. The table turns out to be a 19th century handcarved piece worth $1,000. After Darcy files for bankruptcy, the court orders Catherine to return the table to the bankruptcy estate. However, she will retain a lien against the table equal to what she paid for it, plus compensation for any improvements she made to it. In the event that Catherine had already sold the table for more than she paid for it, the court would order her to turn over the difference between what she paid and what she received.

If you acquired the debtor's property at a regularly scheduled foreclosure sale conducted pursuant to state law, then the price you paid for the property is its reasonably equivalent value. This rule holds true even if that price was only a small percentage of the property's fair market value, according to the U.S. Supreme Court. (See *BFP v. RTC*, 114 S.Ct. 1757 (1994).)

C. Avoidance Actions Against Your Fellow Creditors

When directed at you, preferential or fraudulent transfer actions can seem unfair and dictatorial. On the other hand, you may be justifiably outraged at instances of preferential dealing with, or fraud by, other creditors in the pool. In this section, we'll take a look at how you can help the trustee uncover avoidable transfers to other creditors.

The bankruptcy schedules and statements filed by most debtors indicate that they own no property that the trustee can sell. In Chapter 5, we talked about how to review these schedules to find unreported assets and reasons to challenge the debtor's ability to discharge your claim. It's going to take a similar analysis to find indications of preferential and fraudulent transfers to other creditors. Start with what you know, and consider:

- how you got into this creditor/debtor relationship (Subsection 1, below), and
- what the debtor's schedules and statements reveal (Subsection 2, below).

Not All Avoidable Transfers Are Worth Pursuing

There's no need to act like a dog with a bone here—the fact that a transfer can be recovered doesn't necessarily mean it's worth the effort. In practice, trustees rarely pursue transfers of less than $1,000, because the amount recovered will be less than the expense of prosecuting the action. (You'll remember that the Bankruptcy Code itself acknowledges this issue, by stating that consumer payments totaling less than $600 cannot be avoided as preferential transfers.)

Even for a valuable item of property, be sure to check on whether the debtor would be able to exempt it after it is recovered. Once the debtor exempts it, it's of little use to any creditor. Debtors may exempt property recovered through avoided transfers if the transfer was made involuntarily and disclosed on their schedules and if the property could have been claimed as exempt if it was in the debtor's possession when the bankruptcy was filed. Garnished wages are the most common example of an involuntary prepetition transfer of property that the debtor can exempt.

⚠️ **Debtors can try to avoid their own transfers.** If you're the recipient of a seemingly preferential or fraudulent transfer, don't assume that you're safe from avoidance just because the trustee decides it's not worth the effort. The debtor may be the one to pursue avoidance, but only if the transfer was involuntary and the debtor can claim the property as exempt. Debtors most commonly use the trustee's avoidance powers to recover garnished wages.

1. How You Became a Creditor

If there's one thing you should know, it's what you gave to the debtor that got you into your role as a creditor. Perhaps you loaned the debtor actual cash, or perhaps you sold the debtor something on credit. Since you know what you're looking for, you're in a good position to trace it to its ultimate destination.

If you loaned money to the debtor, take a look at the bankruptcy schedules for information on what the money was spent on. If it went to pay bills, these payments may be recoverable as fraudulent transfers. So, how do you find out what the money was spent on? Start enquiring early in the proceedings: Ask the debtor at the Section 341 creditors' meeting for a breakdown of who got what and when. If the debtor is not cooperative, you might want to schedule a Rule 2004 examination (see Chapter 6). But you would prefer if the trustee followed up on the matter, especially since any money recovered is going to benefit all creditors, not just you.

EXAMPLE: Charlie loans Delia $5,000, which Delia uses to pay five creditors $1,000 each. Delia files for bankruptcy two months later. At the creditors' meeting, Charlie discovers where the money went. Because the transfers took place within 90 days of the bankruptcy, Charlie can convince the trustee to go after each of those creditors with a preferential transfer action. If successful, the $5,000 will come back into the bankruptcy estate. This doesn't mean Charlie will get his $5,000 back. The money will be distributed among the creditors in the bankruptcy proceedings.

Preferential transfers are not unusual. People on the brink of bankruptcy often rob Peter to pay Paul in an effort to avoid bankruptcy. The Bankruptcy Code, through the avoidance of preferential transfers, can force Paul to repay what was taken from Peter.

If the debtor gave away the money you loaned him, that gift may be recoverable as a fraudulent transfer (as discussed in Section A2, above). Just as with the recovery of preferential transfers, any money recovered will be shared by all creditors.

If the debtor is unable to account for what happened to the money, then you may have a reason to challenge the debtor's ability to obtain a discharge. (See Chapter 12 for a discussion of this topic.)

If, instead of cash, you sold something valuable to the debtor, you should again look at the bankruptcy schedules to see whether it is listed as an asset. If the debtor doesn't own it anymore, ask the debtor during the Section 341 creditors' meeting what happened to it. If the debtor gave it away or sold it for less than fair value, the property may be recovered as a fraudulent transfer.

You should also review what the debtor told you about herself and her financial situation that convinced you to extend the credit. If she said she had assets that you don't now find listed in the bankruptcy schedules, ask her during the Section 341 meeting what happened to them. Again, the trustee may be able to recover these assets as fraudulent transfers.

2. The Trustee's Examination of the Schedules and Statements

Trustees meet debtors for the first time at the Section 341 creditors' meeting. All they know about the debtor comes from the bankruptcy schedules and statements. Sometimes creditors—particularly former spouses—tip them off to hidden assets, underreported income, and bogus transfers. But frequently, trustees find money and property to build an estate by knowing what to look for and what questions to ask.

Some questions are obvious. For example, the trustee is going to be all over the debtor if the schedules show that a valuable asset was transferred to a family member but the schedules give no details. Gifts made during the year preceding the bankruptcy filing are listed under Question 7 of the Statement of Financial Affairs filed by the debtor (see Chapter 5). The trustee will ask how much the asset was worth, what was paid by the family member and when the transfer was made. If the answers to these questions make out a case for a preferential transfer, the answers will go right into the trustee's complaint seeking the recovery of that asset.

Some questions are less obvious. For example, the schedules may show that an asset was transferred for apparently fair value. However, under questioning, it may turn out that the debtor didn't receive a cash payment for the asset. Instead, the asset was transferred in exchange for the satisfaction of a debt. As such, the transaction can be cancelled as a preferential transfer.

But what if the debtor received cash in exchange for the asset? Then the trustee knows that the debtor had money, which will lead to questions about what the debtor did with the money. Was it used to pay bills in a preferential manner? Was it given away? Was it used to buy other assets? Are these assets disclosed?

Debtors can't just ignore these questions, since they have a duty to cooperate with the trustee's investigation. Failure to cooperate could cause the bankruptcy court to deny their discharge (see Chapter 12). Debtors can also be denied a discharge if they are unable to provide the

trustee with evidence to support their account of what happened to the property.

Trustees also ferret out preferential and fraudulent transfers by asking how debts were incurred. For example, a credit card debt that was created as the result of transferring the balance owed on one credit card to another credit card can lead to the recovery of preferential transfers. The fact that the debtor never actually received the money from the creditor who paid off the balances on the debtor's other cards doesn't mean there wasn't a transfer from the debtor to those creditors. All that matters is that the debtor had control over how the money was to be used. The debtor exercised this control by telling the new creditor which old bills to pay. That's enough to create a preferential transfer.

The fact that the trustee appears to have gathered enough information to pursue a preferential or fraudulent transfer action doesn't mean she will. Therefore, you should pay close attention to what is being said in case the trustee decides not to pursue the action.

Sample Answer To Complaint to Avoid Preferential Transfer

IN THE UNITED STATES BANKRUPTCY COURT

FOR THE DISTRICT OF WYOMING

In re: Detward Smith)	**CASE NO.:** WHO-03-3434
———————————————)	**ANSWER TO TRUSTEE'S COMPLAINT**
)	**TO AVOID PREFERENTIAL TRANSFER**
Becky Todd, Trustee)	**CH 7**
v.)	
Andy Creditor)	
———————————————)	

1. Admitted that Plaintiff is the Trustee in this case

2. Admitted that Defendant is a creditor in this case.

3. Admitted that this adversary proceeding is a core matter arising in a case filed under title 11 of the United States Code.

4. Admitted that venue is proper in the Bankruptcy Court for the District of Wyoming because this adversary proceeding arises in a case pending in this court.

5. Admitted that Defendant received $3,000 from Debtor on or about March 13, 2003.

6. Admitted that Debtor was indebted to Defendant prior to the transfer referenced in paragraph 5.

7. Denied that the transfer referenced in paragraph 5 was outside of the ordinary course of business. On the contrary, Debtor usually paid Defendant's invoices 30 to 45 days after they were issued and it is customary in the industry to treat payments up to 60 after invoicing as current.

WHEREFORE, Defendant requests the court to deny Trustee's request to avoid the payment received by Defendant as preferential.

Dated: May 15, 2004

Andy Creditor
————————————————
Andy Creditor

Sample Answer To Avoid Fraudulent Transfer

1	**IN THE UNITED STATES BANKRUPTCY COURT**
2	**FOR THE DISTRICT OF WYOMING**
3	

In re: Detward Smith   )   **CASE NO.:** WHO-03-3434
)
_____   )   **ANSWER TO TRUSTEE'S COMPLAINT**
)   **TO AVOID FRAUDULENT TRANSFER**
Becky Todd, Trustee   )   **CH 7**
)
v.   )
)
Andy Creditor   )
)
_____   )

1. Admitted that Plaintiff is the Trustee in this case

2. Admitted that Defendant is a creditor in this case.

3. Admitted that this adversary proceeding is a core matter arising in a case filed under title 11 of the United States Code.

4. Admitted that venue is proper in the Bankruptcy Court for the District of Wyoming because this adversary proceeding arises in a case pending in this court.

5. Admitted that Defendant received title to Debtor's hunting lodge on or about May 2, 2003.

6. Denied that Defendant paid less than the hunting lodge's fair value. On the contrary, the appraised value of the hunting lodge is reasonably equivalent to the value paid by Defendant and Defendant accepted Debtor's payment in good faith.

WHEREFORE, Defendant requests the court to deny Debtor's or Trustee's request to avoid the transfer of Debtor's hunting lodge as being fraudulent.

Dated: May 15, 2004   *Andy Creditor*
                                                         Andy Creditor

Creditors' Rights After the Bankruptcy Ends

At long last, the bankruptcy proceedings are over. Perhaps you
were paid some or all of your
claim—or perhaps you received nothing
at all. You may, however, still have a
chance to collect some or all of what's
owed to you, depending on various factors addressed in this chapter. If you're
alert, prepared, and involved, your
chances will certainly improve—especially since most creditors have by now
written the debtor off. In this chapter
we'll cover:

- the legal implications of a bankruptcy
  discharge, for creditors and debtors
  (Section A)
- creditors' rights to resume collection
  activities in cases where a full discharge was not granted (Section B)
- when creditors can take action to recover the collateral (Section C)
- when creditors can seek payment
  from codebtors who weren't part of
  the bankruptcy (Section D)
- when creditors can accept voluntary
  payments from the debtor (Section E)
- when creditors can seek criminal
  prosecution of the debtor (Section F),
  and
- when creditors can ask the court to
  revoke the bankruptcy discharge
  (Section G).

A. The Effect of the Bankruptcy Discharge

For the person or business that has fallen
into debt, a discharge is the main goal of
filing for bankruptcy. The discharge is a
federal court order that legally cancels the
person or business's debts. This order
comes with a permanent injunction that
prohibits creditors holding discharged
claims from ever attempting to collect
those claims from the debtor. (See 11
U.S.C. § 524.) In order that you fully understand your rights and obligations as a
creditor, we're going to focus this section
on the injunction portion of the discharge, including:

- checking whether your claim was included in the discharge (Subsection 1)
- avoiding activities that violate the discharge injunction (Subsection 2), and
- what happens if you violate the discharge injunction (Subsection 3).

1. Checking Whether Your Claim Was Discharged

If you were active in the bankruptcy proceedings, and you know that the debtor
listed your claim in the schedules filed with
the court, and if your claim wasn't ex-

cepted from discharge, you can assume your claim was discharged. That makes you subject to the discharge injunction—a fact you don't want to ignore, given the penalties for violating the injunction, which we'll discuss further along in this chapter.

If the bankruptcy court was never asked to rule on whether your claim was excepted from discharge, there are still circumstances in which you may sue the debtor in state court and ask the court to determine whether your claim was discharged. The possible conditions for doing so are that your claim:

- was not scheduled in the bankruptcy and you didn't learn of the bankruptcy in time to file a complaint challenging the discharge of your claim
- is for alimony, maintenance, or support owed as the result of a separation agreement, divorce, or other domestic court order
- is based on the debtor having caused death or personal injury by operating a motor vehicle while intoxicated

- is for restitution ordered in a federal criminal proceeding, or
- is for condominium or homeowners' association fees that came due after the debtor filed for bankruptcy and while the unit was occupied by the debtor or by the debtor's tenant.

➡ If you know that your claim was discharged, you can skip to the next section.

Not every case ends with a discharge, however—or with the discharge of your claim. In Section B, below, we'll talk about your rights and responsibilities if the debtor was denied a discharge, your claim was excepted from discharge, or the case was dismissed. You may, in the circumstances described in that section, be able to resume your collection activities.

If You've Come Late to the Bankruptcy Table

Some readers may have come late to the bankruptcy proceedings, and are just now trying to catch up with the entire process. If, for example, the debtor didn't list your claim in her schedules, then you probably didn't receive an official notice of the bankruptcy filing. The fate of your claim now depends on what bankruptcy chapter the debtor filed under.

If the debtor filed under Chapter 7 without notifying you, your claim may be excepted from—that is, not subject to—the discharge. This would occur if your claim is of a type that would be excepted from discharge under Section 523(a)(2), (a)(4), or (a)(6) of the Code (see Chapter 9 of this book for details) and you didn't learn of the case in time to file a complaint to challenge the discharge of your claim. Your claim will also be excepted from discharge if a distribution was made to unsecured creditors and you didn't receive notice in time to file a proof of claim. You may ask either the state court or the bankruptcy court for a determination that your claim was excepted from discharge, based on the debtor's failure to tell you about the bankruptcy. (For details on this and other discharge exceptions, see Chapter 9.)

It's also possible that your name could have been omitted from the schedules but included in the mailing matrix the bankruptcy clerk used for mailing notices. If that's the case, for example you received notice of the bankruptcy even though your claim wasn't scheduled, then the fact that your claim isn't listed in the debtor's schedules is irrelevant to the issue of whether your claim was discharged. You knew of the bankruptcy even if the bankruptcy court didn't know about you. Consequently, your claim is discharged, because you had the chance to let the bankruptcy court know about your claim but didn't do so.

If the debtor filed under one of the reorganization chapters, the important question is not whether your claim was scheduled, but whether it was referred to in the debtor's reorganization plan. Your claim must have been mentioned in order to be discharged. This doesn't mean that you must have been mentioned by name. It is enough if the debtor referenced your claim in a group or class of claims. Still, it must be clear to you that you were included in the group.

Under no circumstance should you attempt to collect on your claim based on its omission from the debtor's schedules or plan without being absolutely positive that your claim was excepted from discharge. Consult an attorney to be sure.

2. Avoiding Violations of the Discharge Injunction

Much like the automatic stay, the discharge injunction provides debtors with blanket protection against direct and indirect collection efforts. It gives the debtor a fresh economic start. And like the automatic stay, creditors who think they can get away with violations by acting carelessly or blindly are in for an unpleasant surprise. Let's start by looking at your general obligations as a creditor, then move to your specific obligations under each bankruptcy chapter.

a. Creditors' Postdischarge Obligations Under All Bankruptcy Chapters

Regardless of which bankruptcy chapter the debtor filed under, you don't want to go back to "business as usual" collection efforts if the bankruptcy ended with the debtor receiving a discharge. Sending a bill or filing a lawsuit are the two most ob-

vious ways to violate the discharge injunction. However, creditors more often get in trouble with subtler sorts of violations. As the following actual court cases show, violations of the discharge injunction don't need to be serious to be actionable.

- A creditor tried to collect for excess mileage on a car that the debtors leased before they filed for bankruptcy and kept during the bankruptcy. The court found that this violated the discharge injunction because the claim was a discharged debt. Although the amount of the creditor's claim couldn't be determined until after the debtors received their discharge, the court said the claim arose prepetition because it was rooted in the prepetition contract. The debtor's relief was limited to preventing the creditor from collecting the claim. (See *Beck v. Gold Key Lease, Inc. (In re Beck)*, 272 B.R. 112 (Bankr. E.D. Pa. 2002).)

- During her ex-husband's bankruptcy, a woman asked the bankruptcy court to rule that the debtor's obligation to pay certain credit card debts that he assumed in the course of their divorce was excepted from discharge. The court refused. After the bankruptcy, the woman asked a state court to hold her ex-husband in contempt for violating the divorce judgment by not paying the credit card debts. The bankruptcy court said this action violated the discharge injunction and ordered the woman to pay her ex-husband $564, which was the amount of his attorney's fees. (See *In re Ray*, No. 00-10287 (Bankr. Me. 2001).)

- Prior to filing for bankruptcy, the debtor borrowed money from a credit union. He had a friend cosign the promissory note. After the debtor received a discharge, the credit union went after the friend for payment. The friend agreed to sign a new note to repay the debt, but the credit union demanded a cosigner. Guess who that turned out to be? The bankruptcy court said that by getting the debtor to cosign his friend's obligation to pay the discharged debt, the credit union had violated the discharge injunction. (See *Mickens v. Waynesboro Dupont Employees Credit Union, Inc., et al. (In re Mickens)*, 229 B.R. 114 (Bankr. W.D. Va. 1999).)

- A debtor filed for bankruptcy alone, even though he and his wife were both obligated on a mortgage. While the debtor's obligation to pay the mortgage was discharged, his wife still owed the debt. The lender foreclosed on the mortgage, sold the collateral and tried to collect what was still owed on the mortgage from the debtor's wife. The lender agreed to give the debtor and his wife a new mortgage when the debtor agreed to repay what was left on the old mortgage. The bankruptcy court said the debtor's promise to repay the discharged debt could not be enforced, because it violated the discharge injunction. The court refused to punish the lender, however, because the offer had been made in good faith. (See *Smith v. First Suburban National Bank (In re Smith)*, 224 B.R. 388 (Bankr. N.D. Ill. 1998).)

- An Alabama credit union was ordered to pay $15,000 in punitive damages and $2,431 in attorneys fees for violating the discharge injunction, after it obtained a judgment against the debtor's wife—who hadn't been part of the bankruptcy filing. It wasn't the judgment alone that caused the problem, however. In an attempt to settle the judgment without the wife's wages being garnished, the debtor had offered to allow the credit union to deduct the judgment from his own paycheck. The credit union said it wouldn't agree to this unless the debtor agreed to repay his discharged debt. Although the credit union had every right to collect its judgment from the debtor's wife and could have accepted payments from the debtor on his wife's debt, it crossed the line when it made the discharged debt part of the bargain. (See *In the Matter of Arnold*, 206 B.R. 560 (Bankr. N.D. Ala. 1997).)

b. Creditors' Obligations After a Chapter 7 Discharge

If your debtor received a Chapter 7 discharge, you must follow the general rules described above. (However, if the debtor was a corporation or a partnership, there is no discharge. But then again, there's no debtor after the bankruptcy to go after.) You'll recall that only individuals can receive a discharge under Chapter 7. Corporations and partnerships can sell off all their assets and go out of business through Chapter 7, but they cannot receive a discharge. Corporations and partnerships file for Chapter 7 relief so they can have the trustee sell their assets free and clear of creditors' claims and so they can move on to new ventures without the burden of the old one's unpaid bills. Once corporations and partnerships complete the liquidation process, they then follow state law to dissolve their business. While this process may have the same consequence as a bankruptcy discharge, it is not governed by bankruptcy law.

An individual Chapter 7 debtor may voluntarily recommit to paying a discharged debt by signing a reaffirmation agreement before the discharge is entered. With such an agreement, the debtor agrees to repay all or part of debts that would otherwise be discharged. These reaffirmation agreements are usu-

ally signed to allow debtors to keep property that is subject to a lien. (See discussion in Chapter 8 and 11 U.S.C. § 524, particularly to be certain the agreement was properly signed, executed, and filed with the court.)

If the debtor then fails to make payments as promised in the agreement, you may resume collection activities. This is based on the idea that the debtor's obligation to pay you comes from the reaffirmation agreement, not from the obligation that was discharged in bankruptcy. In fact, if the debtor defaults on the terms of the reaffirmation agreement, you can sue to collect the unpaid balance of the obligation owed on the reaffirmation agreement. Just make sure that you don't revert to trying to collect any portion of the discharged debt.

> **EXAMPLE:** Dagmar, who is in bankruptcy proceedings, owes Coley $10,000, repayable at a 15% interest rate. Dagmar signs an agreement reaffirming the principal portion of the debt but not the interest. After the bankruptcy, Dagmar makes the first few payments on the reaffirmation agreement, for a total of $3,000, but then stops. Coley can now sue for the remaining $7,000, but cannot sue for

any unpaid interest, because Dagmar didn't reaffirm the unpaid interest.

⚠ Not every repayment agreement qualifies as a reaffirmation agreement. As discussed in Chapter 8, a reaffirmation agreement must be written in accordance with the rules set out in Section 524 of the Code. In particular, it must be signed by the debtor and by the debtor's attorney if the debtor is represented by an attorney before the discharge order is entered. Also, it must be filed with the court. Unless all these requirements are met, the reaffirmation agreement is not valid and anything you do to collect on it will be viewed as a violation of the discharge injunction. Even if you've received the debtor's promise to repay you in writing, you can't enforce it unless it meets the requirements of a valid reaffirmation agreement.

c. Creditors' Obligations After a Chapter 11 Discharge

Confirmation of a Chapter 11 plan creates a new legal relationship between you and the reorganized debtor. Whatever the debtor owed you prior to the bankruptcy filing is wiped out. In its place is a new obligation created by the plan. Perhaps your debt has been replaced by an ownership interest in the reorganized debtor.

Perhaps your debt was paid in full at the time of confirmation or will be paid over time. Perhaps you received some money plus a stake in the new business. To the extent that the plan doesn't pay all or some of your claim, your claim is discharged as soon as the debtor's plan is confirmed.

Whatever happened to your claim, your relationship with the reorganized debtor is established and will be governed by the terms of the confirmed plan. The existence of this plan gives you two possible paths for getting around the discharge injunction, including enforcing the reorganization plan and pursuing a corporation or partnership that attempts to use Chapter 11 to circumvent Chapter 7's no-discharge rule.

i. Enforcing the reorganization plan

Because the confirmed Chapter 11 plan is a new contract between you and the debtor, you can enforce it without worrying about the discharge injunction. If the debtor fails to do what was promised, you may sue the debtor. When you sue, you treat the plan as a contract.

A debtor's failure to abide by the terms of the plan does not give you the ability to sue to collect on your old debt, however. That debt remains discharged. However, if you believe that the debtor didn't tell the truth in proposing the plan or in soliciting its approval, you may ask the court to revoke confirmation of the plan. You must do this within 180 days of when the plan was confirmed. (See Chapter 13 for a discussion of challenging reorganization plans.)

ii.   Resuming collection when the debtor liquidates through Chapter 11

Though Chapter 7 bankruptcy would be the usual choice of debtors wanting to liquidate their assets, some debtors will choose to liquidate through Chapter 11. The advantage is that, under Chapter 11, they can handle the asset sales themselves rather than turning their property over to a trustee. (Creditors may also prefer a Chapter 11 plan if they can name the person responsible for conducting the sale or if the plan provides that the creditors acquire the debtor's assets.)

When debtors use Chapter 11 to liquidate, confirmation of the plan is treated the same as a Chapter 7 discharge. That means that only individuals may receive a discharge, and then only under the terms and conditions that apply in Chapter 7 cases. The same collection rules apply as in Chapter 7 cases, which means that only claims that are reaffirmed or excepted from discharge can be collected from individuals. It also means that debts owed by corporations and partnerships survive bankruptcy, but the debtor doesn't.

d.   Creditors' Obligations After a Chapter 12 or 13 Discharge

Debtors do not receive a discharge of their debts under Chapters 12 and 13 until they complete their plan payments. If the debtor completes the payments called for in the plan, then the money you received from the Chapter 13 trustee will be all the money you receive on your claim. The balance of the claim is discharged and subject to the discharge injunction.

3.   Penalties for Violating the Discharge Injunction

Violations of the discharge injunction expose the offender to penalties similar to those imposed against violators of the automatic stay. In fact, the discharge injunction is really a permanent extension of the automatic stay. (See Chapter 4 for more on the automatic stay). The automatic stay prevents creditors from pursuing collection efforts during the bankruptcy or until the debtor receives a discharge, when the discharge injunction replaces the stay.

If you violate the discharge injunction, you can be ordered to return any money collected in violation of the stay, and to reimburse the debtor for the cost of getting you to repay the money. You also can be ordered to pay punitive damages, depending on how serious the violation was.

B. Opportunities for Creditors When Not All Claims Were Discharged

Not every case ends with a discharge of all claims. In this section, we'll discuss the extent of your rights to pursue collection in cases where:

- your claim was excepted from discharge (Subsection 1)
- the court refused to issue a discharge to the debtor (Subsection 2), or
- the court dismisses the debtor's case (Subsection 3).

Be sure that your claim wasn't discharged before taking any action that would violate the automatic stay or the discharge injunction. Consult an attorney if you are not sure. It's better to pay for legal advice than be forced to pay damages to the debtor.

1. If Your Claim Was Excepted from Discharge

If your claim was excepted from discharge, you may resume collection efforts as soon as the debtor's case is closed. In fact, you may begin collection efforts sooner, if you receive relief from the automatic stay (see Chapter 4 for instructions). Normal collection activity might include suing the debtor to collect your

money, which you would normally do in state court.

How a claim gets excepted from discharge was covered in Chapter 9 of this book. By way of reminder, many types of claims are not discharged in bankruptcy, though the discharge exception is not always automatic. If, for example, you wished to base an exception on the debtor's fraud or other misconduct, you would have had to bring this up with the bankruptcy judge. Other claims, such as for child support, are automatically excepted from discharge.

All the discharge exceptions apply to individuals who file under Chapters 7, 11, and 12. All the discharge exceptions also apply to corporations and partnerships that qualify for a discharge under Chapter 12. Corporations and partnerships cannot receive a Chapter 7 discharge, so the discharge exceptions don't apply. The discharge exceptions also do not apply to corporations and partnerships that reorganize under Chapter 11.

For a Chapter 13 bankruptcy, see our discussion in Chapter 13. By way of reminder, the discharge under Chapter 13 is broader than under Chapter 7—meaning fewer exceptions for creditors. As a nongovernmental creditor, the only exception that you're likely to benefit from in Chapter 13 is the one for alimony, maintenance, or support. Even fraud or wrongful conduct by the debtor won't provide grounds for exceptions in a Chapter 13.

The rules are slightly different if your Chapter 13 debtor received a hardship discharge—meaning a discharge before the debtor completed all payments under the plan. Such debtors do not receive the broad benefits of the normal Chapter 13 discharge. They may, however, receive the equivalent of a Chapter 7 discharge if their creditors have received at least as much as they would have had the case proceeded under Chapter 7. If the debtor receives a hardship discharge, follow the rules set forth for collecting your claim after the debtor receives a Chapter 7 discharge (as described in Subsection A2, above).

2. If the Debtor Was Denied a Chapter 7 Discharge

Not all debtors are entitled to receive a Chapter 7 discharge. In Chapter 12, we discussed the types of behavior that can cost a Chapter 7 debtor the ability to discharge debts. Behavior such as fraudulent transfers (see Chapter 15), improper bookkeeping and other types of dishonest or improper behavior can lead a court to deny the debtor's discharge. After a denial of the discharge, you are free to pursue your claim as if the bankruptcy never happened.

Denial of discharge only happens in Chapter 7 cases. That doesn't mean only

Chapter 7 debtors do things that warrant denial of discharge. Instead, when Chapter 11, 12, or 13 debtors are found to have engaged in that type of activity, their cases are converted to Chapter 7 and then their discharge is denied. It's a two-step process for them.

3. If the Debtor's Case Was Dismissed

Sometimes the court determines that the debtor should not be allowed to stay in bankruptcy, but doesn't decide that the debtor should be denied a discharge. When business bankruptcies are dismissed, it is usually because the debtor acted in bad faith. In general, bad faith means filing for bankruptcy to accomplish a purpose other than the liquidation of the company's assets.

Consumer bankruptcies are usually dismissed based on the debtor's ability to make payments on a reorganization plan. This will cut both ways. Chapter 7 cases are usually dismissed because the court believes the debtor can repay some or all of his debts. Chapter 12 family farmer cases and Chapter 13 consumer cases are usually dismissed because the debtor is unable to make the payments promised in their plans. Chapter 11 cases are usually dismissed only at the debtor's request. If a creditor has a problem with a Chapter 11 debtor, such as its taking too much time to file a reorganization plan, the usual remedy is conversion to Chapter 7 and not dismissal.

If the debtor's case was dismissed by the bankruptcy court, you may resume normal collection activity. This can include suing the debtor to collect your money, which you would most likely do in state court. One word of caution, however. It's not unusual for cases to be dismissed and then reinstated, especially when the case was dismissed because the debtor fell behind on plan payments. You may get notice of the dismissal but be unaware of the reinstatement. When that happens, your collection activity may inadvertently violate the automatic stay that went back into effect when the case was reinstated. While inadvertence will shield you from being ordered to pay damages to the debtor, the court will undo any success your collection activity may have had. If you foreclosed on the debtor's property the foreclosure will be set aside. And, if you acquired a lien it will be voided. (See Chapter 4 for a complete discussion of what happens when the automatic stay is violated.)

You can learn the status of the debtor's case by calling the bankruptcy clerk's office or using an online service, if your court offers one. It's always a good idea to make sure the debtor's case has been dismissed before resuming collection activity.

If the bankruptcy court never voided your lien before the debtor's case was dismissed, then you may enforce it against the collateral after the debtor's case is dismissed if:

- **Your lien was voided because your claim was undersecured.** If the bankruptcy court ordered your lien reduced to the collateral's value, your lien returns to its full value when the debtor's case is dismissed. See Chapter 13 for particulars of what happens in reorganization cases where the case is dismissed after the secured claim is fully paid.

- **Your lien was voided because it was created by a judgment that reduced the value of the debtor's exempt property, or**

- **Your lien was voided because it created a nonpossessory, nonpurchase-money security interest in the debtor's household property.** (See Chapter 8.)

C. Recovering Your Collateral

After the court closes the file on a bankruptcy, you may be able to recover your collateral from the debtor. You can act sooner if your collateral was abandoned by the trustee in a Chapter 7 case or if the property reverted to the debtor's possession as part of a reorganization plan. The discharge injunction doesn't prevent you from enforcing a lien against the debtor's property that was not avoided (cancelled) during the bankruptcy. If you have a security interest in the debtor's property, you may sue to recover the collateral. Be careful that your suit clearly states that you are interested only in getting your collateral (rather than money).

Remember, however: The discharge injunction has subtle traps for the unwary creditor. Asking for money as part of a suit to recover collateral is one of those traps. Even asking for compensation for the cost of recovering the collateral runs afoul of the discharge injunction, because your right to ask for this money is based on the debt that was discharged. Your right to enforce the discharged debt is gone. All that's left is your right to retrieve your collateral. This rule doesn't mean you can't accept a cash settlement of your suit, but you can't ask for cash—either in the suit or in settlement negotiations. So, you would sue to recover the collateral. If the debtor offers you cash instead, you may take it, but you can't ask for it.

Also understand that if you obtained a state court judgment before the debtor filed for bankruptcy, the judgment can't create a lien against property the debtor acquired after the filing. This is because the lien that flows from the judgment doesn't exist without the judgment, and the judgment disappeared in the bank-

ruptcy. If the judgment lien attached prior to the bankruptcy, however, and the debtor didn't avoid the lien, then you can still pursue it.

> **EXAMPLE:** Christabel sues Dixon to collect the $800 he owes her. She receives a judgment against Dixon before he files for bankruptcy. However, when the judgment is entered, Dixon doesn't own anything to which the judgment lien could attach. After he files bankruptcy, he buys a house. Christabel's judgment lien could not attach to Dixon's house because he acquired it after the bankruptcy discharged Christabel's judgment claim. If Dixon had bought the house before filing bankruptcy, then Christabel's judgment lien would have attached prior to the bankruptcy and would be enforceable after the bankruptcy as long as Dixon didn't avoid the lien during the bankruptcy.

D. Collecting Claims from Nonbankrupt Codebtors

The bankruptcy discharge is personal to the debtor—it doesn't affect anyone else who was jointly responsible for repaying your loan. You may seek payment from any of those codebtors (assuming they did not themselves file for bankruptcy) after the bankruptcy is over, subject to the exceptions described below. In fact, you can seek payment at any time unless the debtor filed for Chapter 12 or 13 relief.

1. Special Rules for Chapter 13 Codebtors

When a debtor files under Chapter 7 or Chapter 11, creditors are free to pursue their claims against anyone who is liable for the payment of a claim that the debtor is trying to discharge. However, this rule doesn't apply to consumer loans when the debtor is trying to reorganize under Chapter 12 or 13, because pressure for payment placed on a codebtor can easily translate into pressure on the debtor and make it difficult for the debtor to reorganize. Instead, when debtors file under Chapter 12 or 13, the automatic stay protects nonfiling cosigners as well as the debtor. The codebtor's stay ends when the case ends, whether the case is closed, dismissed or converted. The codebtor stay does not apply at all to loans made to Chapter 12 or 13 debtors in the ordinary course of the debtor's business.

2. Exception for Community Property

If the cosigner is the debtor's spouse, then you cannot collect your claim from property that was community property

(generally, property acquired during the marriage in states that recognize community property). You can go after the nonfiling spouse, but you can't levy on any property that the debtor and the nonfiling spouse owned as community property when the bankruptcy was filed.

3. Exception for Certain Married Joint Tenants

A few noncommunity-property states recognize a form of joint property ownership by married couples known as tenancy by the entireties. When spouses own property as tenants by the entirety, each spouse owns the entire property—meaning that no one can say who owns what percentage of the property for as long as the marriage lasts. Creditors of only one spouse can never reach the property as long it is jointly owned.

Each spouse also owns what's known as a "residual interest"—that is, the right to own the entire asset if he or she outlives the other spouse. This interest may have some monetary value in the marketplace. If you have a claim against the spouse who didn't file bankruptcy, then you can sue that spouse for payment of your claim and you may be able to get a lien against that spouse's residual interest in the property. However, whether you can do so depends on state law, and is beyond the scope of this book.

4. Exception for Business Partners and Principals

If you're the creditor in a bankruptcy filed by a partnership or a small business, you may have made loans to that business onto which the partners, officers, or directors signed, accepting individual responsibility. If so, the bankruptcy court may extend the automatic stay to prevent suits against these partners or principals. The court's injunction does not come automatically, however. The bankruptcy judge would impose this extension of the stay based on the necessity of giving the debtor, who probably filed under Chapter 11, a chance to reorganize without its key people being sued.

E. Accepting Voluntary Payments from the Debtor

The bankruptcy discharge ends the debtor's legal obligation to repay you. That does not, however, mean the debtor can't volunteer to repay you. Unlikely though this might sound, some debtors might wish to reestablish their business reputation or your personal relationship. If the debtor decides to repay you after receiving a discharge, it's too late to have the debtor sign a reaffirmation agreement, but you can still keep any payments the debtor decides to send you. You may not, however, ask the debtor whether she

plans to send you another check. You may not send the debtor a statement of account or in any way acknowledge payment or take any other action that could be construed as an attempt to collect more money on a discharged debt. The payment must be strictly voluntary.

There is one exception to this rule. If the debtor has kept your collateral, and has not reaffirmed your claim but has continued to make regular payments to you, consistent with your original agreement, you may send informational notices to the debtor informing him of the status of the account. These statements may remind the debtor that if the next payment is not received by a certain date you can repossess the collateral. The statements may not ask for payment, but can remind the debtor of the consequences of nonpayment. The following was found to be an acceptable statement: It was titled "Transaction Summary of Voluntary Payments" and included this warning, "Voluntary payments must be timely received if you wish to retain possession of your vehicle." (See *Ramirez v. GMAC*, 272 B.R. 620 (Bankr. C.D. Cal. 2002).)

F. Seeking Criminal Prosecution of the Debtor

If your claim is based on illegal action by the debtor—such as a bounced check—you may ask the local police department or district attorney to bring criminal charges against the debtor. Your request will not violate the automatic stay or the discharge injunction. The technical reason is that state and local officials are immune from operation of the discharge injunction.

This option may be of small comfort to you if your claim was not excepted from discharge and you'd rather get paid than see the debtor go to jail. Also, if you do decide to seek prosecution, make sure it's clear that you're interested only in punishment of the debtor's criminal behavior. If you attempt to use the criminal justice system to collect a purely civil judgment, you may open yourself up to liability for malicious prosecution.

G. Requesting Revocation of the Discharge

If you learn that the debtor lied to the court or otherwise committed fraud in obtaining the discharge, you may ask the court to revoke the discharge. Revocation means canceling the discharge and everything that happened during the proceedings. It puts the debtor and creditors back to where they were on the day the bankruptcy was filed.

You don't have forever to request a revocation, however. In cases under bankruptcy Chapters 7, 12, and 13, you must bring your action to revoke the discharge within one year of when the case was closed or the debtor received a discharge, whichever happened later. In cases under Chapter 11, you must bring the action within 180 days of when the debtor's plan was confirmed.

By putting a deadline on discharge revocation actions, the law gives finality to the bankruptcy. If the fraud wasn't detected during the case and remained hidden for another year, then it may be time for everyone to move on. If discharges could be revoked at any time, then the debtor's fresh start would never really start, and the main purpose for bankruptcy would be frustrated. ■

Minimizing Future Bankruptcy Losses

If you own or run a business, a customer's bankruptcy filing can catch you by surprise. Sure, you'll sometimes get warning signs, such as increasingly late payments and dishonored checks. But, depending on the nature of your business and the peculiarities of the customer's financial situation, it's possible you'll get no apparent warning at all. By the time you know there's a problem, it may be too late to protect yourself. The lesson here is that the best time to shield your accounts receivable from bankruptcy losses is before the receivable is created.

Make a habit of asking yourself a simple question every time you extend credit: "What will happen to me if this person files for bankruptcy?" Very few businesses can operate on a strictly cash basis, and no one expects that you will. On the other hand, it is foolish for any business to ignore the very real possibility that any customer can file for bankruptcy.

This chapter will provide some concrete suggestions to help you minimize your business's exposure to future bankruptcy losses, including:

- diversifying your customer base (Section A)
- requiring new customers to submit credit applications (Section B)
- requiring cosigners or guarantors for risky transactions (Section C)
- obtaining collateral (Section D)
- cashing checks promptly (Section E)

- keeping an eye on customer behavior patterns (Section F), and
- suing when necessary (Section G).

A. Diversify Your Customer Base

You know the old saying: Don't put all your eggs in one basket. If you're supplying goods or services to larger businesses, this can be all too easy to forget. When Kmart filed for bankruptcy, many small manufacturing companies lost their one and only customer. Invoices went unpaid. Orders were cancelled. Inventory piled up. Some companies closed, others went bankrupt and a few lucky others found new customers.

This story was repeated when Enron and WorldCom filed for bankruptcy. It will be repeated over and over again when other big companies file. Don't put yourself in a position where someone else's problem becomes your own. The time to look for new customers is while you still have old ones.

B. Get Credit Applications from New Customers

Lending money or extending credit to customers without checking their creditworthiness is asking for trouble. First of all, you run the risk of not getting paid if the customer files for bankruptcy. But, perhaps worse, you may not be able to recover extraordinary losses caused by a customer who runs up a huge bill just before filing for bankruptcy. Although last-minute charges would usually be excepted from discharge as fraud—if you successfully convince the bankruptcy judge of that fact—it's fraud only if you reasonably relied on something the debtor told you. Blithely extending credit based on the debtor's winning smile will get you nowhere in court.

You can protect yourself from the risk of nonpayment, and preserve your ability to challenge fraudulently incurred charges, by having the customer give you a detailed, written, and signed credit application.

For a sample credit application form, see *Legal Guide for Starting & Running a Small Business*, by Fred S. Steingold (Nolo).

Be serious about the credit application—don't allow the customer to fill in some blanks and not others, or to sign an incomplete form. Your desire to make a sale might thus decrease your chances of getting paid.

Your next step will be to take the completed credit application form and verify the information with a credit-reporting agency. The three major national sources of this information about consumers are:

- Equifax, at 888-202-4025 or www.equifax.com
- Experian, at 888-217-6064 or www.experian.com, and
- TransUnion, at 312-466-7363 or www.transunion.com.

In order to receive consumer credit reports, you'll need to subscribe to the reporting agency's service. For example, Equifax provides a "business partners" program that costs about $300 to join. Half of this fee is for membership and the other half is to cover the cost of conducting a federally mandated on-site investigation of your business. The investigators will make sure that you are who you say you are, and that you have a legitimate use for the information. Once you've been cleared, you can order credit reports at a cost of about $4 each. Each credit report comes with a credit risk score, which predicts how likely this person is to default on a loan.

Credit reports on businesses can be obtained from Dun & Bradstreet (888-814-1435). This information can be obtained without joining an association or subscribing to a service. However, you will need to register with the service provider.

Once you've followed these steps, you'll be better protected if and when your customer files for bankruptcy. You'll be able to show the court the completed and signed credit application as an indication of exactly what information you relied on in extending credit to the customer. If this information wasn't accurate, you can challenge the debtor's ability to discharge your claim (see Chapter 9). Also, the credit report will hopefully show the court that your reliance on the information provided by the debtor was reasonable.

In order for your credit relationship with the customer to remain reasonable, you'll need to periodically review the credit application and ask for updates on applications that have become stale. How long it takes for staleness to set in depends on whether your contacts with the customer are frequent and intimate enough that you have a good idea of how the customer is doing. Some businesses might never ask a good customer to update their credit application; others might ask each time a new loan is made or whenever the credit limit is extended. If you see a customer irregularly, it's wise to ask him to update his records each time he asks for credit.

C. Require a Cosigner or Guarantor

You need not rely on just one person to pay a debt. If the credit application is from an individual, you can ask that someone else cosign for the debt. If the credit application is from a business, see if one of the principals will guarantee the debt.

Obviously, you're not going to ask for a cosigner or a guarantor for every credit transaction. If the applicant has a good credit history, you want to encourage that person to become a regular customer. Only you, with the help of credit risk scores supplied along with credit reports, can judge who is a good credit risk for your business.

⚠️ **If you ask for a cosigner and the person you provided credit to files for bankruptcy under Chapter 12 or Chapter 13, the automatic stay will prevent you from collecting the debt from the cosigner.** See Chapter 4 for details.

D. Obtain Collateral

You can also look to the debtor's property for payment, by asking the debtor to give you a security interest. A security interest allows you to sell the property that is collateral for the loan, in order to collect your claim if the debtor doesn't fully repay you. Even property that is worthless to you may be sufficiently valuable to the debtor that the thought of losing it will encourage payment of a delinquent debt. And, in the event of bankruptcy, you'll start in a better position as a secured creditor than as an unsecured creditor.

What size debt merits asking for collateral is up to you. Some lenders won't provide any loan without taking something as collateral. Other lenders find it's too much of a hassle to ask for collateral for small loans.

If you do get collateral, remember that you don't need to take physical possession of the property. However, if you don't, make sure you follow your state's laws for recording your lien. The paperwork must be properly completed and promptly filed in the correct place. Don't lose your valuable protection by messing up the loan documents. (See Chapter 8 for a discussion of how you can lose your lien if the papers creating your security interest are not properly filed.)

E. Cash All Checks Promptly

Don't let checks sit around your office. You may think you've been paid as soon as the check arrives, but the law says the money isn't yours until the debtor's bank honors the check. (And some debtors actually operate on a belief that whoever gets to the bank first, wins!) If the debtor is sliding toward bankruptcy—a fact you may not know until it's too late—you're better off getting that check through the system as soon as possible. Not only will you eliminate the risk that the money in the debtor's bank account will be exhausted paying other checks, but you will

reduce the risk that you have to return the money as a preferential transfer.

As discussed in detail in Chapter 15, the preferential transfer rules say that payments made by an insolvent debtor on existing debts within 90 days prior to the bankruptcy filing can be recovered by the bankruptcy trustee. When the payment is made by check, transfer of the money from the debtor to the creditor is said to occur on the date the check is honored by the debtor's bank. Given the 90-day window, this payment date becomes very important. In other words, you can be forced to return the debtor's money if the debtor files for bankruptcy within 90 days after the debtor's bank honors the check.

Stop for a second and think about all the money that has been paid to you over the past 90 days. How many of those payments were past due? Where would you be if one or more of the customers who made late payments were to file for bankruptcy today? You could be forced to return the money that was paid to you.

As you can see, you want to start the clock running on potentially preferential payments as quickly as possible. So, deposit all your checks every day.

Start the clock even sooner by requiring customers to pay by cashier's check or money order. Since these forms of payment are treated the same as cash, the transfer occurs as soon as the payment is given to you.

F. Keep Close Tabs on Customers

Even in our automated, computerized, legality-ridden world, there's no substitute for common sense and personal interaction. A customer who is at risk of filing for bankruptcy may exhibit warning signs, which you can catch if your radar is up. Given the turbulence of our economy, it's wise not to become complacent. A person or business who was a good credit risk a few years ago may now be teetering on the edge of bankruptcy.

Some potential warning signs include your customer's:

- pattern of late payments (Subsection 1)
- selling off of assets (Subsection 2)
- changes in company personnel (Subsection 3)
- changes in payment practices (Subsection 4)
- changes in buying patterns (Subsection 5), or
- doing business in an industry or region that's undergoing economic decline (Subsection 6).

1. Payments that Are Slow in Coming

If your standard business practice is to receive payment within 30 days, then watch for customers who tend to get their payments in beyond this period. You may be forced to return any payment made more than 30 days late if the customer files for bankruptcy within 90 days of when you received the cash or the bank honored the customer's check. By ignoring your 30-day limit, you may be creating preferential transfer exposure.

If a certain customer just can't seem to pay on time, demand cash on delivery or retain a security interest in the property until payment is received. But run a credit check as soon as you find yourself waiting for payment, so that you'll know whether there's going to be a problem with the account.

2. Customers Selling Off Assets

If you see a "For Sale" sign in front of your customer's store, it may be a sign that the customer is going out of business. Then again, the customer may just be moving to a bigger location. Make a note to ask what's up. At the very least, a change in location will require you to update the information in the customer's credit file.

Be vigilant for more subtle warning signs of trouble ahead. Any sale of assets outside your customer's normal course of business should be questioned. For example, a bakery that sells one of its delivery trucks may be losing business.

If you have sales representatives who visit your customers, tell them to let you know about any signs of trouble, such as empty shelves in retail or wholesale locations, or facilities that look rundown and in need of maintenance.

3. Personnel Changes

Layoffs are almost always an indication that a business is hurting. The reduction in staff may be all the business needs to keep going, or it may just be the first domino to fall on the path to bankruptcy. You won't know which until you ask. Innocently asking "How's business?" often produces the most reliable answer. Also watch for changes in key personnel. Ask questions and run a credit check if there's somebody new signing the customer's checks, especially if it's someone you don't know.

You should also ask questions whenever there's a change in upper management. Instability at the top can be a sign of problems below.

4. Changes in Payment Practices

People or businesses in financial trouble often start moving their money around or drawing on backup sources of cash. If a customer who has always paid cash starts using credit, it may signify that cash is tight. If your customer's check is drawn on a new bank or from a new account, be cautious. Be particularly concerned if your customer's bill is paid by a related company or by a personal check from the company's owner.

Not only does a payment from someone other than the debtor indicate that the debtor may not have the money to pay you, if that other entity files for bankruptcy within one year, the payment can be recovered as a fraudulent transfer, because the entity that paid your bill didn't owe you the money. (See Chapter 15 for a complete discussion of fraudulent transfers.) In fact, the payment may be at risk of loss for a longer period than one year. While federal bankruptcy law allows trustees to avoid fraudulent transfers made up to one year before the bankruptcy filing, there are times when trustees can use state fraudulent transfer laws to recover payments made even more than one year before the petition.

5. Changes in Buying Patterns

A sudden surge or decline in buying on credit may indicate problems with your customer's account. A surge could be an indication of fraud. Check to make sure your customer was actually the one who made the purchases, in order to guard against fraudulent transactions. If the customer clears the charges, run a credit check to see if the customer is overextended. The credit check will show how much debt the customer has incurred and whether the customer is keeping up with other payments. There are lots of good reasons for a spike in a customer's buying tendencies, but there is also the possibility of fraud. Rule it out before extending more credit to the customer. On the other side of the coin, a drop in credit purchases may be an indication that the customer's business is slow or is being wrapped up.

6. Economic Decline in the Customer's Industry or Region

What's going on in the universe where your debtor does business? It's more likely than not that your customer is typical of other businesses in that industry and region. If either is experiencing a downturn, run a credit check to see how your customer is doing.

G. Know When to Sue

If a customer has a delinquent account, don't let a threat of bankruptcy stop you from suing. The worst that's going to happen is that the customer will file for bankruptcy before you receive a judgment, in which case the automatic stay will simply stop matters in their tracks. The best that could happen is that you'll get a judgment and get paid by enforcing it against the debtor's income or property. The upside clearly outweighs the downside. ■

Forcing Debtors Into Bankruptcy

So far, we've talked only about bankruptcies filed by debtors. These are voluntary petitions in which the debtor has willingly decided that bankruptcy is best for him. There are times, however, when you might actually wish that a debtor would file for bankruptcy. For example, if you're not getting paid and there are indications that the debtor is liquidating, it may be clear to you that only a bankruptcy is going to resolve this matter in an orderly and equitable manner. In fact, you do, under certain circumstances, have the power to file an involuntary bankruptcy petition against the debtor.

Involuntary bankruptcy is an unusual and extreme measure. Fewer than one in 1,000 bankruptcy cases are started this way. Involuntary bankruptcy should not be viewed as a standard collection technique, and should never be used in bad faith, to harass, or to revenge yourself upon the debtor.

This chapter explains how the involuntary bankruptcy process works. However, we don't recommend filing an involuntary petition without the help of an attorney, mainly because of the costs and penalties you'd face if your petition is unsuccessful (see Section C, below). To help you consider whether it's time to call your lawyer about filing an involuntary petition, this chapter will cover:

- the legal grounds for filing an involuntary petition (Section A)

- who can bring such a petition (Section B)
- the benefits and risks of bringing such a petition (Section C)
- the immediate effect of the filing (Section D)
- how creditors with claims arising after the filing and before the court's decision will be treated (Section E), and
- the impact of the court's decision (Section F).

To see the official form used for filing an involuntary petition (Form B5), go the U.S. courts' website at www.uscourts.gov/bankform/b5.pdf.

A. Grounds for Filing an Involuntary Bankruptcy Petition

In order for you to file an involuntary petition against a debtor, the debtor must be either an individual who is not a farmer, or a for-profit corporation or partnership. Any of these can be forced to liquidate under Chapter 7 or to reorganize under Chapter 11 if either of the following is true:

- **The person or business is not staying current on its legitimate bills.** The court will look over the previous 120 days to see whether the debtor is generally paying bills as they come due. If the debtor is failing to do so, then the court will force the debtor into bankruptcy.

- **Someone took possession of the person, or business's assets (without authorization from a court).** The "someone" in this instance is likely to be a creditor. In other words, the debtor may have turned property over to a single creditor or sold off assets to pay the creditor's claim. If this has happened, then the bankruptcy court will force the debtor into bankruptcy.

B. Who Can File an Involuntary Bankruptcy Petition?

Not just anyone can push a debtor into bankruptcy proceedings. Involuntary bankruptcy cases can be filed only by the parties most interested in the debtor's bill payments, namely the creditors. That doesn't mean that a lone creditor can always bring a petition, however. If the debtor has fewer than 12 creditors (up to 11), then a single creditor would have to hold an unsecured, nondisputed claim worth at least $11,625 in order to initiate an involuntary bankruptcy. An unsecured creditor with a claim of less than $11,625 could, however, join other unsecured creditors to file an involuntary petition if their aggregate claim is at least $11,625. If the debtor has 12 or more creditors, at

least three creditors holding unsecured claims worth at least $11,625 in total must sign the involuntary bankruptcy petition.

When determining whether the debtor has 12 or more creditors, you don't need to count employees, insiders, or any creditor who received a transfer that may be avoided by the trustee. Also, the creditors who band together to file the petition must be sufficiently independent of each other that their cooperation shows the seriousness of the debtor's financial situation and the legitimacy of the creditors' concern. If the petitioning creditors have common ownership or are related enterprises, then the court may treat them as a single creditor.

Don't miscount. One surefire way to have the court find that your involuntary petition was filed in bad faith is to file it alone when the debtor has well over 11 creditors.

Not surprisingly, it must be clear to the court that the creditors have real claims, and aren't just suing over some argument. In fact, the claims of the petitioning creditors cannot be subject to any bona fide dispute. A bona fide dispute is one in which the debtor can objectively support his argument that he is not responsible for paying the claim. If you happen also to owe money to the debtor, that doesn't mean that your claim is subject to a bona fide dispute. The legitimacy of your claim is determined apart from any claims for payment that the debtor has against you.

Some special rules apply in cases where the debtor is a partnership. Any general partner who has not filed for bankruptcy may file an involuntary bankruptcy against the partnership. If all the general partners have filed for bankruptcy, then the trustee of any of the general partners may file an involuntary petition against the partnership.

C. Considering Whether to File an Involuntary Petition

Filing an involuntary petition carries certain risks, whether or not the court grants your request. In this section, we'll look at what might happen in the event of a positive or negative court decision, and end by describing some situations that might nevertheless warrant asking the court to consider the matter.

1. Downside Risks of a Successful Involuntary Petition

Let's start by assuming that the court will grant your request to put the debtor into bankruptcy proceedings. Consider that these proceedings will cost the debtor money—and that these various administrative costs will then reduce the amount of money available to pay claims. You'll need to weigh whether the certainty of recovering something in bankruptcy is preferable to the hassle of trying to collect on a larger amount outside of bankruptcy. We can't evaluate this for you—your decision will depend on your circumstances as well as the debtor's. An involuntary petition may be advisable against a debtor that is wrapping up its business, but not advisable against a debtor with an ongoing business. An involuntary bankruptcy may be more advisable against a creditor with a large, unsecured claim than against one with a smaller, partially secured claim.

There is also the risk that successfully putting the debtor into bankruptcy will also put the debtor right out of business—earlier than might have otherwise occurred.

EXAMPLE: Donatelli's Shoes keeps its extra inventory in Clancy's warehouse. Donatelli's has always been slow in paying its bill, but when it got to be several months old Clancy got concerned. He noticed that Donatelli's had few shoes in storage. When he went to Donatelli's store, he found the shelves nearly empty. Donatelli's said it was just waiting for a new shipment, but Clancy found out that it was selling off shoes to other stores. Clancy concluded that Donatelli's was going out of business and was cashing out its inventory first. Clancy decided that the best way to protect his claim was to force Donatelli's into bankruptcy. As it turned out, Donatelli's was selling its inventory. But it was also waiting for a new shipment, which it would have to pay for in cash so that it could sell the store as a going concern. However, the involuntary bankruptcy prevented this and forced Donatelli's to convert the case to a voluntary Chapter 7.

You can avoid the scenario in the example above by talking to the debtor before filing an involuntary petition. The legitimate threat of an involuntary case being filed should encourage the debtor to give honest answers.

2. Penalties for Filing an Unsuccessful Involuntary Petition

If you have misread the situation, and the bankruptcy court concludes that the debtor should not be forced into bankruptcy, you may face some dire consequences. The court will, without a doubt, require you to pay the debtor's cost of defending the court action. In addition, if the court finds that you acted out of vengeance or with malice towards the debtor, your costs might rise even higher. You could be ordered to compensate the debtor for the damage the filing did to the debtor's reputation, and ordered to

pay punitive damages. It will help if you acted on the advice of legal counsel, however. That will reduce the likelihood that the court orders punitive damages against you.

3. Situations Where Involuntary Petitions Are Appropriate

Now that you've been fully warned, let's look at some situations in which the filing of an involuntary case against a debtor may be appropriate:

- **The debtor is paying some creditors but not others.** If you believe the debtor is freezing you out, and you fear that the situation is going to get worse, you might be in a good position to file an involuntary petition. When you're counting creditors, remember that any creditor who is getting paid should be excluded from the determination of whether the debtor has 12 or more creditors if any of those payments can be avoided by a trustee (see Chapter 15).

- **The debtor acts like he's working for one creditor.** Sometimes one secured creditor will be able to exert so much leverage over the debtor through the amount of debt owed and the importance of the collateral that the debtor can be forced to do whatever that creditor wants. If it appears that the debtor is doing things for the secured creditor's benefit that harm you and other creditors, then an involuntary filing may be appropriate.

• **The debtor isn't paying anybody and doesn't seem to moving toward bankruptcy.** Sometimes you wonder how a debtor does it. He's not paying his bills, but people still lend him money or sell him stuff on credit. If you reach a point where you're fed up and you want to get paid whatever you can and move on, then filing an involuntary petition may be appropriate. But be careful that it's not a vindictive act.

D. Immediate Effect of Filing an Involuntary Petition

Even when it wasn't the debtor's choice to file for bankruptcy, the debtor receives the standard protections immediately after the filing. The automatic stay kicks in and a bankruptcy estate is created. However, unlike a voluntary filing, the filing of an involuntary petition does not stop the debtor from conducting his business or selling assets. So, if you're concerned that the debtor is or will be selling off assets or transferring property, accompany the involuntary petition with a request that the court appoint a trustee. The trustee's

role would be to oversee the debtor's transactions until the court can decide whether the debtor should, in fact, be forced into bankruptcy.

The debtor has an opportunity to file a response to the involuntary petition. That response will typically challenge the basis on which the petition was filed (claiming, for example, that the debtor was current on all bills or has not been transferring assets) or questioning whether the creditors meet the requirements for filing an involuntary petition in the first place.

> **EXAMPLE:** Cunningham's Pest Control files an involuntary bankruptcy against Darling's Pets. Cunningham says Darling's owes him $15,000 for one year's worth of bug treatments. But Darling's says Cunningham's treatments killed their supply of gerbils and cost them $10,000. Since Cunningham's claim is subject to a legitimate dispute, the company is not eligible to file an involuntary petition against Darling's.

Some debtors won't file a response, however, and will actually opt to proceed into bankruptcy voluntarily. The debtor can then convert the involuntary petition into a voluntary petition under any chapter that the debtor is eligible to file under.

Once the ball gets rolling, additional unsecured creditors may want to add their names to the petition. Unsecured creditors can do so after the involuntary petition has been filed up to the point when the court rules on its merits. The addition of creditors makes it harder for the debtor to have the involuntary case dismissed, especially if the debtor's only challenge was the validity or amount of a particular creditor's claim.

In some cases, the debtor will pay off the claims of creditors who have signed the involuntary petition, hoping that the creditor will then withdraw support for the petition. However, the law doesn't allow creditors to back out like this. Once a creditor decides to force a debtor into bankruptcy, she is acting on behalf of all creditors. The creditor cannot end what she started just because she's happy now. However, creditors may withdraw for other reasons, such as a misunderstanding of the law or a misrepresentation made by the debtor or another creditor. Withdrawal will not prevent a petitioning creditor from being liable to the debtor for damages if the case is dismissed. Withdrawal should, however, reduce the amount of damages owed.

E. Treatment of Creditors with Postpetition, Predecision Claims

There's a period of time between when the involuntary petition is filed and when the bankruptcy court enters the order forcing the debtor into bankruptcy. During this time gap, the debtor is allowed to run her business and incur debt. If your claim arises during this intermediate time period, you are what's called a "gap period creditor."

Gap period creditors are treated as if their claims arose before the involuntary petition was filed. This means their claims will be discharged if and when a discharge is entered. However, if there is money available to pay creditors' claims, their claims will be paid ahead of all unsecured claims except for those incurred for administrative expenses. So, suppliers who continue to stock a financially troubled store after an involuntary petition has been filed will get paid ahead of everyone else—except the lawyers—if the case goes forward. The case could go forward either because the court approves the involuntary petition or because the debtor voluntarily files a bankruptcy petition.

F. The Court's Decision

The court's decision whether to force the debtor into bankruptcy will be based on the facts and circumstances of the case. If the correct number of creditors holding legitimate, unsecured claims request the relief, and the evidence supports their allegations, then the court will enter the requested order. After entry of the order, the debtor has 15 days in which to file the same schedules, statements, and other papers that a debtor would file in a vol-untary case. From that point forward, the case proceeds in the same manner as a voluntary case.

If the court denies the petition, then the bankruptcy will be dismissed. If the case is dismissed for any reason other than the consent of all parties, including the debtor, then the petitioning creditors can be made to reimburse the debtor for the cost of defending the bankruptcy. If any petitioning creditor acted in bad faith, the court can order that creditor to pay punitive damages to the debtor as well. ■

Legal Help Beyond This Book

lthough we've tried to make the information in this book as comprehensive as possible, we can't anticipate every question you might have. If we tried, this book would weigh a ton, cost a fortune, and be practically useless. Also, as we've pointed out along the way, not all bankruptcy proceedings go smoothly—and when things get adversarial, a lawyer can be well worth the cost, for both complex legal questions and for dealing with procedural and paperwork requirements. So, here are some suggestions on how to get the additional information or advice specific to your needs. We'll cover:

- when to use a bankruptcy lawyer (Section A)
- how to do your own legal research (Section B), and
- what legal research tools are available online (Section C).

A. When to Use Bankruptcy Lawyers

Bankruptcy lawyers can be valuable sources of information and advice, analyzing how the law applies to your situation or how you might best proceed. They are also the only people to whom you can turn when you need or want someone to represent your interests in bankruptcy court. The lawyer doesn't have to handle every part of your case—you should be able to work out an agreement with the lawyer to merely consult with you, or to handle only certain procedures. In the latter case, however, the lawyer will probably insist upon reviewing work that you do yourself, and on being paid for that time.

There are several tasks involved in protecting your claim that you should be comfortable doing yourself. For example, you should be confident that you can file a proof of claim, review the bankruptcy schedules, and attend the meeting of creditors without the help of an attorney. Experienced business creditors might also feel comfortable handling certain additional items, while others will prefer to hire a lawyer for help with:

- asking the debtor to sign a reaffirmation agreement
- obtaining relief from the automatic stay, or
- objecting to the confirmation of the debtor's reorganization plan.

After that, we're getting into territory where the risks inherent in making a mistake grow larger. That means that the benefits of hiring professional help increase. For example, you'll probably want a lawyer's help if you choose to:

- ask the court to dismiss the debtor's case
- challenge the discharge of your claim
- challenge the debtor's right to receive a discharge, or
- file an involuntary petition against a debtor.

1. How to Find a Good Bankruptcy Lawyer

You'll see a lot of advertisements for bankruptcy lawyers in the newspaper, on television, and in the yellow pages. The problem is, most of these lawyers represent debtors. You want a lawyer who has experience representing creditors in bankruptcy. Here's how to find one:

- **Get a personal referral.** Ask your business colleagues and friends who they use to represent them against bankrupt debtors. This is your best approach, because you'll not only be referred to someone who does the type of work you're looking for, you'll know he or she has at least one satisfied customer.
- **Get a referral from a trade association.** If you belong to a trade association, ask whether it has any affiliation with bankruptcy lawyers in your area.
- **Contact the American Board of Certification (ABC).** This is a nonprofit group that certifies bankruptcy and creditors' rights lawyers as specialists in their fields. They have both an online directory (at www.abc.org) and a paper version, free for the asking. You can also contact them at 44 Canal Center Plaza #404, Alexandria, VA 22314, 703-739-1023.

- **Contact an attorney trade association.** Some specialized lawyers join trade associations—which not only give out the lawyers' names, but usually help the lawyers keep up on important legal changes. Try, for example, the National Association of Retail Collection Attorneys, at 1620 I Street NW, Suite 615, Washington, DC 20006; 202-861-0706; www.narca.org. Or, there's the Commercial Law League of America, which represents creditors in collection and bankruptcy matters, at 150 N. Michigan Avenue, Suite 600, Chicago, Illinois. 606061; 312-781-2000; www.clla.org.
- **Check out the court's hearing lists.** Since you're looking for a lawyer experienced with bankruptcy court proceedings, why not look for a lawyer who already has matters scheduled before the court? Every bankruptcy court publishes a list of motions and complaints that will be heard during the upcoming week. These lists describe the action and identify the lawyers. Call the bankruptcy clerk's office or check the court's website to see where the list is published for your court, then look for names of attorneys representing a creditor in an action similar to yours. You can even watch the proceedings to see which lawyers' styles you like.

- **Contact a lawyer referral panel.**
  Most county bar associations will give
  you the names of lawyers who practice bankruptcy law (though it's doubtful they can identify those concentrat-
  ing on creditors' rights). Another problem is that bar associations usually
  provide only minimal screening for the
  attorneys listed, which means not all
  those who participate are the most experienced or competent.
- **If all else fails, try the yellow
  pages.** The few bankruptcy attorneys
  who represent creditors usually identify their practice as including "creditors' rights."

2. What to Look for in a Bankruptcy Lawyer

No matter what approach you take in
finding a lawyer, just getting a name isn't
enough. No matter where you got the
lawyer's name, take the time to check out
his or her credentials and experience. In
fact, plan on starting with a list of a few
lawyers and narrowing it down to the
one who is the best fit for you. Remember, you're hiring a lawyer to provide a
service for you, so shop around if the
price or personality isn't right.

One of the most important consider-
ations is that you feel comfortable with
the lawyer you hire. For most people,
that means hiring someone you can talk
to and who will take the time to answer
your questions. Start by making an appointment with the lawyer to discuss your
situation. Your goal at the initial conference is to find out what the lawyer is like
personally, what she recommends, and
how much it will cost. Don't be afraid to
ask for references or to find out when the
lawyer is handling a similar matter in
court that you can watch.

An attorney with a successful creditors'
rights practice will have dozens of clients
and lots going on. Don't be surprised by a
busy, somewhat cluttered office. Chances
are it won't resemble the office of the attorney you used to incorporate your business, unless the office is big enough that
the real work is done behind the scenes.

Also don't be surprised if a paralegal
working under the attorney's supervision
handles a great deal of your work. What
you need done is unique to you, but com-
monplace to the attorney. By allowing
paralegals to handle the routine aspects of
the job, particularly the preparation of standard forms, you should be able to reduce
your costs and maximize your recovery
from the debtor. (Of course, if you're paying top dollar and feel that the attorney has
handed the matter over to a less-than-expe-
rienced paralegal, it's time to complain.)

⚠️ **Don't hand your whole case
over to a nonlawyer.** Though
some consultants and document
preparers may offer bankruptcy-related
services at cheaper prices than lawyers,

they won't be able to handle every part of your case. Here's what a nonlawyer may do for you:

- type a document per your instructions
- file a document with the court, or
- attend the meeting of creditors.

Here's what a nonlawyer may not do for you:

- advise you regarding your legal rights, including telling you what to put in a document the nonlawyer is preparing for you, or
- attend the hearing on a motion or the trial of a complaint as your representative.

3. How Much Bankruptcy Lawyers Charge

Most bankruptcy lawyers charge flat rates for routine services such as filing a proof of claim or attending a creditors' meeting. However, given that you're using this book, it's probable that you won't be hiring an attorney to handle such matters.

Instead, you'll want help filing motions and complaints, for which the attorney will probably charge you at an hourly rate. This rate varies widely from one region and court to another. Since these rates also vary lawyer by lawyer, don't be afraid to price shop. While hourly fees for bankruptcy attorneys range from $150 to $300 per hour, the at-

torney you're likely to hire will probably charge about $225 per hour, give or take $25 depending on the attorney's experience and your location.

There is no legal limit on what a bankruptcy lawyer can charge you. While the court reviews the fees paid to the attorneys representing the debtor and the trustee, there is no court supervision of the fees paid by creditors. This is because you, not the bankruptcy estate, will be responsible for paying the bill. There are, however, two situations in which your attorney will be allowed to get paid from the bankruptcy estate for services provided to you after the bankruptcy was filed:

- If your attorney provides a service that benefits the bankruptcy estate, such as helping the trustee locate hidden assets, then your attorney can get paid from the estate.
- If your claim is secured and the collateral is worth more than you are owed, you may include your attorney's fee as part of your claim if the debtor is required to pay that fee under the agreement that created your claim.

In both of these situations, the court will review the amount of the fees for reasonableness, just as it does for fees paid to attorneys working for the debtor or the trustee.

4. Get Your Agreement in Writing

Get a written fee agreement whenever you hire a lawyer. You need to know what services are being provided and at what cost. Though this information may seem clear to you after talking to the lawyer, surprises might be in store for both of you when you try to commit your understanding to writing. Written agreements are especially important if disputes arise later.

If the lawyer is charging you a fixed fee for services, the agreement must state the amount of the fee, detail the services being performed and explain what happens if additional services are required.

If the lawyer is charging you at an hourly rate, the agreement must state the amount of the retainer you'll give the lawyer, the hourly rate being charged by the lawyer and any assistants, the billing protocol, and how any unused portion of the retainer fee will be disposed of. (For those of you unfamiliar with retainer fees, they're an initial deposit that the lawyer can tap into for payment as the hours are worked.)

B. Law Libraries

Often, you can answer your own legal questions if you're willing to do some research. The best place to find all the resources you need—plus human help in accessing them—is a law library. The trick is in knowing what types of information you can find there. Sometimes, what you need to know isn't written down. For instance, the law library won't tell you how closely Judge So-And-So scrutinizes a debtor's expenses in a Chapter 7 bankruptcy. You'll probably need to ask a bankruptcy lawyer that type of question.

Library research can help you, however, if your question involves a legal interpretation, such as how the judge is likely to rule if you challenge one of the debtor's exemptions. You can find out how similar questions have been decided by bankruptcy courts and courts of appeal.

To find a local law library, check your county courthouses and public law schools. In addition, bigger public libraries sometimes have legal reference books that may be useful to you. The key to using these resources is knowing what types of questions can be answered through library research.

Here's what you should find in the typical law library:

- books and guides, as well as a reference librarian, that explain the legal research process (Subsection 1)
- books and articles by bankruptcy experts on almost every aspect of bankruptcy law and practice, including many of the local procedures peculiar to each court (Subsection 2)
- federal bankruptcy statutes, which govern the bankruptcy process, and state statutes, which govern secured

transactions and may establish what property the debtor may protect (Subsection 3)

- federal bankruptcy rules, which govern bankruptcy court procedures in more detail (Subsection 4)
- published decisions of bankruptcy court judges and appellate courts that interpret the bankruptcy statutes and rules (Subsection 5), and
- specific instructions for handling routine and nonroutine bankruptcy procedures (Subsection 6).

In addition, the library will probably have Internet access, with which you can pursue the types of research described in Section C, below.

1. Legal Research Resources

To find the answer to a legal question (as opposed to simply looking up a statute or case to which you already have the citation), you may need some guidance in basic legal research techniques. Don't skip this step—it's what law students spend the better part of three years learning how to do. Good resources that may be available in your law library include:

- *Legal Research: How to Find and Understand the Law*, by Stephen Elias and Susan Levinkind (Nolo)
- *How to Find the Law*, by Morris L. Cohen, Robert C. Berring, and Kent C. Olson (West Wadsworth), and

- *Legal Research in a Nutshell*, by Morris L. Cohen and Kent C. Olson (West Wadsworth).

The reference librarian will be able to guide you to these resources, and also to help you embark on your research trail.

2. Materials by Bankruptcy Experts

It's good to get an overview of your subject before trying to find a precise answer to a specific question. The best way to do this is to find a general commentary by a bankruptcy expert. For example, if you want more information about whether your claim deserves to be excepted from discharge, you should start by reading a discussion about your type of claim. Or, if you don't know whether the debtor is entitled to claim certain property as exempt, an overview of your state's exemption laws will put you on the right track.

The most complete source of this type of background information is a multi-volume treatise known as *Collier on Bankruptcy*, by Lawrence P. King, et al. (Matthew Bender). It's available in virtually all law libraries. *Collier* is both incredibly thorough and meticulously up to date. In addition to comments on every aspect of bankruptcy law, *Collier* contains the bankruptcy statutes, rules, and exemption lists for every state.

Collier is organized by bankruptcy statute. This means that the quickest way to find information within it is to know what statute you're looking for. See the list of statutes and their accompanying subject matter at the end of this chapter. If you still don't know the governing statute, start with the *Collier* subject matter index. Be warned, however, that the index can be difficult for the layperson to use, since it contains a lot of bankruptcy jargon.

For general discussions of bankruptcy issues, you can also turn to the following sources:

- *Automatic Stay Litigation in Bankruptcy,* by Mark A. Shaiken (Aspen Publishers). This is a how-to book for presenting and defending motions to lift the automatic stay.
- *Chapter 13 Bankruptcy,* by Keith M. Lundin (Bankruptcy Press). Judge Lundin is one of the country's most respected authorities on consumer bankruptcy in general and Chapter 13 in particular. Although this five-volume treatise is written for lawyers, you shouldn't hesitate to refer to it.
- *Creditors' Rights in Bankruptcy,* by Patrick A. Murphy (Clark Boardman Callahan Publishing). This looseleaf publication is designed to help lawyers determine the appropriate approach for resolving issues faced by creditors in bankruptcy.

3. Federal and State Statutes

After consulting *Collier* or one of the other bankruptcy guides, you may need to look up a federal statute (a law passed by the U.S. Congress). Federal statutes are collected in a multivolume set of books known as the United States Code (U.S.C.) and divided into 50 numbered titles. Title 11 contains the bankruptcy statutes (referred to in this book as the Bankruptcy Code).

Unfortunately, the Bankruptcy Code is too long and involved to simply thumb through in search of information. You'll need to use outside sources to direct you toward a section of the Code that covers your issue or question. Sometimes you'll find out the section from the references (citations) in this book. For instance, in Chapter 9 we consider whether your claim will be excepted from discharge. The statutory references in that chapter are to 11 U.S.C. § 523(a). The citation means Title 11 of the United States Code, Section 523(a).

If you need to research a question and don't know what portion of the statute to start with, there are two ways to find out. First, check the sidebar at the end of this chapter, "Significant Bankruptcy Code Sections," which will tell you what's covered by most of the bankruptcy statutes that might affect your case.

If that list doesn't help, go to *U.S. Code Annotated* published by West. It contains not just the statutes, but clarifying information, including summaries of cases interpreting the law.

To read a bankruptcy statute, find the U.S. Code (preferably the annotated version, or "U.S.C.A.") in your law library. Go to Title 11, turn to the section number and begin reading. After you read the statute in the hardcover portion of the book, turn to the very back of the book. There should be an insert pamphlet (called a pocket part) for the current year. Look to see whether the statute is in the pocket part. If it is, that's probably because this section of the statute has been amended, or additional court cases have come out interpreting the statute, since the hardcover volume was published. (For online access to statutes, see Section C, below.)

When you first read a bankruptcy statute you'll probably be totally confused, if not close to tears. Relax. No one understands these statutes as they're written. You can go either to *Colliers* and read its interpretation or directly to court opinions that have interpreted the statute. You can locate these opinions in the case summaries that directly follow the statute.

You may also need to look at the laws for your particular state to determine your rights in bankruptcy. Although the Bankruptcy Code is federal, and most of your research will involve federal law, the Bankruptcy Code relies on state law to determine secured property rights, such as how a lien is perfected. The Bankruptcy Code also allows states to opt out of the federal exemption scheme. If your state has opted out, then you'll need to reference state law to determine what property the debtor is allowed to protect. Ask the reference librarian for help, or see the legal research resources described in Subsection 1, above. (For online access to state statutes, see Section C, below.)

4. Procedural Bankruptcy Rules

If you have a question about court procedures—for example, the deadline for filing your proof of claim—you'll need to look at the federal bankruptcy rules. They govern the procedural aspects of bankruptcy cases, such as time limits and the process of filing papers. The rules cover other issues, too, which may seem like questions of substance, not procedure, such as when debtors can pay the filing fee in installments. If you can't find your answer in the Bankruptcy Code, it may be in the rules.

You can find a copy of the bankruptcy rules in *Collier*, discussed in Subsection 2, above. They're also available online, at a Cornell website, www.law.cornell.edu/topics/bankruptcy.html, and at the Government Printing Office's website at www.access.gpo.gov/uscode/title11a/11a_1_.html.

5. Published Court Decisions

To understand bankruptcy statutes and rules, it's usually necessary to read a case (court decision) or two that have dealt with how the particular statute applies to situations like yours. Published court decisions are of two types: those decided by a single bankruptcy judge and those decided by a court of appeal.

A bankruptcy judge who resolves a particular issue in a case may write a statement explaining the decision. If this statement, usually called a "memorandum opinion" or "findings of fact and conclusions of law," appears to be of interest to those who practice bankruptcy law, it will be published. If you want to persuade your bankruptcy judge on a particular point, it's to your advantage to find a supportive case that has been decided by another bankruptcy judge considering similar facts.

Several publications include bankruptcy cases. The one most commonly found in law libraries is the *Bankruptcy Reporter* (published by West), abbreviated as *B.R.* You can find summaries of cases published in the *Bankruptcy Reporter* directly following each bankruptcy statute in the *U.S. Code Annotated*. (You won't find much free online access to bankruptcy court decisions, as described in Section C, below.)

If one of the parties to a bankruptcy dispute appeals the bankruptcy judge's ruling, the appeal will be decided by a federal district court or a bankruptcy appellate panel. These are also published in the *Bankruptcy Reporter*. If a further appeal is taken, the matter will be heard by a federal circuit court. This court's decisions are published in the *Federal Reporter*, third series, (published by West), which is abbreviated F.3d.

Once you find a relevant case or two, you're hot on your research trail. Your next step is to find similar cases by using cross-reference tools known as digests and *Shepard's*. These tools are also useful for making sure your case is up to date—that is, hasn't been overturned by a higher court. These are explained in *Legal Research: How to Find and Understand the Law*, by Stephen Elias and Susan Levinkind (Nolo) and in other legal research texts.

6. Specific Instructions for Bankruptcy Procedures

Your best source for how-to help on basic bankruptcy procedures in your court is your court's website. You can locate the websites for all bankruptcy courts by going to www.uscourts.gov and following the links. Once there, look under the local rules for instructions on how to do things like file a motion for stay relief.

C. Online Legal Resources

You can accomplish a good deal of legal research through the Internet. However, you can't do it all for free, especially in the bankruptcy area. Although state and federal statutes are available on the Web at no cost, decisions by bankruptcy judges are usually not available in the free databases—rather, you have to subscribe to services like Westlaw or Lexis to access them.

Still, there are a number of useful free sites, such as:

- www.nolo.com. The *Statutes & Cases* area of Nolo's *Plain-English Law Center* links to state cases and statutes, U.S. Supreme Court cases and the federal code (including the Bankruptcy Code at Title 11). This area also explains how to do basic legal research. Nolo's free *Legal Encyclopedia* (also on the website) contains articles about bankruptcy. Finally, check out Nolo's *Legal Updates* section for recent changes in bankruptcy laws that affect this and related products.

- www.findlaw.com. Findlaw links to each state's online legal material, such as statutes and cases, as well as to federal statutes and cases. It also links to many online bankruptcy resources, including government documents, journals, and newsletters. However, as we've said, decisions

published by the bankruptcy courts themselves are not available through this otherwise excellent free database of legal materials.

- www.uscourts.gov/bankform. You can download all bankruptcy court forms from this site.

- www.abiworld.org. This is the home page of the American Bankruptcy Institute. It includes daily news updates, information, and commentary on bankruptcy legislation.

- www.bernsteinlaw.com/publications/ index_pubs.html. The Bernstein law firm provides an online version of their handy book, *Bernstein's Dictionary of Bankruptcy Terminology.* You'll also find several articles of interest to bankruptcy creditors, on topics such as defending against preferential transfer complaints and handling tenant bankruptcies.

- www.high-tech-law.com/lawfind/. This site, by the law firm of Swiggart and Agin, provides an extensive list of online bankruptcy-related materials, such as frequently asked questions, important bankruptcy cases, the U.S. Bankruptcy Code, federal bankruptcy rules, background on bankruptcy lawyers, and links to other online bankruptcy sites.

Summary of Major Bankruptcy Code and Rule Sections

For quick reference, the following list summarizes the contents of the most important sections of the federal Bankruptcy Code (at 11 U.S.C.) and the Bankruptcy Rules.

Significant Bankruptcy Codes

§ 101	Definitions used in the Code
§ 109	Who may file for which type of bankruptcy
§ 303	Involuntary bankruptcy
§ 341	Meeting of creditors
§ 342	Getting notice of the meeting of creditors
§ 343	Examination of the debtor at the meeting of creditors
§ 348	Converting from one type of bankruptcy to another
§ 349	Dismissing a case
§ 350	Closing and reopening a case
§ 361	Receiving adequate protection on your secured claim
§ 362	The automatic stay
§ 363	The debtor's ability to use, lease, and sell property
§ 365	Executory contracts and unexpired leases
§ 501	Filing your proof of claim
§ 502	Establishing the amount of your claim
§ 506	Establishing the amount of your secured claim
§ 507	Description of claims with priority
§ 522	Exemptions
§ 523	Description of nondischargeable claims
§ 524	Rules governing reaffirmation of debts
§ 525	Rules against discrimination
§ 541	Property of the estate (general)
§ 545	Ability to avoid statutory liens
§ 546	Restrictions on avoiding powers
§ 547	Ability to avoid preferential transfers
§ 548	Ability to avoid fraudulent transfers
§ 549	Ability to avoid postpetition transfers
§ 550	Liability of person who receives transfer
§ 552	Postpetition preservation of security interest

Summary of Major Bankruptcy Code and Rule Sections, continued

§ 553	Setoffs
§ 706	Conversions from Chapter 7
§ 707	Dismissal of Chapter 7 case
§ 722	Redemption of collateral
§ 727	Chapter 7 discharge
§ 1102	Creditors' committees in Chapter 11
§ 1103	Powers and duties of creditors' committees
§ 1111	Filing proofs of claim in Chapter 11
§ 1112	Conversion or dismissal of Chapter 11 case
§ 1114	Payment of insurance benefits to retired employees
§ 1121	Who may file a plan
§ 1122	Classification of claims in Chapter 11 plans
§ 1123	Contents of Chapter 11 plans
§ 1126	Voting on Chapter 11 plans
§ 1129	Confirmation of Chapter 11 plan
§ 1141	Effect of confirmation of Chapter 11 plan
§ 1201	Codebtor stay in Chapter 12 cases
§ 1205	Adequate protection of your secured claim in Chapter 12 cases
§ 1207	Property of the Chapter 12 estate
§ 1208	Conversion or dismissal of Chapter 12 case
§ 1222	Contents of Chapter 12 plan
§ 1225	Confirmation of Chapter 12 plan
§ 1228	Chapter 12 discharge
§ 1230	Revocation of Chapter 12 discharge
§ 1301	Codebtor stay in Chapter 13 cases
§ 1305	Treatment of postpetition claims
§ 1306	Property of the Chapter 13 estate
§ 1307	Conversion or dismissal of Chapter 13 case
§ 1322	Contents of Chapter 13 plan
§ 1325	Confirmation of Chapter 13 plan
§ 1328	Chapter 13 discharge
§ 1330	Revocation of Chapter 13 discharge

Summary of Major Bankruptcy Code and Rule Sections, continued

Significant Bankruptcy Rules

§ 1003	Starting an involuntary case
§ 1010	Service of involuntary petition
§ 1017	Conversion or dismissal of case (general)
§ 1019	Conversion of reorganization case to Chapter 7
§ 2002	Notice to creditors regarding bankruptcy filing
§ 2003	Meeting of creditors
§ 2004	Examination of debtor by creditor
§ 2005	Order to compel debtor's cooperation with examination
§ 2007.1	Appointment of trustee or examiner in Chapter 11 case
§ 3001	Rules for preparing proof of claim
§ 3002	Rules for filing proof of claim (general)
§ 3003	Rules for filing proof of claim in Chapter 11 case
§ 3006	Withdrawal of proof of claim
§ 3007	Objection to proof of claim
§ 3010	Small payments to creditors
§ 3013	Classification of claims
§ 3015	Objection to confirmation in Chapter 12 and 13 cases
§ 4001	Relief from the automatic stay
§ 4003	Objections to exemption claims
§ 4004	Procedure for objecting to discharge of debtor
§ 4007	Procedure for objecting to discharge of claim
§ 6004	Procedure for objecting to debtor's use of property
§ 6006	Assumption, rejection, or assignment of executory contracts
§ 7001, et seq.	Rules governing adversary proceedings
§ 8001, et seq.	Rules governing appellate proceedings
§ 9004	Style for presenting documents to court
§ 9006	How to compute time limits
§ 9010	Powers of attorneys
§ 9011	Truthfulness of representations made to court
§ 9013	Form and notice of motions
§ 9014	Form and notice of contested proceedings
§ 9017	Rules of evidence

Appendix

This Appendix contains reprints of the federal schedule and statement forms that the debtor must fill out to accompany the bankruptcy petition. How to read and interpret the contents of these forms is discussed in Chapter 5 of this book. The forms are also available online, at www.uscourts.gov/bankform/index.html.

FORMS INCLUDED:

Schedule A: Real Property

Schedule B: Personal Property

Schedule C: Property Claimed as Exempt

Schedule D: Creditors Holding Secured Claims

Schedule E: Creditors Holding Unsecured Priority Claims

Schedule F: Creditors Holding Unsecured Nonpriority Claims

Schedule G: Executory Contracts and Unexpired Leases

Schedule H: Codebtors

Schedule I: Current Income of Individual Debtor(s)

Schedule J: Current Expenditures of Individual Debtor(s)

Statement of Financial Affairs

Statement of Intention

FORM B6A
(6/90)

In re _____,   Case No. _____

　　　　　　Debtor   (If known)

SCHEDULE A - REAL PROPERTY

　　　Except as directed below, list all real property in which the debtor has any legal, equitable, or future interest, including all property owned as a co-tenant , community property, or in which the debtor has a life estate. Include any property in which the debtor holds rights and powers exercisable for the debtor's own benefit. If the debtor is married, state whether husband, wife, or both own the property by placing an "H," "W," "J," or "C" in the column labeled "Husband, Wife, Joint, or Community." If the debtor holds no interest in real property, write "None" under "Description and Location of Property."

　　　Do not include interests in executory contracts and unexpired leases on this schedule. List them in Schedule G - Executory Contracts and Unexpired Leases.

　　　If an entity claims to have a lien or hold a secured interest in any property, state the amount of the secured claim. See Schedule D. If no entity claims to hold a secured interest in the property, write "None" in the column labeled "Amount of Secured Claim."

　　　If the debtor is an individual or if a joint petition is filed, state the amount of any exemption claimed in the property only in Schedule C - Property Claimed as Exempt.

DESCRIPTION AND LOCATION OF PROPERTY	NATURE OF DEBTOR'S INTEREST IN PROPERTY	HUSBAND, WIFE, JOINT, OR COMMUNITY	CURRENT MARKET VALUE OF DEBTOR'S INTEREST IN PROPERTY, WITHOUT DEDUCTING ANY SECURED CLAIM OR EXEMPTION	AMOUNT OF SECURED CLAIM

Total▶

(Report also on Summary of Schedules.)

FORM B6B
(10/89)

In re _____ ,   Case No. _____
          Debtor   **(If known)**

SCHEDULE B - PERSONAL PROPERTY

Except as directed below, list all personal property of the debtor of whatever kind. If the debtor has no property in one or more of the categories, place an "x" in the appropriate position in the column labeled "None." If additional space is needed in any category, attach a separate sheet properly identified with the case name, case number, and the number of the category. If the debtor is married, state whether husband, wife, or both own the property by placing an "H," "W," "J," or "C" in the column labeled "Husband, Wife, Joint, or Community." If the debtor is an individual or a joint petition is filed, state the amount of any exemptions claimed only in Schedule C - Property Claimed as Exempt.

Do not list interests in executory contracts and unexpired leases on this schedule. List them in Schedule G - Executory Contracts and Unexpired Leases.

If the property is being held for the debtor by someone else, state that person's name and address under "Description and Location of Property."

TYPE OF PROPERTY	N O N E	DESCRIPTION AND LOCATION OF PROPERTY	HUSBAND, WIFE, JOINT, OR COMMUNITY	CURRENT MARKET VALUE OF DEBTOR'S INTEREST IN PROPERTY, WITH-OUT DEDUCTING ANY SECURED CLAIM OR EXEMPTION
1. Cash on hand.				
2. Checking, savings or other financial accounts, certificates of deposit, or shares in banks, savings and loan, thrift, building and loan, and homestead associations, or credit unions, brokerage houses, or cooperatives.				
3. Security deposits with public utilities, telephone companies, landlords, and others.				
4. Household goods and furnishings, including audio, video, and computer equipment.				
5. Books; pictures and other art objects; antiques; stamp, coin, record, tape, compact disc, and other collections or collectibles.				
6. Wearing apparel.				
7. Furs and jewelry.				
8. Firearms and sports, photographic, and other hobby equipment.				
9. Interests in insurance policies. Name insurance company of each policy and itemize surrender or refund value of each.				
10. Annuities. Itemize and name each issuer.				

FORM B6C
(6/90)

In re _____,   Case No. _____

  Debtor   **(If known)**

SCHEDULE C - PROPERTY CLAIMED AS EXEMPT

Debtor elects the exemptions to which debtor is entitled under:

(Check one box)

☐ 11 U.S.C. § 522(b)(1): Exemptions provided in 11 U.S.C. § 522(d). **Note: These exemptions are available only in certain states.**

☐ 11 U.S.C. § 522(b)(2): Exemptions available under applicable nonbankruptcy federal laws, state or local law where the debtor's domicile has been located for the 180 days immediately preceding the filing of the petition, or for a longer portion of the 180-day period than in any other place, and the debtor's interest as a tenant by the entirety or joint tenant to the extent the interest is exempt from process under applicable nonbankruptcy law.

DESCRIPTION OF PROPERTY	SPECIFY LAW PROVIDING EACH EXEMPTION	VALUE OF CLAIMED EXEMPTION	CURRENT MARKET VALUE OF PROPERTY WITHOUT DEDUCTING EXEMPTION

FORM B6D
(6/90)

In re _____,   Case No. _____

Debtor   (If known)

SCHEDULE D - CREDITORS HOLDING SECURED CLAIMS

State the name, mailing address, including zip code, and account number, if any, of all entities holding claims secured by property of the debtor as of the date of filing of the petition. List creditors holding all types of secured interests such as judgment liens, garnishments, statutory liens, mortgages, deeds of trust, and other security interests. List creditors in alphabetical order to the extent practicable. If all secured creditors will not fit on this page, use the continuation sheet provided.

If any entity other than a spouse in a joint case may be jointly liable on a claim, place an "X" in the column labeled "Codebtor," include the entity on the appropriate schedule of creditors, and complete Schedule H - Codebtors. If a joint petition is filed, state whether husband, wife, both of them, or the marital community may be liable on each claim by placing an "H," "W," "J," or "C" in the column labeled "Husband, Wife, Joint, or Community."

If the claim is contingent, place an "X" in the column labeled "Contingent." If the claim is unliquidated, place an "X" in the column labeled "Unliquidated." If the claim is disputed, place an "X" in the column labeled "Disputed." (You may need to place an "X" in more than one of these three columns.)

Report the total of all claims listed on this schedule in the box labeled "Total" on the last sheet of the completed schedule. Report this total also on the Summary of Schedules.

☐ Check this box if debtor has no creditors holding secured claims to report on this Schedule D.

CREDITOR'S NAME AND MAILING ADDRESS INCLUDING ZIP CODE	CODEBTOR	HUSBAND, WIFE, JOINT, OR COMMUNITY	DATE CLAIM WAS INCURRED, NATURE OF LIEN, AND DESCRIPTION AND MARKET VALUE OF PROPERTY SUBJECT TO LIEN	CONTINGENT	UNLIQUIDATED	DISPUTED	AMOUNT OF CLAIM WITHOUT DEDUCTING VALUE OF COLLATERAL	UNSECURED PORTION, IF ANY
ACCOUNT NO.								
			VALUE $					
ACCOUNT NO.								
			VALUE $					
ACCOUNT NO.								
			VALUE $					
ACCOUNT NO.								
			VALUE $					

_____ continuation sheets attached

Subtotal ➤ (Total of this page) $ _____

Total ➤ (Use only on last page) $ _____

(Report total also on Summary of Schedules)

Form B6F
(Rev.4/01)

In re _____ ,   Case No._____
                          Debtor   (if known)

☐ **Alimony, Maintenance, or Support**

   Claims of a spouse, former spouse, or child of the debtor for alimony, maintenance, or support, to the extent provided in 11 U.S.C. § 507(a)(7).

☐ **Taxes and Certain Other Debts Owed to Governmental Units**

   Taxes, customs duties, and penalties owing to federal, state, and local governmental units as set forth in 11 U.S.C. § 507(a)(8).

☐ **Commitments to Maintain the Capital of an Insured Depository Institution**

   Claims based on commitments to the FDIC, RTC, Director of the Office of Thrift Supervision, Comptroller of the Currency, or Board of Governors of the Federal Reserve System, or their predecessors or successors, to maintain the capital of an insured depository institution. 11 U.S.C. § 507 (a)(9).

* Amounts are subject to adjustment on April 1, 2004, and every three years thereafter with respect to cases commenced on or after the date of adjustment.

_____ continuation sheets attached

Form B6E
(Rev. 4/01)

In re _____,   Case No. _____
                     Debtor   (if known)

SCHEDULE E - CREDITORS HOLDING UNSECURED PRIORITY CLAIMS

A complete list of claims entitled to priority, listed separately by type of priority, is to be set forth on the sheets provided. Only holders of unsecured claims entitled to priority should be listed in this schedule. In the boxes provided on the attached sheets, state the name and mailing address, including zip code, and account number, if any, of all entities holding priority claims against the debtor or the property of the debtor, as of the date of the filing of the petition.

If any entity other than a spouse in a joint case may be jointly liable on a claim, place an "X" in the column labeled "Codebtor," include the entity on the appropriate schedule of creditors, and complete Schedule H-Codebtors. If a joint petition is filed, state whether husband, wife, both of them or the marital community may be liable on each claim by placing an "H,""W,""J," or "C" in the column labeled "Husband, Wife, Joint, or Community."

If the claim is contingent, place an "X" in the column labeled "Contingent." If the claim is unliquidated, place an "X" in the column labeled "Unliquidated." If the claim is disputed, place an "X" in the column labeled "Disputed." (You may need to place an "X" in more than one of these three columns.)

Report the total of claims listed on each sheet in the box labeled "Subtotal" on each sheet. Report the total of all claims listed on this Schedule E in the box labeled "Total" on the last sheet of the completed schedule. Repeat this total also on the Summary of Schedules.

☐ Check this box if debtor has no creditors holding unsecured priority claims to report on this Schedule E.

TYPES OF PRIORITY CLAIMS (Check the appropriate box(es) below if claims in that category are listed on the attached sheets)

☐ **Extensions of credit in an involuntary case**

Claims arising in the ordinary course of the debtor's business or financial affairs after the commencement of the case but before the earlier of the appointment of a trustee or the order for relief. 11 U.S.C. § 507(a)(2).

☐ **Wages, salaries, and commissions**

Wages, salaries, and commissions, including vacation, severance, and sick leave pay owing to employees and commissions owing to qualifying independent sales representatives up to $4,650* per person earned within 90 days immediately preceding the filing of the original petition, or the cessation of business, whichever occurred first, to the extent provided in 11 U.S.C. § 507(a)(3).

☐ **Contributions to employee benefit plans**

Money owed to employee benefit plans for services rendered within 180 days immediately preceding the filing of the original petition, or the cessation of business, whichever occurred first, to the extent provided in 11 U.S.C. § 507(a)(4).

☐ **Certain farmers and fishermen**

Claims of certain farmers and fishermen, up to $4,650* per farmer or fisherman, against the debtor, as provided in 11 U.S.C. § 507(a)(5).

☐ **Deposits by individuals**

Claims of individuals up to $2,100* for deposits for the purchase, lease, or rental of property or services for personal, family, or household use, that were not delivered or provided. 11 U.S.C. § 507(a)(6).

FORM B6F (Official Form 6F) (9/97)

In re _____,   Case No. _____
          Debtor   (If known)

SCHEDULE F- CREDITORS HOLDING UNSECURED NONPRIORITY CLAIMS

State the name, mailing address, including zip code, and account number, if any, of all entities holding unsecured claims without priority against the debtor or the property of the debtor, as of the date of filing of the petition. Do not include claims listed in Schedules D and E. If all creditors will not fit on this page, use the continuation sheet provided.

If any entity other than a spouse in a joint case may be jointly liable on a claim, place an "X" in the column labeled "Codebtor," include the entity on the appropriate schedule of creditors, and complete Schedule H - Codebtors. If a joint petition is filed, state whether husband, wife, both of them, or the marital community maybe liable on each claim by placing an "H," "W," "J," or "C" in the column labeled "Husband, Wife, Joint, or Community."

If the claim is contingent, place an "X" in the column labeled "Contingent." If the claim is unliquidated, place an "X" in the column labeled "Unliquidated." If the claim is disputed, place an "X" in the column labeled "Disputed." (You may need to place an "X" in more than one of these three columns.)

Report total of all claims listed on this schedule in the box labeled "Total" on the last sheet of the completed schedule. Report this total also on the Summary of Schedules.

☐ Check this box if debtor has no creditors holding unsecured claims to report on this Schedule F.

CREDITOR'S NAME AND MAILING ADDRESS INCLUDING ZIP CODE	CODEBTOR	HUSBAND, WIFE, JOINT, OR COMMUNITY	DATE CLAIM WAS INCURRED AND CONSIDERATION FOR CLAIM. IF CLAIM IS SUBJECT TO SETOFF, SO STATE.	CONTINGENT	UNLIQUIDATED	DISPUTED	AMOUNT OF CLAIM
ACCOUNT NO.							
ACCOUNT NO.							
ACCOUNT NO.							
ACCOUNT NO.							

_____ continuation sheets attached

Subtotal ➤ | $

Total ➤ | $

(Report also on Summary of Schedules)

B6G
(10/89)

In re _____ ,   Case No._____
　　　　　　　Debtor　　　　　　　　　　　　　　　　　　　　　　　(if known)

SCHEDULE G - EXECUTORY CONTRACTS AND UNEXPIRED LEASES

　　Describe all executory contracts of any nature and all unexpired leases of real or personal property. Include any timeshare interests.

　　State nature of debtor's interest in contract, i.e., "Purchaser," "Agent," etc. State whether debtor is the lessor or lessee of a lease.

　　Provide the names and complete mailing addresses of all other parties to each lease or contract described.

NOTE: A party listed on this schedule will not receive notice of the filing of this case unless the party is also scheduled in the appropriate schedule of creditors.

☐ Check this box if debtor has no executory contracts or unexpired leases.

NAME AND MAILING ADDRESS, INCLUDING ZIP CODE, OF OTHER PARTIES TO LEASE OR CONTRACT.	DESCRIPTION OF CONTRACT OR LEASE AND NATURE OF DEBTOR'S INTEREST. STATE WHETHER LEASE IS FOR NONRESIDENTIAL REAL PROPERTY. STATE CONTRACT NUMBER OF ANY GOVERNMENT CONTRACT.

B6H
(6/90)

In re _____ ,   Case No. _____
            Debtor   **(if known)**

SCHEDULE H - CODEBTORS

Provide the information requested concerning any person or entity, other than a spouse in a joint case, that is also liable on any debts listed by debtor in the schedules of creditors. Include all guarantors and co-signers. In community property states, a married debtor not filing a joint case should report the name and address of the nondebtor spouse on this schedule. Include all names used by the nondebtor spouse during the six years immediately preceding the commencement of this case.

☐ Check this box if debtor has no codebtors.

NAME AND ADDRESS OF CODEBTOR	NAME AND ADDRESS OF CREDITOR

FORM B6I
(6/90)

In re _____ ,   Case No._____
          Debtor   (if known)

SCHEDULE I - CURRENT INCOME OF INDIVIDUAL DEBTOR(S)

The column labeled "Spouse" must be completed in all cases filed by joint debtors and by a married debtor in a chapter 12 or 13 case whether or not a joint petition is filed, unless the spouses are separated and a joint petition is not filed.

Debtor's Marital Status:	DEPENDENTS OF DEBTOR AND SPOUSE		
	NAMES	AGE	RELATIONSHIP

Employment:	DEBTOR	SPOUSE
Occupation		
Name of Employer		
How long employed		
Address of Employer		

Income: (Estimate of average monthly income)   DEBTOR   SPOUSE
Current monthly gross wages, salary, and commissions
  (pro rate if not paid monthly.) $ _____ $ _____
Estimated monthly overtime $ _____ $ _____

SUBTOTAL $ _____ $ _____

  LESS PAYROLL DEDUCTIONS
  a. Payroll taxes and social security $ _____ $ _____
  b. Insurance $ _____ $ _____
  c. Union dues $ _____ $ _____
  d. Other (Specify: _____) $ _____ $ _____

  SUBTOTAL OF PAYROLL DEDUCTIONS $ _____ $ _____

TOTAL NET MONTHLY TAKE HOME PAY $ _____ $ _____

Regular income from operation of business or profession or farm $ _____ $ _____
(attach detailed statement)
Income from real property $ _____ $ _____
Interest and dividends $ _____ $ _____
Alimony, maintenance or support payments payable to the debtor for the
debtor's use or that of dependents listed above. $ _____ $ _____
Social security or other government assistance
(Specify) _____ $ _____ $ _____
Pension or retirement income $ _____ $ _____
Other monthly income $ _____ $ _____
(Specify) _____ $ _____ $ _____
                                                         $ _____ $ _____

TOTAL MONTHLY INCOME $ _____ $ _____

TOTAL COMBINED MONTHLY INCOME $_____   (Report also on Summary of Schedules)

Describe any increase or decrease of more than 10% in any of the above categories anticipated to occur within the year following the filing of this document:

FORM B6J
(6/90)

In re _____ ,   Case No._____

               Debtor   (if known)

SCHEDULE J - CURRENT EXPENDITURES OF INDIVIDUAL DEBTOR(S)

Complete this schedule by estimating the average monthly expenses of the debtor and the debtor's family. Pro rate any payments made bi-weekly, quarterly, semi-annually, or annually to show monthly rate.

— Check this box if a joint petition is filed and debtor's spouse maintains a separate household. Complete a separate schedule of
— expenditures labeled "Spouse."

Rent or home mortgage payment (include lot rented for mobile home)	$ _____
Are real estate taxes included? Yes _____ No _____	
Is property insurance included? Yes _____ No _____	
Utilities Electricity and heating fuel	$ _____
Water and sewer	$ _____
Telephone	$ _____
Other _____	$ _____
Home maintenance (repairs and upkeep)	$ _____
Food	$ _____
Clothing	$ _____
Laundry and dry cleaning	$ _____
Medical and dental expenses	$ _____
Transportation (not including car payments)	$ _____
Recreation, clubs and entertainment, newspapers, magazines, etc.	$ _____
Charitable contributions	$ _____
Insurance (not deducted from wages or included in home mortgage payments)	
Homeowner's or renter's	$ _____
Life	$ _____
Health	$ _____
Auto	$ _____
Other _____	$ _____
Taxes (not deducted from wages or included in home mortgage payments) (Specify) _____	$ _____
Installment payments: (In chapter 12 and 13 cases, do not list payments to be included in the plan)	
Auto	$ _____
Other _____	$ _____
Other _____	$ _____
Alimony, maintenance, and support paid to others	$ _____
Payments for support of additional dependents not living at your home	$ _____
Regular expenses from operation of business, profession, or farm (attach detailed statement)	$ _____
Other _____	$ _____
TOTAL MONTHLY EXPENSES (Report also on Summary of Schedules)	$ _____

[FOR CHAPTER 12 AND 13 DEBTORS ONLY]
Provide the information requested below, including whether plan payments are to be made bi-weekly, monthly, annually, or at some other regular interval.

A. Total projected monthly income	$ _____
B. Total projected monthly expenses	$ _____
C. Excess income (A minus B)	$ _____
D. Total amount to be paid into plan each _____	$ _____
(interval)	

Form 7
(9/00)

FORM 7. STATEMENT OF FINANCIAL AFFAIRS

UNITED STATES BANKRUPTCY COURT

_____ DISTRICT OF _____

In re: _____ ,   Case No. _____
         (Name)   (if known)
                        Debtor

STATEMENT OF FINANCIAL AFFAIRS

This statement is to be completed by every debtor. Spouses filing a joint petition may file a single statement on which the information for both spouses is combined. If the case is filed under chapter 12 or chapter 13, a married debtor must furnish information for both spouses whether or not a joint petition is filed, unless the spouses are separated and a joint petition is not filed. An individual debtor engaged in business as a sole proprietor, partner, family farmer, or self-employed professional, should provide the information requested on this statement concerning all such activities as well as the individual's personal affairs.

Questions 1 - 18 are to be completed by all debtors. Debtors that are or have been in business, as defined below, also must complete Questions 19 - 25. **If the answer to an applicable question is "None," mark the box labeled "None."** If additional space is needed for the answer to any question, use and attach a separate sheet properly identified with the case name, case number (if known), and the number of the question.

DEFINITIONS

"In business." A debtor is "in business" for the purpose of this form if the debtor is a corporation or partnership. An individual debtor is "in business" for the purpose of this form if the debtor is or has been, within the six years immediately preceding the filing of this bankruptcy case, any of the following: an officer, director, managing executive, or owner of 5 percent or more of the voting or equity securities of a corporation; a partner, other than a limited partner, of a partnership; a sole proprietor or self-employed.

"Insider." The term "insider" includes but is not limited to: relatives of the debtor; general partners of the debtor and their relatives; corporations of which the debtor is an officer, director, or person in control; officers, directors, and any owner of 5 percent or more of the voting or equity securities of a corporate debtor and their relatives; affiliates of the debtor and insiders of such affiliates; any managing agent of the debtor. 11 U.S.C. § 101.

_____

1. Income from employment or operation of business

None
☐

State the gross amount of income the debtor has received from employment, trade, or profession, or from operation of the debtor's business from the beginning of this calendar year to the date this case was commenced. State also the gross amounts received during the **two years** immediately preceding this calendar year. (A debtor that maintains, or has maintained, financial records on the basis of a fiscal rather than a calendar year may report fiscal year income. Identify the beginning and ending dates of the debtor's fiscal year.) If a joint petition is filed, state income for each spouse separately. (Married debtors filing under chapter 12 or chapter 13 must state income of both spouses whether or not a joint petition is filed, unless the spouses are separated and a joint petition is not filed.)

          AMOUNT   SOURCE (if more than one)

2

2. Income other than from employment or operation of business

None
☐

State the amount of income received by the debtor other than from employment, trade, profession, or operation of the debtor's business during the **two years** immediately preceding the commencement of this case. Give particulars. If a joint petition is filed, state income for each spouse separately. (Married debtors filing under chapter 12 or chapter 13 must state income for each spouse whether or not a joint petition is filed, unless the spouses are separated and a joint petition is not filed.)

AMOUNT   SOURCE

---

3. Payments to creditors

None
☐

a. List all payments on loans, installment purchases of goods or services, and other debts, aggregating more than $600 to any creditor, made within **90 days** immediately preceding the commencement of this case. (Married debtors filing under chapter 12 or chapter 13 must include payments by either or both spouses whether or not a joint petition is filed, unless the spouses are separated and a joint petition is not filed.)

NAME AND ADDRESS OF CREDITOR	DATES OF PAYMENTS	AMOUNT PAID	AMOUNT STILL OWING

None
☐

b. List all payments made within **one year** immediately preceding the commencement of this case to or for the benefit of creditors who are or were insiders. (Married debtors filing under chapter 12 or chapter 13 must include payments by either or both spouses whether or not a joint petition is filed, unless the spouses are separated and a joint petition is not filed.)

NAME AND ADDRESS OF CREDITOR AND RELATIONSHIP TO DEBTOR	DATE OF PAYMENT	AMOUNT PAID	AMOUNT STILL OWING

---

4. Suits and administrative proceedings, executions, garnishments and attachments

None
☐

a. List all suits and administrative proceedings to which the debtor is or was a party within **one year** immediately preceding the filing of this bankruptcy case. (Married debtors filing under chapter 12 or chapter 13 must include information concerning either or both spouses whether or not a joint petition is filed, unless the spouses are separated and a joint petition is not filed.)

CAPTION OF SUIT AND CASE NUMBER	NATURE OF PROCEEDING	COURT OR AGENCY AND LOCATION	STATUS OR DISPOSITION

3

None ☐   b.   Describe all property that has been attached, garnished or seized under any legal or equitable process within **one year** immediately preceding the commencement of this case. (Married debtors filing under chapter 12 or chapter 13 must include information concerning property of either or both spouses whether or not a joint petition is filed, unless the spouses are separated and a joint petition is not filed.)

NAME AND ADDRESS OF PERSON FOR WHOSE BENEFIT PROPERTY WAS SEIZED	DATE OF SEIZURE	DESCRIPTION AND VALUE OF PROPERTY

5. Repossessions, foreclosures and returns

None ☐   List all property that has been repossessed by a creditor, sold at a foreclosure sale, transferred through a deed in lieu of foreclosure or returned to the seller, within **one year** immediately preceding the commencement of this case. (Married debtors filing under chapter 12 or chapter 13 must include information concerning property of either or both spouses whether or not a joint petition is filed, unless the spouses are separated and a joint petition is not filed.)

NAME AND ADDRESS OF CREDITOR OR SELLER	DATE OF REPOSSESSION, FORECLOSURE SALE, TRANSFER OR RETURN	DESCRIPTION AND VALUE OF PROPERTY

6. Assignments and receiverships

None ☐   a.   Describe any assignment of property for the benefit of creditors made within **120 days** immediately preceding the commencement of this case. (Married debtors filing under chapter 12 or chapter 13 must include any assignment by either or both spouses whether or not a joint petition is filed, unless the spouses are separated and a joint petition is not filed.)

NAME AND ADDRESS OF ASSIGNEE	DATE OF ASSIGNMENT	TERMS OF ASSIGNMENT OR SETTLEMENT

None ☐   b.   List all property which has been in the hands of a custodian, receiver, or court-appointed official within **one year** immediately preceding the commencement of this case. (Married debtors filing under chapter 12 or chapter 13 must include information concerning property of either or both spouses whether or not a joint petition is filed, unless the spouses are separated and a joint petition is not filed.)

NAME AND ADDRESS OF CUSTODIAN	NAME AND LOCATION OF COURT CASE TITLE & NUMBER	DATE OF ORDER	DESCRIPTION AND VALUE OF PROPERTY

7. Gifts   4

None
☐

List all gifts or charitable contributions made within **one year** immediately preceding the commencement of this case except ordinary and usual gifts to family members aggregating less than $200 in value per individual family member and charitable contributions aggregating less than $100 per recipient. (Married debtors filing under chapter 12 or chapter 13 must include gifts or contributions by either or both spouses whether or not a joint petition is filed, unless the spouses are separated and a joint petition is not filed.)

NAME AND ADDRESS OF PERSON OR ORGANIZATION	RELATIONSHIP TO DEBTOR, IF ANY	DATE OF GIFT	DESCRIPTION AND VALUE OF GIFT

8. Losses

None
☐

List all losses from fire, theft, other casualty or gambling within **one year** immediately preceding the commencement of this case **or since the commencement of this case.** (Married debtors filing under chapter 12 or chapter 13 must include losses by either or both spouses whether or not a joint petition is filed, unless the spouses are separated and a joint petition is not filed.)

DESCRIPTION AND VALUE OF PROPERTY	DESCRIPTION OF CIRCUMSTANCES AND, IF LOSS WAS COVERED IN WHOLE OR IN PART BY INSURANCE, GIVE PARTICULARS	DATE OF LOSS

9. Payments related to debt counseling or bankruptcy

None
☐

List all payments made or property transferred by or on behalf of the debtor to any persons, including attorneys, for consultation concerning debt consolidation, relief under the bankruptcy law or preparation of a petition in bankruptcy within **one year** immediately preceding the commencement of this case.

NAME AND ADDRESS OF PAYEE	DATE OF PAYMENT, NAME OF PAYOR IF OTHER THAN DEBTOR	AMOUNT OF MONEY OR DESCRIPTION AND VALUE OF PROPERTY

10. Other transfers

None
☐

List all other property, other than property transferred in the ordinary course of the business or financial affairs of the debtor, transferred either absolutely or as security within **one year** immediately preceding the commencement of this case. (Married debtors filing under chapter 12 or chapter 13 must include transfers by either or both spouses whether or not a joint petition is filed, unless the spouses are separated and a joint petition is not filed.)

NAME AND ADDRESS OF TRANSFEREE, RELATIONSHIP TO DEBTOR	DATE	DESCRIBE PROPERTY TRANSFERRED AND VALUE RECEIVED

11. Closed financial accounts   5

None
☐

List all financial accounts and instruments held in the name of the debtor or for the benefit of the debtor which were closed, sold, or otherwise transferred within **one year** immediately preceding the commencement of this case. Include checking, savings, or other financial accounts, certificates of deposit, or other instruments; shares and share accounts held in banks, credit unions, pension funds, cooperatives, associations, brokerage houses and other financial institutions. (Married debtors filing under chapter 12 or chapter 13 must include information concerning accounts or instruments held by or for either or both spouses whether or not a joint petition is filed, unless the spouses are separated and a joint petition is not filed.)

NAME AND ADDRESS OF INSTITUTION	TYPE AND NUMBER OF ACCOUNT AND AMOUNT OF FINAL BALANCE	AMOUNT AND DATE OF SALE OR CLOSING

12. Safe deposit boxes

None
☐

List each safe deposit or other box or depository in which the debtor has or had securities, cash, or other valuables within **one year** immediately preceding the commencement of this case. (Married debtors filing under chapter 12 or chapter 13 must include boxes or depositories of either or both spouses whether or not a joint petition is filed, unless the spouses are separated and a joint petition is not filed.)

NAME AND ADDRESS OF BANK OR OTHER DEPOSITORY	NAMES AND ADDRESSES OF THOSE WITH ACCESS TO BOX OR DEPOSITORY	DESCRIPTION OF CONTENTS	DATE OF TRANSFER OR SURRENDER, IF ANY

13. Setoffs

None
☐

List all setoffs made by any creditor, including a bank, against a debt or deposit of the debtor within **90 days** preceding the commencement of this case. (Married debtors filing under chapter 12 or chapter 13 must include information concerning either or both spouses whether or not a joint petition is filed, unless the spouses are separated and a joint petition is not filed.)

NAME AND ADDRESS OF CREDITOR	DATE OF SETOFF	AMOUNT OF SETOFF

14. Property held for another person

None
☐

List all property owned by another person that the debtor holds or controls.

NAME AND ADDRESS OF OWNER	DESCRIPTION AND VALUE OF PROPERTY	LOCATION OF PROPERTY

6

15. Prior address of debtor

None
☐

If the debtor has moved within the **two years** immediately preceding the commencement of this case, list all premises which the debtor occupied during that period and vacated prior to the commencement of this case. If a joint petition is filed, report also any separate address of either spouse.

ADDRESS   NAME USED   DATES OF OCCUPANCY

16. Spouses and Former Spouses

None
☐

If the debtor resides or resided in a community property state, commonwealth, or territory (including Alaska, Arizona, California, Idaho, Louisiana, Nevada, New Mexico, Puerto Rico, Texas, Washington, or Wisconsin) within the **six-year period** immediately preceding the commencement of the case, identify the name of the debtor's spouse and of any former spouse who resides or resided with the debtor in the community property state.

NAME

17. Environmental Information.

For the purpose of this question, the following definitions apply:

"Environmental Law" means any federal, state, or local statute or regulation regulating pollution, contamination, releases of hazardous or toxic substances, wastes or material into the air, land, soil, surface water, groundwater, or other medium, including, but not limited to, statutes or regulations regulating the cleanup of these substances, wastes, or material.

"Site" means any location, facility, or property as defined under any Environmental Law, whether or not presently or formerly owned or operated by the debtor, including, but not limited to, disposal sites.

"Hazardous Material" means anything defined as a hazardous waste, hazardous substance, toxic substance, hazardous material, pollutant, or contaminant or similar term under an Environmental Law

None
☐

a.   List the name and address of every site for which the debtor has received notice in writing by a governmental unit that it may be liable or potentially liable under or in violation of an Environmental Law. Indicate the governmental unit, the date of the notice, and, if known, the Environmental Law:

SITE NAME   NAME AND ADDRESS   DATE OF   ENVIRONMENTAL
AND ADDRESS   OF GOVERNMENTAL UNIT   NOTICE   LAW

None
☐

b.   List the name and address of every site for which the debtor provided notice to a governmental unit of a release of Hazardous Material. Indicate the governmental unit to which the notice was sent and the date of the notice.

SITE NAME   NAME AND ADDRESS   DATE OF   ENVIRONMENTAL

AND ADDRESS   OF GOVERNMENTAL UNIT   NOTICE   LAW   7

None ☐   c.   List all judicial or administrative proceedings, including settlements or orders, under any Environmental Law with respect to which the debtor is or was a party. Indicate the name and address of the governmental unit that is or was a party to the proceeding, and the docket number.

NAME AND ADDRESS   DOCKET NUMBER   STATUS OR
OF GOVERNMENTAL UNIT   DISPOSITION

18 . Nature, location and name of business

None ☐   a.   If the debtor is an individual, list the names, addresses, taxpayer identification numbers, nature of the businesses, and beginning and ending dates of all businesses in which the debtor was an officer, director, partner, or managing executive of a corporation, partnership, sole proprietorship, or was a self-employed professional within the **six years** immediately preceding the commencement of this case, or in which the debtor owned 5 percent or more of the voting or equity securities within the **six years** immediately preceding the commencement of this case.
>   If the debtor is a partnership, list the names, addresses, taxpayer identification numbers, nature of the businesses, and beginning and ending dates of all businesses in which the debtor was a partner or owned 5 percent or more of the voting or equity securities, within the **six years** immediately preceding the commencement of this case.
>   If the debtor is a corporation, list the names, addresses, taxpayer identification numbers, nature of the businesses, and beginning and ending dates of all businesses in which the debtor was a partner or owned 5 percent or more of the voting or equity securities within the **six years** immediately preceding the commencement of this case.

| | TAXPAYER | | | BEGINNING AND ENDING |
| NAME | I.D. NUMBER | ADDRESS | NATURE OF BUSINESS | DATES |

None ☐   b.   Identify any business listed in response to subdivision a., above, that is "single asset real estate" as defined in 11 U.S.C. § 101.

NAME   ADDRESS

The following questions are to be completed by every debtor that is a corporation or partnership and by any individual debtor who is or has been, within the **six years** immediately preceding the commencement of this case, any of the following: an officer, director, managing executive, or owner of more than 5 percent of the voting or equity securities of a corporation; a partner, other than a limited partner, of a partnership; a sole proprietor or otherwise self-employed.

*(An individual or joint debtor should complete this portion of the statement **only** if the debtor is or has been in business, as defined above, within the six years immediately preceding the commencement of this case. A debtor who has not been in business within those six years should go directly to the signature page.)*

8

19. Books, records and financial statements

None ☐

a. List all bookkeepers and accountants who within the **two years** immediately preceding the filing of this bankruptcy case kept or supervised the keeping of books of account and records of the debtor.

NAME AND ADDRESS   DATES SERVICES RENDERED

None ☐

b. List all firms or individuals who within the **two years** immediately preceding the filing of this bankruptcy case have audited the books of account and records, or prepared a financial statement of the debtor.

NAME   ADDRESS   DATES SERVICES RENDERED

None ☐

c. List all firms or individuals who at the time of the commencement of this case were in possession of the books of account and records of the debtor. If any of the books of account and records are not available, explain.

NAME   ADDRESS

None ☐

d. List all financial institutions, creditors and other parties, including mercantile and trade agencies, to whom a financial statement was issued within the **two years** immediately preceding the commencement of this case by the debtor.

NAME AND ADDRESS   DATE ISSUED

20. Inventories

None ☐

a. List the dates of the last two inventories taken of your property, the name of the person who supervised the taking of each inventory, and the dollar amount and basis of each inventory.

DATE OF INVENTORY   INVENTORY SUPERVISOR   DOLLAR AMOUNT OF INVENTORY
                                                    (Specify cost, market or other basis)

None ☐

b. List the name and address of the person having possession of the records of each of the two inventories reported in a., above.

DATE OF INVENTORY   NAME AND ADDRESSES OF CUSTODIAN
                                                    OF INVENTORY RECORDS

21 . Current Partners, Officers, Directors and Shareholders   9

None ☐

a. If the debtor is a partnership, list the nature and percentage of partnership interest of each member of the partnership.

NAME AND ADDRESS   NATURE OF INTEREST   PERCENTAGE OF INTEREST

None ☐

b. If the debtor is a corporation, list all officers and directors of the corporation, and each stockholder who directly or indirectly owns, controls, or holds 5 percent or more of the voting or equity securities of the corporation.

NAME AND ADDRESS   TITLE   NATURE AND PERCENTAGE OF STOCK OWNERSHIP

22 . Former partners, officers, directors and shareholders

None ☐

a. If the debtor is a partnership, list each member who withdrew from the partnership within **one year** immediately preceding the commencement of this case.

NAME   ADDRESS   DATE OF WITHDRAWAL

None ☐

b. If the debtor is a corporation, list all officers, or directors whose relationship with the corporation terminated within **one year** immediately preceding the commencement of this case.

NAME AND ADDRESS   TITLE   DATE OF TERMINATION

23 . Withdrawals from a partnership or distributions by a corporation

None ☐

If the debtor is a partnership or corporation, list all withdrawals or distributions credited or given to an insider, including compensation in any form, bonuses, loans, stock redemptions, options exercised and any other perquisite during **one year** immediately preceding the commencement of this case.

NAME & ADDRESS OF RECIPIENT, RELATIONSHIP TO DEBTOR   DATE AND PURPOSE OF WITHDRAWAL   AMOUNT OF MONEY OR DESCRIPTION AND VALUE OF PROPERTY

10

24. Tax Consolidation Group.

None

☐

If the debtor is a corporation, list the name and federal taxpayer identification number of the parent corporation of any consolidated group for tax purposes of which the debtor has been a member at any time within the **six-year period** immediately preceding the commencement of the case.

NAME OF PARENT CORPORATION   TAXPAYER IDENTIFICATION NUMBER

25. Pension Funds.

None

☐

If the debtor is not an individual, list the name and federal taxpayer identification number of any pension fund to which the debtor, as an employer, has been responsible for contributing at any time within the **six-year period** immediately preceding the commencement of the case.

NAME OF PENSION FUND   TAXPAYER IDENTIFICATION NUMBER

* * * * * *

11

[If completed by an individual or individual and spouse]

I declare under penalty of perjury that I have read the answers contained in the foregoing statement of financial affairs and any attachments thereto and that they are true and correct.

Date _____   Signature _____
                                  of Debtor

Date _____   Signature _____
                                  of Joint Debtor
                                  (if any)

[If completed on behalf of a partnership or corporation]

I, declare under penalty of perjury that I have read the answers contained in the foregoing statement of financial affairs and any attachments thereto and that they are true and correct to the best of my knowledge, information and belief.

Date _____   Signature _____

                                  _____
                                  Print Name and Title

[An individual signing on behalf of a partnership or corporation must indicate position or relationship to debtor.]

_____ continuation sheets attached

Penalty for making a false statement: Fine of up to $500,000 or imprisonment for up to 5 years, or both. 18 U.S.C. § 152 and 3571

CERTIFICATION AND SIGNATURE OF NON-ATTORNEY BANKRUPTCY PETITION PREPARER (See 11 U.S.C. § 110)

I certify that I am a bankruptcy petition preparer as defined in 11 U.S.C. § 110, that I prepared this document for compensation, and that I have provided the debtor with a copy of this document.

_____
Printed or Typed Name of Bankruptcy Petition Preparer   _____
                                                                Social Security No.

_____

_____
Address

Names and Social Security numbers of all other individuals who prepared or assisted in preparing this document:

If more than one person prepared this document, attach additional signed sheets conforming to the appropriate Official Form for each person.

X _____
Signature of Bankruptcy Petition Preparer   _____
                                                                Date

A bankruptcy petition preparer's failure to comply with the provisions of title 11 and the Federal Rules of Bankruptcy Procedure may result in fines or imprisonment or both. 18 U.S.C. § 156.

114-1

Form B8 (Official Form 8)
(9/97)

Form 8. INDIVIDUAL DEBTOR'S STATEMENT OF INTENTION

[Caption as in Form 16B]

CHAPTER 7 INDIVIDUAL DEBTOR'S STATEMENT OF INTENTION

1. I have filed a schedule of assets and liabilities which includes consumer debts secured by property of the estate.

2. I intend to do the following with respect to the property of the estate which secures those consumer debts:

    a. *Property to Be Surrendered.*

Description of Property	Creditor's name

    b. *Property to Be Retained*   *[Check any applicable statement.]*

Description of Property	Creditor's Name	Property is claimed as exempt	Property will be redeemed pursuant to 11 U.S.C. § 722	Debt will be reaffirmed pursuant to 11 U.S.C. § 524(c)

Date: _____

_____
Signature of Debtor

CERTIFICATION OF NON-ATTORNEY BANKRUPTCY PETITION PREPARER (See 11 U.S.C. § 110)

I certify that I am a bankruptcy petition preparer as defined in 11 U.S.C. § 110, that I prepared this document for compensation, and that I have provided the debtor with a copy of this document.

_____   _____
Printed or Typed Name of Bankruptcy Petition Preparer   Social Security No.

_____

Address

Names and Social Security Numbers of all other individuals who prepared or assisted in preparing this document.

If more than one person prepared this document, attach additional signed sheets conforming to the appropriate Official Form for each person.

X_____   _____
Signature of Bankruptcy Petition Preparer   Date

A bankruptcy petition preparer's failure to comply with the provisions of title 11 and the Federal Rules of Bankruptcy Procedure may result in fines or imprisonment or both. 11 U.S.C. § 110; 18 U.S.C. § 156.

Index

B

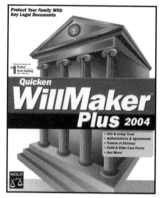

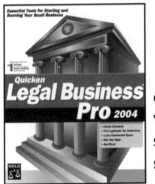